intel

LITERATURE SALES ORDER FORM

NAME: ____________________

COMPANY: ____________________

ADDRESS: ____________________

CITY: ____________________ STATE: ____________________

COUNTRY: ____________________

PHONE NO.: (   ) ____________________

ORDER NO.	TITLE	QTY.		PRICE		TOTAL
			×		=	
			×		=	
			×		=	
			×		=	
			×		=	
			×		=	
			×		=	
			×		=	
			×		=	
			×		=	

Subtotal ________

Must Add Your Local Sales Tax ________

Must add appropriate postage to subtotal (10% U.S. and Canada, 20% all other) → Postage ________

Total ________

Pay by Visa, MasterCard, American Express, Check, Money Order, or company purchase order payable to Intel Literature Sales. Allow 2-4 weeks for delivery.

☐ Visa ☐ MasterCard ☐ American Express Expiration Date ________

Account No. ____________________

Signature: ____________________

Mail To: Intel Literature Sales
P.O. Box 58130
Santa Clara, CA
95052-8130

International Customers outside the U.S. and Canada should contact their local Intel Sales Office or Distributor listed in the back of most Intel literature.

European Literature Order Form in back of book.

Call Toll Free: (800) 548-4725 for phone orders

Prices good until 12/31/88.

Source HB

Mail To: Intel Literature Sales
P.O. Box 58130
Santa Clara, CA 95052-8130

80960KB PROGRAMMER'S REFERENCE MANUAL

1988

Intel Corporation makes no warranty for the use of its products and assumes no responsibility for any errors which may appear in this document nor does it make a commitment to update the information contained herein.

Intel retains the right to make changes to these specifications at any time, without notice.

Contact your local sales office to obtain the latest specifications before placing your order.

The following are trademarks of Intel Corporation and may only be used to identify Intel Products:

> Above, BITBUS, COMMputer, CREDIT, Data Pipeline, FASTPATH, GENIUS, i, $\overset{\Delta}{\text{i}}$, ICE, iCEL, iCS, iDBP, iDIS, I^2ICE, iLBX, i_m, iMDDX, iMMX, Insite, Intel, int_el, int_elBOS, Intelevision, int_eligent Identifier, int_eligent Programming, Intellec, Intellink, iOSP, iPDS, iPSC, iRMX, iSBC, iSBX, iSDM, iSXM, KEPROM, Library Manager, MAP-NET, MCS, Megachassis, MICROMAINFRAME, MULTIBUS, MULTICHANNEL, MULTIMODULE, ONCE, OpenNET, OTP, PC-BUBBLE, Plug-A-Bubble, PROMPT, Promware, QUEST, QueX, Quick-Pulse Programming, Ripplemode, RMX/80, RUPI, Seamless, SLD, UPI, and VLSiCEL, and the combination of ICE, iCS, iRMX, iSBC, iSBX, MCS, or UPI and a numerical suffix, 4-SITE.

Ethernet is a trademark of Xerox.

DEC is a trademark of Digital Equipment Corporation.

VAX is a trademark of Digital Equipment Corporation.

MDS is an ordering code only and is not used as a product name or trademark. MDS® is a registered trademark of Mohawk Data Sciences Corporation.

MULTIBUS is a patented Intel bus.

Additional copies of this manual or other Intel literature may be obtained from:

Intel Corporation
Literature Distribution
Mail Stop SC6-59
P.O. Box 58130
Santa Clara, CA 95052-8130

TABLE OF CONTENTS

APPENDIX D
INITIALIZATION CODE

APPENDIX E
CONSIDERATIONS FOR WRITING PORTABLE SOFTWARE

Figures

Tables

Preface

PREFACE

This manual provides detailed programming information for the Intel 80960KB processor, which is part of the 80960K series of embedded-processor products. All of the processors in the 80960K series of products are based on the Intel 80960 architecture.

Most of the information in this manual also pertains to the Intel 80960KA processor, which will be available from Intel in the near future. The only difference between the 80960KB and 80960KA processors, is that the 80960KA does not provide on-chip support for floating-point operations or operations on decimal numbers.

Guide to Manual 1

CHAPTER 1
GUIDE TO MANUAL

This chapter describes this manual. It explains the organization of the manual, describes the contents of each chapter, and discusses terminology used in the manual. It also shows the chapters of the manual that should be of most interest to applications programmers, compiler designers, and designers of operating-system kernels (or system executives).

MANUAL STRUCTURE

This manual is a reference manual for the Intel 80960KB processor. It has been designed to serve two functions:

1. To give programmers and system designers detailed information about the processor's programming environment and kernel (or executive) support facilities.
2. To provide reference information on the Intel 80960 architecture, the architecture on which the 80960KB processor is based.

To meet these two goals, the manual is organized to describe the various elements of the 80960 architecture first (in Chapters 2 through 11), then to describe those additional features that are included in the 80960KB implementation of the architecture (in Chapters 12 and 13). A summary of those features of the 80960KB processor that are implementation dependent is provided in Appendix E.

Some other useful features of this manual are as follows:

- Detailed reference information for all the 80960KB instructions is given in Chapter 11. The instructions are arranged alphabetically.
- A quick reference for all of the 80960KB instructions, sorted both alphabetically and by opcode, is given in Appendix A. Also in this chapter are a collection of illustrations of all the system-data structures.

Table 1-1 shows those chapters that will be of most interest to applications programmers, compiler designers, or kernel designers.

Table 1-1: Chapters of Interest for Specific Users

User	Chapters
Applications Programmer	Chapters 2 through 6, Chapter 11, Chapter 12, and Appendices A and C
Compiler Designer	Chapters 2 through 6, Chapter 8, Chapter 9, Chapter 11, Chapter 12, and Appendices A, B, C and E
Kernel Designer	Chapters 2 through 13, and Appendices A through E

CHAPTER OVERVIEW

The following is a brief overview of the contents of each chapter:

Chapter 1 – Guide to Manual. Overview of this manual.

Chapter 2 – Introduction to the 80960 Architecture. Overview of the Intel 80960 architecture, the architecture on which the 80960KB processor is based.

Chapter 3 – Execution Environment. Description of the environment in which instructions are executed. The topics discussed in this chapter include the address space, registers, instruction pointer, and arithmetic controls.

Chapter 4 – Procedure Calls. Description of the various mechanisms available for making procedure calls. The topics discussed here include the local call/return mechanism, procedure stack, branch-and-link procedure calls, procedure table calls, and supervisor call mechanism.

Chapter 5 – Data Types and Addressing Modes. Description of the non-floating-point data types and of how bits and bytes are addressed. The addressing modes provided for addressing data in memory are also described in this chapter.

Chapter 6 – Instruction Set Summary. Overview of all the non-floating point instructions in the 80960KB instruction set, arranged by functional groups. Also included is a brief description of the assembly language instruction format.

Chapter 7 – Processor Management and Initialization. Description of the processor management facilities. Included is a discussion of the system data structures required to operate the processor, the software requirements for processor management, and the requirements for physical memory. Processor initialization is described at the end of the chapter.

Chapter 8 – Interrupts. Description of the interrupt mechanism, interrupt priority, interrupt table, interrupt-handling procedures, and the software requirements for handling interrupts.

Chapter 9 – Fault Handling. Description of the processor's fault-handling mechanism. Included here is a discussion of the fault-table structure, fault-handling procedures, and the software requirements for handling faults. A detailed description of each fault is given in a reference section at the end of the chapter.

Chapter 10 – Debugging. Description of the debugging and monitoring support facilities, including the trace control register.

Chapter 11 – Instruction Set Reference. Alphabetical listing of the complete 80960KB instruction set with detailed descriptions of each instruction, assembly-language syntax, examples, and algorithms.

Chapter 12 – Floating-Point Operation. Description of the floating-point processing facilities of the processor. This chapter includes an overview of floating-point numbers and a description of the 80960KB floating-point data types and their relationship to the IEEE floating-point standard. Also included is a description of the floating-point instructions, exceptions, and faults.

Chapter 13 — Interagent Communication. Description of the interprocessor communication (IAC) mechanism, which allows several processors to communicate with one another on the bus. The topics covered in this chapter include the IAC mechanism and software requirements for using internal IACs. A detailed description of each IAC is given in a reference section at the end of the chapter.

Appendix A — Instruction and Data Structure Quick Reference. Two lists of the 80960KB instructions: one sorted alphabetically by assembly-language mnemonic and one sorted by machine language opcode. A collection of illustrations showing the system data structures is also provided here.

Appendix B — Machine-Level Instruction Formats. Description of the machine-level instruction formats.

Appendix C — Instruction Timing. Description of the 80960KB processor's instruction pipeline and how it affects the timing of instructions. The number of clock cycles required for each instruction are also given in this appendix.

Appendix D — Initialization Code. Listing of code to initialize the 80960KB processor.

Appendix E — Considerations for Writing Portable Software. Discussion of various aspects of the 80960 architecture that should be considered if code written for the 80960KB processor is intended to be ported at a later date to other implementations of the 80960 architecture.

NOTATION AND TERMINOLOGY

The following paragraphs describe the notation and terminology used in this manual that have special meaning.

Reserved and Preserved

Certain fields in the processor's system data structures are described as being either *reserved* fields or *preserved* fields. A reserved field is one that other implementations of the 80960 architecture can use. To help insure that a current software design is compatible with future processors based on the 80960 architecture, the bits in reserved fields should be set to 0 when the data structure is initially created. Thereafter, software should not access these fields.

Some fields in system data structures are shown as being required to be set to either 1 or 0. These fields should be treated as if they were reserved fields. They should be set to the specified value when the data structure is created and not accessed by software thereafter.

A preserved field is one that the processor does not use. Software may use preserved fields for any function.

Set and Clear

The terms *set* and *clear* are used in this manual to refer to the value of a bit field in a system data structure. If a bit is set, its value is 1; if the bit is clear, its value is 0. Likewise, setting a bit means giving it a value of 1 and clearing a bit means giving it a value of 0.

Introduction to the 80960 Architecture

2

CHAPTER 2
INTRODUCTION TO THE 80960 ARCHITECTURE

This chapter provides an overview of the architecture on which the 80960K series of processors is based.

A NEW 32-BIT ARCHITECTURE FROM INTEL

The 80960KB processor marks the introduction of the 80960 architecture – a new 32-bit architecture from Intel. This architecture has been designed specifically to meet the needs of embedded applications such as machine control, robotics, process control, avionics, and instrumentation. It represents a renewed commitment from Intel to provide reliable, high-performance processors and controllers for the embedded processor marketplace.

The 80960 architecture can best be characterized as a high-performance computing engine. It features high-speed instruction execution and ease of programming. It is also easily extensible, allowing processors and controllers based on this architecture to be conveniently customized to meet the needs of specific processing and control applications.

Some of the important attributes of the 80960 architecture include:

- full 32-bit registers
- high-speed, pipelined instruction execution
- a convenient program execution environment with 32 general-purpose registers and a versatile set of special-function registers
- a highly optimized procedure call mechanism that features on-chip caching of local variables and parameters
- extensive facilities for handling interrupts and faults
- extensive tracing facilities to support efficient program debugging and monitoring
- register scoreboarding and write buffering to permit efficient operation with lower performance memory subsystems

The following sections describe those features of the 80960 architecture that are provided to streamline code execution and simplify programming. Also described are those features that allow extensions to be added to the architecture.

HIGH PERFORMANCE PROGRAM EXECUTION

Much of the design of the 80960 architecture has been aimed at maximizing the processor's computational and data processing speed through increased parallelism. The following paragraphs describe several of the mechanisms and techniques used to accomplish this goal, including:

- an efficient load and store memory-access model
- caching of code and procedural data
- overlapped execution of instructions
- many one or two clock instructions

Load and Store Model

One of the more important features of the 80960 architecture is that most of its operations are performed on operands in registers, rather than in memory. For example, all the arithmetic, logic, comparison, branching, and bit operations are performed with registers and literals.

This feature provides two benefits. First, it increases program execution speed by minimizing the number of memory accesses required to execute a program. Second, it reduces memory latency encountered when using slower, lower-cost memory parts.

To support this concept, the architecture provides a generous supply of general-purpose registers. For each procedure, 32 registers are available (28 of which are available for general use). These registers are divided into two types: global and local. Both these types of registers can be used for general storage of operands. The only difference is that global registers retain their contents across procedure boundaries, whereas the processor allocates a new set of local registers each time a new procedure is called.

The architecture also provides a set of fast, versatile load and store instructions. These instructions allow burst transfers of 1, 2, 4, 8, 12, or 16 bytes of information between memory and the registers.

On-Chip Caching of Code and Data

To further reduce memory accesses, the architecture offers two mechanisms for caching code and data on chip: an instruction cache and multiple sets of local registers. The instruction cache allows prefetching of blocks of instruction from memory, which helps insure that the instruction execution pipeline is supplied with a steady stream of instructions. It also reduces the number of memory accesses required when performing iterative operations such as loops. (The size of the instruction cache can vary. With the 80960KB processor, it is 512 bytes.)

To optimize the architecture's procedure call mechanism, the processor provides multiple sets of local registers. This allows the processor to perform most procedure calls without having to write the local registers out to the stack in memory.

(The number of local-register sets provided depends on the processor implementation. The 80960KB processor provides four sets of local registers.)

Overlapped Instruction Execution

Another technique that the 80960 architecture employs to enhance program execution speed is overlapping the execution of some instructions. This is accomplished through two mechanisms: register scoreboarding and branch prediction.

Register scoreboarding permits instruction execution to continue while data is being fetched from memory. When a load instruction is executed, the processor sets one or more scoreboard bits to indicate the target registers to be loaded. After the target registers are loaded, the scoreboard bits are cleared. While the target registers are being loaded, the processor is allowed to execute other instructions that do not use these registers. The processor uses the scoreboard bits to insure that target registers are not used until the loads are complete. (The checking of scoreboard bits is carried out transparently from software.) The net result of using this technique is that code can often be optimized in such a way as to allow some instructions to be executed in zero clock cycles (that is, executed for free).

Conditional branch instructions commonly cause bottlenecks in the instruction execution pipeline, since the instruction decoder cannot decode instructions past the branch instruction until it knows the direction the branch is going to take. The 80960 architecture solves this problem with a technique called branch prediction. Branch prediction allows a programmer or compiler to select conditional branch instructions that indicate to the processor the direction a branch is likely to go. The decoder can then continue decoding instructions beyond the branch, even though the branch condition has not yet been tested. This technique eliminates waits between the decoder and execution unit, while branch conditions are being evaluated.

Note

The branch prediction mechanism is not implemented in the 80960K series of processors.

Single-Clock Instructions

It is the intent of the 80960 architecture that a processor be able to execute commonly used instructions such as moves, adds, subtracts, logical operations, and branches in a minimum number of clock cycles (preferable one clock cycle). The architecture supports this concept in several ways. For example, the load and store model described earlier in this chapter (with its concentration on register-to-register operations) eliminates the clock cycles required to perform memory-to-memory operations.

Also, all the instructions in the 80960 architecture are 32-bits long and aligned on 32-bit boundaries. This feature allows instructions to be decoded in one clock cycle. It also eliminates the need for an instruction-alignment stage in the pipeline.

The design of the 80960KB processor takes full advantage of these features of the architecture, resulting in over 50 instructions that can be executed in a single clock-cycle.

Efficient Interrupt Model

The 80960 architecture provides an efficient mechanism for servicing interrupts from external sources. To handle interrupts, the processor maintains an interrupt table of 248 interrupt vectors (240 of which are available for general use). When an interrupt is signaled, the processor uses a pointer from the interrupt table to perform an implicit call to an interrupt handler procedure. In performing this call, the processor automatically saves the state of the processor prior to receiving the interrupt; performs the interrupt routine; and then restores the state of the processor. A separate interrupt stack is also provided to segregate interrupt handling from application programs.

The interrupt handling facilities also feature a method of evaluating interrupts by priority. The processor is then able to store interrupt vectors that are lower in priority than the task that the processor is currently working on in a pending interrupt section of the interrupt table. At certain defined times, the processor checks the pending interrupts and services them.

SIMPLIFIED PROGRAMMING ENVIRONMENT

Partly as a side benefit of its streamlined execution environment and partly by design, processors based on the 80960 architecture are particularly easy to program. For example, the large number of general purpose registers allows relatively complex algorithms to be executed with a minimum number of memory accesses. The following paragraphs describe some of the other features for the architecture that simplify programming.

Highly Efficient Procedure Call Mechanism

The procedure call mechanism makes procedure calls and parameter passing between procedures simple and compact. Each time a call instruction is issued, the processor automatically saves the current set of local registers and allocates a new set of local registers for the called procedure. Likewise, on a return from a procedure, the current set of local registers is deallocated and the local registers for the procedure being returned to are restored. On a procedure call, the program thus never has to explicitly save and restore those local variables and parameters that are stored in local registers.

Versatile Instruction Set and Addressing

The selection of instructions and addressing modes also simplifies programming. The architecture offers a full set of load, store, move, arithmetic, comparison, and branch instructions, with operations on both integer and ordinal data types. It also provides a complete set of Boolean and bit-field instructions, to simplify operations on bits and bit strings.

The addressing modes are efficient and straightforward, while at the same time providing the necessary indexing and scaling modes required to address complex arrays and record structures.

The large 4-gigabyte address space provides ample room to store programs and data. The availability of 32 addressing lines allows some address lines to be memory-mapped to control hardware functions.

Extensive Fault Handling Capability

To aid in program development, the 80960 architecture defines a wide selection of faults that the processor detects, including arithmetic faults, invalid operands, invalid operations, and machine faults. When a fault is detected, the processor makes an implicit call to a fault handler routine, using a mechanism similar to that described above for interrupts. The information collected for each fault allows program developers to quickly correct faulting code. It also allows automatic fault recovery from some faults.

Debugging and Monitoring

To support debugging systems, the 80960 architecture provides a mechanism for monitoring processor activity by means of trace events. The processor can be configured to detect as many as seven different trace events, including the instruction execution, branch events, calls, supervisor calls, returns, prereturns, and breakpoints. When the processor detects a trace event, it signals a trace fault and calls a fault handler. Intel provides several tools that use this feature, including an in-circuit emulator (ICE) device.

SUPPORT FOR ARCHITECTURAL EXTENSIONS

The 80960 architecture described earlier in this chapter provides a high-performance computing engine for use as the computational and data processing core of embedded processors or controllers. The architecture also provides several features that enable processors based on this architecture to be easily customized to meet the needs of specific embedded applications, such as signal processing, array processing, or graphics processing.

The most important of these features is a set of 32 special function registers. These registers provide a convenient interface to circuitry in the processor or to pins that can be connected to external hardware. They can be used to control timers, to perform operations on special data types, or to perform I/O functions.

The special function registers are similar to the global registers. They can be addressed by all the register-access instructions.

EXTENSIONS INCLUDED IN THE 80960K SERIES PROCESSORS

The 80960K series of processors offer a complete implementation of the 80960 architecture, plus several extensions to the architecture. These extensions fall into two categories: floating-point processing and interagent communication.

On-Chip Floating Point

The 80960KB processor provides a complete implementation of the IEEE standard for binary floating-point arithmetic (IEEE 754-185). This implementation includes a full set of floating-point operations, including add, subtract, multiply, divide, trigonometric functions, and logarithmic functions. These operations are performed on single precision (32-bit), double precision (64-bit), and extended precision (80-bit) real numbers.

One of the benefits of this implementation is that the floating-point handling facilities are completely integrated into the normal instruction execution environment. Single- and double-precision floating-point values are stored in the same registers as non-floating point values. The four, 80-bit floating-point registers are provided to hold extended-precision values.

Interagent Communication

All of the processors in the 80960K series provide an interagent communication (IAC) mechanism, which allows agents connected to the processor's bus to communicate with one another. This mechanism operates similarly to the interrupt mechanism, except that IAC messages are passed through dedicated sections of memory. The sorts of tasks handled with IAC messages are processor reinitialization, stopping the processor, purging the instruction cache, and forcing the processor to check pending interrupts.

LOOK FOR MORE IN THE FUTURE

As has been shown in the preceding discussion, the 80960 architecture offers lots of possibilities and lots of room to grow. The first implementation of this architecture (the 80960KB processor) provides average instruction processing rates of 7.5 million instructions per second (7.5 MIPS) at 20 MHz clock rate and 10 MIPS at a 25 MHz clock rate[1]. This performance places the 80960KB at the top of the performance range for advanced, VLSI processor architectures.

However, the 80960KB is only the beginning. With improvements in VLSI technology, future implementation of this architecture will offer even greater performance. They will also offer a variety of useful extensions to solve specific control and monitoring needs in the field of embedded applications.

[1] 1 MIP is equivalent to the performance of a Digital Equipment Corp. VAX 11/780.

Execution Environment 3

CHAPTER 3
EXECUTION ENVIRONMENT

This chapter describes how the 80960KB processor stores and executes instructions and how it stores and manipulates data. The parts of the execution environment that are discussed include the address space, the register model, the instruction pointer, and the arithmetic controls.

The execution environment's procedure stack and procedure-call mechanism are described in Chapter 4.

OVERVIEW OF THE EXECUTION ENVIRONMENT

When the 80960KB processor is initialized, it sets up an execution environment. It then begins executing instructions from a program, using this execution environment to store and manipulate data.

Figure 3-1 shows the part of the execution environment that the processor sets up to execute a procedure within a program. This environment consists of a 2^{32}-byte address space, a set of global and floating-point registers, a set of local registers, a set of arithmetic-controls bits, the instruction pointer, a set of process-controls bits, and a set of trace-controls bits. All of these items, except the address space, reside on the 80960KB chip.

Note

The floating-point registers shown in Figure 3-1 are not defined in the 80960 architecture. They are extensions to the architecture that have been added to the 80960KB processor to support floating-point operations on the extended-real (floating point) data type. (The 80960KA processor does not provide floating-point registers.)

The 32 special-function registers (shown in Figure 3-1 in a dashed box) are defined in the 80960 architecture. These registers are not implemented in the 80960KB and 80960KA processors.

When the instruction stream includes a procedure call, a procedure stack and some additional elements are added to this execution environment. These procedure-call related elements are shown and discussed in Chapter 4.

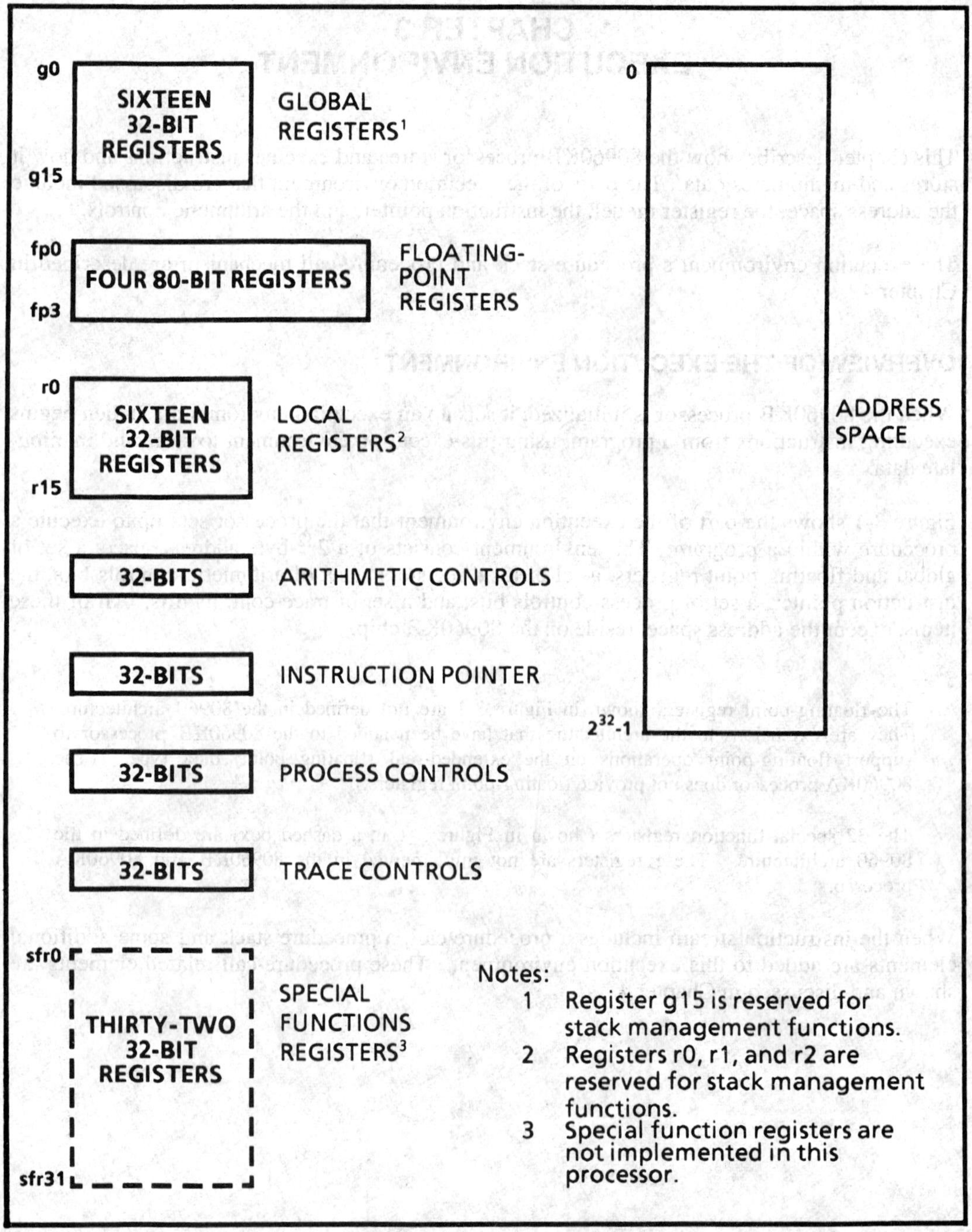

Figure 3-1: Execution Environment

ADDRESS SPACE

From the point of view of the processor, the address space is flat (unsegmented) and byte addressable, with addresses running contiguously from 0 to 2^{32} - 1. Programs and the kernel can allocate space for data, instructions, and the stack anywhere within this space, with the following exceptions:

- Instructions must be aligned on word boundaries.
- Some of the addresses in the upper 16M Bytes of the address space (addresses $FF000000_{16}$ through $FFFFFFFF_{16}$) are reserved for specific functions. In general, programs and the kernel should not use this section of the address space.

The memory requirements to support this address space are given in Chapter 7 in the section titled "Memory Requirements."

REGISTER MODEL

The processor provides three types of data registers: global, floating-point, and local. The 16 global registers constitute a set of general-purpose registers, the contents of which are preserved across procedure boundaries. The 4 floating-point registers are provided to support extended floating-point arithmetic. Their contents are also preserved across procedure boundaries. The 16 local registers are provided to hold parameters specific to a procedure (i.e., local variables). For each procedure that is called, the processor allocates a separate set of 16 local registers.

For any one procedure within a program, 36 registers are thus available (as shown in Figure 3-2): the 16 global registers, the 4 floating-point registers, and the 16 local registers. All of these registers are maintained on the processor chip.

Global Registers

The 16 global registers (g0 through g15) are 32-bit registers. Each register can thus hold a word (32 bits) of data. Registers g0 through g14 are general-purpose registers; g15 is reserved for the current frame pointer (FP). The FP contains the address of the first byte in the current (topmost) stack frame. (The FP and the procedure stack are discussed in detail in Chapter 4.)

The general-purpose global registers (g0 through g14) can hold any of the data types that the processor recognizes (i.e., ordinals, integers, reals).

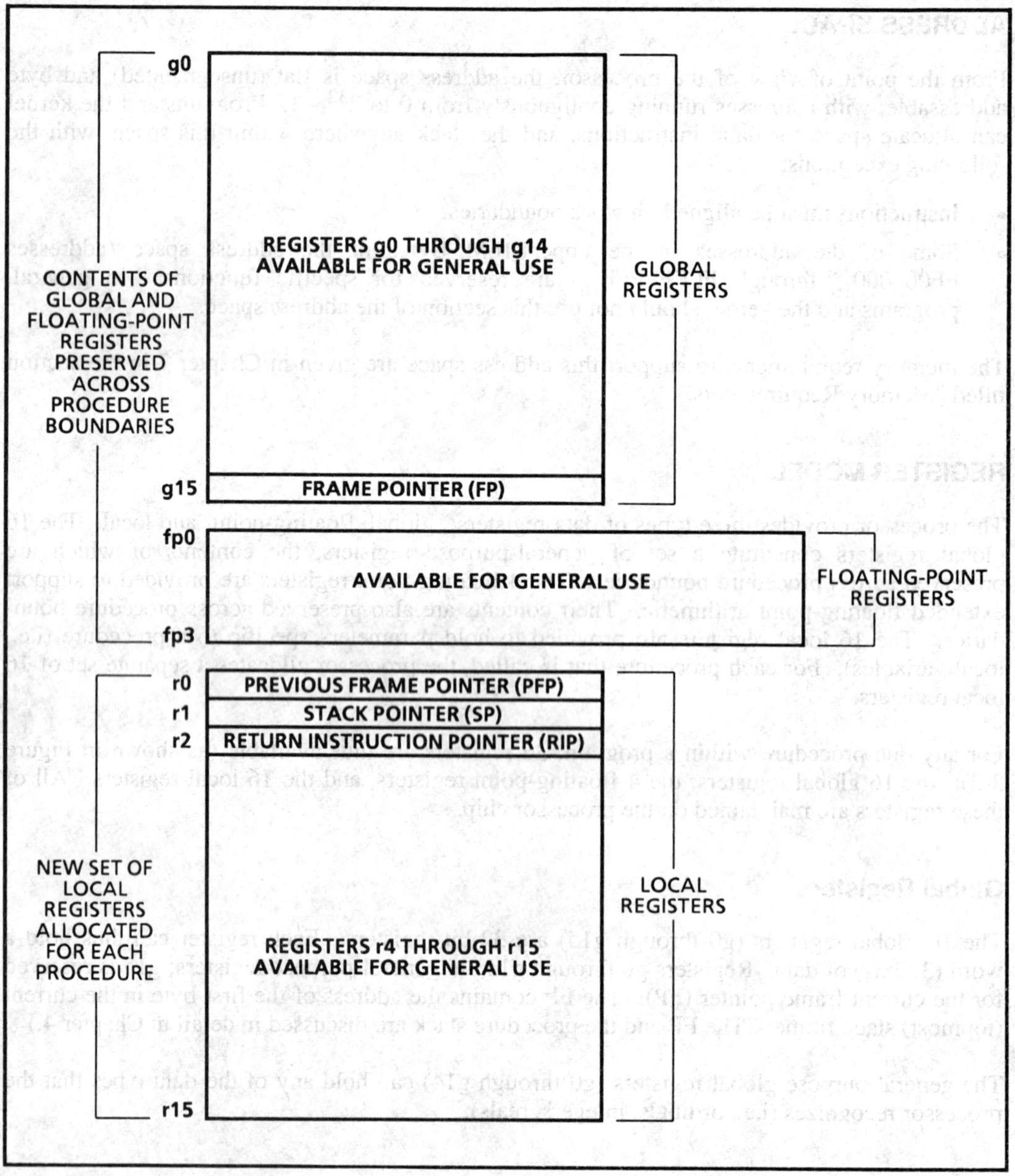

Figure 3-2: Registers Available to a Single Procedure

Floating-Point Registers

The four floating-point registers (fp0 through fp3) are 80-bit registers. These registers can be accessed only as operands of floating-point instructions. All numbers stored in these registers are stored in extended-real format. (This format is described in Chapter 12.) The processor automatically converts floating-point values from real or long-real format into extended-real format when a floating-point register is used as a destination for an instruction.

Note

> The floating-point registers are defined in the 80960 architecture as an option for processors such as the 80960KB that support floating-point operations. These registers may be omitted from implementations of the architecture that do not support floating-point operations.

Local Registers

The 16 local registers (r0 through r15) are 32-bit registers, like the global registers. The purpose of the local registers is to provide a separate set of registers, aside from the global and floating-point registers, for each active procedure. Each time a procedure is called, the processor automatically sets up a new set of local registers for that procedure and saves the local registers for the calling procedure. The program does not have to explicitly save and restore these registers.

Local registers r3 through r15 are general-purpose registers. Registers r0 through r2 are reserved for special functions, as follows: register r0 contains the previous frame pointer (PFP); r1 contains the stack pointer (SP); and r2 contains the return instruction pointer (RIP). (The PFP, SP, and RIP are discussed in detail in Chapter 4.) The processor accesses the local registers at the same speed as it does the global registers.

Register Alignment

Several of the processor's instructions operate on multiple-word operands. For example, the load-long instruction (**ldl**) loads two words from memory into two consecutive registers. Here, the register number for the least significant word is specified in the instruction and the most significant word is automatically loaded into the next higher numbered register.

In cases where an instruction specifies a register number and multiple, consecutive registers are implied, the register number must be even if two registers are accessed (e.g., g0, g2) and an integral multiple of four if three or four registers are accessed (e.g., g0, g4). If a register reference for a source value is not properly aligned, the value is undefined. If a register reference for a destination value is not properly aligned, the registers that the processor writes to are undefined.

Register Scoreboarding

The 80960KB provides a mechanism called *register scoreboarding* that in certain situations permits instructions to be executed concurrently. This mechanism works as follows. While an instruction is being executed, the processor sets a scoreboard bit to indicate that a particular register or group of registers is being used in an operation. If the instructions that follow do not use registers in that group, the processor in some instances is able to execute those instructions before execution of the prior instruction is complete. In effect, the register scoreboarding mechanism allows some instructions to be executed for free (zero clock cycles).

A common application of this feature is to execute one or more fast instructions (instructions that take one to three clock cycles) concurrently with load instructions. A load instruction typically takes 3 to 9 clock cycles (depending on the design of system memory). Register scoreboarding allows other instructions to be executed concurrently with the load instruction, providing that the other instructions do not affect the registers being loaded. For example, the following group of instructions loads a group of local registers while performing some other operations on data in global registers.

```
ld xyz, r6              # r6 ← data from address xyz
addi g4, g6, g7         # g7 ← g4 + g6
addi g9, g10, g11       # g11 ← g9 + g10
ld abc, r8              # r6 ← data from address abc
and g0, 0xffff, g1      # g1 ← g0 AND 0xffff
addi r6, r8, r7         # r7 ← r6 + r8
```

Here, the two **addi** instructions following the first load and the **and** instruction following the second load are performed for free.

The other situation where scoreboarding can be useful for procedure optimization is when floating-point instructions are being executed. Floating-point operations are handled by a separate execution unit in the processor. So, non-floating point instructions can often be executed concurrently with floating-point instructions, providing that they do not use the same registers and do not use the arithmetic-logic unit (ALU).

(A detailed description of the register-scoreboarding mechanism is given in Appendix C.)

INSTRUCTION POINTER

The instruction pointer (IP) is the address (in the address space) of the instruction currently being executed. This address is 32 bits; however, since instructions are required to be aligned on word boundaries in memory, the 2 least-significant bits of the IP are always zero.

Instructions in the processor are one or two words long. The IP gives the address of the lowest order byte of the first word of the instruction.

The IP is stored in the processor and cannot be read directly. However, the IP-with-displacement addressing mode allows the IP to be used as an offset into the address space. This addressing mode can also be used with the **lda** (load address) instruction to read the current value of the IP.

When a break occurs in the instruction stream (due to an interrupt or a procedure call), the IP of the next instruction to be executed (i.e., the RIP) is stored in local register r2, which is then stored on the stack. Refer to Chapter 4 for further discussion of this operation.

ARITHMETIC CONTROLS

The processor's arithmetic controls are made up of a set of 32 bits, which are cached on the processor chip in the arithmetic-controls register. Figure 3-3 shows the arrangement of the arithmetic controls bits. The arithmetic controls bits include condition code bits; floating-point control and status bits; integer control and status bits; and a bit that controls faulting on imprecise faults.

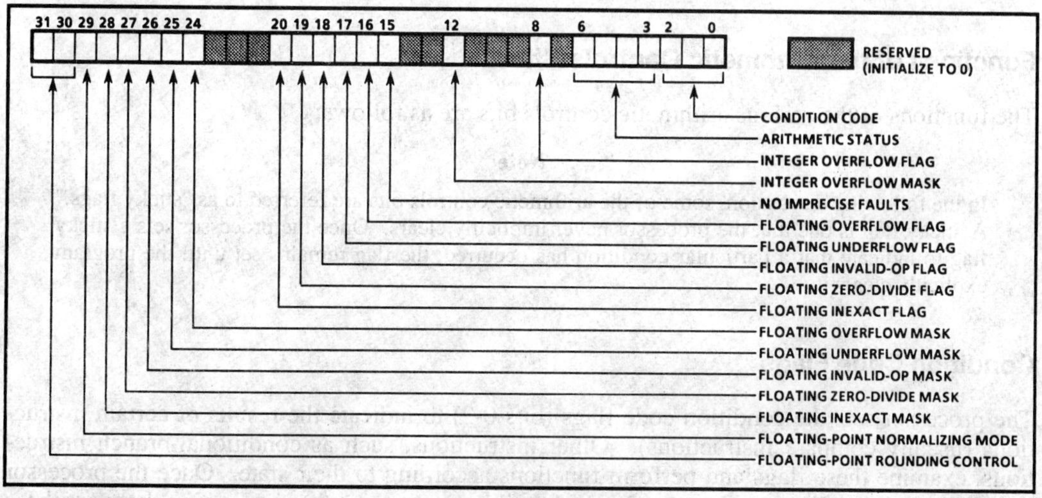

Figure 3-3: Arithmetic Controls

The processor sets or clears these bits to show the results of certain operations. For example, the processor modifies the condition code bits after each comparison operation to show the result of the comparison. Other arithmetic control bits, such as the floating-point fault masks, are set by the currently running program to tell the processor how to respond to certain fault conditions.

Note

The arithmetic status flags and the floating-point flags and masks are not defined in the 80960 architecture. They are an extension to the architecture, which is provided in the 80960KB processor to support floating-point operations. For implementations of the architecture that do not support floating-point operations, these flags and masks are reserved bits.

Initializing and Modifying the Arithmetic Controls

The state of the processor's arithmetic controls is undefined at processor initialization or on a processor reinitialize (initiated with a reinitialize processor IAC). Part of the initialization code should thus be to set the arithmetic controls to a specific state.

The arithmetic controls can be examined and modified using the modify AC (**modac**) instruction. This instruction uses a mask to allow specific bits to be checked and changed.

The processor automatically saves and restores the arithmetic controls when it services an interrupt or handles a fault. Here, the processor saves the current state of the arithmetic controls in an interrupt record or fault record, then restores the arithmetic controls upon returning from the interrupt or fault handler, respectively.

The **modac** instruction can be used to explicitly save and restore the contents of the arithmetic controls.

Functions of the Arithmetic Controls Bits

The functions of the various arithmetic controls bits are as follows:

Note

In the following discussion, some of the arithmetic controls bits are referred to as "sticky flags." A sticky flag is one that the processor never implicitly clears. Once the processor sets a sticky flag to indicate that a particular condition has occurred, the flag remains set until the program explicitly clears it.

Condition Code Flags

The processor sets the condition code flags (bits 0-2) to indicate the results of certain instructions (usually compare instructions). Other instructions, such as conditional-branch instructions, examine these flags and perform functions according to their state. Once the processor has set these flags, it leaves them unchanged until it executes another instruction that uses these flags to store results.

These flags are used to show either true or false conditions or inequalities (greater-than, equal, or less-than conditions). To show true or false conditions, the flags are set as shown in Table 3-1.

Table 3-1: Condition Codes for True or False Conditions

Condition Code	Condition
010	true
000	false

The condition code flags are set as shown in Table 3-2 to show inequalities.

Table 3-2: Condition Codes for Inequality Conditions

Condition Code	Condition
000	unordered
001	greater than
010	equal
011	greater than or equal
100	less than
101	not equal
110	less than or equal
111	ordered

The terms ordered and unordered are used when comparing floating-point numbers. If, when comparing two floating-point values, one of the values is a NaN (not a number), the relationship is said to be "unordered." Refer to the section in Chapter 12 titled "Comparison and Classification" for further information about the ordered and unordered conditions.

Arithmetic Status Flags

The processor uses the arithmetic status field (bits 3-6) in conjunction with the classify instructions (**classr** and **classrl**) to show the class of a floating-point number. When executing these instructions, the processor sets the arithmetic status bits as shown in Table 3-3, according to the class of the value being classified.

Table 3-3: Encoding of Arithmetic Status Field

Arithmetic Status	Classification
s000	zero
s001	denormalized number
s010	normal finite number
s011	infinity
s100	quiet NaN
s101	signaling NaN
s110	reserved operand

The "s" bit is set to the sign of the value being classified.

Integer Overflow Mask

The integer overflow mask (bit 12) and the integer overflow flag (bit 8) are used in conjunction with the arithmetic integer-overflow fault. The mask bit masks the integer-overflow fault.

When the fault is masked, the processor sets the integer overflow flag whenever an integer or decimal overflow occurs, to indicate that the fault condition has occurred even though the fault has been masked. If the fault is not masked, the fault is allowed to occur and the flag is not set. The integer overflow flag is a sticky flag. (Refer to the discussion of the arithmetic integer-overflow fault in Chapter 9 for more information about the integer overflow mask and flag.)

No Imprecise Faults Flag

The no imprecise faults flag (bit 15) determines whether or not imprecise faults are allowed to be raised. If set, faults are required to be precise; if clear, certain faults can be imprecise. (Refer to the section in Chapter 9 titled "Precise and Imprecise Faults" for more information about this flag.)

Floating-Point Flags and Masks

The floating-point flags (bits 16 through 20) and masks (bits 24 through 28) perform the same functions as the integer overflow flag and mask, except they are used for operations on real (floating point) numbers. When a mask bit is set, its associated floating-point fault is masked. If a mask bit is set, the processor sets the flag for the associated fault whenever the fault condition occurs. All the floating-point flag bits are sticky bits. Refer to the section in Chapter 12 titled "Exceptions and Fault Handling" for a detailed discussion of the floating-point faults and their associated flag and mask bits in the arithmetic controls.

Floating-Point Normalizing Mode Flag

The floating-point normalizing mode flag (bit 29) determines whether or not floating-point instructions are allowed to operate on denormalized numbers. If set, floating-point instructions are allowed to operate on denormalized numbers; if clear, the processor generates a floating reserved-operand fault when it detects denormalized numbers that are used as operands for floating-point instructions. (Refer to the section in Chapter 12 titled "Normalizing Mode" for more information on the use of this flag.)

Floating-Point Rounding Control

The floating-point rounding control field (bits 31-30) indicates which rounding mode is in effect for floating point computations. These bits are set as shown in Table 3-4, depending on the rounding mode to be selected.

Table 3-4: Encoding of Rounding Control Field

Rounding Control	Rounding Mode
00	round to nearest (even)
01	Round down (toward negative infinity)
10	Round up (toward positive infinity)
11	Truncate (round toward zero)

(Refer to the section in Chapter 12 titled "Rounding Control" for more information on the use of the floating-point rounding control bits.)

All the unused bits in the AC register are reserved and must be set to 0.

PROCESS AND TRACE CONTROLS

The processor's process controls and trace controls are also cached on the processor chip. The process controls are a set of 32 bits that control or show the current execution state of the processor. The process controls are described in detail in Chapter 7.

The trace controls are a set of 32 bits that control the tracing facilities of the processor. The trace controls are described in Chapter 10.

INSTRUCTION CACHING

The processor provides a 512-byte cache for instructions. When the processor fetches an instruction or group of instructions from memory, they are stored in this cache before being fed into the instruction-execution pipeline. The processor manages this cache transparently from the program being run.

This instruction cache is a read-only cache, meaning that once bytes from the instruction stream are written into the instruction cache, they cannot be changed. Because of this, the processor does not support self-modified programs in a transparent fashion. The only way to change the instruction stream once it has been written into the instruction cache is to purge the instruction cache. The IAC message "purge instruction cache" is provided for this purpose, as described in Chapter 13.

Note

The purge instruction cache IAC is not defined in the 80960 architecture. It is an implementation-dependent feature of the 80960KB processor.

Procedure Calls **4**

CHAPTER 4
PROCEDURE CALLS

This chapter describes the 80960KB processor's procedure call and stack mechanism. It also describes the supervisor call mechanism, which provides a means of calling privileged procedures such as kernel services.

TYPES OF PROCEDURE CALLS

The processor supports three types of procedure calls:

- Local call
- System call
- Branch and link

A local call uses the processor's call/return mechanism, in which a new set of local registers and a new frame on the stack are allocated for the called procedure. A system call is similar to a local call, however, it provides access to procedures through a system procedure table. The most important use of a system call is to call privileged procedures called supervisor procedures. A system call to a supervisor procedure is called a *supervisor call.* A branch and link is merely a branch to a new instruction with the return IP stored in a global register.

In this chapter, the call/return mechanism is introduced first and is followed by a discussion of how this mechanism is used to make local calls and system calls.

Note

The processor's interrupt- and fault-handling mechanisms use implicit procedure calls. These implicit calls are described in detail in Chapters 8 and 9, respectively.

CALL/RETURN MECHANISM

The processor's call/return mechanism has been designed to simplify procedure calls and to provide a flexible method for storing and handling variables that are local to a procedure.

Two structures support this mechanism: the local registers (on the processor chip) and the procedure stack (in memory). Figure 4-1 shows the relationship of the local registers to the procedure stack.

For each procedure, the processor automatically allocates a set of local registers and a frame on the procedure stack. Since the local registers are on-chip, they provide fast-access storage for local variables. If additional space for local variables is required, it can be allocated in the stack frame.

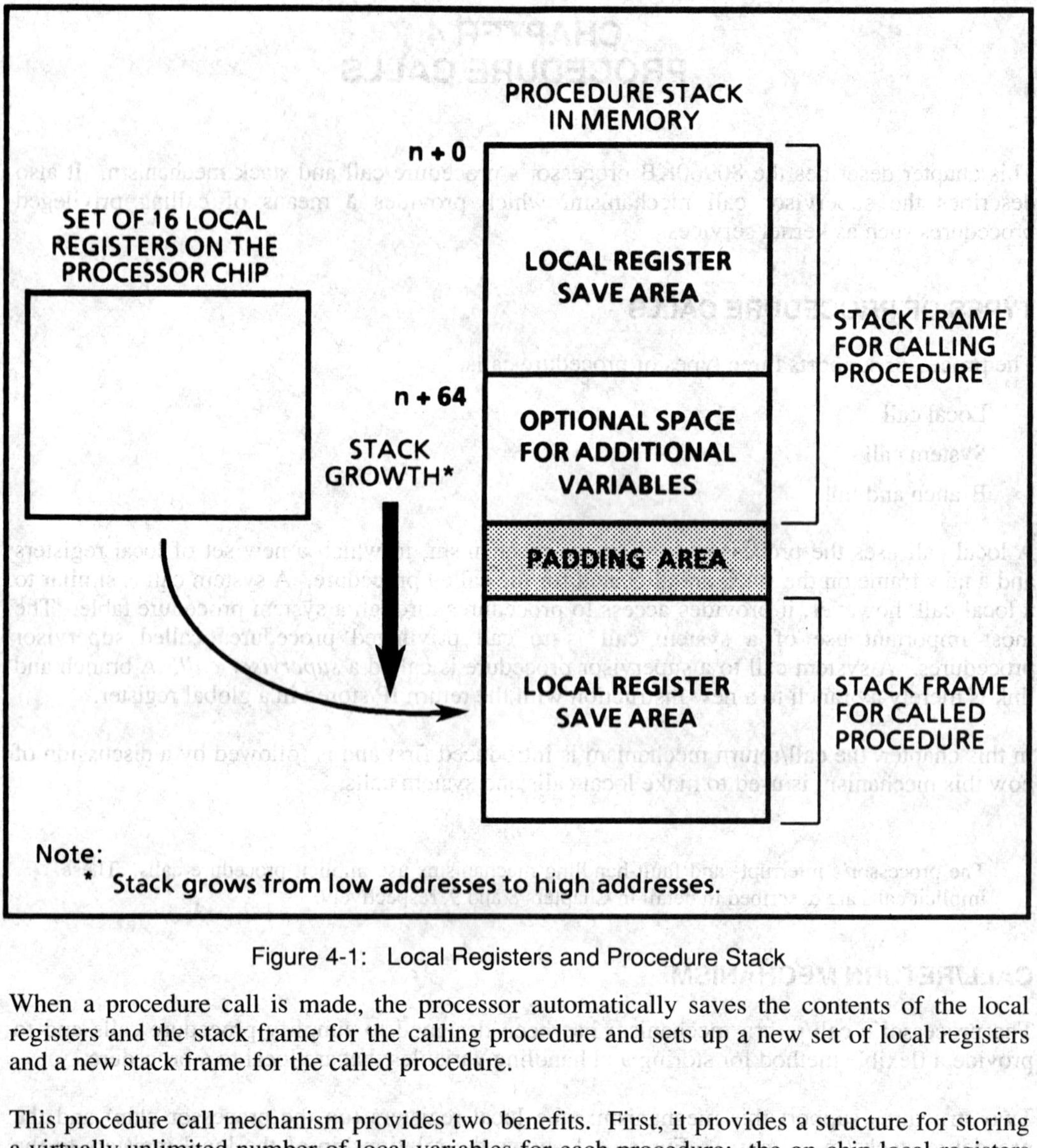

Figure 4-1: Local Registers and Procedure Stack

When a procedure call is made, the processor automatically saves the contents of the local registers and the stack frame for the calling procedure and sets up a new set of local registers and a new stack frame for the called procedure.

This procedure call mechanism provides two benefits. First, it provides a structure for storing a virtually unlimited number of local variables for each procedure: the on-chip local registers provide quick access to often-used variables and the stack provides space for additional variables.

Second, a program does not have to explicitly save and restore the variables stored in the local registers and stack frames. The processor does this implicitly on procedure calls and on returns.

A detailed description of the call/return mechanism is given in the following paragraphs.

Local Registers and the Procedure Stack

For each procedure, the processor allocates a set of 16 local registers. Three of these registers (r1, r2, and r3) are reserved for linkage information to tie procedures together. The remaining 13 local registers are available for general storage of variables.

The processor maintains a procedure stack in memory for use when performing local calls. This stack can be located anywhere in the address space and grows from low addresses to high addresses.

The stack consists of contiguous frames, one frame for each active procedure. As shown in Figure 4-2, each stack frame provides a save area for the local registers and an optional area for additional variables.

To increase the speed of procedure calls, the 80960KB processor provides four sets of local registers. Thus, when a procedure call is made, the contents of the current set of local registers often do not have to be stored in the procedure stack. Instead, a new set of local registers is assigned to the called procedure. When procedure calls are made greater than four deep, the processor automatically stores the contents of the oldest set of local registers on the stack to free up a set of local registers for the most recently called procedure.

Refer to the section later in this chapter titled "Mapping the Local Registers to the Procedure Stack" for further discussion of the relationship between the local register sets and the procedure stack.

Procedure Linking Information

Global register g15 (FP) and local registers r0 (PFP), r1 (SP), and r2 (RIP) contain information to link procedures together and to link the local registers to the procedure stack. The following paragraphs describe this linkage information.

Frame Pointer

The FP is the address of the first byte of the current (topmost) stack frame. On procedure calls, the FP for the new frame is stored in global register g15; on returns, the FP for the previous frame is restored in g15.

The 80960KB processor aligns each new stack frame on a 64-byte boundary. Since the resulting FP always points to a 64-byte boundary, the processor ignores the 6 low-order bits of the FP and interprets them to be zero.

Note

The alignment boundary for new frames is defined by means of an implementation-dependent parameter called SALIGN. The relationship of SALIGN to the frame alignment boundary is described in Appendix E.

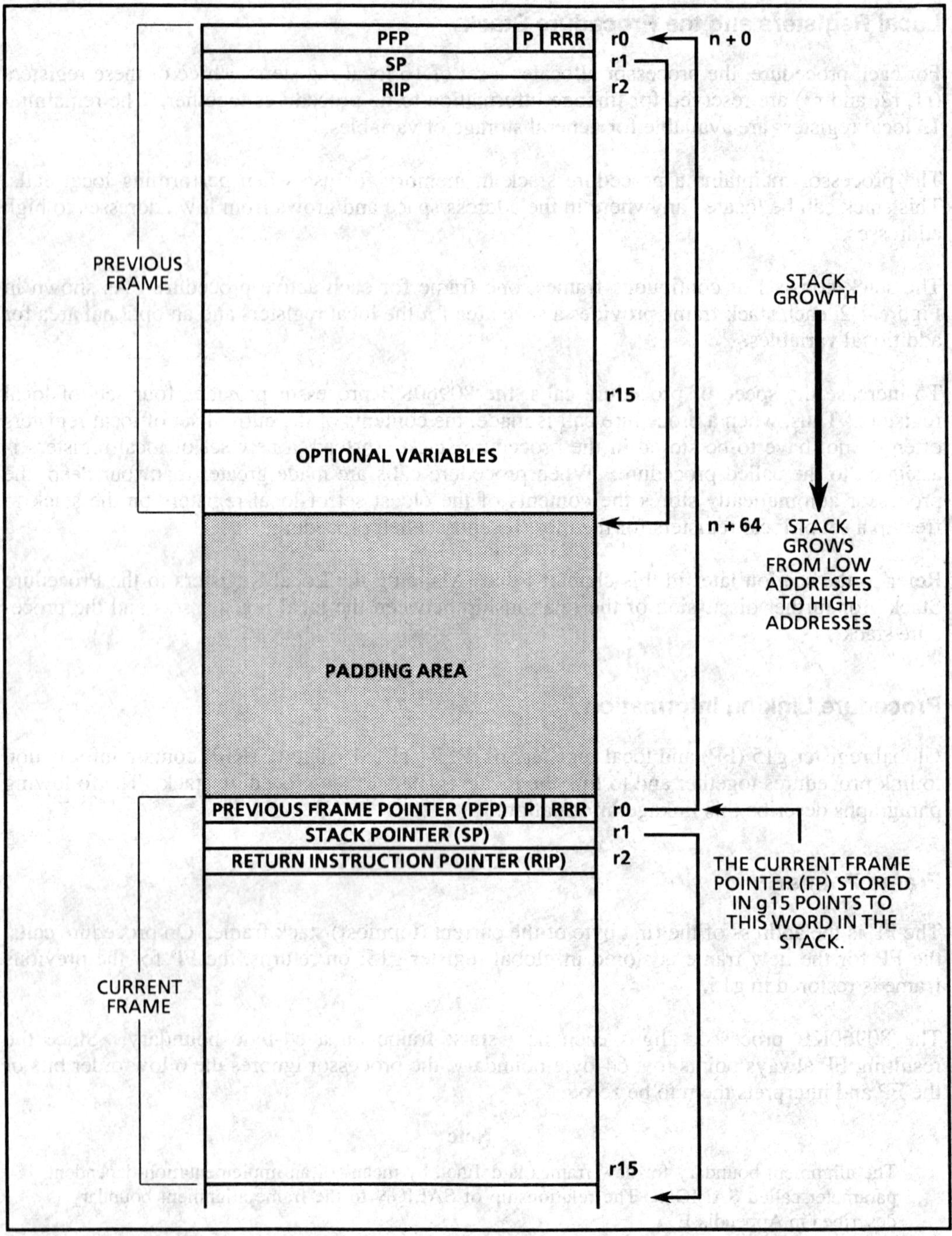

Figure 4-2: Procedure Stack Structure

Stack Pointer

The procedure stack grows upward (i.e., toward higher addresses). The SP points to the next available byte of the stack frame, which can also be thought of as the last byte of the stack frame plus one. To determine the initial SP value, the processor adds 64 to the FP.

If additional space is needed on the stack for local variables, the SP may be incremented in one-byte increments. For example, the following instruction adds six words of additional space to the stack:

```
addo sp, 24, sp     #  sp ← sp + 24
```

With the Intel 80960KB Assembler, the keyword "sp" stands for register r1.

Padding Area

When the processor creates a new frame on a procedure call, it will, if necessary, add a padding area to the stack so that the new frame starts on a 64 byte boundary. To create the padding area, the processor rounds off the SP for the current stack frame (the value in r1) to the next highest 64 byte boundary. This value becomes the FP for the new stack frame.

Previous Frame Pointer

The PFP is the address of the first byte of the previous stack frame. Since the 80960KB ignores the 6 low-order bits of the FP, only the 26 most-significant bits of the PFP are stored here. The 4 least-significant bits of r0 are then used to store return status information.

Return Status and Prereturn-Trace Information

Bits 0 through 2 of local register r0 contain return status information for the calling procedure and bit 3 contains the prereturn-trace flag. When a procedure call is made (either explicit or implicit), the processor records the call type in the return status field. The processor then uses this information to select the proper return mechanism when returning to the calling procedure.

Table 4-1 shows the encoding of the return status field according to the different types of calls that the processor supports. Of the five types of calls allowed, the fault call (described in Chapter 9) and the interrupt and stopped-interrupt calls (described in Chapter 8) are implicit calls that the processor initiates. The local call (described in this section) is an explicit call that a program initiates using the **call** or **callx** instruction. The supervisor call (described at the end of this chapter in the section titled "User-Supervisor Protection Model") is an explicit call that a program makes using the **calls** instruction.

Table 4-1: Encoding of Return Status Field

Encoding	Call Type	Return Action
000	Local call or supervisor call made from the supervisor mode	Local return
001	Fault call	Fault return
010	Supervisor call from user mode, trace was disabled before call	Supervisor return, with the trace enable flag in the process controls set to 0 and the execution mode flag set to 0
011	Supervisor call from user mode, trace was enabled before call	Supervisor return, with the trace enable flag in the process controls set to 1 and the execution mode flag set to 0
100	reserved	
101	reserved	
110	Stopped-interrupt call	Stopped-interrupt return
111	Interrupt call	Interrupt return

The third column of Table 4-1 shows the type of a return action that the processor takes depending on the state of the return status field.

The processor records two versions of the supervisor call: one for when the trace-enable flag in the process controls is set prior to a supervisor call and one for when the flag is clear prior to the call. The trace controls are described in detail in Chapter 10.

The prereturn-trace flag is used in conjunction with the call-trace and prereturn-trace modes. If the call-trace mode is enabled when a call is made, the processor sets the prereturn-trace flag; otherwise it clears the flag. Then, if this flag is set and the prereturn-trace mode is enabled, a prereturn trace event is generated on a return before any actions associated with the return operation are performed. Refer to Chapter 10 for a detailed discussion of the interaction of the call-trace and prereturn-trace modes and the prereturn-trace flag.

Return Instruction Pointer

The RIP is the address of the instruction that the processor is to execute after returning from a procedure call. This instruction is the instruction that follows the procedure call instruction.

Since the processor uses the same procedure call mechanism to make implicit procedure calls to service faults and interrupts, programs should not use register r2 for purposes other than to hold the RIP.

Mapping the Local Registers to the Procedure Stack

The availability of multiple register sets cached on the processor chip and the saving and restoring of these register sets in stack frames should be transparent to most programs. However, the following additional information about how the local registers and procedure stack are mapped to one another can help avoid problems.

Since the local-register sets reside on the processor chip, the processor will often not have to access the stack frame in the procedure stack, even though space has been allocated on the stack for the current frame. The processor only accesses the current frame in the procedure stack in the following instances:

1. to read or write variables other than those held in the local registers, or
2. to read local registers that were stored in the procedure stack due to the nesting of procedures calls more than four deep.

This method of mapping the local registers to the register-save areas in the procedure stack has several implications. First, storing information in a local register does not guarantee that it will be stored in its associated word in the current stack frame. Likewise, storing information in the first 16 words of a stack frame does not guarantee that the local registers associated with the stack frame are modified.

Second, if you try to read the contents of the current set of local registers through a memory access to the first 16 words of the current stack frame, you may not get the expected result. This is also true if you try to read the contents of a previously stored set of local registers through a memory address to its associated stack frame.

The processor automatically stores the contents of a local register set into the register-save area of its associated stack frame only if the nesting of procedure calls (local or supervisor) is deeper than the number of local register sets.

Occasionally, it is necessary to have the contents of all local register sets match the contents of the register-save areas in their associated stack frames. For example, when debugging software it may be necessary to trace the call history back through the nested procedures. This can not be done unless the cached local-register frames are flushed (i.e., written out to the procedure stack).

The processor provides the **flushreg** (flush local registers) instruction to allow voluntary flushing of the local registers. This instruction causes the contents of all the local-register sets, except the current set, to be written to their associated stack frames in memory.

Third, if you need to modify the previous FP in register r0, you should precede this operation with the **flushreg** instruction, or else the behavior of the **ret** (return) instruction is not predictable.

Fourth, local registers should not be used for passing parameters between procedures. (Parameter passing is discussed in the following section.)

Fifth, when a set of local registers is assigned to a new procedure, the processor may not clear or initialize these registers. The initial contents of these registers are therefore unpredictable. Also, the processor does not initialize the local register-save area in the newly created stack frame for the procedure, so its contents are equally unpredictable.

LOCAL CALL

A local call is made using either of two local call instructions: **call** and **callx**. These instructions initiate a procedure call using the call/return mechanism described earlier in this chapter.

The **call** instruction specifies the address of the called procedures as the IP plus a signed, 24-bit displacement (i.e., -2^{23} to $2^{23} - 4$).

The **callx** instruction allows any of the addressing modes to be used to specify the procedure address. The *IP with displacement* addressing mode allows full 32-bit IP relative addressing.

The **ret** instruction initiates a procedure switch back to the last procedure that issued a call.

Local Call Operation

During a local call, the processor performs the following operations:

1. Stores the RIP in current local-register r2.
2. Allocates a new set of local registers for the called procedure.
3. Allocates a new frame on the procedure stack.
4. Changes the instruction pointer to point to the first instruction in the called procedure.
5. Stores the PFP in new local-register r0.
6. Stores the FP for the new frame in global register g15.
7. Allocates a save area for the new local registers in the new stack frame.
8. Stores the SP in new local-register r1.

Local Return Operation

On a return, the processor performs these operations:

1. Sets the FP in global register g15 to the value of the PFP in current local-register r0.
2. Deallocates the current local registers for the procedure that initiated the return and switches to the local registers assigned to the procedure being returned to.
3. Deallocates the stack frame for the procedure that initiated the return.
4. Sets the IP to the value of the RIP in new local-register r2.

The algorithms that the **call**, **callx**, and **ret** instructions use are described in greater detail in Chapter 11.

PARAMETER PASSING

The processor supports two mechanisms for passing parameters between procedures: global registers and argument list.

Passing Parameters in Global Registers

The global registers provide the fastest method of passing parameters. Here, the calling procedure copies the parameters to be passed into global registers. The called procedure then copies the parameters (if necessary) out of the global registers after the call.

On a return, the called procedure can copy result parameters into global registers prior to the return, with the calling procedure copying them out of the global registers after the return.

Passing Parameters in an Argument List

When more parameters need to be passed than will fit in the global registers, they can be placed in an argument list. This argument list can be stored anywhere in memory providing that the procedure being called has a pointer to the list. Commonly, a pointer to the argument list is placed in a global register.

Parameters can also be returned to the calling procedure through an argument list. Here again, a pointer to the argument is generally returned to the calling procedure through a global register.

The argument list method of passing parameters should be thought of as an escape mechanism and used only when there are not enough global registers available for passing parameters.

Passing Parameters Through the Stack

A convenient place to store an argument list is in the stack frame for the calling procedure. Storing the argument list in the stack provides the benefit of having the list automatically deallocated upon returning from the procedure that set up the list. Space for the argument list is created by incrementing the SP, as described earlier in this chapter in the section titled "Stack Pointer."

Parameters can also be returned to the calling procedure through an argument list in the stack. However, care should be taken when doing this. The return argument list must not be placed in the frame for the called procedure, since this frame is deallocated on the return. Also, if the return list is to be placed in the frame of the calling procedure, the calling procedure must allocate space for this list prior to making the call.

SYSTEM CALL

A system call is made using the call system instruction **calls**. This call is similar to a local call except that the processor gets the IP for the called procedure from a data structure called the system procedure table. (System calls are sometimes referred to in this manual as "system procedure-table calls.")

Figure 4-3 illustrates the use of the system procedure table in a system call. The **calls** instruction requires a procedure-number operand. This procedure number provides an index into the system procedure table, which contains IPs for specific procedures.

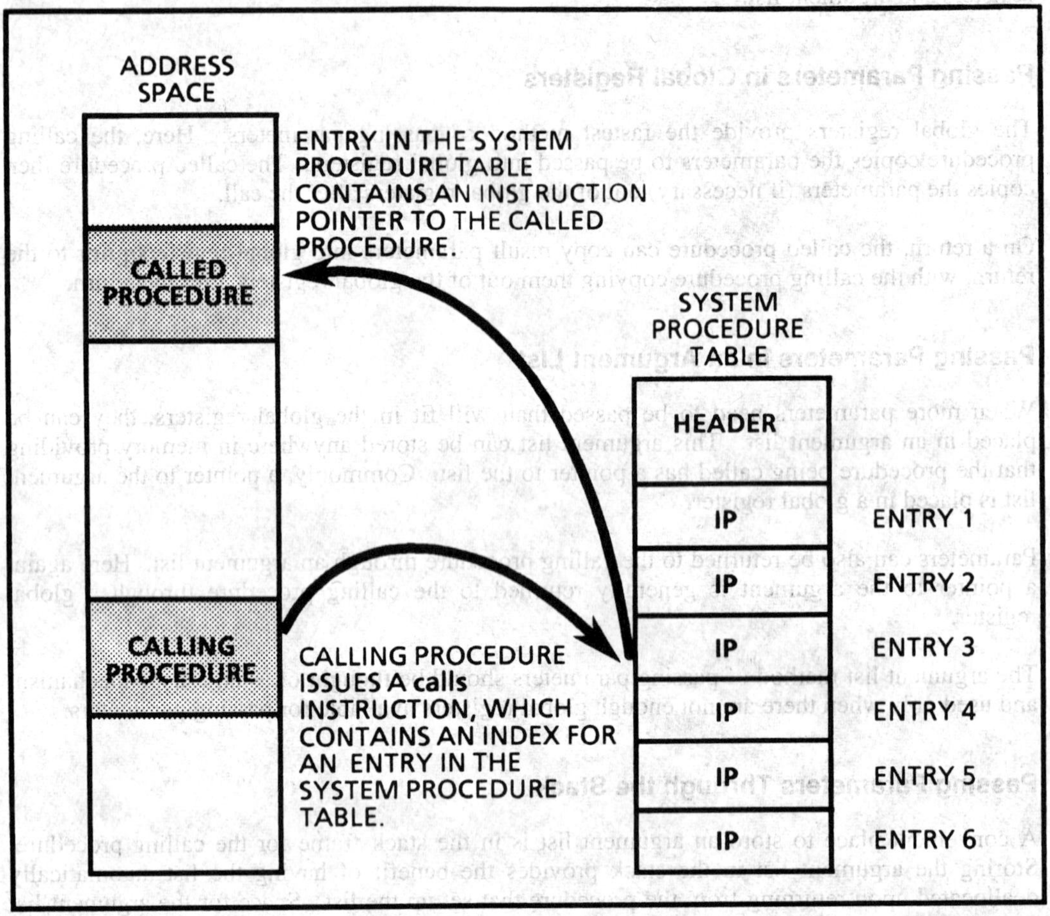

Figure 4-3: System Call Mechanism

The system call mechanism supports two types of procedure calls: local calls and supervisor calls. A local call is the same as that made with the **call** and **callx** instructions, except that the processor gets the IP of the called procedure from the system procedure table. The supervisor call differs from the local call in two ways: (1) it causes the processor to switch to another stack (called the supervisor stack), and (2) it causes the processor to switch to a different execution mode.

The system call mechanism offers two benefits. First, it supports portability for application software. System calls are commonly used to call kernel services. By calling these services with a procedure number rather than a specific IP, applications software does not have to be changed each time the implementation of the kernel services is modified.

Second, the ability to switch to a different execution mode and stack allows kernel procedures and data to be insulated from applications code. This benefit is describe in more detail later in this chapter in the section titled "User-Supervisor Protection Model".

SYSTEM PROCEDURE TABLE

The system procedure table is a general structure, which the processor uses in two ways. The first way is as a place for storing IPs for kernel procedures, which can then be accessed through the system call mechanism. The processor gets a pointer to the system procedure table from the initial memory image (IMI) as described in Chapter 7 in the section titled "System Data-Structure Pointers."

The second way a system procedure table is used is as a place for storing IPs for fault handler procedures. Here, the processor gets a pointer to the system procedure table from entries in the fault table, as described in Chapter 9 in the section titled "Fault-Table Entries."

The structure of the system procedure table is shown in Figure 4-4. The following sections describe the fields in this table.

Procedure Entries

The procedure entries specify the target IPs for the procedures that can be accessed through the system procedure table. Each entry is made up of an address (or IP) field and a type field. The address field gives the address of the first instruction of the target procedure. Since all instructions are word aligned, only the 30 most-significant bits of the address are given. The processor automatically provides zeros for the least-significant bits.

The procedure entry type field indicates the type of call to execute: local or supervisor. The encodings of this field are shown in Table 4-2.

Table 4-2: Encodings of Entry Type Field in System Procedure Table Entry

Entry Type Field	Procedure Type
00	local procedure
01	reserved
10	supervisor procedure
11	reserved

Supervisor Stack Pointer

When a supervisor call is made, the processor switches to a new stack called the *supervisor stack*. The processor gets a pointer to this stack from the supervisor-stack-pointer entry (bytes 12-15, bits 2-31) in the system procedure table. Since stack frames are word aligned, only the 30 most-significant bits of the supervisor stack pointer are given.

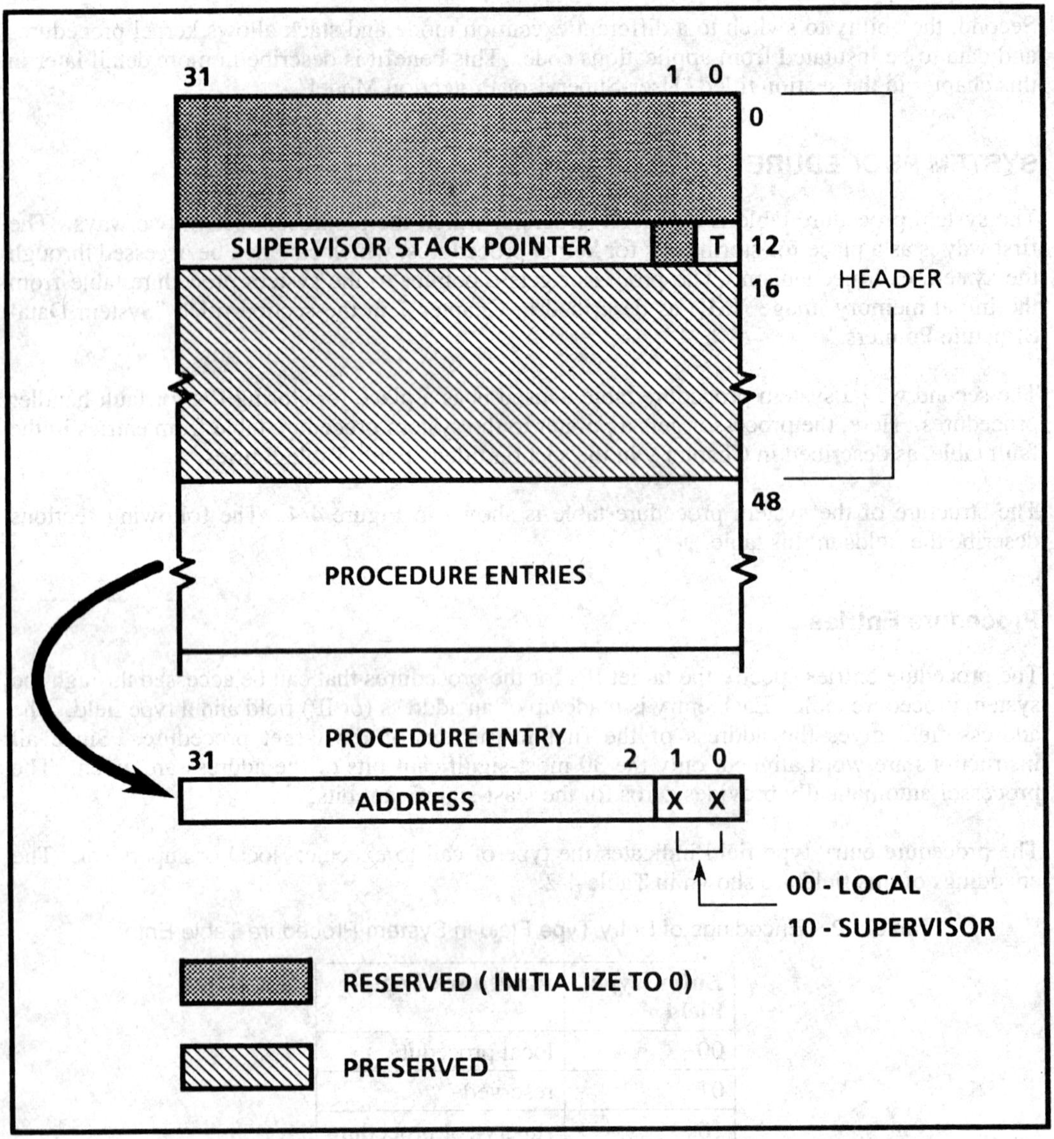

Figure 4-4: Procedure Table Structure

Trace Control Flag

The trace-control flag (byte 12, bit 0) specifies the new value of the trace-enable flag when a supervisor call causes a switch from user mode to supervisor mode. The use of this bit is described in Chapter 10.

System Call to a Local Procedure

When a **calls** instruction references a procedure entry designated as a local type (00_2), the processor executes a local call to the procedure selected from the system procedure table. Neither a mode switch nor a stack switch occurs.

The **ret** instruction permits returns from either a local procedure or a supervisor procedure. The return status field in local register r0 determines the type of return action that the processor is to take. If the return status field is set to 000_2, a local return is executed. In a local return, no stack or mode switching is carried out.

USER-SUPERVISOR PROTECTION MODEL

The processor provides a mode and stack switching mechanism called the user-supervisor protection model. This protection model allows a system to be designed in which kernel code and data reside in the same address space as user code and data, but access to the kernel procedures (called supervisor procedures) is only allowed through a tightly controlled interface. This interface is provided by the system procedure table.

The user-supervisor protection model also allows kernel procedures to be executed using a different stack (the supervisor stack) than is used to execute applications program procedures. The ability to switch stacks helps maintain the integrity of the kernel. For example, it would allow system debugging software or a system monitor to be accessed, even if an applications program crashes.

User and Supervisor Modes

When using the user-supervisor protection model, the processor can be in either of two execution modes: user or supervisor. The difference between the two modes is that when in the supervisor mode, the processor

- switches to the supervisor stack, and
- may execute a set of supervisor only instructions.

Note

In the 80960KB implementation of the 80960 architecture, the only supervisor-only instruction is the modify process controls instruction (**modpc**).

Supervisor Calls

Mode switching between the user and supervisor execution modes is accomplished through a supervisor call. A supervisor call is a call executed with the **calls** instruction that references a supervisor procedure in the system procedure table (i.e., a procedure with an entry type 10_2).

When the processor is in the user mode and it executes a **calls** instruction, the processor performs the following actions:

- It switches to supervisor mode
- It switches to the supervisor stack
- It sets the return status field in register R0 of the calling procedure to $01X_2$, indicating that a mode and stack switch has occurred.

The processor remains in the supervisor mode until a return is performed from the procedure that caused the original mode switch. While in the supervisor mode, either the local call instructions (**call** and **callx**) or the **calls** instruction can be used to call supervisor procedures.

(The **call** and **callx** instructions call local (or user) procedures in user mode and supervisor procedures in supervisor mode. There is no stack or processor state switching associated with these instructions.)

When a **ret** instruction is executed and the return status field is set to $01X_2$, the processor performs a supervisor return. Here, the processor switches from the supervisor stack to the local stack, and the execution mode is switched from supervisor to user.

Supervisor Stack

When using the user-supervisor mechanism, the processor maintains separate stacks in the address space, one for procedures executed in the user mode (local procedures) and another for procedures executed in the supervisor mode (supervisor procedures). When in the user mode, the local procedure stack described at the beginning of this chapter is used. When a supervisor call is made, the processor switches to the supervisor stack. It continues to use the supervisor stack until a return is made to the user mode.

The structure of the supervisor stack is identical to that of the local procedure stack (shown in Figure 4-2). The processor obtains the SP for the supervisor stack from the system procedure table. When a supervisor call is executed while in the user mode (causing a switch to the supervisor stack), the processor aligns this SP to the next 64 byte boundary to form the new FP for the supervisor stack. When a local call or supervisor call is made while in the supervisor mode, the processor aligns the SP in the current frame of the supervisor stack to the next 64 byte boundary to form the FP pointer. This operation allows supervisor procedures to be called from supervisor procedures.

Hints on Using the User-Supervisor Protection Model

The user-supervisor has three basic uses in an embedded system application:

1. to allow the **modpc** instruction to be used,
2. to allow kernel code to use a separate stack from the applications code, and
3. to allow an external memory management unit (MMU) to provide protection for kernel code and data.

If an application does not require any of the above features, it can be designed to not use the user-supervisor protection model. Here, all procedure calls are to local procedures. If the system table is used, all the entries must be the local type (i.e., entry type 00_2).

If access to the **modpc** instruction is required, but the other two features are not, it is suggested that the system be designed to always run in supervisor mode. At initialization, the processor automatically places itself in supervisor mode, prior to executing the first instruction. The processor then remains in supervisor mode indefinitely, as long as no action is taken to change the execution mode to user mode (i.e., using the **modpc** instruction to change the execution mode bit of the process controls to 0). With this technique, all of the procedure calling instructions (**call**, **callx**, and **calls**) can be used. The processor only uses one stack, which is considered the supervisor stack. It gets the supervisor stack pointer from local register r2. (Prior to making the first procedure call, the supervisor stack pointer must be loaded into r2.)

The processor does not support the last use of the user-supervisor protection model directly. In other words, the processor does not provide a pin or other device that indicates to external hardware when a mode switch has occurred. Several techniques are available to perform this operation, which are beyond the scope of this manual.

BRANCH AND LINK

The **bal** (branch and link) and **balx** (branch and link extended) instructions provide an alternate method of making procedure calls. These instructions save the address of the next instruction (RIP) in a specified location, then branch to a target instruction or set of instructions. The state of the local registers and stack remains unchanged. (For the **bal** instruction, the RIP is automatically stored in global register g14; for the **balx** instruction, the location of the RIP is specified with one of the instruction operands.)

A return is accomplished with a **bx** (branch extended) instruction, where the address of the target instruction is the one saved with the branch and link instruction.

Branch and link procedure calls are recommended for calls to procedures that (1) do not call other procedures (i.e., for procedure calls that do not result in nesting of procedures) and (2) do not need many local variables (i.e., allocation of a new set of local registers does not provide any benefit). Here, local registers as well as global registers can be used for parameter passing.

Data Types and Addressing Modes 5

CHAPTER 5
DATA TYPES AND ADDRESSING MODES

This chapter describes the data types that the 80960KB processor recognizes and the addressing modes that are available for accessing memory locations.

DATA TYPES

The processor defines and operates on the following data types:

- Integer (8, 16, 32, and 64 bits)
- Ordinal (8, 16, 32, and 64 bits)
- Real (32, 64, and 80 bits)
- Decimal (ASCII digits)
- Bit Field
- Triple-Word (96 bit)
- Quad-Word (128 bit)

Note

The real and decimal data types are not defined in the 80960 architecture. They are supported in the 80960KB processor, but not in the 80960KA processor.

The integer, ordinal, real, and decimal data types can be thought of as numeric data types because some operations on these data types produce numeric results (e.g., add, subtract).

The remaining data types (bit field, triple word, and quad word) represent groupings of bits or bytes that the processor can operate on as a whole, regardless of the nature of the data contained in the group. These data types facilitate the moving of blocks of bits or bytes.

Integers

Integers are signed whole numbers, which are stored and operated on in two's complement format. The processor recognizes four sizes of integers: 8 bit (byte integers), 16 bit (short integers), 32 bit (integers), and 64 bit (long integers). Figure 5-1 shows the formats for the four integer sizes and the ranges of values allowed for each size.

Ordinals

Ordinals are a general-purpose data type. The processor recognizes four sizes of ordinals: 8 bit (byte ordinals), 16 bit (short ordinals), 32 bit (ordinals), and 64 bit (long ordinals). Figure 5-2 shows the formats for the four ordinal sizes and the ranges of numeric values allowed for each size.

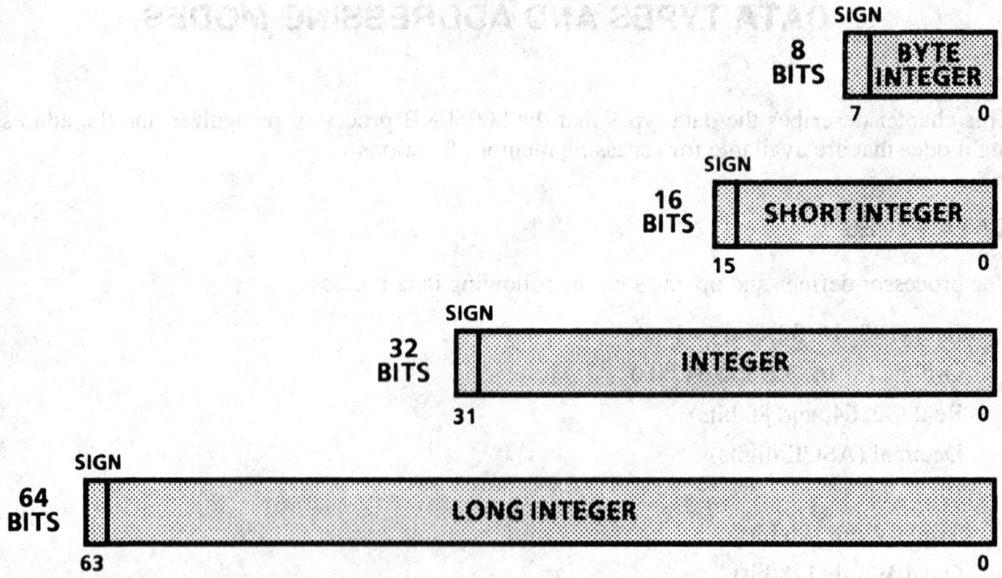

DATA TYPE	RANGE	DECIMAL EQUIVALENT
Byte Integer	-2^7 to 2^7-1	-128 to 127
Short Integer	-2^{15} to $2^{15}-1$	-32,768 to 32,767
Integer	-2^{31} to $2^{31} - 1$	-2.14×10^9 to 2.14×10^9
Long Integer	-2^{63} to $2^{63} - 1$	-9.22×10^{18} to 9.22×10^{18}

Figure 5-1: Integer Format and Range

The processor uses ordinals for both numeric and non-numeric operations. For numeric operations, ordinals are treated as unsigned whole numbers. The processor provides several arithmetic instructions that operate on ordinals. For non-numeric operations, ordinals contain bit fields, byte strings, and Boolean values.

When ordinals are used to represent Boolean values, a 1_2 represents a TRUE and a 0_2 represents a FALSE.

Reals

Reals are floating-point numbers. The processor recognizes three sizes of reals: 32 bit (reals), 64 bit (long reals), and 80 bit (extended reals). The real-number format conforms to ANSI/IEEE Std. 754-1985, the IEEE Standard For Binary Floating-Point Arithmetic. Real numbers are discussed in greater detail in Chapter 12.

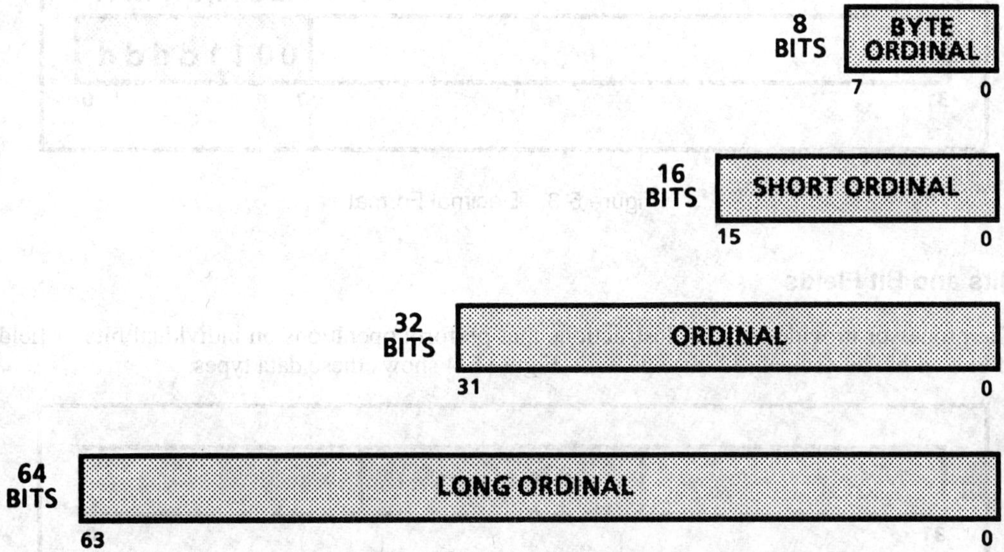

DATA TYPE	RANGE	DECIMAL EQUIVALENT
Byte Ordinal	0 to 2^{8}-1	0 to 255
Short Ordinal	0 to 2^{16}-1	0 to 65,535
Ordinal	0 to 2^{32} - 1	0 to 4.29×10^{9}
Long Ordinal	0 to 2^{64} - 1	0 to 1.84×10^{19}

Figure 5-2: Ordinal Format and Range

Decimals

The processor provides three instructions that perform operations on decimal values when the values are presented in ASCII format. Figure 5-3 shows the ASCII format for decimal digits. Each decimal digit is contained in the least-significant byte of an ordinal (32 bits). The decimal digit must be of the form $0011dddd_2$, where $dddd_2$ is a binary-coded decimal value from 0 to 9. For decimal operations, bits 8 through 31 of the ordinal containing the decimal digit are ignored.

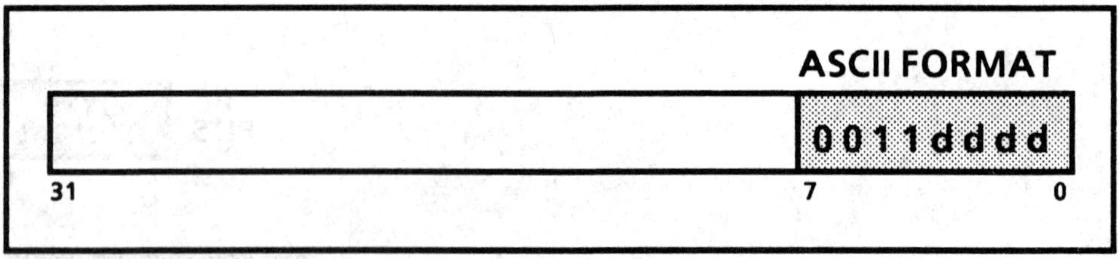

Figure 5-3: Decimal Format

Bits and Bit Fields

The processor provides several instructions that perform operations on individual bits or fields of bits within an ordinal (32 bit) operand. Figure 5-4 shows these data types.

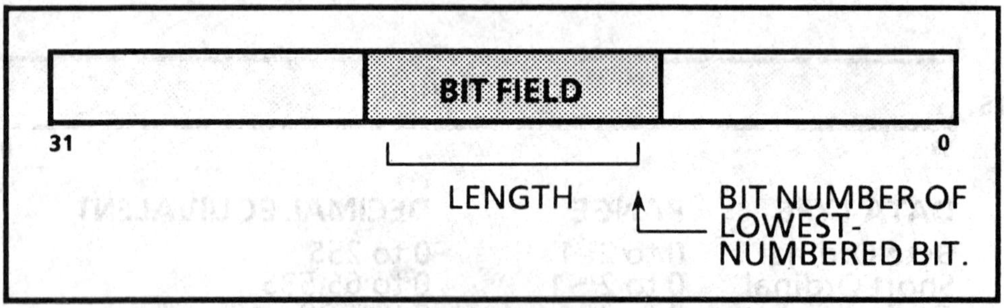

Figure 5-4: Bits and Bit Fields

An individual bit is specified for a bit operation by giving its bit number in the ordinal in which it resides. The least-significant bit of a 32-bit ordinal is bit 0; the most-significant bit is bit 31.

A bit field is a contiguous sequence of bits of from 0 to 32 bits in length within a 32-bit ordinal. A bit field is defined by giving its length in bits and the bit number of its lowest-numbered bit.

A bit field cannot span a register boundary.

Triple and Quad Words

Triple and quad words refer to consecutive bytes in memory or in registers: a triple word is 12 bytes and a quad word is 16 bytes. These data types facilitate the moving of blocks of bytes. The triple-word data type is useful for moving extended-real numbers (80 bits).

The quad-word instructions (**ldq**, **stq**, and **movq**) offer the most efficient way to move large blocks of data.

BYTE, WORD, AND BIT ADDRESSING

The processor provides instructions for moving blocks of data values of various lengths from memory to registers (load) and from registers to memory (store). The allowable sizes for blocks are bytes, half-words (2 bytes), words (4 bytes), double words, triple words, and quad words. For example, the **stl** (store long) instruction stores an 8-byte (double word) block of data in memory.

When a block of data is stored in memory, the least-significant byte of the block is stored at a base memory address and the more significant bytes are stored at successively higher addresses.

When loading a byte, half-word, or word from memory to a register, the least-significant bit of the block is always loaded in bit 0 of the register. When loading double words, triple words, and quad words, the least-significant word is stored in the base register. The more significant words are then stored at successively higher numbered registers. Double words, triple words, and quad words must also be aligned in registers to natural boundaries as described in Chapter 3 in the section titled "Register Alignment."

Bits can only be addressed in data that resides in a register. Bit 0 in a register is the least-significant bit and bit 31 is the most-significant bit.

ADDRESSING MODES

The processor offers 11 modes for addressing operands. These modes are grouped as follows:

- Literal
- Register
- Absolute
- Register Indirect
- Register Indirect with Index
- Index with Displacement
- IP with Displacement

Most of the instructions use only the first two modes (literal and register). The remaining modes are used for memory related instructions.

Table 5-1 shows all the addressing modes, a brief description of the elements of the address in each mode, and the assembly-code syntax for each mode.

Table 5-1: Addressing Modes

Mode	Description	Assembler Syntax
Literal	value	value
Register	register	reg
Absolute offset	offset	exp
Register Indirect	abase	(reg)
Register Indirect with offset	abase + offset	exp (reg)
Register Indirect with index	abase + (index*scale)	(reg) [reg*scale]
Register Indirect with index and displacement	abase + (index*scale) + displacement	exp (reg) [reg*scale]
Index with displacement	(index*scale) + displacement	exp [reg*scale]
IP with displacement	IP + displacement + 8	exp (IP)

Where:
reg is register and exp is expression

Literals

The processor recognizes two types of literals: ordinal literal and floating-point literal. An ordinal literal can range from 0 to 31 (5 bits). When an ordinal literal is used as an operand, the processor expands it to 32 bits by adding leading zeros. If the instruction defines an operand larger than 32 bits, the processor zero-extends the value to the operand size. If an ordinal literal is used in an instruction that requires integer operands, the processor treats the literal as a positive integer value.

The processor also recognizes two floating-point literals (+0.0 and +1.0). These floating-point literals can only be used with floating-point instructions. As with the ordinal literals, the processor converts the floating-point literals to the operand size specified by the instruction.

A few of the floating-point instructions use both floating-point and non-floating-point operands (e.g., the convert integer-to-real instructions). Ordinal literals can be used in these instructions for non-floating-point operands.

Note

Floating-point literals are not defined in the 80960 architecture.

Register

A register is referenced as an operand by giving the register number (e.g., g0, r5, fp3). Both floating-point and non-floating-point instructions can reference global and local registers in this way. However, floating-point registers can only be referenced in conjunction with a floating-point instruction.

Absolute

Absolute addressing is used to reference a memory location directly as an offset from address 0 of the address space, ranging from -2^{31} to $2^{31} - 1$. Typically, an assembler will allow absolute addresses to be specified through arithmetic expressions (e.g., x + 44), symbolic labels, and absolute values.

At the machine-level, two absolute-addressing modes are provided, depending on the instruction format (i.e., MEMA or MEMB). For the MEMA format, the offset is an ordinal number ranging from 0 to 2048; for the MEMB format, the offset is an integer (called a displacement) ranging from -2^{31} to $2^{31} -1$. After evaluating an absolute address, the assembler will convert the address into an offset and select the appropriate machine-level instruction type and addressing mode. (The machine-level addressing modes and instruction formats are described in Appendix B.)

Register Indirect

The register indirect addressing modes allow an address to be specified with an ordinal value (32 bits) in a register or with an offset or a displacement added to a value in a register. Here, the value in the register is referred to as the address base (abase).

Again, an assembler will allow the offset and displacement to be specified with an expression or symbolic label, then evaluate the address to determine whether an offset or a displacement is appropriate.

Register Indirect with Index

The register indirect with index addressing modes allow a scaled index to be added to the value in a register. The index is specified by means of a value placed in a register. This index value is then multiplied by the scale factor. The allowable scale factors are 1, 2, 4, 8, and 16.

A displacement may also be added to the abase value and scaled index.

Index with Displacement

A scaled index can also be used with a displacement alone. Again, the index is contained in a register and is multiplied by a scaling constant before the displacement is added to it.

IP with Displacement

The IP with displacement addressing mode is often used with load and store instructions to make them IP relative.

Note that with this mode the displacement plus a constant of 8 is added to the IP of the instruction.

Instruction Set Summary 6

CHAPTER 6
INSTRUCTION SET SUMMARY

This chapter provides an overview of the instruction set for the 80960KB processor. Included is a discussion of the instruction format and a summary of the instruction groups and the instructions in each group.

Chapter 11 gives detailed descriptions of each of the instructions. The instructions are listed in this chapter in alphabetical order. Included for each instruction are the assembly-language format, the action taken when the instruction is executed, and examples of how the instruction might be used.

Appendix C provides a detailed description of the factors that affect instruction timing. It also gives the number of clock cycles required for each instruction.

INSTRUCTION FORMATS

Instructions are described in this reference manual in two formats: assembly language and machine level.

Assembly-Language Format

Throughout most of this manual, the instructions are referred to by their assembly-language mnemonics. For example, the add ordinal instruction is referred to as the **addo** instruction.

An assembly-language statement consists of an instruction mnemonic, followed by from 0 to 3 operands, separated by commas. The following example shows the assembly-language statement for the **addo** instruction:

```
addo g5, g9, g7
```

Here, the ordinal operands in global registers g5 and g9 are added together and the result is stored in g7.

A detailed description of the nomenclature used to describe assembly-language instructions is given in Chapter 11.

Machine Formats

At the machine level of the processor, all instructions are word aligned. Most of the instructions are one word long, although some addressing modes make use of a two-word format.

There are four instruction formats: register (REG), compare and branch (COBR), control (CTRL), and memory (MEM). Each instruction uses one of these formats, which is determined by the opcode field of the instruction.

The machine-level formats for the instructions are described in detail in Appendix B.

INSTRUCTION GROUPS

The 80960KB processor implements all the instructions in the 80960 instruction set, which includes all of the data movement, arithmetic, logical, and program control instructions commonly found in computer architectures. The processor also includes a set of floating-point instructions and several instructions to handle architectural extensions found in the processor.

The 80960 instruction set is made up of the following groups of instructions:

- Data Movement
- Arithmetic (Ordinal and Integer)
- Logical
- Bit and Bit Field
- Comparison
- Branch
- Call/Return
- Fault
- Debug
- Processor Management

The instruction-set extensions found in the 80960KB processor include the following groups of instructions:

- Integer to Real Conversion
- Floating Point
- Synchronous Move and Load
- Decimal

Tables 6-1 and 6-2 give a summary of the 80960 instructions and the 80960KB instruction-set extensions, respectively. The actual number of instructions is greater than those shown in this list, because for some operations, several different instructions are provided to handle different operand sizes, data types, or branch conditions.

Table 6-1: Summary of the 80960 Instruction Set

Data Movement	**Arithmetic**	**Logical**	**Bit and Bit Field**
Load Store Move Load Address	Add Subtract Multiply Divide Remainder Modulo Shift Extended Multiply Extended Divide	And Not And And Not Or Exclusive Or Not Or Or Not Nor Exclusive Nor Not Nand Rotate	Set Bit Clear Bit Not Bit Check Bit Alter Bit Scan For Bit Scan Over Bit Extract Modify
Comparison	**Branch**	**Call/Return**	**Fault**
Compare Conditional Compare Compare and Increment Compare and Decrement	Unconditional Branch Conditional Branch Compare and Branch	Call Call Extended Call System Return Branch and Link	Conditional Fault Synchronize Faults
Debug	**Processor**	**Miscellaneous**	
Modify Trace Controls Mark Force Mark	Modify Arithmetic Controls Modify Process Controls Flush Local Registers Test Condition Code	Atomic Add Atomic Modify Scan Byte For Equal	

Table 6-2: Summary of the 80960KB Instruction-Set Extensions

Conversion	Floating Point	Synchronous	Decimal
Convert Real to Integer	Move Real	Synchronous Load	Move
Convert Integer to Real	Add	Synchronous Move	Add With Carry
	Subtract		Subtract With Carry
	Multiply		
	Divide		
	Remainder		
	Scale		
	Round		
	Square Root		
	Sine		
	Cosine		
	Tangent		
	Arctangent		
	Log		
	Log Binary		
	Log Natural		
	Exponent		
	Classify		
	Copy Real Extended		
	Compare		

The following sections give a brief overview of the instructions in each of these groups. The floating-point instructions are described in Chapter 12.

DATA MOVEMENT

The data movement instructions include those instructions that move data from memory to the global and local registers; that move data from the global and local registers to memory; and that move data among these registers.

Load

The load instructions (listed below) copy bytes or words from memory to a selected register or group of registers:

ld	load
ldob	load byte ordinal
ldos	load short ordinal
ldib	load byte integer
ldis	load short integer
ldl	load long
ldt	load triple
ldq	load quad

For the **ld**, **ldob**, **ldos**, **ldib**, and **ldis** instructions, a memory address and a register are specified in the instruction and the value at the memory address is copied into the register. Zero and sign extending is performed automatically for byte and short (half-word) operands.

The **ld**, **ldl**, **ldt**, and **ldq** instructions copy 4, 8, 12, and 16 bytes from memory into successive registers.

Note

When using the load, store, and move instructions that move 8, 12, or 16 bytes at a time, the rules for register alignment must be followed. Refer to the section in Chapter 3 titled "Register Alignment" for a discussion of these rules.

Store

For each load instruction there is a corresponding store instruction (listed below), which copies bytes or words from a selected register or group of registers to memory:

st	store
stob	store byte ordinal
stos	store short ordinal
stib	store byte integer
stis	store short integer
stl	store long
stt	store triple
stq	store quad

For the **st**, **stob**, **stos**, **stib**, and **stis** instructions, a register and memory address are specified in the instruction and the value in the register is copied into memory. For the byte and short instructions, the value in the register is automatically reformatted for the shorter memory location. For the **stib** and **stis** instructions, this reformatting can lead to overflow if the register value is too large to be represented in the shorter memory location.

The **st**, **stl**, **stt**, and **stq** instructions copy 4, 8, 12, and 16 bytes from successive registers into memory.

Move

The move instructions, listed below, copy data from a register or group of registers to another register or group of registers.

mov	move word
movl	move long word
movt	move triple word
movq	move quad word

These move instructions can only be used to move data among the global and local registers. A set of move-real instructions (**movr**, **movrl**, and **movre**) are provided for moving real number values between the global and local registers and the floating-point registers. The move-real instructions are described in Chapter 12.

Load Address

The **lda** instruction computes an effective address in the address space from an operand presented in one of the addressing modes. A common use of this instruction is to load a constant into a register.

ARITHMETIC

Table 6-3 lists all the arithmetic operations for which the 80960KB processor provides instructions and the data types that the instructions operate on. An "X" in this table indicates that the 80960 architecture provides an instruction for the specified operation and data type; an "E" indicates that an 80960KB instruction-set extension provides an instruction for the specified operation and data type. An "E*" indicates that the specified operation can be performed on the specified data type using 80960KB extended instructions, but that a unique instruction for this operation is not provided. For example, a specific instruction is not provided to add two extended-real values. However, this operation can be carried out with either the add real (**addr**) or the add long real (**addrl**) instruction.

With two exceptions, all the processor's arithmetic operations are carried out on operands in registers. The processor does not provide instructions that perform arithmetic operations on operands in memory.

The two instructions that are exceptions are the **atadd** (atomic add) and **atmod** (atomic modify) instructions, which are discussed later in this chapter.

A summary of the arithmetic instructions for real (floating-point) data types is provided in Chapter 12. The following sections describe the arithmetic instructions for ordinal and integer data types.

Add, Subtract, Multiply, and Divide

The following instructions perform add, subtract, multiply, or divide operations on integers and ordinals:

addi	add integer
addo	add ordinal
subi	subtract integer
subo	subtract ordinal
muli	multiply integer
mulo	multiply ordinal
divi	divide integer
divo	divide ordinal

These instructions perform operations on one-word operands in registers and store the results in a register.

Table 6-3: Arithmetic Operations

Arithmetic Operations	Integer	Ordinal	Real	Long Real	Extended Real
Add	X	X	E	E	E*
Subtract	X	X	E	E	E*
Multiply	X	X	E	E	E*
Divide	X	X	E	E	E*
Remainder	X	X	E	E	E*
Modulo	X				
Shift Left	X	X			
Shift Right	X	X			
Shift Right Dividing	X				
Scale			E	E	E*
Round			E	E	E*
Square Root			E	E	E*
Sine			E	E	E*
Cosine			E	E	E*
Tangent			E	E	E*
Arctangent			E	E	E*
Exponent			E	E	E*
Log			E	E	E*
Log Binary			E	E	E*
Log Epsilon			E	E	E*
Classify			E	E	E*
Copy Sign					E
Copy Reversed Sign					E

Extended Arithmetic

The following four instructions are provided to support extended arithmetic operations to be performed (i.e., arithmetic operations on operands greater than one word in length):

addc	add ordinal with carry
subc	subtract ordinal with carry
emul	extended multiply
ediv	extended divide

The **addc** and **subc** instructions add or subtract two words (contained in registers) plus a condition code bit (used as a carry bit). If the result has a carry, the carry bit in the condition code is set. Also, a second condition code bit is set if the operation would have resulted in an integer overflow condition. (The three-bit condition code is contained in the arithmetic controls as described in Chapter 3.)

These instructions treat the operands as ordinals, however, the indication of overflow in the condition code facilitates a software implementation of extended-integer arithmetic.

The **emul** instruction multiplies two ordinals (each contained in a register), producing long ordinal result (stored in two registers). The **ediv** instruction divides a long ordinal by an ordinal, producing an ordinal quotient and an ordinal remainder.

Remainder and Modulo

The following instructions divide one operand by another and retain the remainder of the operation:

remi	remainder integer
remo	remainder ordinal
modi	modulo integer

The difference between the remainder and modulo instructions lies in the sign of the result. For the **remi** and **remo** instructions, the result has the same sign as the dividend; for the **modi** instruction, the result has the same sign as the divisor.

Shift and Rotate

The processor provides the following five shift instructions:

shlo	shift left ordinal
shro	shift right ordinal
shli	shift left integer
shri	shift right integer
shrdi	shift right dividing integer

These instructions shift the operand a specified number of bits to the left or to the right. The **shlo**, **shli**, **shro**, and **shrdi** instructions are equivalent to multiplying (shift left) or dividing (shift right) by the power of 2. Bits shifted beyond the register boundary are discarded

The **shri** instruction performs a conventional arithmetic shift right. However, when this instruction is used to divide an integer operand by the power of 2, it produces an incorrect quotient for negative operands. (The **shrdi** instruction produces the correct quotient when this divide operation is used on negative operands.)

The **rotate** instruction rotates the bits of the operand to the left (toward higher significance) by a specified number of bits. Bits shifted beyond the left boundary of the register (bit 31) appear at the right boundary (bit 0).

LOGICAL

The following instructions perform bitwise Boolean operations on the specified operands:

and	A and B
notand	(not A) and B
andnot	A and (not B)
xor	not (A = B)
or	A or B
nor	(not A) and (not B)
xnor	A = B
not	not A
notor	(not A) or B
ornot	A or (not B)
nand	(not A) or (not B)

COMPARISON

The processor provides several types of instructions that are used to compare two operands. The following sections describe the compare instructions for ordinal and integer data types. The compare instructions for real data types are discussed in Chapter 12.

Compare and Conditional Compare

The compare instructions listed below, compare two operands then set the condition-code bits in the arithmetic controls according to the results.

cmpi	compare integer
cmpo	compare ordinal
concmpi	conditional compare integer
concmpo	conditional compare ordinal

The condition-code bits are set to indicate whether one operand is less than, equal to, or greater than the other operand. (Refer to the section in Chapter 3 titled "Functions of the Arithmetic Controls Bits" for a discussion of meanings of the condition-code bits for conditional operations.)

The **cmpi** and **cmpo** instructions simply compare the two operands and set the condition-code bits accordingly.

The **concmpi** and **concmpo** instructions first check the status of bit 2 of the condition code. If it is not set, the operands are compared as with the **cmpi** and **cmpo** instructions. If bit 2 is set, no comparison is performed and the condition-code bits are not changed.

The conditional compare instructions are provided specifically to optimize two-sided range comparisons to check if A is between B and C (i.e., B ≤ A ≤ C). Here, a compare instruction (**cmpi** or **cmpo**) is used to check one side of the range (e.g., A ≥ B) and a conditional compare instruction (**concmpi** or **concmpo**) is used to check the other side (e.g., A ≤ C) according to the result of the first comparison.

Compare and Increment or Decrement

The following instructions compare two operands, set the condition-code bits according to the results, then increment or decrement one of the operands:

cmpinci	compare and increment integer
cmpinco	compare and increment ordinal
cmpdeci	compare and decrement integer
cmpdeco	compare and decrement ordinal

These instructions are intended for use at the end of iterative loops.

BRANCH

The branch instructions allow the direction of program flow to be changed by explicitly modifying the IP. The processor provides three types of branch instructions:

- unconditional branch
- conditional branch
- compare and branch

Most of the branch instructions specify the target IP by specifying a signed displacement to be added to the current IP. Other branch instructions specify the memory address of the target IP using one of the processor's addressing modes. This latter group of instructions are called extended-addressing instructions (e.g., branch extended, branch and link extended)

Unconditional Branch

The following four instructions are used for unconditional branching:

b	Branch
bx	Branch Extended
bal	Branch and Link
balx	Branch and Link Extended

The **b** and **bx** instructions cause program execution to jump to the specified target IP. As described in Chapter 11, these two instructions perform the same function; however, they use different machine-level instruction formats.

The **bal** and **balx** instructions store the address of the next instruction in a specified register, then jump to the specified target IP. (For the **bal** instruction, the RIP is automatically stored in register G14; for the **balx** instruction the location of the RIP is specified with an instruction operand.) As described in Chapter 4, the branch and link instructions provide a method of performing procedure calls that does not use the processor's call/return mechanism. Here, the saved instruction address is used as a return IP.

The **bx** and **balx** instructions can be made IP-relative by using the IP with displacement addressing mode.

Conditional Branch

With the conditional branch (branch if) instructions, the processor checks the condition-code bits in the arithmetic controls. If these bits match the value specified with the instruction, the processor jumps to the target IP. These instructions use the displacement plus IP method of specifying the target IP:

be	branch if equal
bne	branch if not equal
bl	branch if less
ble	branch if less or equal
bg	branch if greater
bge	branch if greater or equal
bo	branch if ordered
bno	branch if unordered

(Refer to the section in Chapter 3 titled "Functions of the Arithmetic Controls Bits" for a discussion of meanings of the condition-code bits for conditional operations.)

The **bo** and **bno** instructions refer to comparisons of real numbers. Ordered and unordered real numbers are described in Chapter 12.

Compare and Branch

The compare and branch instructions compare two operands, then branch according to the results. There are three subtypes of instructions in this group: compare integer, compare ordinal, and check bit:

cmpibe	compare integer and branch if equal
cmpibne	compare integer and branch if not equal
cmpibl	compare integer and branch if less
cmpible	compare integer and branch if less or equal
cmpibg	compare integer and branch if greater
cmpibge	compare integer and branch if greater or equal
cmpibo	compare integer and branch if ordered
cmpibno	compare integer and branch if unordered
cmpobe	compare ordinal and branch if equal
cmpobne	compare ordinal and branch if not equal
cmpobl	compare ordinal and branch if less
cmpoble	compare ordinal and branch if less or equal
cmpobg	compare ordinal and branch if greater
cmpobge	compare ordinal and branch if greater or equal
bbs	check bit and branch if set
bbc	check bit and branch if clear

With the compare-ordinal-and-branch and compare-integer-and-branch instructions, two operands are compared and the condition-code bits are set, as with the compare instructions described earlier in this chapter. A conditional branch is then executed as with the conditional branch (branch if) instructions.

With the check-bit-and-branch instructions, one operand specifies a bit to be checked in the other operand. The condition-code bits are set according to the state of the specified bit (i.e., 010_2 if the bit is set and 000_2 if the bit is clear). A conditional branch is then executed according to the setting of the condition-code bits.

BIT AND BIT FIELD

The bit instructions perform operations on a specific bit in an ordinal operand or on a bit field.

Bit Operations

The following instructions operate on a specified bit:

setbit	set bit
clrbit	clear bit
notbit	not bit
chkbit	check bit
alterbit	alter bit
scanbit	scan for bit
spanbit	span over bit

The **setbit**, **clrbit**, and **notbit** instructions set, clear, or complement (toggle) a specified bit in an ordinal.

The **chkbit** instruction causes the condition-code bits to be set according to the state of a specified bit in a register. The condition code is set to 010_2 if the bit is set and 000_2 otherwise.

The **alterbit** instruction alters the state of a specified bit in an ordinal according to the condition code. If the condition code is 010_2, the bit is set; if the condition code is 000_2, the bit is cleared.

The **scanbit** and **spanbit** instructions find the most significant set bit and clear bit, respectively, in an ordinal.

Bit Field Operations

There are two bit field instructions **extract** and **modify**. The **extract** instruction converts a specified bit field, taken from an ordinal value, into an ordinal value. In essence, this instruction shifts a bit field in a register to the right and fills in the bits to the left of the bit field with zeros.

The **modify** instruction copies bits from one register, under control of a mask, into another register. Only the unmasked bits in the destination register are modified.

BYTE OPERATIONS

The **scanbyte** instruction performs a byte-by-byte comparison of two ordinals to determine if any two corresponding bytes are equal. The condition code is set according to the results of the comparison.

CONVERSION

Data can be converted from one length to another by means of the load and store instructions. For example, the **ldis** instruction loads a short integer from memory to a register and automatically converts the integer from a half word to a full word.

The 80960KB extended instruction set provides instructions to perform conversions between integer and real data types. These instructions are described in Chapter 12.

CALL AND RETURN

The processor offers an on-chip call/return mechanism for making procedure calls to local procedures and kernel procedures. This call/return mechanism is described in detail in Chapter 4. The following four instructions are provided to support this mechanism.

call	call
callx	call extended
calls	call system
ret	return

The **call** and **callx** instructions call local procedures. The **call** instruction specifies the target procedure (the first instruction of the procedure) by adding a signed displacement to the IP. The **callx** instruction uses extended addressing, as described for the **bx** and **balx** instructions, to specify the target procedure. For both of these instructions, a new set of local registers and a new stack frame are allocated for the called procedure.

The **calls** instruction operates similarly to the **call** and **callx** instructions, except that it gets its target procedure address from the system procedure table. An index number included as an operand in the instruction provides an entry point into the procedure table.

Depending on the type of entry being pointed to in the procedure table, the **calls** instruction can cause a supervisor call to be executed. A supervisor call causes the processor to switch to the supervisor stack and to switch to supervisor mode. The supervisor call is described in detail in Chapter 4.

The **ret** instruction performs a return from a called procedure to the calling procedure (the procedure that made the call). This instruction obtains its target IP (return IP) from linkage information that was saved for the calling procedure. The **ret** instruction is used to return from local and supervisor calls and from implicit calls to interrupt and fault handlers.

ATOMIC INSTRUCTIONS

The atomic instructions perform read-modify-write operations on operands in memory. They insure that an operation on a specified memory location is completed before another agent with access to memory is allowed to access that memory location. These instructions are particularly useful in systems in which several agents have access to system memory.

There are two atomic instructions: atomic add (**atadd**) and atomic modify (**atmod**). The **atadd** instruction causes an operand to be added to the value in the specified memory location. The **atmod** causes bits in the specified memory location to be modified under control of a mask.

CONDITIONAL FAULTS

Generally, the processor generates faults automatically as the result of certain operations. Fault handling routines are then invoked to handle the various types of faults without explicit intervention by the currently running process. (Faults are discussed in detail in Chapter 9.)

The following conditional fault instructions permit a fault to be generated explicitly according to the state of the condition-code bits:

faulte	fault if equal
faultne	fault if not equal
faultl	fault if less
faultle	fault if less or equal
faultg	fault if greater
faultge	fault if greater or equal
faulto	fault if ordered
faultno	fault if unordered

DEBUG

The processor supports debugging and monitoring of program activity through the use of trace events. The following instructions support these debugging and monitoring tools:

modtc	modify trace controls
mark	mark
fmark	force mark

The trace functions are controlled through the processor's trace controls bits. Some of these bits allow various types of tracing to be enabled or disabled. Other bits act as flags to indicate when an enabled trace event has been detected. (Trace controls are described in detail in Chapter 10.)

The **modtc** instruction permits the trace controls bits to be modified.

The **mark** instruction causes a breakpoint trace event to be generated if the breakpoint trace mode is enabled. The **fmark** instruction generates a breakpoint trace independent of the state of the breakpoint trace mode flag. The latter two instructions allow a breakpoint to be placed anywhere in a program.

PROCESSOR MANAGEMENT

The processor provides several instructions for use in controlling processor-related functions.

The **modpc** instruction provides a method of reading and modifying the contents of the process controls.

In certain instances, it is necessary to insure that the contents of the local-register save area of the stack frames are the same as the local registers. The flush local registers instruction (**flushreg**) automatically stores the contents of all the local register sets, except the current set, in the register save area of their associated stack frames.

The arithmetic controls cannot be addressed with the load, move, and store instructions or the bit instructions. Instead, special instructions are provided for this purpose.

The modify arithmetic controls instruction (**modac**) permits bits in the arithmetic controls register to be modified under the control of a mask.

The following test instructions allow the state of the condition-code bits to be tested:

teste	test if equal
testne	test if not equal
testl	test if less
testle	test if less or equal
testg	test if greater
testge	test if greater or equal
testo	test if ordered
testno	test if unordered

These instructions cause a TRUE (010_2)to be stored in a destination register if the condition code matches the condition specified with the instruction. Otherwise, a FALSE (000_2) is stored in the register.

80960KB NON-FLOATING-POINT INSTRUCTION-SET EXTENSIONS

The following non-floating-point instructions are extensions to the 80960 architecture instruction set. The synchronous load and move instructions are provided in both the 80960KB and 80960KA processors; the decimal instructions are provided only in the 80960KB processor.

Synchronous Load and Move

The processor's store instructions are executed asynchronously with the memory controller. Once the processor sends data out on its bus for storage in main memory, it continues with the next instruction in the instruction stream, assuming that its bus control logic will carry out the operation.

The 80960KB processor provides four special instructions for performing memory operations that perform store and move operations synchronously with memory.

The synchronous load instruction (**synld**) loads a word from a register into memory. When this instruction is performed, the processor waits until a condition code bit is set in the arithmetic controls, indicating that the operation has been completed, before it begins executing the next instruction.

The synchronous move instructions (**synmov**, **synmovl**, and **synmovq**) perform synchronous moves of data from one location in memory to another.

These instructions are used primarily for sending IAC messages, as described in Chapter 13.

Decimal

The following three instructions are provided for use in decimal-arithmetic algorithms:

dmovt	move and test decimal
daddc	decimal add with carry
dsubc	decimal subtract with carry

These instructions operate on 32-bit decimal operands that contain an 8-bit, ASCII-coded decimal in the least-significant byte of the word (as shown in Figure 5-3).

The **dmovt** instruction moves a decimal operand from one register to another and tests the least significant byte of the operand to determine if it is a decimal digit (0 to 9). It sets the condition code according to the results of the test: 010_2 if the operand contains a decimal digit and 000_2 otherwise.

The **daddc** and **dsubc** instructions operate similarly to the **addc** and **subc** instructions. They add or subtract two decimal digits plus bit 1 of the condition code (used as a carry-in bit). If the operation produces a decimal carry, the condition code is set accordingly. The subtraction operation is carried out in 10's complement arithmetic.

These instructions can be used iteratively to add or subtract decimal values of any length.

With the 80960KB processor, the most efficient method of multiplying or dividing decimal numbers is to convert them into extended-real numbers and use the **mulr** and **divr** instructions. Decimal values of up to 18 decimal digits can be handled with this technique.

Processor Management and Initialization

7

CHAPTER 7
PROCESSOR MANAGEMENT AND INITIALIZATION

This chapter describes the facilities for initializing and managing the operation of the 80960KB processor. Included is a description of the processor-management facilities and the steps required to initialize the processor. Appendix D gives a listing of the necessary 80960KB code to initialize the processor.

OVERVIEW OF PROCESSOR MANAGEMENT FACILITIES

This chapter and Chapters 8, 9, 10, and 13 describe the 80960KB's processor-management facilities. These facilities are primarily software-related, although some hardware considerations are also discussed.

For the purpose of discussion in these chapters, it is assumed that the processor is going to execute a program made up of a system kernel (or executive) and applications code. This program may be located in ROM or RAM.

Such a program has the following facilities available to it to initialize, communicate with, and control the processor:

- Instruction List
- System Data Structures
- Interrupts
- IACs
- Faults

These facilities allow system hardware and the kernel to initialize the processor and initiate instruction execution. They also provide software or external agents with methods of interrupting the processor to service external I/O devices.

The following paragraphs give an overview of these processor-management facilities.

Instruction List

At the most rudimentary level, the processor is controlled through a stream of instructions that the processor fetches from memory and executes one at a time. Once the processor is initialized, it begins executing instructions and continues until it is stopped.

System Data Structures

The processor defines several system data structures that reside in memory. These data structures (shown in Figure 7-1) offer a means of configuring the processor to operate in a specific way.

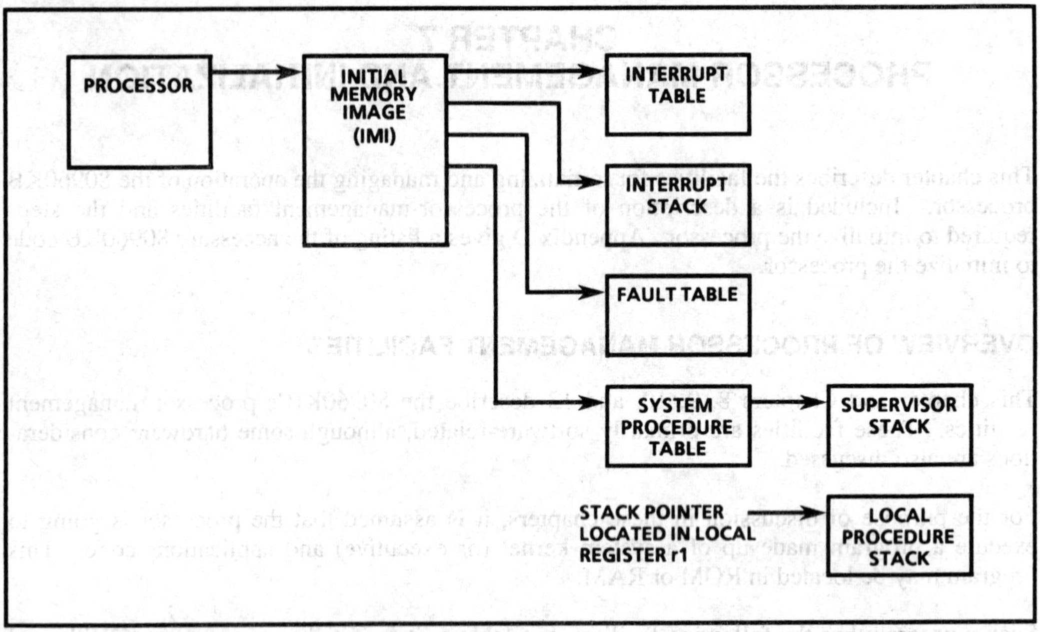

Figure 7-1: System Defined Data Structures

The system data structures can be located anywhere in the processor's address space. The processor gets pointers to most of these data structures from the initial memory image (IMI). The IMI is described later in this chapter in the section titled "Initial Memory Image."

The interrupt table provides pointers to interrupt-handling procedures. The interrupt vector numbers act as indices into this table. For the purpose of handling interrupts, a separate interrupt stack is maintained in the address space. The interrupt mechanism is described in Chapter 8.

The fault table provides pointers to fault-handling procedures. When the processor detects a fault, it generates a fault vector number internally that provides an index into the fault table. The fault mechanism is described in Chapter 9.

The system procedure table contains pointers to the kernel procedures, which are accessed using the system call (**calls**) mechanism. The system table structure is described in Chapter 4 in the section titled "System Procedure Table."

The processor uses two stacks for procedures calls: the local procedure stack and the (optional) supervisor stack. These stacks are described in Chapter 4.

The processor also contains a register, called the process controls register, that it uses to store information about the current state of the processor and the program it is executing. The process controls are described later in this chapter in the section titled "Process Controls."

Interrupts

The processor defines two methods of asynchronously requesting services from the processor: interrupts and IAC messages. Interrupts are the more common of the two.

An interrupt is a break in the control flow of a program so that the processor can handle a more urgent chore. Interrupt requests are generally sent to the processor from an external source, often to request I/O services. When the processor receives an interrupt request, it temporarily stops work on its current task and begins work on an interrupt-handling procedure. Upon completion of the interrupt-handling procedure, the processor generally returns to the task that was interrupted and continues work where it left off.

Interrupts also have a priority, which the processor uses to determine whether to service the interrupt immediately or to postpone service until a later time.

IACs

The 80960KB processor provides an alternate method of communicating with other agents in the system called IAC messages, or simply IACs. Using the IAC mechanism, other agents on the system bus are able to communicate with the processor through messages that are exchanged in a reserved section of memory.

Like interrupts, IACs are used to request that the processor stop work on its current task and begin work on another task. However, where an interrupt generally causes a temporary break in the execution of a program, an IAC often causes a permanent change in the control flow of the processor.

The IAC mechanism is described in Chapter 13.

Faults

While executing instructions, the processor is able to recognize certain conditions that could cause it to return an inappropriate result or that could cause it to go down a wrong and possibly disastrous path. One example of such a condition is a divisor operand of zero in a divide operation. Another example is an instruction with an invalid opcode. These conditions are called faults.

The processor handles faults almost the same way that it handles interrupts. When the processor detects a fault, it automatically stops its current processing activity and begins work on a fault-handling procedure.

PROCESS CONTROLS

The process-controls word (shown in Figure 7-2) contains miscellaneous pieces of information to control processor activity and show the current state of the processor. The various functions of this field are described in the following paragraphs.

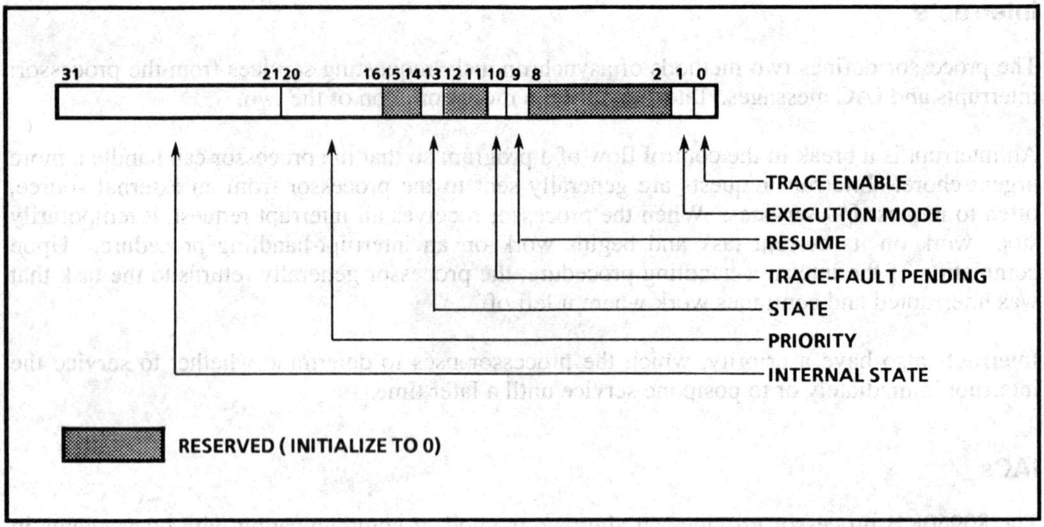

Figure 7-2: Process-Controls Word

The *execution mode* flag determines whether the processor is operating in the user mode (clear) or supervisor mode (set). The processor automatically sets this bit on a supervisor call and clears it on a return from supervisor mode.

The *priority* field determines the priority (from 0 to 31) of the processor. When the processor is in the executing state, it sets its priority according to this value.

The *state* flag determines the state of the processor. The encoding of this bit is shown in Table 7-1.

Table 7-1: Encoding of Processor State Field

State Field	Processor State
0	Executing
1	Interrupted

This bit tells software whether the processor

- is currently executing a program (0) or
- has been interrupted so the it can service an interrupt (1).

The *trace-enable* and *trace-fault-pending* flags control tracing. The trace-enable field determines whether trace faults are to be generated (set) or not-generated (clear). The trace-fault-pending field is a flag that the processor uses to determine if a trace event has been detected (set) or not (clear). The use of these fields is discussed in detail in Chapter 10.

The *resume* flag signals the processor that an instruction has been suspended. The processor sets this flag whenever it suspends an instruction to handle an interrupt or fault. On a return from the interrupt or fault handler, the processor checks this flag and performs an instruction resumption action if the flag is set.

All of the bits in the process controls are set to zero as part of the initialization procedure. Bits 2 through 8, 11, 12, 15, and 21 through 31 are reserved. These bits should not be altered following initialization.

Changing the Process Controls

The kernel can change the process controls using any of the following three methods:

- Modify-process-controls instruction (**modpc**)
- Alter the saved process controls prior to a return from an interrupt handler
- Alter the saved process controls prior to a return from a fault handler

The **modpc** instruction reads and modifies the process controls cached in the processor.

In the latter two methods, the kernel changes the process controls in the interrupt or fault record that is saved on the stack. On the return from the interrupt or fault handler, the modified process controls are copied into the processor's internal process controls.

Note

Changing the saved process controls by means of a fault handler can only be used if the fault handler was invoked by means of an implicit supervisor call.

When the process controls are changed as described above, the processor acts on the changes as soon as it receives the new information, except for the following situation.

If the **modpc** instruction is used to change the trace-enable flag, the processor does not guarantee to act on the change until after up to four more instructions have been executed.

PRIORITIES

The processor defines a priority mechanism for determining the order in which programs, interrupts, and IACs are worked on. Priorities range from 0 to 31, with 31 being the highest priority. Each interrupt vector is assigned a priority. Also, when the processor is executing a program, it sets its priority according to the priority field of the process controls.

Interrupt priorities serve two functions. First, they determine if the processor will service an interrupt immediately or delay servicing it with respect to its current priority. Second, they determine which interrupt of several interrupts is serviced first.

When the processor receives an IAC, it always services it immediately (i.e., treats the IAC as if it has a priority of 31). A mechanism is provided that allows priorities to be assigned to IACs. When using this mechanism, external hardware is required to intercept all IACs sent to the processor and to check their priority. This hardware then determines whether to send the IAC to the processor for servicing or delay it according to the current priority of the processor. (The *80960KB Hardware Designer's Reference Manual* provides a more complete description of this mechanism.)

PROCESSOR STATES

The processor has four different operating states: executing, interrupted, stopped, and stopped-interrupted. The processor is placed in one of two states (executing or stopped) at initialization. After that, the processor and software control the processor's state.

The processor can switch between the executing and interrupted states or between the stopped and stopped-interrupted states. However, the processor never switches from the executing state to the stopped state, unless it detects a series of fault conditions that it cannot handle.

Software can change the state of the processor in either of two ways: (1) issue a reinitialize IAC or (2) issue a freeze IAC. The reinitialize IAC forces the processor to reread the pointers from the IMI and begin executing instructions from a new IP. The freeze IAC forces the processor into the stopped state.

Executing and Interrupted State

In the executing state, the processor is executing the program.

If the processor is interrupted while in the executing state, it saves the current state of the program, switches to the interrupted state, and services the interrupt. Upon returning from the interrupt handler, the processor resumes work on the program.

Stopped and Stopped-Interrupted States

In the stopped state the processor ceases all activity. The only tasks it can perform while in this state are to service an interrupt or an IAC. While servicing an interrupt, the processor switches to the stopped-interrupted state. It then switches back to the stopped state upon completion of the interrupt routine. Likewise, while servicing an IAC, the processor switches to the stopped-interrupted state. If the IAC handling action does not result in a change in the processor's state, the processor switches back to the stopped state when it finishes the IAC handling action.

The only way to get the processor out of the stopped state (other than to service an interrupt) is to reinitialize the processor, either with a hardware reset or by sending it an external reinitialize IAC.

INSTRUCTION SUSPENSION

When the processor is interrupted while it is in the midst of executing an instruction, it does one of three things before it services the interrupt:

1. It completes the instruction.
2. It terminates the instruction and sets the processor state so that it is as if execution of that instruction had not yet begun.
3. It suspends the instruction and saves the necessary resumption information so that execution of the instruction can be continued when the processor begins work on the program again. This course of action is generally reserved for instructions that have a long execution time and that alter the internal and external processor state as they execute.

Which of these steps the processor takes depends on the instruction being executed. However, whichever step it takes is transparent to the software. The processor automatically saves the necessary state information so that work on the program can be resumed with no loss of information.

Refer to the section in Chapter 8 titled "Interrupt Handling Action" for more information on how resumption information is saved when an interrupt is serviced.

MEMORY REQUIREMENTS

The processor provides a 2^{32}-byte address space. This address space can be mapped to read-write memory, read-only memory, and memory-mapped I/O. (The processor does not provided a dedicated, addressable I/O space.)

The address space is linear (or flat): there are no subdivisions of the address space such as segments. For the purpose of memory management, an external memory management unit (MMU) may subdivide memory into pages or restrict access to certain areas of memory to protect kernel code and data. But from the point of view of the processor, the address space is linear.

All of the address space is available for general use except the upper 16M bytes ($FF000000_{16}$ to $FFFFFFFF_{16}$), which are reserved for special functions. (These functions are described in Chapter 13.)

An address in memory is a 32-bit value in the range 0 to $FFFFFFFF_{16}$. It can be used to reference a single byte, 2 bytes, 4 bytes, 8 bytes, 12 bytes or 16 bytes of memory depending on the instruction being used. (Refer to the descriptions of the load and store instructions in Chapter 11 for information on multiple-byte addressing.)

Memory Restrictions

The processor requires that the memory to which the address space is mapped has the following capabilities.

- It must be byte addressable.
- It must support burst transfers (i.e., transfers of blocks of contiguous bytes up to 16 bytes in length).

- It must guarantee *indivisible* access (read or write) for memory addresses that fall within 16-byte boundaries.
- It must guarantee *atomic* access for memory addresses that fall within 16-byte boundaries.

The latter two capabilities are required to allow multiple processors to share a common memory conveniently.

An indivisible access guarantees that a processor reading or writing a set of memory locations will complete the operation before another processor can read or write the same location. The processor requires indivisible access within an aligned, 16-byte block of memory.

An atomic access is a read-modify-write operation. Here external logic must guarantee that once a processor begins a read-modify-write operation on a set of memory locations, it is allowed to complete the operation before another processor is allowed to access the same location.

As described above, the processor requires that when one processor is performing an atomic operation within an aligned, 16-byte block, other processors are delayed from performing another atomic operation within that block until the first operation has been completed.

The 80960KB processor provides two features to aid in implementing the memory requirements described above: SIZE lines and a LOCK line on the local bus.

The SIZE lines indicate the length of a memory access in bytes. These lines can be used to specify 1-, 2-, 4-, 8-, 12-, or 16-byte lengths. When making a multiple-byte access, the processor thus sends the memory controller a base address, on the address lines, and a length, on the SIZE lines.

The LOCK line is used to synchronize atomic operations. When a processor performs an atomic operation, it first examines the LOCK line. If it is asserted, the processor waits until the line is not asserted (i.e., spins on the LOCK line). If the line is not asserted, the processor asserts the LOCK line when it is performing an atomic read and deasserts the line when it performs the companion atomic write.

The LOCK line mechanism allows only one atomic operation to be carried out in memory at one time.

SOFTWARE REQUIREMENTS FOR PROCESSOR MANAGEMENT

The processor-management facilities described earlier in this chapter allow the processor to be configured and operated in several ways. This section lists the data structures that the kernel must supply to operate the processor.

To use the processor, the kernel must provide the following items:

- IMI
- Other System Data Structures

- Address Space
- Stacks
- Code

The IMI comprises the minimum data structures that the processor needs to initialize the system.

As part of the initialization procedure, a more complete set of system data structures are established in memory. These data structures include an interrupt table and a fault table. If the system call mechanism is going to be used, a system procedure table is required.

Two stacks are also required: an interrupt stack and a local (or user) procedure stack. The initial stack pointer for the interrupt stack is given in the IMI. The initial stack pointer (SP) for the local-procedure stack is given in local register r1; the initialization code is required to establish the SP value in this register.

If the supervisor call mechanism is to be used, a supervisor stack must also be provided. The initial stack pointer for this stack is given in the system-procedure table. The supervisor stack can be placed anywhere in the address space.

Note

The section in Chapter 4 titled "Hints on Using the User-Supervisor Protection Model" describes an application of the user-supervisor protection model, in which the processor is always in supervisor mode. When using this application, the local stack and the supervisor stack are the same. The processor gets the initial stack pointer for this stack from register r1.

Finally, three levels of code are required: initialization code, kernel code, and applications code. The initialization code is part of the IMI. (Appendix D gives an initialization code example.) The starting IP for the initialization code is also provided in the IMI.

PROCESSOR INITIALIZATION

This section describes how to initialize the 80960KB processor. It defines the mechanism that the processor uses to establish its initial state and begin instruction execution. It also describes some general guidelines for writing code to complete the initialization of the processor for specific applications.

Note

The 80960 architecture does not define an initial memory image or an initialization procedure. The following initialization requirements are specific to the 80960KB processor.

Initial Memory Image

The IMI performs three functions for the processor: (1) it provides check-sum words that the processor uses in its self-test routine at start-up, (2) it provides pointers to the system data structures, and (3) it provides scratch space that the processor uses to perform certain internal functions. Figure 7-3 shows the structure of the IMI.

The IMI is made up of four parts: the check-sum word, the system address table (SAT), and the processor control block (PRCB), and the initialization code. In an embedded application, all of the parts of this image will generally be held in ROM, except the scratch space of the PRCB. For this reason, the PRCB should be copied from ROM to RAM after system initialization. (The reinitialize IAC, described in Chapter 13, is used to give the processor the PRCB pointer for the relocated PRCB.)

Check-Sum Words

The check-sum words must be in memory locations 00000000_{16} to $0000001F_{16}$. The first of these words is a pointer to the base of the SAT. The second word is a pointer to the base of the PRCB. The fourth word is the instruction pointer to the first instruction of the initialization code.

The remaining words (word 3 and words 5 through 8) are check words, which must be chosen such that the one's complement of the sum of the eight words plus $FFFFFFFF_{16}$ equals 0.

System Address Table

The SAT is 158 bytes in size and can be located anywhere in the address space. It has four required entries. The word beginning at byte 136 must contain a pointer to the base (first byte) of the SAT. This pointer is identical to the pointer given in the first word of the check-sum words. The word beginning at byte 152 must contain a pointer to the base of the system procedure table. The words beginning at byte 140 and 156 must contain $00FC00FB_{16}$ and $304400FB_{16}$, respectively.

All of the other words in the SAT are preserved and can be used by software.

Processor Control Block

The PRCB is 174 bytes long and can also be located anywhere in the address space. It has seven required entries and one reserved space.

Bits 0 through 30 of the word beginning at byte 4 must be zero.

The *write-external-priority flag* (bit 31 of the word beginning at byte 4) instructs the processor to write the priority of the processor to the IAC message control field whenever an interrupt (not caused by an IAC) or the execution of the **modpc** instruction occurs. When this bit is set, the write-external-priority mechanism is enabled; when the bit is clear, the mechanism is disabled. The use of this flag is described in Chapter 13.

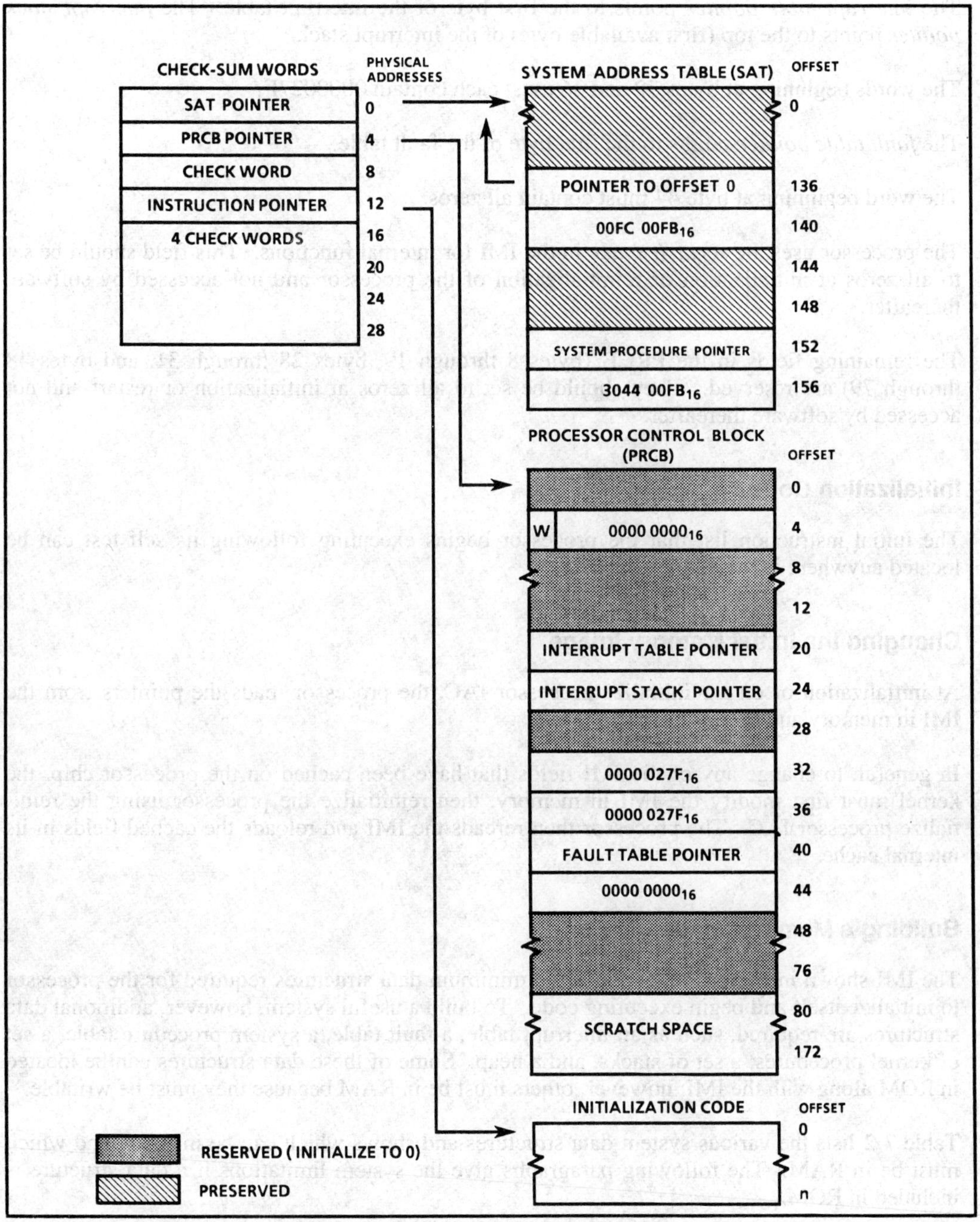

Figure 7-3: Initial Memory Image

The *interrupt table pointer* points to the first byte of the interrupt table. The *interrupt stack pointer* points to the top (first available byte) of the interrupt stack.

The words beginning at bytes 32 and 36 must each contain $0000027F_{16}$.

The *fault table pointer* points to the first byte of the fault table.

The word beginning at byte 44 must contain all zeros.

The processor uses the *scratch space* in the IMI for internal functions. This field should be set to all zeros at initialization or reinitialization of the processor and not accessed by software thereafter.

The remaining fields in the PRCB (bytes 8 through 19, bytes 28 through 31, and bytes 48 through 79) are reserved. They should be set to all zeros at initialization or restart and not accessed by software thereafter.

Initialization Code

The initial instruction list that the processor begins executing following its self test can be located anywhere in the address space.

Changing the Initial Memory Image

At initialization or on a reinitialize processor IAC, the processor reads the pointers from the IMI in memory and caches them.

In general, to change any of the IMI fields that have been cached on the processor chip, the kernel must first modify the IMI in memory, then reinitialize the processor using the reinitialize processor IAC. The processor then rereads the IMI and reloads the cached fields in its internal cache.

Building a Memory Image

The IMI shown in Figure 7-3 contains the minimum data structures required for the processor to initialize itself and begin executing code. To build a useful system, however, additional data structures are required, such as an interrupt table, a fault table, a system procedure table, a set of kernel procedures, a set of stacks, and a heap. Some of these data structures can be located in ROM along with the IMI; however, others must be in RAM because they must be writable.

Table 7-2 lists the various system data structures and shows which can be in ROM and which must be in RAM. The following paragraphs give the system limitations if a data structure is included in ROM.

Table 7-2: ROM and RAM Resident Data Structures

Data Structure	May Be in ROM	May Be in ROM with Limitations	Must Be in RAM
IMI	X		
PRCB		X	
SAT		X	
Interrupt table			X
Fault table	X		
Kernel Procedures	X		
Stacks and heap			X

All of the PRCB except the scratch space area must be in ROM. The scratch space must be in RAM.

The interrupt table must be in RAM for the processor to operate properly, because it contains the interrupt pending fields, which the processor must be able to write to.

The fault table can be in ROM, providing it will never be necessary to relocate the fault handler routines.

The kernel procedures can be in either ROM or RAM or both, depending on the design of the kernel.

Typical Initialization Scenario

Initialization of the 80960KB processor typically is handled in two stages. In the first stage of initialization the processor performs a self test and reads pointers from the IMI. During the second stage, the processor executes initialization code designed to build the remainder of the memory image so that execution of applications code can begin.

First Stage of Initialization

The following procedure shows the steps that system hardware and the processor go through in the first stage of initialization. The algorithm in Figure 7-4 gives the details of this procedure.

```
assert FAILURE pin;
perform self test;
if self test fails
    then enter stopped state;
    else
        deassert FAILURE pin;
        enter predefined state;
        if STARTUP pin = 0
            then enter stopped state;
            else
                x ← memory(0);  read 8 words beginning
                    at address 0
                AC.cc ← 000₂;
                temp ← FFFFFFFF₁₆ add_with_carry x(0);
                temp ← temp add_with_carry x(1);
                temp ← temp add_with_carry x(2);
                temp ← temp add_with_carry x(3);
                temp ← temp add_with_carry x(4);
                temp ← temp add_with_carry x(5);
                temp ← temp add_with_carry x(6);
                temp ← temp add_with_carry x(7);
                if temp ≠ 0
                    then
                        assert FAILURE pin;
                        enter stopped state;
                    else
                        prcb_address ← memory(4);
                        IP ← memory (12)
                        fetch IMI;
                        processor.priority ← 31;
                        processor.state ← interrupted;
                        FP ← IMI.interrupt_stack_pointer;
                        clear any latched external interrupt/IAC
                            signals;
                        begin execution;
                endif;
        endif;
endif;
```

Figure 7-4: Algorithm for First Stage of Initialization Procedure

1. Hardware asserts the RESET pin on the processor.
2. The processor samples LPN to get its local processor number (1 or 0). (LPN and STARTUP are signals that come from multiplexed information received on several processor pins.)
3. The processor asserts the $\overline{\text{FAILURE}}$ pin and performs a self test. If the processor passes the self test, it deasserts the $\overline{\text{FAILURE}}$ pin.

4. The processor samples STARTUP to determine whether it is the initializing processor (1) or not (0). If the processor is the initializing processor, it continues with the initialization procedure; if it is not, it goes into the stopped state. (In multiprocessing systems, all processors except the initializing processor are put in the stopped state.)
5. The processor reads the 8 check-sum words and checks that the check sum is 0.
6. Using the contents of the check-sum words, the processor determines the location of the SAT, the PRCB, and the first instruction to be executed.
7. The processor sets its process priority to 31 (highest possible) and its state to interrupted.
8. The processor clears any latched external interrupt or IAC signals. This means that the processor will not service any interrupts or IACs prior to beginning instruction execution.
9. The processor begins execution of the initialization instruction list.

After self test, the processor establishes its own state. For the initializing processor this state is interrupted; for any other processors in the system this state is stopped. Also at initialization, the trace controls are set to zero; the process controls are set to zero (except for the execution mode, which is set to supervisor, and the priority, which is set to 31); and the breakpoint registers are disabled.

Since the processor places itself in the interrupted state during the first stage of initialization, the initialization code is essentially a special interrupt-handler procedure.

Second Stage of Initialization

The processor activity during the second stage of initialization, which occurs once the processor begins instruction execution, is up to software. In general, this stage of initialization is used to copy or create additional data structures in memory, such as the interrupt table, the system-procedure table, and the fault table (if not in the initial memory image), and the kernel procedures.

Once these jobs are completed, the processor can then begin executing applications code.

Appendix D gives an example of the 80960KB code that might be used to carry out this second stage of initialization.

A common initialization technique is to create a new PRCB and interrupt table in RAM along with the other system data structures that are placed in memory in the second stage of initialization. The processor is then reinitialized to point to the PRCB and interrupt table. (The code in Appendix D uses this technique.)

The processor is reinitialized using the reinitialize IAC. This reinitialize IAC message includes new pointers to the SAT and PRCB. The processor reads the new PRCB, then begins instruction execution according to the control information contained in the PRCB.

Interrupts 8

CHAPTER 8
INTERRUPTS

This chapter describes the 80960KB processor's interrupt handling facilities. It also describes how interrupts are signaled.

OVERVIEW OF THE INTERRUPT FACILITIES

An interrupt is a temporary break in the control stream of a program so that the processor can handle another chore. Interrupts are generally requested from an external source. The interrupt request either contains a vector number or else points to a vector that tells the processor what chore to do while in the interrupted state. When the processor has finished servicing the interrupt, it generally returns to the program that it was working on when the interrupt occurred and resumes execution where it left off.

The processor provides a mechanism for servicing interrupts, which uses an implicit procedure call to a selected interrupt handling procedure, called an *interrupt handler*.

When an interrupt occurs, the current state of the program is saved. If the interrupt occurs during an instruction that requires many machine cycles, the instruction state is also saved and execution of the instruction is suspended.

The processor then creates a new frame on the interrupt stack and executes an implicit call to the interrupt handler selected with the interrupt vector.

Upon returning from the interrupt handler, the processor switches back to the program that was running when the interrupt occurred, restores it to the state it was in when the interrupt occurred, and resumes work on it.

Another feature of this interrupt handling mechanism is that it allows interrupts to be prioritized. If an interrupt is signaled that has the same or a lower priority than the processor's current priority, the processor will save the interrupt vector and service the interrupt at a later time. Interrupts that are waiting to be serviced are called pending interrupts.

SOFTWARE REQUIREMENTS FOR INTERRUPT HANDLING

To use the processor's interrupt handling facilities, software must provide the following items in memory:

- Interrupt Table
- Interrupt Handler Routines
- Interrupt Stack

These items are generally established in memory as part of the initialization procedure. Once these items are present in memory and pointers to them have been entered in the appropriate system data structures, the processor then handles interrupts automatically and independently from software.

The requirements for these items are given in following sections of this chapter.

VECTORS AND PRIORITY

Each interrupt vector is 8 bits in length, which allows up to 256 unique vectors to be defined. In practice, vectors 0 through 7 cannot be used, and vectors 244 through 251 are reserved and should not be used by software.

Each vector has a predefined priority, which is defined by the following expression:

priority = vector/8

Thus, at each priority level, there are 8 possible vectors (e.g., vectors 8 through 15 have a priority of 1, vectors 16 through 23 a priority of 2, and so on to vectors 246 through 255, which have a priority of 31).

The processor uses the priority of an interrupt to determine whether or not to service the interrupt immediately or to delay service. If the interrupt priority is greater than the processor's current priority, the processor services the interrupt immediately; if the interrupt priority is equal to or less than the processor's current priority, the processor saves the interrupt vector as a pending interrupt so that it can be serviced at a later time.

A priority-31 interrupt is always serviced immediately.

Note that the lowest program priority allowed is 0. If the current program has a 0 priority, a priority-0 interrupt will never be accepted. This is why vectors 0 through 7 cannot be used. In fact, there are no entries provided for these vectors in the interrupt table.

INTERRUPT TABLE

The interrupt table contains instruction pointers (addresses in the address space) to interrupt handlers. It must be aligned on a word boundary. The processor determines the location of the interrupt table by means of a pointer in the IMI.

As shown in Figure 8-1, the interrupt table contains one entry (i.e., one pointer) for each allowable vector. The structure of an interrupt-table entry is given at the bottom of Figure 8-1. Each interrupt procedure must begin on a word boundary, so the two least-significant bits of the entry are set to 0.

The first 36 bytes of the interrupt table are used to record pending interrupts. This section of the table is divided into two fields: pending priorities (byte-offset 0 through 3) and pending interrupts (byte-offset 4 through 35).

The pending priorities field contains a 32-bit string in which each bit represents an interrupt priority. The bit number in the string represents the priority number. When the processor posts a pending interrupt in the interrupt table, the bit corresponding to the interrupt's priority is set. For example, if an interrupt with a priority of 10 is posted in the interrupt table, bit 10 is set.

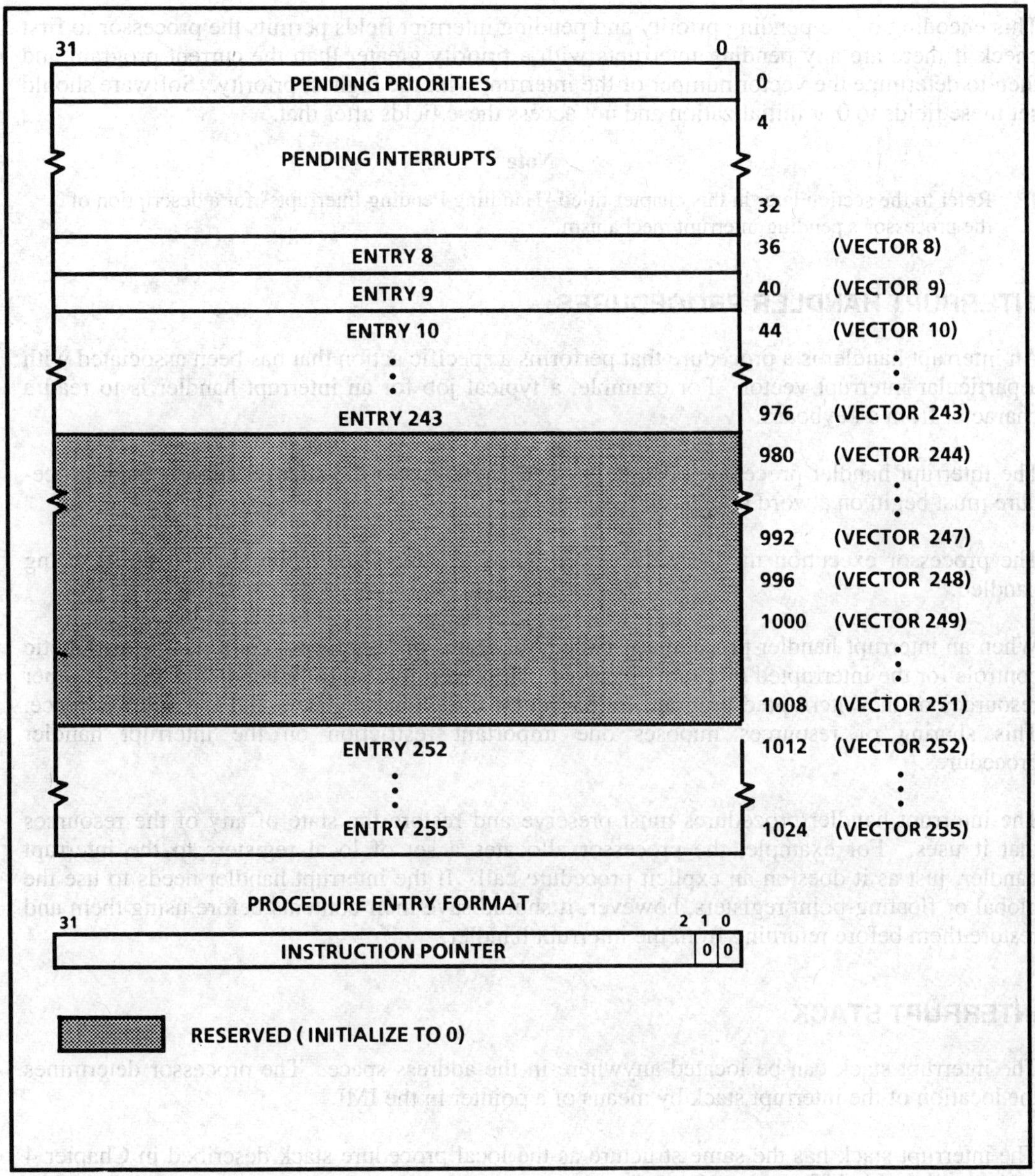

Figure 8-1: Interrupt Table

The pending interrupts field contains a 256-bit string in which each bit represents an interrupt vector. For example, byte-offset 4 is reserved, byte-offset 5 is for vectors 8 through 15, byte-offset 6 is for vectors 16 through 23, and so on. When a pending interrupt is logged, its corresponding bit in the pending interrupt field is set.

This encoding of the pending priority and pending interrupt fields permits the processor to first check if there are any pending interrupts with a priority greater than the current program and then to determine the vector number of the interrupt with the highest priority. Software should set these fields to 0 at initialization and not access these fields after that.

Note

Refer to the section later in this chapter titled "Handling Pending Interrupts" for a description of the processor's pending interrupt mechanism.

INTERRUPT HANDLER PROCEDURES

An interrupt handler is a procedure that performs a specific action that has been associated with a particular interrupt vector. For example, a typical job for an interrupt handler is to read a character from a keyboard.

The interrupt handler procedures can be located anywhere in the address space. Each procedure must begin on a word boundary.

The processor execution mode is always switched to supervisor while an interrupt is being handled.

When an interrupt-handler procedure is called, the states of the process controls and arithmetic controls for the interrupted program are saved. However, the interrupt handler shares the other resources of the interrupted program, in particular the global registers and the address space. This sharing of resources imposes one important restriction on the interrupt handler procedures.

The interrupt handler procedures must preserve and restore the state of any of the resources that it uses. For example, the processor allocates a set of local registers to the interrupt handler, just as it does on an explicit procedure call. If the interrupt handler needs to use the global or floating-point registers, however, it should save their contents before using them and restore them before returning from the interrupt handler.

INTERRUPT STACK

The interrupt stack can be located anywhere in the address space. The processor determines the location of the interrupt stack by means of a pointer in the IMI.

The interrupt stack has the same structure as the local procedure stack described in Chapter 4 in the section titled "Procedure Stack."

INTERRUPT HANDLING ACTIONS

When the processor receives an interrupt, it handles it automatically. The processor takes care of saving the processor state, calling the interrupt-handler routine, and restoring the processor state once the interrupt has been serviced. Software support is not required.

The following section describes the actions the processor takes while handling interrupts. It is not necessary to read this section to use the interrupt mechanism or write an interrupt handler routine. This discussion is provided for those readers who wish to know the details of the interrupt handling mechanism.

Receiving an Interrupt

Whenever the processor receives an interrupt signal, it performs the following action:

1. It temporarily stops work on its current task, whether it is working on a program or another interrupt procedure.
2. It reads the interrupt vector.
3. It compares the priority of the vector with the processor's current priority.
4. If the interrupt priority is higher than that of the processor, the processor services the interrupt immediately as described in the next sections.
5. If the interrupt priority is equal to or less than that of the processor, the processor sets the appropriate priority bit and vector bit in pending interrupt record and continues work on its current task.

Servicing an Interrupt

The method that the processor uses to service an interrupt depends on the state the processor is in when it receives the interrupt. The following sections describe the interrupt handling actions for various states of the processor. In all of these cases, it is assumed that the interrupt priority is higher than that of the processor and will thus be serviced immediately after the processor receives it. The handling of lower priority interrupts is described later in this chapter in the section titled "Pending Interrupts."

Executing State Interrupt

When the processor receives an interrupt while it is in the executing state (i.e., executing a program), it performs the following actions to service the interrupt; this procedure is the same regardless of whether the processor is in the user or the supervisor mode when the interrupt occurs:

1. The processor saves the current state of process controls and arithmetic controls in an interrupt record on the stack that the processor is currently using. This stack can be the local-procedure stack or the supervisor stack. (The interrupt record is described in the following section.)
2. If the execution of an instruction was suspended, the processor includes a resumption record for the instruction in the current stack and sets the resume flag in the saved process controls. (Refer to the section in Chapter 7 titled "Instruction Suspension" for a discussion of the criteria for suspending instructions.)
3. The processor switches to the interrupted state.

4. The processor sets the state flag in the process controls to interrupted, its execution mode to supervisor, and its priority to the priority of the interrupt. Setting the processor's priority to that of the interrupt insures that lower priority interrupts can not interrupt the servicing of the current interrupt.
5. Also in its internal process controls, the processor clears the trace-fault-pending and trace-enable flags. Clearing these flags allows the interrupt to be handled without trace faults being raised.
6. The processor allocates a new frame on the interrupt stack and switches to the interrupt stack.
7. The processor sets the frame return status field (associated with the PFP) to 111_2.
8. The processor performs an implicit call-extended operation (similar to that performed for the **callx** instruction). The address for the procedure that is called is that which is specified in the interrupt table for the specified interrupt vector.

Once the processor has completed the interrupt procedure, it performs the following action on the return:

1. The processor deallocates the stack frame from the interrupt stack and switches to the local or supervisor stack (whichever one it was using when it was interrupted).
2. The processor copies the arithmetic controls field from the interrupt record into its arithmetic controls register.
3. The processor copies the process controls field from the interrupt record into its internal process controls.
4. If the resume flag of the process controls is set, the processor copies the resumption record from the interrupt record to the resumption record field of the PRCB.
5. The processor checks the interrupt table for pending interrupts that are higher then the priority of the program being returned to. If a higher-priority pending interrupt is found, it is handled as if the interrupt occurred at this point.
6. Assuming that there are not pending interrupts to be serviced, the processor switches to the executing state and resumes work on the program.

Interrupted State Interrupt

If the processor receives an interrupt while it is servicing an interrupt, and the new interrupt has a higher priority than the interrupt currently being serviced, the current interrupt-handler routine is interrupted. Here the processor performs the same action to save the state of the interrupted interrupt-handler routine as is described at the beginning of this section. Here, the interrupt record is saved on the top of the interrupt stack, prior to the new frame that is created for use in servicing the new interrupt.

Interrupt Record

The processor saves the state of an interrupted program (or interrupt-handler) routine in an interrupt record. Figure 8-2 shows the structure of this interrupt record.

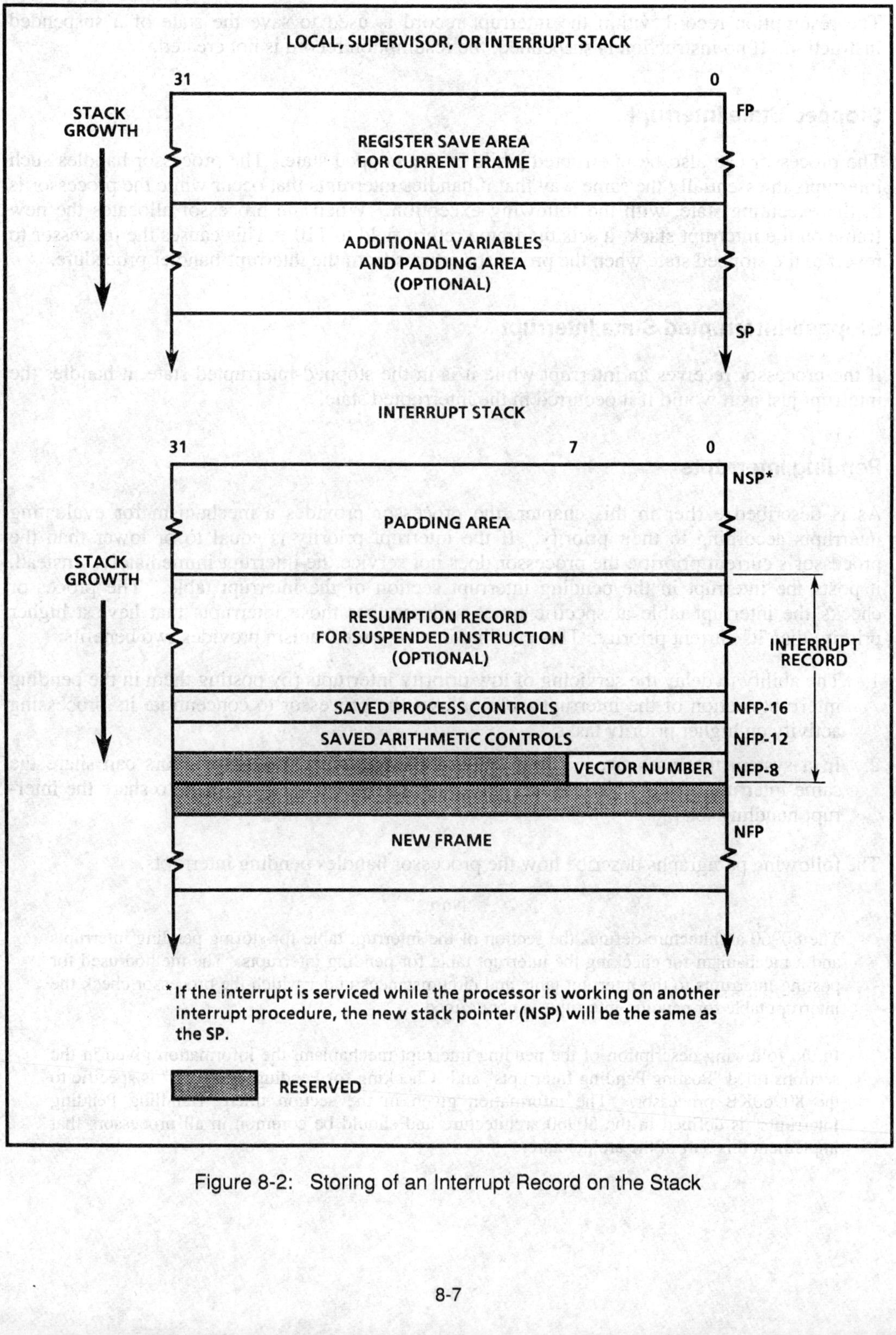

Figure 8-2: Storing of an Interrupt Record on the Stack

The resumption record within the interrupt record is used to save the state of a suspended instruction. If no instruction is suspended, the resumption record is not created.

Stopped State Interrupt

The processor can also be interrupted while in the stopped state. The processor handles such interrupts in essentially the same way that it handles interrupts that occur while the processor is in the executing state, with the following exception. When the processor allocates the new frame on the interrupt stack, it sets the frame return field to 110_2. This causes the processor to revert to the stopped state when the processor returns from the interrupt-handler procedure.

Stopped-Interrupted State Interrupt

If the processor receives an interrupt while it is in the stopped-interrupted state, it handles the interrupt just as it would if it occurred in the interrupted state.

Pending Interrupts

As is described earlier in this chapter, the processor provides a mechanism for evaluating interrupts according to their priority. If the interrupt priority is equal to or lower than the processor's current priority, the processor does not service the interrupt immediately. Instead, it posts the interrupt in the pending interrupt section of the interrupt table. The processor checks the interrupt table at specific times and services those interrupts that have a higher priority than its current priority. This pending interrupt mechanism provides two benefits:

1. The ability to delay the servicing of low priority interrupts (by posting them in the pending interrupt section of the interrupt table) allows the processor to concentrate its processing activity on higher priority tasks.
2. In a system that uses two or more 80960KB processors, both processors can share the same interrupt table. This interrupt-table sharing allows the processors to share the interrupt handling load.

The following paragraphs describe how the processor handles pending interrupts.

Note

The 80960 architecture defines the section of the interrupt table for storing pending interrupts and a mechanism for checking the interrupt table for pending interrupts. The method used for posting interrupts to the interrupt table and circumstances under which the processor check the interrupt table for pending interrupts is not defined.

In the following description of the pending interrupt mechanism, the information given in the sections titled "Posting Pending Interrupts" and "Checking for Pending Interrupts" is specific to the 80960KB processor. The information given in the section titled "Handling Pending Interrupts" is defined in the 80960 architecture and should be common in all processors that implement this part of the architecture.

Posting Pending Interrupts

An interrupt can be posted in the pending-interrupt record of the interrupt table in either of the following two ways:

1. The processor receives an interrupt with a priority equal to or lower than that of the program the processor is currently working on. The processor then automatically posts the interrupt in the pending-interrupt record.
2. The kernel can set the desired pending-interrupt and pending-priority bits in the interrupt table.

Using the first method, the processor performs an atomic read/write operation that locks the interrupt table until the posting operation has been completed. Locking the interrupt table prevents other agents on the bus from accessing the interrupt table during this time.

The second method of posting an interrupt is risky, because it does not use this locking technique. (The processor's atomic instructions are not able to perform a locking operation that spans several instructions.) This method will work only if the kernel can insure the following:

- that no external I/O agent will attempt to post a pending interrupt simultaneously with the processor, and
- that an interrupt cannot occur after one bit (e.g., the pending priority bit) of the pending-interrupt record is set but before the other bit (the pending interrupt vector) is set.

Checking for Pending Interrupts

The processor automatically checks the interrupt table for pending interrupts at the following times:

- After returning from an interrupt-handler procedure
- While executing a modify-process-controls instruction (**modpc**), if the instruction causes the program's priority to be lowered.
- After receiving a test pending interrupts IAC message.

Handling Pending Interrupts

The processor uses the same type of atomic read/write operation to check the interrupt table for pending interrupts as it does for posting pending interrupts. Again, this technique prevents other agents on the bus from accessing the interrupt table until the pending-interrupt check has been completed.

When the processor finds a pending interrupt, it handles it as if it had just received the interrupt. The handling mechanism is the same as is described earlier in this chapter for interrupts that are serviced as soon as they are received.

If the processor finds two pending interrupts at the same priority, it services the interrupt with the highest vector number first.

SIGNALING INTERRUPTS

Note

The 80960 architecture does not define a mechanism for signaling interrupts to the processor. The methods of signaling interrupts described in the following section are specific to the 80960KB processor.

The 80960KB processor can be interrupted in any of the following five ways:

- Signal on its interrupt pins
- Signal on its interrupt pins from an external interrupt controller
- An IAC message from external source
- An IAC message from a program in the processor
- A pending interrupt (described earlier in this chapter)

Interrupts From Interrupt Pins

The processor has four interrupt pins, called INT0, INT1, INT2, and INT3. These pins can be configured in either of the following three ways:

- as four interrupt-signal inputs;
- as two interrupt inputs and two pins for handshaking with an interrupt controller such as the Intel 8259A Programmable Interrupt Controller; or
- as one IAC input and three interrupt inputs.

A 32-bit, interrupt-control register in the processor determines how these pins are used. Each interrupt pin is associated with one 8-bit field in the register, as shown in Figure 8-3.

31 … 24	23 … 16	15 … 8	7 … 0
INT3 VECTOR	INT2 VECTOR	INT1 VECTOR	INT0 VECTOR

Figure 8-3: Interrupt-Control Register

If the interrupt pins are to be used as four inputs, a different interrupt vector is stored in each of the four fields in the interrupt-control register. Then, when an interrupt is signaled on one of the pins, the processor reads the vector from the pin's associated field in the register. For example, if an interrupt is signaled on pin INT0, the processor reads the vector from bits 0 through 7.

The processor assumes that the interrupt vectors in the interrupt register are arranged in descending order from the INT0 field to the INT3 field (e.g., the priority of INT0 ≥ INT1 ≥ INT2 ≥ INT3). To insure that interrupts are handled in the proper order, software should follow this convention.

If the INT0 vector field is set to 0, the function of the INT0 pin is changed to IAC, and it is used to signal the processor that an external IAC message has been sent to it. In fact, the INT0 pin must be configured in this manner for the processor to service external IAC messages.

If the INT2 vector field is set to 0, the functions of the INT2 and INT3 pins are changed to INTR and $\overline{\text{INTA}}$, respectively. Here, the INTR pin is used to receive signals from an interrupt controller and the $\overline{\text{INTA}}$ pin is used to send acknowledge signals back to the controller. When the processor receives a signal on the INTR pin, it reads an interrupt vector from the least-significant 8 bits of its bus, then sends an acknowledge signal to the controller through $\overline{\text{INTA}}$. When the INT2 and INT3 pins are configured in this manner, the processor ignores the INT3 vector field.

Note

Refer to the *80960KB Hardware Designer's Reference Manual* for more information on the use of INT2 and INT3 pins with an interrupt controller.

The interrupt-control register is memory mapped to addresses $FF000004_{16}$ through $FF000007_{16}$. Only the processor can read or write this register using the synchronous load (**synld**) and synchronous move (**synmov**) instructions. External agents on the bus cannot access this register.

The value in the interrupt-control register after the processor is initialized is $FF000000_{16}$.

IAC Interrupts

The processor can also receive an interrupt request by means of the IAC mechanism. (The IAC mechanism is described in detail in Chapter 13.) The interrupt IAC message can be sent to the processor either from an external bus agent, such as an I/O processor or another 80960KB processor, or internally as part of the currently running program. The interrupt vector is contained in the interrupt IAC message.

As with any other IAC message, the processor receives notice of an external interrupt-IAC message through the INT0 pin, which has been configured as an IAC pin, as described in the previous section. The processor then reads the IAC message to get the interrupt vector.

A program running on the processor can signal an interrupt through an internal interrupt-IAC message. An internal IAC is sent to the processor by means of a synchronous move instruction. When the processor executes a synchronous move to its IAC message space, it signals an IAC message internally. The processor then reads the IAC message as it would for an external IAC.

Fault Handling 9

CHAPTER 9
FAULT HANDLING

This chapter describes the fault handling facilities of the 80960KB processor. The subjects covered include the fault-handling data structures, the software support required for fault handling, and the fault handling mechanism. A reference section that contains detailed information on each fault type is provided at the end of the chapter.

OVERVIEW OF THE FAULT-HANDLING FACILITIES

The processor is able to detect various conditions in code or in its internal state (called "fault conditions") that could cause the processor to deliver incorrect or inappropriate results or that could cause it to head down an undesirable control path. For example, the processor recognizes divide-by-zero and overflow conditions on integer calculations. It also detects inappropriate operand values, uncompleted memory accesses, or references to incomplete or non-existent system-data structures.

The processor can detect a fault while it is executing a program, an interrupt handler, or a fault handler. (In this chapter, when a program is referred to, it generally also means any interrupt handler or fault handler that may have been invoked while the processor was working on the program.)

When the processor detects a fault, it handles the fault immediately and independently of the program or handler it is currently working on, using a mechanism similar to that used to service interrupts.

A fault is generally handled with a fault-handling procedure (called a fault handler), which the processor invokes through an implicit procedure call. Prior to making the call, the processor saves the state of the current program and in some cases the state of an incomplete instruction. It also saves information about the fault, which the fault handler can use to correct or recover from the condition that caused the fault.

If the fault handler is able to recover from the fault, the processor can then restore the program to its state prior to the fault and resume work on the program. If the fault handler is not able to recover from the fault, it can take any of several actions to gracefully shut down the processor.

FAULT TYPES

All of the faults that the processor detects are predefined. These faults are divided into types and subtypes, each of which is given a number. The processor uses the type number to select a fault handler. The fault handler then uses the subtype number to select a specific fault-handling procedure.

Table 9-1 lists the faults that the processor detects, arranged by type and subtype. For convenience, individual faults are referred to in this manual by their fault-subtype name. Thus a *machine bad-access fault* is referred to as simply a *bad-access fault*, or an *arithmetic integer overflow fault* is referred to as an *integer overflow fault*.

The fifth column of Table 9-1 shows each fault as it appears in the fault record (the word at offset 40 of the fault record is shown later in this chapter).

Table 9-1: Fault Types and Subtypes

Fault Type		Fault Subtype		Fault Record
No.	**Name**	**No./Bit Position**	**Name**	
1	Trace	Bit 1	Instruction Trace	0xXX01 0002
		Bit 2	Branch Trace	0xXX01 0004
		Bit 3	Call Trace	0xXX01 0008
		Bit 4	Return Trace	0xXX01 0010
		Bit 5	Prereturn Trace	0xXX01 0020
		Bit 6	Supervisor Trace	0xXX01 0040
		Bit 7	Breakpoint Trace	0xXX01 0080
2	Operation	1	Invalid Opcode	0xXX02 0001
		2	Unimplemented	0xXX02 0002
		4	Invalid Operand	0xXX02 0004
3	Arithmetic	1	Integer Overflow	0xXX03 0001
		2	Arithmetic Zero-Divide	0xXX03 0002
4	Floating Point	Bit 0	Floating Overflow	0xXX04 0001
		Bit 1	Floating Underflow	0xXX04 0002
		Bit 2	Floating Invalid-Operation	0xXX04 0004
		Bit 3	Floating Zero-Divide	0xXX04 0008
		Bit 4	Floating Inexact	0xXX04 0010
		Bit 5	Floating Reserved-Encoding	0xXX04 0020
5	Constraint	1	Constraint Range	0xXX05 0001
		2	Privileged	0xXX05 0002
7	Protection	Bit 1	Length	0xXX07 0001
8	Machine	1	Bad Access	0xXX08 0001
9	Structural	3	IAC	0xXX09 0003
A	Type	1	Type Mismatch	0xXX0A 0001

Note

The 80960 architecture defines a basic set of fault types and subtypes. Processors that provide extensions to the architecture may recognize additional fault conditions. The encoding of fault types and subtypes allows any of these extensions to be included in the fault table along with the basic faults. Space in the fault table will be reserved in such a way that processors that recognize the same fault types and subtypes will encode them in the same way.

For example, the floating-point faults (fault type 4) are an extension provided in the 80960KB processor (but not in the 80960KA processor). Any other processors based on the 80960 architecture that also recognize floating-point faults will also encode them as fault type 4.

FAULT-HANDLING METHOD

The processor handles all faults through an implicit procedure call to a fault handler. When a fault occurs while the processor is executing a program, the processor creates a fault record on its current stack. This record includes information on the state of the program and data on the fault. If the fault occurred while the processor was in the midst of executing an instruction, a resumption record for the instruction may also be saved on the stack.

Following the creation of the fault and resumption records, the processor selects a fault handler from a system-data structure called the *fault table*. It then invokes the fault handler (by means of an implicit call) and begins executing the handler procedure. As is described later in this chapter, the fault-handler call can be a local call (call-extended operation), a local system-procedure-table call (local system-call operation), or a supervisor call.

This same procedure call method is used to handle faults that occur while the processor is servicing an interrupt or that occur while the processor is working on a fault handler.

Multiple Fault Conditions

It is possible for multiple fault conditions to occur simultaneously. For certain fault types, such as trace faults or protection faults, bit positions in the fault-subtype field are used to indicate the occurrence of multiple faults of the same type. As a general rule, however, the processor does not indicate situations where multiple faults occur. Instead, it records one of the faults and does not report on the faults that were not recorded.

If a fault occurs while the processor is executing a fault handling routine, the operating of the processor is not predictable.

Faults and Interrupts

If an interrupt occurs during an instruction that will fault, that has just faulted, or that has faulted while the processor is in the midst of selecting the fault handler, the processor will handle the fault in either of the following ways:

- It includes the fault information as part of its interrupt record and services the interrupt immediately. After it has serviced the interrupt, it handles the fault.
- It completes the selection of the fault handler, then services the interrupt just prior to executing the first instruction of the fault handler.

SOFTWARE REQUIREMENTS FOR HANDLING FAULTS

To use the processor's fault-handling facilities, the following system-data structures and procedures must be present in memory:

- Fault Table
- Fault-Handler Procedures

- Interrupt Table
- Interrupt Stack

Software should generally load these items in memory as part of the initialization procedure. Once they are present in memory and pointers to them have been included in the IMI, the processor then handles faults automatically and independently from software.

Requirements for the fault table and fault-handler procedures are given in the following sections.

FAULT TABLE

The fault table provides the processor with a pathway to the fault handlers when the processor is using the implicit procedure-call method of handling faults. As shown in Figure 9-1, there is one entry in the fault table for each fault type. When a fault occurs, the processor uses the fault type to select an entry in the fault table. From this entry, the processor then obtains a pointer to the fault handler for the type of fault that occurred.

The fault handler reads the fault subtype or subtypes from the fault record to determine the appropriate fault recovery action.

Location of the Fault Table in Memory

The fault table can be located anywhere in the address space. The processor obtains a pointer to the fault table from the IMI.

Fault-Table Entries

Each entry in the fault table is two words long. As shown at the bottom of Figure 9-1, there are two types of fault-table entries allowed: local-procedure entry and system-procedure-table entry. The entry-type field determines the entry type.

A local-procedure entry (entry type 00_2) provides an instruction pointer (address in the address space) for the fault-handler procedure. Using this entry, the processor invokes the specified fault handler by means of an implicit call-extended operation (similar to that performed for the **callx** instruction). The second word of a local-procedure entry is reserved. It should be set to zero when the fault table is created and not accessed after that.

A system-procedure-table entry (entry type 10_2) provides a procedure number in the system procedure table. Using this entry, the processor invokes the specified fault handler by means of an implicit call-system operation (similar to that performed for the **calls** instruction).

Fault-handling procedures in the system procedure table can be local procedures or supervisor procedures. A fault handler can thus be invoked through the fault table in any of three ways: implicit local-procedure call, implicit local procedure-table call, or implicit supervisor call.

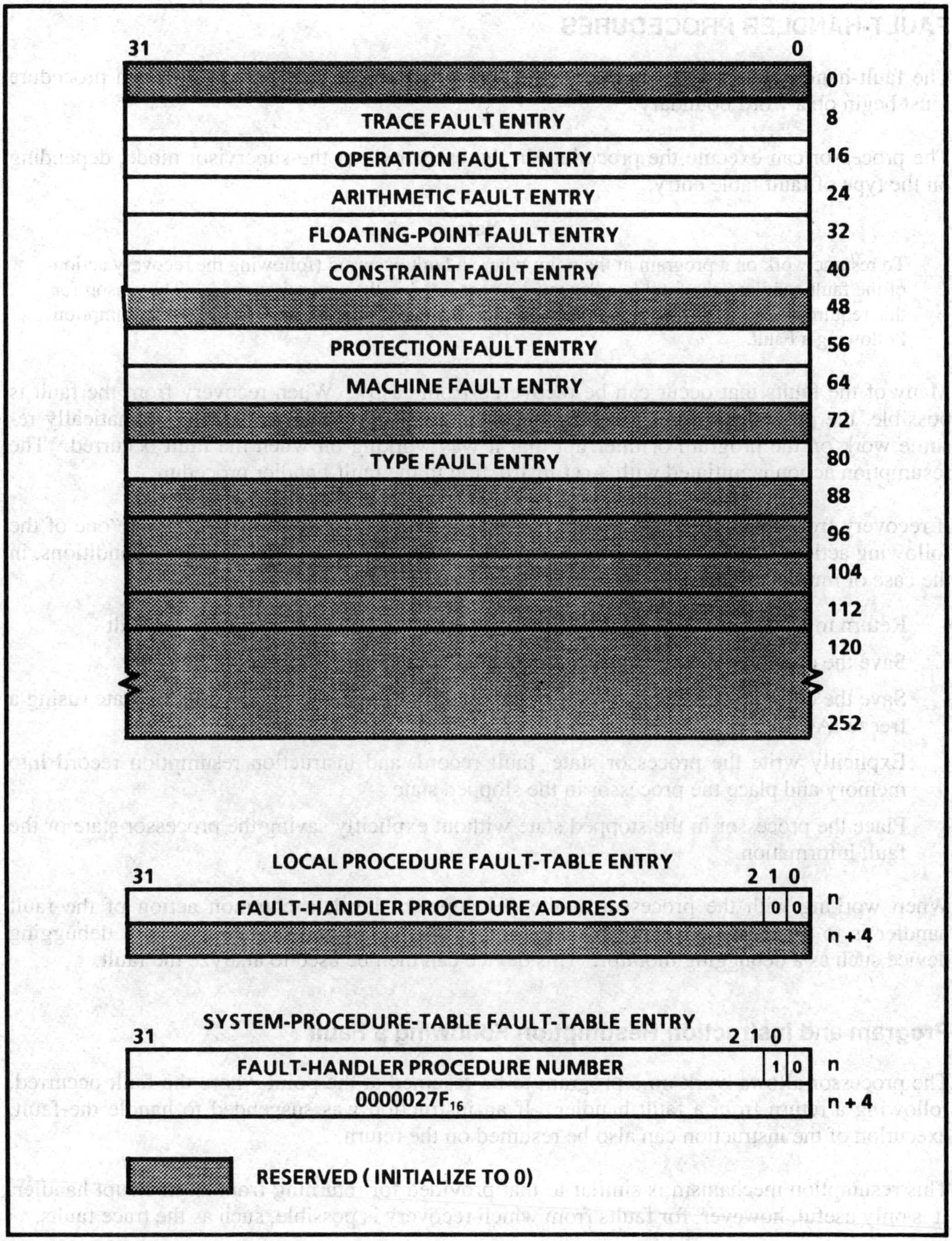

Figure 9-1: Fault Table and Fault-Table Entries

FAULT-HANDLER PROCEDURES

The fault-handler procedures can be located anywhere in the address space. Each procedure must begin on a word boundary.

The processor can execute the procedure in the user mode or the supervisor mode, depending on the type of fault table entry.

Note

To resume work on a program at the point where a fault occurred (following the recovery action of the fault handler), the fault handler must be executed in the supervisor mode. The reason for this requirement is described in a following section titled "Program and Instruction Resumption Following a Fault."

Many of the faults that occur can be recovered from easily. When recovery from the fault is possible, the processor's fault-handling mechanism allows the processor to automatically resume work on the program or interrupt that it was working on when the fault occurred. The resumption action is initiated with a **ret** instruction in the fault-handler procedure.

If recovery from the fault is not possible or not desirable, the fault handler can take one of the following actions, depending on the nature and severity of the fault condition (or conditions, in the case of multiple faults):

- Return to a point in the program or interrupt code other than the point of the fault
- Save the current state of the processor and call a debug monitor
- Save the current state of the processor and place the processor in the stopped state (using a freeze IAC)
- Explicitly write the processor state, fault record, and instruction resumption record into memory and place the processor in the stopped state
- Place the processor in the stopped state without explicitly saving the processor state or the fault information.

When working with the processor at the development level, a common action of the fault handler is to save the fault and processor state information and make a call to a debugging device such as a debugging monitor. This device can then be used to analyze the fault.

Program and Instruction Resumption Following a Fault

The processor allows work on a program to be resumed at the point where the fault occurred, following a return from a fault handler. If an instruction was suspended to handle the fault, execution of the instruction can also be resumed on the return.

This resumption mechanism is similar to that provided for returning from an interrupt handler. It is only useful, however, for faults from which recovery is possible, such as the trace faults.

To use this mechanism, the fault handler must be invoked using an implicit supervisor procedure-table call. This method is required because to resume work on the program and a suspended instruction at the point where the fault occurred, the saved process controls in the fault record must be copied back into the processor on the return from the fault handler. The processor only performs this action if the processor is in the supervisor mode on the return.

If the fault handler is invoked with an implicit local-procedure call or an implicit local-procedure-table call, the return IP determines where in the program the processor resumes work, following a return from a fault handler. Here, the return is handled in a similar manner to a return from an explicit call with a **call** or **callx** instruction.

The return IP (referred to later in this chapter as the saved IP) is saved in the RIP register (r2) of the stack frame that was in use when the fault occurred. This IP may be the instruction the processor faulted on or the next instruction that the processor would have executed if the fault had not occurred. In either case, the resumption record is not used, so the processor might continue work on the program without completing the instruction that the fault occurred on.

A fault handler should thus be invoked with an implicit local-procedure or local-procedure-table call only if it is not required or desirable to resume the program at the point of the fault. The section later in this chapter titled "Return Without Resumption" discusses returning to a point in the program code other than the point of the fault.

FAULT CONTROLS

Certain fault types and subtypes have masks or flags associated with them that determine whether or not a fault is signaled when a fault condition occurs. Table 9-2 lists these flags and masks, the system data structures in which they are located, and the fault subtype they affect.

Table 9-2: Fault Flags or Masks

Flag or Mask Name	Location	Fault Affected
Integer Overflow Mask	Arithmetic Controls	Integer Overflow
Floating Overflow Mask	Arithmetic Controls	Floating Overflow
Floating Underflow Mask	Arithmetic Controls	Floating Underflow
Floating Invalid Operation Mask	Arithmetic Controls	Floating Invalid Operation
Floating Zero-Divide Mask	Arithmetic Controls	Floating Zero-Divide
Floating-point Inexact Mask	Arithmetic Controls	Floating Inexact
No Imprecise Faults Flag	Arithmetic Controls	All Imprecise Faults
Trace-Enable Flag	Process Controls	All Trace Faults
Trace-Mode Flags	Trace Controls	All Trace Faults

The integer and floating-point mask bits inhibit faults from being raised for specific fault conditions (i.e., integer overflow and floating-point overflow, underflow, zero divide, invalid operation, and inexact). The use of these masks is discussed in the fault-reference section at the end of this chapter. Also, the floating-point fault masks are described in Chapter 12 in the section titled "Exceptions and Fault Handling."

The no-imprecise-faults (NIF) flag controls the synchronizing of faults for a category of faults called imprecise faults. This flag should be set to 1. The function of this flag is described later in this chapter in the section titled "Precise and Imprecise Faults".

The trace-mode flags (in the trace controls) and trace-enable flag (in the process controls) support trace faults. The trace-mode flags enable trace modes; the trace-enable flag enables the generation of trace faults. The use of these flags is described in the fault reference section on trace faults at the end of this chapter. Further discussion of these flags is provided in Chapter 10 in the section titled "Trace-Enable and Trace-Fault-Pending Flags."

SIGNALING A FAULT

The processor generates faults implicitly when fault conditions occur and explicitly at the request of software. Most faults are generated implicitly. The fault control bits described in the previous section allow the implicit generation of some faults to be either enabled (as with the trace faults) or masked (as with the floating-point faults).

Fault-If Instructions

The fault-if instructions (**faulte**, **faultne**, **faultl**, **faultle**, **faultg**, **faultge**, **faulto**, and **faultno**) allow a fault to be generated explicitly anywhere within an application program, kernel procedure, interrupt handler, or fault handler. When one of these instructions is executed, the processor checks the condition code bits in the arithmetic controls, then signals a constraint-range fault if the condition specified with the instruction is met.

FAULT RECORD

When a fault occurs, the processor records information about the fault in a fault record. The fault handler and processor use this information to recover from or correct the fault condition and resume execution of the process. Figure 9-2 shows the structure of the fault record. The use of the fields in this record are described in the following paragraphs.

The type number (byte ordinal) of a fault is stored in the fault-type field; the subtype number or bit positions (byte ordinal) is stored in the fault-subtype field.

The fault-flags field provides a set of general-purpose flags that the processor uses to indicate additional information about a particular fault subtype. Most of the faults do not use these flags, in which case the flags have no defined values.

The address-of-the-faulting-instruction field contains the IP of the instruction that caused the fault or that was being executed when the fault occurred.

The states of the process controls and arithmetic controls at the time that a fault is generated are stored in their respective fields in the fault record. This information is used to resume work on the program after the fault has been handled.

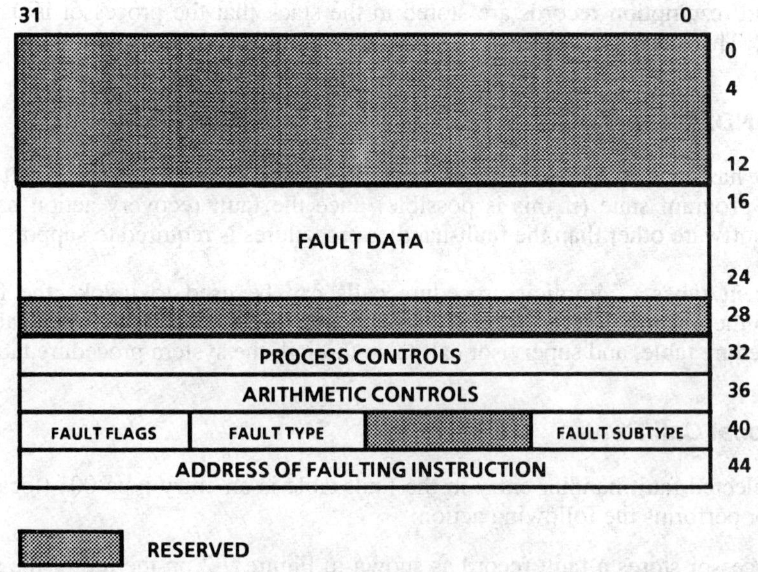

Figure 9-2: Fault Record

Finally, a three-word fault data field is provided for the fault. The information that is stored in these fields depends on the type of fault that occurs. Any part of a fault-data field that is not used for a particular fault has no defined value. The information that is stored in these fields for each fault type is given in the fault reference section at the end of this chapter.

Saved Instruction Pointer

The saved IP (the RIP that is saved in r2 of the stack frame in use when the fault occurred) is also part of the fault information that the processor saves when a fault occurs. This IP generally points to the next instruction that the processor would have executed if the fault had not occurred, although it may point to the faulting instruction. It is this instruction that the processor begins working on when the return from the fault handler is initiated.

Resumption Record

If the processor suspends an instruction as the result of a fault, it creates a 48-byte resumption record. The criteria that the processor uses to determine whether or not to suspend an instruction and the structure of the resumption record are the same as are used when an interrupt occurs.

Location of the Fault and Resumption Records

The fault and resumption records are stored in the stack that the processor is using when the fault occurs. This stack can be the local stack, the supervisor stack, or the interrupt stack.

FAULT HANDLING ACTION

Once a fault has occurred, the processor saves the program state, calls the fault handler, and restores the program state (if this is possible) once the fault recovery action has been completed. No software other than the fault-handler procedures is required to support this activity.

Three different types of implicit procedure calls can be used to invoke the fault handler, according to the information in the selected fault-table entry: local call, local call through the system procedure table, and supervisor call (also through the system procedure table).

Implicit, Local Call/Return

When the selected fault-handler entry in the fault table is an entry type 00_2 (local procedure), the processor performs the following action:

1. The processor stores a fault record as shown in Figure 9-2 on the top of the stack that the processor is currently using. The stack can be the local stack, the supervisor stack, or the interrupt stack.
2. If the fault caused an instruction to be suspended, the processor includes an instruction-resumption record on the current stack and sets the resume flag in the saved process controls.
3. The processor creates a new frame on the current stack, with the frame-return status field set to 001_2.
4. Using the procedure address from the selected fault-table entry, the processor performs an implicit call-extended operation to the fault handler.

If the fault handler is not able to perform a recovery action, it performs one of the actions described in the section earlier in this chapter titled "Possible Fault-Handler Actions."

If the handler action results in a recovery from the fault, a **ret** instruction in the fault handler allows processor control to return to the program that was being worked on when the fault occurred. On the return, the processor performs the following action:

1. The processor deallocates the stack frame created for the fault handler.
2. The processor copies the arithmetic controls field from the fault record into the arithmetic controls register in the processor.
3. The processor then resumes work on the program it was working on when the fault occurred at the instruction in the return IP register.

Implicit, Local Procedure-Table Call/Return

When the fault-handler entry selects an entry in the system procedure table (entry type 10_2) and the system-procedure-table entry is for local procedure, the processor performs the same action as is described in the previous section for a local procedure call/return. The only difference is that the processor gets the address of the fault handler from the system procedure table rather than from the fault table.

Implicit, Supervisor Call/Return

When the fault-handler entry selects an entry in the system procedure table (entry type 10_2) and the system-procedure-table entry is for a supervisor procedure, the processor performs the same action as is described in the previous section for a local procedure call and return, with the exceptions described in the following paragraphs.

On a supervisor fault-handler call, the processor performs the following additional actions:

1. If the processor is in user mode when the fault occurs, the fault record and resumption record are stored in the local stack. The processor then takes the stack pointer from the procedure table and switches to the supervisor stack. The execution mode is then set to supervisor.
2. If the processor is already in supervisor mode when the fault occurs, the fault record is stored in the current stack (which is the supervisor stack). The processor then creates a new frame on the current stack and begins work on the fault-handler procedure selected from the procedure table.
3. In both of the above cases, the processor copies the state of the trace-control flag (byte 12, bit 1) of the procedure table into the trace-enable flag field of the process controls.

On a return from the fault handler, the processor performs the following additional actions:

1. If the processor is in supervisor mode prior to the return from the fault handler (which it should be), it copies the saved process controls into its internal process controls.
2. If the resume flag of the process controls is set, the processor reads the resumption record from the stack.
3. The processor then resumes work on the program at the point it was working on when the fault occurred.

The restoration of the process controls causes any changes in the process controls through the action of the fault handler to be lost. In particular, if the **ret** instruction from the fault handler caused the trace-fault-pending flag in the process controls to be set, this setting would be lost on the return.

Program State After a Fault

As has been described earlier in this chapter, faults can occur prior to the execution of the faulting instruction (i.e., the instruction that causes the fault), during the instruction, or after the instruction. When the fault occurs before the faulting instruction is executed, the instruction can theoretically be executed on the return from the fault handler. So, the fault is not accompanied by a change in the control flow of the program.

When a fault occurs during or after the instruction that caused a fault, the fault may be accompanied by a change in the program's control flow such that the faulting instruction cannot be reexecuted. For example, when an integer-overflow fault occurs, the overflow value is stored in the destination. If the destination register was the same as one of the source registers, the source value is lost, making it impossible to reexecute the faulting instruction.

In general, changes in the program's control flow never accompany the following fault types or subtypes:

- All Operation Subtypes
- Arithmetic Zero-Divide
- All Floating-Point Subtypes Except Floating Inexact
- All Constraint Subtypes
- Prereturn Trace

Changes in the program's control flow always accompany the following fault types and subtypes:

- All Trace Subtypes Except Prereturn Trace
- Integer Overflow
- Floating Inexact

Changes in the program's control flow may or may not accompany the following fault types and subtypes:

- Structural
- Bad Access

The effect that specific fault types have on a program is given in the fault reference section at the end of this chapter under the heading "Program State Changes."

Return Without Resumption

There may be situations where the fault handler needs to return to a point in the program other than where the fault occurred. This can be done by altering the return IP in the previous frame. However, if resumption information was collected with the fault (resulting in the resume flag being set in the saved process controls), such a return can cause unpredictable results.

To predictably perform a return from a fault handler to an alternate point in the program, the fault handler should clear the following information in the process-controls field of the fault record before the return: the resume and trace-fault-pending flags; the internal state field.

Note

A return of this type can only be performed if the processor is in supervisor mode prior to the return.

PRECISE AND IMPRECISE FAULTS

As described in the section in Chapter 3 titled "Register Scoreboarding," the 80960KB processor is, in some instances, able to execute instructions concurrently. When two instructions are being executed concurrently, it is possible for them to generate faults simultaneously. When this occurs, one of the faults may not be signaled or may be signaled out of order, making it impossible to recover from that fault.

The processor provides two mechanisms to allow the circumstances under which faults are signaled to be controlled. These mechanisms are the no imprecise faults flag (NIF flag) in the arithmetic controls and the synchronize faults instruction (**syncf**). The following paragraphs describe how these mechanisms can be used.

Faults are grouped into the following categories: precise, imprecise, and asynchronous.

Precise faults are those that are intended to be recoverable by software. For any instruction that can generate a precise fault, the processor will (1) not execute the instruction if an unfinished prior instruction will fault and (2) not execute subsequent out-of-order instructions that will fault. The following faults are always precise:

- trace
- protection

Imprecise faults are those that in some instances are allowed to occur and not be signaled or be signaled out of order. These faults include the following:

- operation
- arithmetic
- floating point
- constraint
- type

Asynchronous faults are those whose occurrence has no direct relationship to the instruction pointer. This category includes the machine fault.

The NIF flag controls whether or not imprecise faults are allowed. When this flag is set, all faults must be precise. In this mode, the ability to execute instructions concurrently is essentially disabled. All faults that occur are signaled.

When the NIF flag is clear, faults in the imprecise category can in some instances occur and not be signaled. In this mode, the following conditions hold true:

1. When an imprecise fault occurs, the saved IP is undefined (but the address of the faulting instruction in the fault record is valid).
2. If instructions are executed concurrently when an imprecise fault occurs, the results produced by these instructions are undefined.
3. If instructions are executed out-of-order and multiple imprecise faults occur, only one of the faults is generated. The one that is selected is not predictable.

The **syncf** instruction forces the processor to complete execution of all instructions that occur prior to the **syncf** instruction and to generate all faults, before it begins work on instructions that occur after the **syncf** instruction. This instruction has two uses. One use is to force faults to be precise when the NIF is clear. The other use is to insure that all instructions are complete and all faults signaled in one block of code before execution of another block of code (for example, on Ada block boundaries when the blocks have different exception handlers).

The intent of these fault-generating modes is that compiled code should execute with the NIF clear, using the **syncf** instruction where necessary to ensure that faults occur in order. In this mode, imprecise faults are considered as catastrophic errors from which recovery is not needed.

If recovery from one or more of the imprecise faults is required (for example, a program that needs to handle unmasked floating-point exceptions and recover from them) and the fault handler cannot be closely coupled with the application to perform recovery even if the faults are imprecise, the NIF should be set. Executing with the NIF set will likely lead to slower execution times.

FAULT REFERENCE

This section describes each of the fault types and subtypes and gives detailed information about what is stored in the various fields of the fault record. The section is organized alphabetically by fault type.

Fault Reference Notation

The following paragraphs describe the information that is provided for each fault type.

Fault Type and Subtype

The fault-type section gives the number entered in the fault-type field of the fault record for the given fault type. The fault-subtype section lists the fault subtypes and their associated number or bit position in the fault-subtype field of the fault record.

Function

The function section gives a general description of the purpose of the fault type, then describes the purpose of each of the fault subtypes in detail. It also describes how the processor handles each fault subtype.

Fault Record

The fault record section describes how the flags, fault-data, and address-of-faulting-instruction fields of the fault record are used for the fault type and subtypes.

Saved IP

The saved IP section describes what value is saved in the RIP register (r2) of the stack frame the processor was using when the fault occurred.

Program State Changes

The program state changes section describes the effects that the fault subtypes have on the control flow of a program.

Arithmetic Faults

Fault Type: 3_{16}

Fault Subtype:

Number	Name
0	Reserved
1	Integer Overflow
2	Arithmetic Zero-Divide
3-F	Reserved

Function: Indicates that there is a problem with an operand or the result of an arithmetic instruction. This fault type applies only to ordinal and integer instruction, not floating-point instructions.

The integer-overflow fault occurs when the result of an integer instruction overflows the destination and the integer-overflow mask in the arithmetic-controls register is cleared. Here, the *n* least significant bits of the result are stored in the destination, where *n* is the destination size.

The arithmetic zero-divide fault occurs when the divisor operand of an ordinal or integer divide instruction is zero.

Fault Record:

Flags: Not used.

Fault Data: Not used.

Addr. Fault. Inst.: IP for the instruction on which the processor faulted.

Saved IP: IP for the instruction that would have been executed next, if the fault had not occurred.

Prog. State Changes: A change in the program's control flow accompanies the integer-overflow fault, because the result is stored in the destination before the fault is signaled. The faulting instruction can thus not be reexecuted.

A change in the program's control flow does not accompany the arithmetic zero-divide fault, because the fault occurs before the execution of the faulting instruction.

Constraint Faults

Fault Type:	5_{16}	
Fault Subtype:	**Number**	**Name**
	0	Reserved
	1	Constraint Range
	2-F	Reserved

Function: Indicates that the processor is either in or not in the required state for the instruction to be executed.

The constraint-range fault occurs when a fault-if instruction is executed and the condition code in the arithmetic controls matches the condition required by the instruction.

Fault Record:

	Flags:	Not used.
	Fault Data:	Not used.
	Addr. Fault. Inst.:	IP for the instruction on which the processor faulted

Saved IP: Not used.

Prog. State Changes: No changes in the program's control flow accompany the constraint-range fault. This fault occurs after the fault-if instruction has been executed, but the instruction has no effect on the program state.

Floating-Point Faults

Fault Type: 4_{16}

Fault Subtype:

Bit Number	Name
Bit 0	Floating Overflow
Bit 1	Floating Underflow
Bit 2	Floating Invalid-Operation
Bit 3	Floating Zero-Divide
Bit 4	Floating Inexact
Bit 5	Floating Reserved-Encoding
Bits 6 and 7	Reserved

Function: Indicates that there is a problem with an operand or the result of a floating-point instruction. Each floating-point fault is assigned a bit in the fault-subtype field. Multiple floating-point faults can only occur simultaneously, however, with the floating-overflow, floating-underflow, and floating-inexact faults.

The floating-point faults are described in detail in the section in Chapter 12 titled "Exceptions and Fault Handling." The following paragraphs give a brief description of each floating-point fault.

A floating-overflow fault occurs when (1) the floating-point overflow mask is clear and (2) the infinitely precise result of a floating-point instruction exceeds the largest allowable finite value for the specified destination format. This fault interacts with the floating-inexact fault (as described in Chapter 12).

A floating-underflow fault occurs when (1) the floating-point underflow mask is clear and (2) the infinitely precise result of a floating-point instruction is less than the smallest possible normalized, finite value for the specified destination format. This fault interacts with the floating-inexact fault (as described in Chapter 12).

The floating invalid-operation fault occurs when (1) the floating-point invalid-operation mask is clear and (2) one of the source operands for a floating-point instruction is inappropriate for the type of operation being performed.

The floating zero-divide fault occurs when (1) the floating-point zero-divide mask is clear and (2) the divisor operand of a floating-point divide instruction is zero.

The floating-inexact fault occurs when (1) the floating-point inexact mask is clear and (2) an infinitely precise result cannot be encoded in the format specified for the destination operand. This fault interacts with the floating-overflow and floating-underflow faults (as described in Chapter 12).

The floating reserved-encoding fault occurs when a denormalized value is used as an operand in a floating-point instruction and the normalizing-mode bit in the arithmetic controls is clear.

Fault Record:

Flags:

F0 — Used if inexact fault occurs in conjunction with overflow or underflow fault. If set, F0 indicates that the adjusted result has been rounded toward +∞; if clear, F0 indicates that the adjusted result has been rounded toward -∞.

F1 — Used with overflow and underflow faults only. If set, F1 indicates that the adjusted result has been bias adjusted, because its exponent was outside the range of the extended-real format.

Fault Data: Used only with overflow and underflow faults. Adjusted result is stored in this field in extended-real format (as shown in Figure 12-5).

Addr. Fault. Inst.: IP for the instruction on which the processor faulted

Saved IP: IP for the instruction that would have been executed next, if the fault had not occurred.

Prog. State Changes: Changes in the program's control flow accompany the floating-overflow, floating-underflow, and floating-inexact faults, because a result is stored in the destination before the fault is signaled. The faulting instruction can thus not be reexecuted.

Changes in the program's control flow do not accompany the floating invalid-operation, floating zero-divide, and floating reserved-encoding faults, because the faults occur before the execution of the faulting instruction.

Machine Faults

Fault Type: 8_{16}

Fault Subtype:

Number	Name
0	Reserved
1	Bad Access
2-F	Reserved

Function: Indicates that the processor has detected a hardware or memory-system error.

The bad-access fault is the only one of this fault type. This fault occurs whenever an unrecoverable memory error occurs on a memory operation. In the 80960KB processor, the processor receives a signal on its bad access pin (BADAC) to indicate an unrecoverable memory error. Upon receiving this signal, the processor signals a machine bad access fault. There is one exception to this action. The processor will not signal a machine bad access fault while executing any of the synchronous load or move instructions. Instead, it sets the condition code bits to indicate whether or not the memory access was completed successfully.

Fault Record: **Flags:** Not used.

Fault Data: Not used.

Addr. Fault. Inst.: Not used.

Saved IP: Not used.

Prog. State Changes: This fault may occur at any time. When it does occur, the accompanying state of the program's control flow is undefined. As a result, the processor is not able to return predictably from the fault handler to the point in the program where the fault occurred.

If this fault occurs during an atomic operation, there is no guarantee that the locking mechanism that memory uses for synchronization is unlocked.

Operation Faults

Fault Type: 2_{16}

Fault Subtype:

Number	Name
0	Reserved
1	Invalid Opcode
2	Unimplemented
3	Reserved
4	Invalid Operand
5 - F	Reserved

Function: Indicates that the processor cannot execute the current instruction because of invalid instruction syntax or operand semantics.

The invalid-opcode fault occurs when the processor attempts to execute an instruction that contains an undefined opcode or addressing mode.

The unimplemented fault occurs when unaligned memory accesses are not allowed and the processor attempts to access an unaligned word or group of words in memory. (The 80960KB processor does allow unaligned memory accesses, so this fault never occurs.)

The invalid-operand fault occurs when the processor attempts to execute an instruction for which one or more of the operands have special requirements and one or more of the operands do not meet these requirements. This fault subtype is not generated on floating-point instructions.

Fault Record:

Flags: Not used.

Fault Data: Not used.

Addr. Fault. Inst.: IP for the last instruction executed in the process.

Saved IP: IP for the instruction that would have been executed next, if the fault had not occurred.

Prog. State Changes: A change in the program's control flow does not accompany the operation faults, because the faults occur before the execution of the faulting instruction.

Protection Faults

Fault Type: 7_{16}

Fault Subtype:

Bit Number	Name
Bit 0	Reserved
Bit 1	Length
Bit 2-7	Reserved

Function: Indicates that the index operand used in a **calls** instruction points to an entry beyond the extent of the system procedure table.

Fault Flags: Not used.

Fault Data: Not used.

Addr. Fault. Inst.: IP for the instruction on which the processor faulted.

Saved IP: Same as the address-of-faulting-instruction field.

Prog. State Changes: A change in the program's control flow does not accompany the protection length fault.

Trace Faults

Fault Type: 1_{16}

Fault Subtype:

Bit Number	Name
Bit 0	Reserved
Bit 1	Instruction Trace
Bit 2	Branch Trace
Bit 3	Call Trace
Bit 4	Return Trace
Bit 5	Prereturn Trace
Bit 6	Supervisor Trace
Bit 7	Breakpoint Trace

Function: Indicates that the processor has detected one or more trace events. The processor's event tracing mechanism is described in detail in Chapter 10.

A trace event is the occurrence of a particular instruction or type of instruction in the instruction stream. The processor recognizes seven different trace events (instruction, branch, call, return, prereturn, supervisor, and breakpoint). It detects these events, however, only if a mode bit is set for the event in the trace controls word, which is cached in the processor chip. If, in addition, the trace-enable flag in the process controls is set, the processor generates a fault when a trace event is detected.

The fault is generated following the instruction that causes a trace event (or prior to the instruction for the prereturn trace event).

The following trace modes are available:

- **Instruction** — Generate trace event following any instruction.
- **Branch** — Generate trace event following any branch instruction when branch is taken.
- **Call** — Generate trace event following any call or branch-and-link instruction, or implicit procedure call (i.e., call to fault or interrupt handler).
- **Return** — Generate trace event following any return instruction.
- **Prereturn** — Generate trace event prior to any return instruction.
- **Supervisor** — Generate trace event following any call-system instruction.
- **Breakpoint** — Generate trace event following any processor action that causes a breakpoint condition.

There is a trace fault subtype and a bit in the fault-subtype field associated with each of these modes. Multiple fault subtypes can occur simultaneously, with the fault-subtype bit set for each subtype that occurs.

When a fault type other than a trace fault occurs during the execution of an instruction that causes a trace event, the non-trace-fault is handled before the trace fault. An exception to this rule is the prereturn trace fault. The prereturn trace fault will occur before the processor has a chance to detect a non-trace-fault, so it is handled first.

Likewise, if an interrupt occurs during an instruction that causes a trace event, the interrupt is serviced before the trace fault is handled. Again, the prereturn trace fault is an exception. Since it occurs before the instruction, it will be handled before any interrupt that might occur during the execution of the instruction.

Fault Record:

Flags: Not used.

Fault Data: Not used.

Addr. Fault. Inst.: IP for the instruction that caused the trace event, except for the prereturn trace fault. For the prereturn trace fault, this field has no defined value.

Saved IP: IP for the instruction that would have been executed next, if the fault had not occurred.

Prog. State Changes: A change in the program's control flow accompanies all the trace faults (except the prereturn trace fault), because the events that can cause a trace fault occur after the faulting instruction is completed. As a result, the faulting instruction cannot be reexecuted upon returning from the fault handler.

Since the prereturn trace fault occurs before the **return** instruction is executed, a change in the program's control flow does not accompany this fault and the faulting instruction can be executed upon returning from the fault handler.

Type Faults

Fault Type: A_{16}

Fault Subtype:

Number	Name
0	Reserved
1	Type Mismatch
2-F	Reserved

Function: Indicates that an attempt was made to execute the **modpc** instruction while the processor was in the user mode.

Fault Record:

Flags: Not used.

Fault Data: Not used.

Addr. Fault. Inst.: IP for the instruction on which the processor faulted

Saved IP: Not used.

Prog. State Changes: When a type mismatch fault occurs, the accompanying state of the program is undefined. The processor is thus not able to return predictably from the fault handler to the point in the program where the fault occurred.

Debugging 10

CHAPTER 10
DEBUGGING

This chapter describes the tracing facilities of the 80960KB processor, which allow the monitoring of instruction execution.

OVERVIEW OF THE TRACE-CONTROL FACILITIES

The 80960KB processor provides facilities for monitoring the activity of the processor by means of trace events. A trace event in the 80960KB is a condition where the processor has just completed executing a particular instruction or type of instruction, or where the processor is about to execute a particular instruction.

By monitoring trace events, debugging software is able to display or analyze the activity of the processor or of a program. This analysis can be used to locate software or hardware bugs or for general system monitoring during the development of system or applications programs.

The typical way to use this tracing capability is to set the processor to detect certain trace events either by means of the trace-controls word or a set of breakpoint registers. An alternate method of creating a trace event is with the **mark** and force mark **fmark** instructions. These instructions cause an explicit trace event to be generated when the processor detects them in the instruction stream.

If tracing is enabled, the processor signals a trace fault when it detects a trace event. The fault handler for trace faults can then call the debugging monitor software to display or analyze the state of the processor when the trace event occurred.

REQUIRED SOFTWARE SUPPORT FOR TRACING

To use the processor's tracing facilities, software must provide trace-fault handling procedures, perhaps interfaced with a debugging monitor. Software must also manipulate several control flags to enable the various tracing modes and to enable or disable tracing in general. These control flags are located in the system-data structures described in the next section.

TRACE CONTROLS

The following flags or fields control tracing:

- Trace controls
- Trace-enable flag in the process controls
- Trace-fault-pending flag in the process controls
- Trace flag (bit 0) in the return-status field of register r0
- Trace-control flag in the supervisor-stack-pointer field of the system table or a procedure table

Trace-Controls Word

The trace-controls word is cached internally in the processor.

The trace controls allow software to define the conditions under which trace events are generated. Figure 10-1 shows the structure of the trace-controls word.

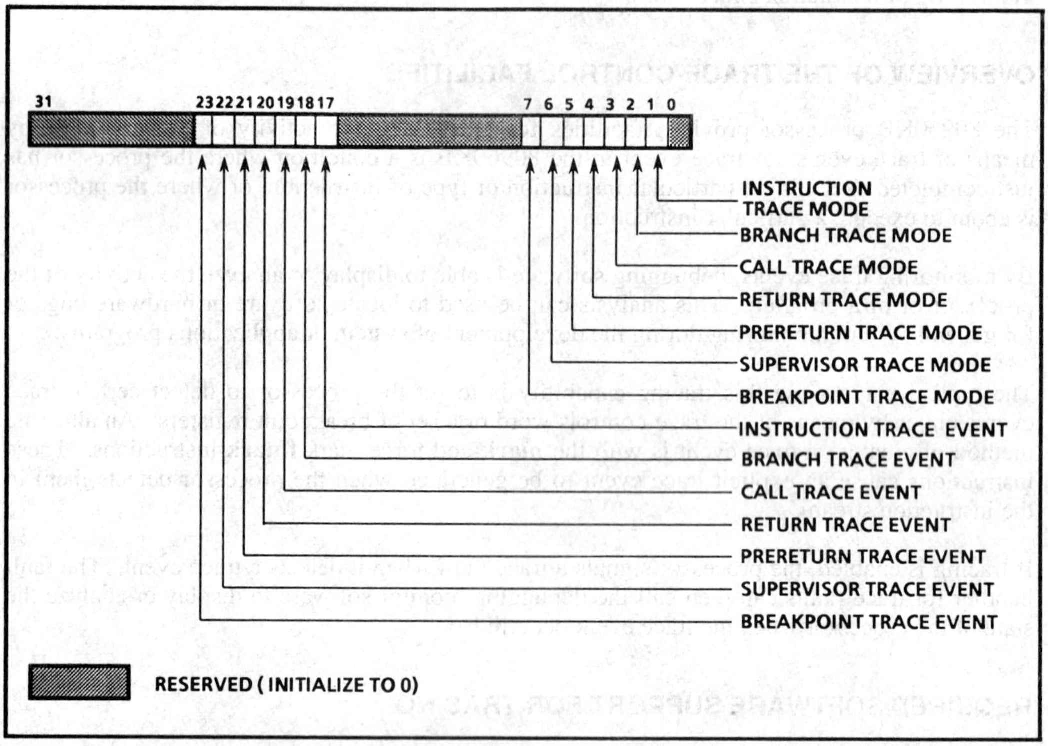

Figure 10-1: Trace-Controls Word

This word contains two sets of bits: the mode flags and the event flags. The mode flags define a set of trace modes that the processor can use to generate trace events. A mode represents a subset of instructions that will cause trace events to be generated. For example, when the call-trace mode is enabled, the processor generates a trace event whenever a call or branch-and-link operation is executed. To enable a trace mode, the kernel sets the mode flag for the selected trace mode in the trace controls. The trace modes are described later in this chapter.

The processor uses the event flags to keep track of which trace events (for those trace modes that have been enabled) have been detected.

A special instruction, the modify-trace-controls (**modtc**) instruction, allows software to set or clear flags in the trace controls. On initialization, all the flags in the processor's internal trace controls are cleared. The **modtc** instruction can then be used to set or clear trace mode flags as required.

Software can access the event flags using the **modtc** instruction, however, there is no reason to. The processor modifies these flags as part of its trace-handling mechanism.

Bits 0, 8 through 16, and 24 through 31 of the trace controls are reserved. Software should initialize these bits to zero and not modify them.

Trace-Enable and Trace-Fault-Pending Flags

The trace-enable flag and the trace-fault-pending flag, in the process controls (shown in Figure 7-2), control tracing. The trace-enable flag enables the processor's tracing facilities. When this flag is set, the processor generates trace faults on all trace events.

Typically, software selects the trace modes to be used through the trace controls. It then sets the trace-enable flag when tracing is to begin. This flag is also altered as part of some of the call and return operations that the processor carries out, as described at the end of this chapter.

The trace-fault-pending flag allows the processor to keep track of the fact that an enabled trace event has been detected. The processor uses this flag as follows. When the processor detects an enabled trace event, it sets this flag. Before executing an instruction, the processor checks this flag. If the flag is set, it signals a trace fault. By providing a means of recording the occurrence of a trace event, the trace-fault-pending flag allows the processor to service an interrupt or handle a fault other than a trace fault, before handling the trace fault. Software should not modify this flag.

Trace Control on Supervisor Calls

The trace flag and the trace-control flag allow tracing to be enabled or disabled when a call-system instruction (**calls**) is executed that results in a switch to supervisor mode. This action occurs independent of whether or not tracing is enabled prior to the call.

When a supervisor call is executed (**calls** instruction that references an entry in the system procedure table with an entry type 11_2), the processor saves the current state of the trace-enable flag (from the process controls) in the trace flag (bit 0) of the return-status field of register r0.

Then, when the processor selects the supervisor procedure from the procedure table, it sets the trace-enable flag in the process controls according to the setting in the trace-control flag in the procedure table (bit 0 of the word that contains the supervisor-stack pointer).

On a return from the supervisor procedure, the trace-enable flag in the process controls is restored to the value saved in the return-status field of register r0.

TRACE MODES

The following trace modes can be enabled through the trace controls:

- Instruction trace

- Branch trace
- Call trace
- Return trace
- Prereturn trace
- Supervisor trace
- Breakpoint trace

These modes can be enabled individually or several modes can be enabled at once. Some of these modes overlap, such as the call-trace mode and the supervisor-trace mode. The section later in this chapter titled "Handling Multiple Trace Events" describes what the processor does when multiple trace events occur.

The following sections describe each of the trace modes.

Instruction Trace

When the instruction-trace mode is enabled, the processor generates an instruction-trace event each time an instruction is executed. This mode can be used within a debugging monitor to single-step the processor.

Branch Trace

When the branch-trace mode is enabled, the processor generates an branch-trace event any time a branch instruction that branches is executed. A branch-trace event is not generated for conditional-branch instructions that do not branch. Also, branch-and-link, call, and return instructions do not cause branch-trace events to be generated.

Call Trace

When the call-trace mode is enabled, the processor generates a call-trace event any time a call instruction (**call**, **callx**, or **calls**) or a branch-and-link instruction (**bal** or **balx**) is executed. An implicit call, such as the action used to invoke a fault handler or an interrupt handler, also causes a call-trace event to be generated.

When the processor detects a call-trace event, it also sets the prereturn-trace flag (bit 3 of register r0) in the new frame created by the call operation or in the current frame if a branch-and-link operation was performed. The processor uses this flag to determine whether or not to signal a prereturn-trace event on a **return** instruction.

Return Trace

When the return-trace mode is enabled, the processor generates a return-trace event any time a **ret** instruction is executed.

Prereturn Trace

The prereturn-trace mode causes the processor to generate a prereturn-trace event prior to the execution of any **ret** instruction, providing the prereturn-trace flag in r0 is set. (Prereturn tracing cannot be used without enabling call tracing.)

The processor sets the prereturn-trace flag whenever it detects a call-trace event (as described above for the call-trace mode). This flag performs a prereturn-trace-pending function. If another trace event occurs at the same time as the prereturn-trace event, the prereturn-trace flag allows the processor to fault on the non-prereturn-trace event first, then come back and fault again on the prereturn-trace event. The prereturn trace is the only trace event that can cause two successive trace faults to be generated between instruction boundaries.

Supervisor Trace

When the supervisor-trace mode is enabled, the processor generates a supervisor-trace event any time (1) a call-system instruction (**calls**) is executed, where the procedure table entry is a supervisor procedure, or (2) when a **ret** instruction is executed and the return-status field is set to 010_2 or 011_2 (i.e., return from supervisor mode).

This trace mode allows a debugging program to determine the boundaries of kernel procedure calls within the instruction stream.

Breakpoint Trace

The breakpoint-trace mode allows trace events to be generated at places other than those specified with the other trace modes. This mode is used in conjunction with the **mark** and force-mark (**fmark**) instructions, and the breakpoint registers.

The **mark** and **fmark** instructions allow breakpoint-trace events to be generated at specific points in the instruction stream. When the breakpoint-trace mode is enabled, the processor generates a breakpoint-trace event any time it encounters a **mark** instruction. The **fmark** causes the processor to generate a breakpoint-trace event regardless of whether the breakpoint-trace mode is enabled or not.

The processor has two, one-word breakpoint registers, designated as breakpoint 0 and breakpoint 1. Using the set-breakpoint-register IAC, one instruction pointer can be loaded into each register. The processor then generates a breakpoint trace any time it executes an instruction referenced in a breakpoint register.

TRACE-FAULT HANDLER

A fault handler is a procedure that the processor calls to handle faults that occur. The requirements for fault handlers are given in Chapter 9 in the section titled "Fault-Handler Procedures."

A trace-fault handler has one additional restriction. It must be called with an implicit supervisor call, and the trace-control flag in the system-procedure-table entry must be clear. This restriction insures that tracing is turned off when a trace fault is being handled, which is necessary to prevent an endless loop.

SIGNALING A TRACE EVENT

To summarize the information presented in the previous sections, the processor signals a trace event when it detects any of the following conditions:

- An instruction included in a trace-mode group is executed or about to be executed (in the case of a prereturn trace event) and the trace mode for that instruction is enabled.
- An implicit call operation has been executed and the call-trace mode is enabled.
- A **mark** instruction has been executed and the breakpoint-trace mode is enabled.
- An **fmark** instruction has been executed.
- An instruction specified in a breakpoint register is executed and the breakpoint-trace mode is enabled.

When the processor detects a trace event and the trace-enable flag in the process controls is set, the processor performs the following action:

1. The processor sets the appropriate trace-event flag in the trace controls. If a trace event meets the conditions of more than one of the enabled trace modes, a trace-event flag is set for each trace mode condition that is met.
2. The processor sets the trace-fault-pending flag in the process controls.

Note

The processor may set a trace-event flag and the trace-fault-pending flag before it has completed execution of the instruction that caused the event. However, the processor only handles trace events in between the execution of instructions.

If, when the processor detects a trace event, the trace-enable flag in the process controls is clear, the processor sets the appropriate event flags, but does not set the trace-fault-pending flag.

HANDLING MULTIPLE TRACE EVENTS

If the processor detects multiple trace events, it records one or more of them based on the following precedence, where 1 is the highest precedence:

1. Supervisor-trace event
2. Breakpoint- (from **mark** or **fmark** instruction, or from a breakpoint register), branch-, call-, or return-trace event
3. Instruction-trace event

When multiple trace events are detected, the processor may not signal each event; however, it will signal at least the one with the highest precedence.

TRACE HANDLING ACTION

Once a trace event has been signaled, the processor determines how to handle the trace event, according to the setting of the trace-enable and trace-fault-pending flags in the process controls and to other events that might occur simultaneously with the trace event such as an interrupt or a non-trace fault.

The following sections describe how the processor handles trace events for various situations.

Normal Handling of Trace Events

Prior to executing an instruction, the processor performs the following action regarding trace events:

1. The processor checks the state of the trace-fault pending flag. If this flag is clear, the processor begins execution of the next instruction. If the flag is set, the processor performs the following actions.
2. The processor checks the state of the trace-enable flag. If the trace-enable flag is clear, the processor clears any trace event flags that have been set, prior to starting execution of the next instruction. If the trace-enable flag is set, the processor performs the following action.
3. The processor signals a trace fault and begins the fault handling action, as described in Chapter 9.

Prereturn Trace Handling

The processor handles a prereturn-trace event the same as described above except when it occurs at the same time as a non-trace fault. Here, the non-trace fault is handled first.

On returning from the fault handler for the non-trace fault, the processor checks the prereturn-trace flag in register r0. If this flag is set, the processor generates a prereturn-trace event, then handles it as described above.

Tracing and Interrupt Handlers

When the processor invokes an interrupt handler to service an interrupt, it disables tracing. It does this by saving the current state of the process controls, then clearing the trace-enable and trace-fault-pending flags in the current process controls.

On returning from the interrupt handler, the processor restores the process controls to the state they were in prior to handling the interrupt, which restores the state of the trace-enable and trace-fault-pending flags. If these two flags were set prior to calling the interrupt handler, a trace fault will be signaled on the return from the interrupt handler.

Tracing and Fault Handlers

The processor can invoke a fault handler with either an implicit local call or an implicit supervisor call. On a local call, the trace-enable and trace-fault-pending flags are neither saved on the call nor restored on the return. The state of these flags on the return is thus dependent on the action of the fault handler.

On a supervisor call, the trace-enable and trace-fault-pending flags are saved, as part of the saved process controls, and restored on the return. So, if these two flags were set prior to calling the fault handler, a trace fault will be signaled on the return from the fault handler.

Note

On a return from an interrupt handler or a fault handler (other than the trace-fault handler), the trace-fault-pending flag is restored. If this flag is set as a result of the handler's **ret** instruction, the detected trace event is lost.

Core Instruction Reference

11

CHAPTER 11
INSTRUCTION SET REFERENCE

This chapter provides detailed information about each of the instructions for the 80960KB processor. To provide quick access to information on a particular instruction, the instructions are listed alphabetically by assembly-language mnemonic. An explanation of the format and abbreviations used in this chapter is given in the following section.

INTRODUCTION

The information in this chapter is oriented toward programmers who are writing assembly-language code for the 80960KB processor. The information provided for each instruction includes the following:

- Alphabetic reference
- Assembly-language mnemonic and name
- Assembly-language format
- Description of the instruction's operation
- Action the instruction carries out when executed (generally presented in the form of an algorithm)
- Faults that can occur during execution
- Assembly-language example
- Opcode and instruction format
- Related instructions

Additional information about the instruction set can be found in the following chapters and appendices in this manual:

- Chapter 6 -- Summary of the instruction set by group and description of the assembly-language instruction format
- Appendix A -- Instruction Quick Reference
- Appendix B -- Machine-Level Instruction Formats

NOTATION

To simplify the presentation of information about the instructions, a simple notation has been adopted in this chapter. The following paragraphs describe this notation.

Alphabetic Reference

The instructions are listed alphabetically by assembly-language mnemonic. If several instructions are related and fall together alphabetically, they are described as a group on a single page.

The reference at the top of each page gives the assembly-language mnemonics for the instructions covered on that page (e.g., **subc**). Occasionally, there are so many instructions covered on the page that it is not practical to give all the mnemonics in the page reference. In these cases, the name of the instruction group is given in capital letters (e.g., BRANCH or FAULT IF)

A box around the alphabetic reference (such as **addr, addrl**) indicates that the instruction or group of instructions are extensions to the 80960 architecture instruction set.

Mnemonic

The Mnemonic section gives the complete mnemonic (in bold-face type) and instruction name for each instruction covered on the page, for example:

subi Subtract Integer

Format

The Format section gives the assembly-language format of the instruction and the type of operands allowed. The format is given in two or three lines. The following is an example of a two line format:

sub*	*src1*,	*src2*,	*dst*
	reg/lit	reg/lit	reg

The first line gives the assembly-language mnemonic (bold-face type) and the operands (italics). When the format is used for two or more instructions, an abbreviated form of the mnemonic is used. The " * " sign at the end of the mnemonic indicates that the mnemonic has been abbreviated.

The operand names are designed to describe the functions of the operands (e.g., *src*, *len*, *mask*).

The second line of the format shows what is allowed to be entered for each operand. The notation used on this line is as follows:

reg Global (g0 ... g15) or local (r0 ... r15) register

freg Global (g0 ... g15) or local (r0 ... r15) register, or floating-point (fp0 ... fp3) register, where the registers contain floating-point numbers

lit Integer or ordinal literal of the range 0 ... 31

flit Floating-point literal of value 1.0 or 0.0

disp Signed displacement of range $-2^{22} \ldots (2^{22} - 1)$

mem Address defined with the full range of addressing modes

In some cases, a third line will be added to show specifically what will be in a register or memory location. For example, it may be useful to know that a register is to contain an address. The notation used in this line is as follows:

addr	Address
efa	Effective address

Description

The Description section describes what the instruction does and the functions of the operands. It also gives programming hints when appropriate.

Action

The Action section gives an algorithm written in a pseudo-code that describes in detail what actions the processor takes when executing the instruction and the precise order of these actions. The main purpose of this section is to show the possible side effects of the instruction. The following is an example of the action algorithm for the **alterbit** instruction:

if (AC.cc **and** 2#010#) = 0
  then *dst* ← *src* **and not** (2^(*bitpos* **mod** 32));
  else *dst* ← *src* **or** 2^(*bitpos* **mod** 32);
end if;

In these action statements, the term AC.cc means the condition-code bits in the arithmetic controls. The notation 2#*value*# means that the value enclosed in the "#" signs is in base 2.

Faults

The Faults section lists the faults that can be signaled as the result of execution of the instruction. Faults listed with all-capital letters refer to a group of faults; faults listed with initial-capital letters refer to a specific fault.

All instructions can signal a group of general faults which are referred to as STANDARD FAULTS. The standard faults include the trace-instruction and machine-bad-access faults. In addition, for all instructions that have a MEM machine-format (such as, load, store, call extended), the invalid-opcode and operation-unimplemented faults are standard faults.

The following list shows the various fault groups and the individual faults in each group:

TRACE FAULTS
- Instruction Trace
- Branch Trace
- Call Trace
- Return Trace
- Prereturn Trace
- Supervisor Trace
- Breakpoint Trace

OPERATION
- Invalid Opcode
- Unimplemented
- Invalid Operand

ARITHMETIC
- Integer Overflow
- Arithmetic Zero-Divide

FLOATING-POINT
- Floating Overflow
- Floating Underflow
- Floating Invalid-Operation
- Floating Zero-Divide
- Floating Inexact
- Floating Reserved-Encoding

CONSTRAINT
- Constraint Range
- Privileged

PROTECTION
- Segment Length

MACHINE
- Bad Access

TYPE
- Type Mismatch

Example

The Example section gives an assembly-language example of an application of the instruction.

Opcode and Instruction Format

The Opcode and Instruction Format section gives the opcode and machine language instruction format for each instruction, for example:

subi	593	REG

The opcode is given in hexadecimal format.

The machine language format is one of four possible formats: REG, COBR, CTRL, and MEM. Refer to Appendix B for more information on the machine-language instruction formats.

See Also

The See Also section gives the mnemonics of related instructions, which can then be looked up alphabetically in this chapter for comparison. For instructions that are grouped on one page (such as **addr** and **addrl**) only the first mnemonic is given.

INSTRUCTIONS

This section contains reference information on the processor's instructions. It is arranged alphabetically by instruction or instruction group.

addc

Mnemonic: **addc** Add Ordinal With Carry

Format: **addc** *src1*, *src2*, *dst*
reg/lit reg/lit reg

Description: Adds the *src2* and *src1* values, and bit 1 of the condition code (used here as a carry in), and stores the result in *dst*. If the ordinal addition results in a carry, bit 1 of the condition code is set; otherwise, bit 1 is cleared. If integer addition results in an overflow, bit 0 of the condition code is set; otherwise, bit 0 is cleared. Regardless of the results of the addition, bits 0 and 1 of the arithmetic controls are always written.

The **addc** instruction can be used for either ordinal or integer arithmetic. The instruction does not distinguish between ordinal and integer source operands. Instead, the processor evaluates the result for both data types and sets bits 0 and 1 of the condition code accordingly.

An integer overflow fault is never signaled with this instruction.

Action:

Let the value of the condition code be xCx.
dst ← *src2* + *src1* + C;
AC.cc ← 2#0CV#;
C is carry from ordinal addition.
V is 1 if integer addition would have generated an overflow.

Faults: STANDARD

Example:

```
# Example of double-precision arithmetic
# Assume 64-bit source operands
# in g0,g1 and g2,g3
cmpo 1, 0           # clears Bit 1 (carry bit) of
                    # the AC.cc
addc g0, g2, g0     # add low-order 32 bits;
                    # g0  ← g2 + g0 + Carry Bit
addc g1, g3, g1     # add high-order 32 bits;
                    # g1  ← g3 + g1 + Carry Bit
# 64-bit result is in g0, g1
```

Opcode: **addc** 5B0 REG

See Also: **addo, subc**

addi, addo

Mnemonic:	**addi**	Add Integer		
	addo	Add Ordinal		
Format:	**add***	*src1*,	*src2*,	*dst*
		reg/lit	reg/lit	reg

Description: Adds the *src2* and *src1* values and stores the result in *dst*.

Action: *dst* ← *src2* + *src1*;

Faults:

STANDARD	Refer to discussion of faults at the beginning of this chapter.
Integer Overflow	Result is too large for destination format. This fault is signaled only when executing the **addi** instruction and if both of the following conditions are met: (1) the integer-overflow mask in the arithmetic-controls registers is clear and (2) the source operands have like signs and the sign of the result operand is different than the signs of the source operands.

Example:

```
addi r4, g5, r9     # r9 ← g5 + r4
```

Opcode:

addi	591	REG
addo	590	REG

See Also: **addc**, **addr**, **subi**, **subo**

addr, addrl

Mnemonics: **addr** Add Real
addrl Add Long Real

Format: **addr*** *src1*, freg/flit *src2*, freg/flit *dst* freg

addr*	*src1*,	*src2*,	*dst*
	freg/flit	freg/flit	freg

Description: Adds the *src2* and *src1* values and stores the result in *dst*.

For the **addrl** instruction, if the *src1*, *src2*, or *dst* operand references a global or local register, this register is the first (lowest numbered) of two successive registers. Also, this register must be even numbered (e.g., g0, g2, g4).

The following table shows the results obtained when adding various classes of numbers, assuming that neither overflow nor underflow occurs.

Src1

Src2		-∞	-F	-0	+0	+F	+∞	NaN
	-∞	-∞	-∞	-∞	-∞	-∞	*	NaN
	-F	-∞	-F	src2	src2	±F or ±0	+∞	NaN
	-0	-∞	src1	-0	±0	src1	+∞	NaN
	+0	-∞	src1	±0	+0	src1	+∞	NaN
	+F	-∞	±F or ±0	src2	src2	+F	+∞	NaN
	+∞	*	+∞	+∞	+∞	+∞	+∞	NaN
	NaN	NaN	NaN	NaN	NaN	NaN	NaN	NaN

Notes:

F Means finite-real number
* Indicates floating invalid-operation exception

When the sum of two operands with opposite signs is zero, the result is +0, except for the round toward -∞ mode, in which case, the result is -0. When zero is added to itself (e.g. *src1* + *src1*, where *src1* is 0), the result retains the sign of the source.

Action: *dst* ← *src2* + *src1*;

addr, addrl

Faults:

STANDARD	Refer to the discussion of faults at the beginning of this chapter.
Floating Reserved Encoding	One or more operands is an unnormalized (including denormalized) value and the normalizing-mode bit in the arithmetic controls is set.

The following floating-point exceptions can be raised. Whether or not an exception results in a fault being raised depends on the state of its associated mask bit in the arithmetic controls.

Floating Overflow	Result is too large for destination format.
Floating Underflow	Normalized result is too small for destination format.
Floating Invalid Operation	Source operands are infinities of unlike sign.
	One or more operands is an SNaN value.
Floating Inexact	Result cannot be represented exactly in destination format.
	Floating overflow occurred and the overflow exception was masked.

Example:

```
addrl g6, g8, fp3    #fp3 ← g6,g7 + g8,g9
```

Opcode:

addr	78F	REG
addrl	79F	REG

See Also: **addi, subr**

alterbit

Mnemonic: **alterbit** Alter Bit

Format: **alterbit** *bitpos*, *src*, *dst*
reg/lit reg/lit reg

Description: Copies the *src* value to *dst* with one bit altered. The *bitpos* operand specifies the bit to be changed; the condition code determines the value the bit is to be changed to. If the condition code is $X1X_2$, the selected bit is set; otherwise, it is cleared.

Action:

if (AC.cc **and** 2#010#) = 0
  then *dst* ← *src* **and not** (2^(*bitpos* **mod** 32));
  else *dst* ← *src* **or** 2^(*bitpos* **mod** 32);
end if;

Faults: STANDARD

Example:

```
# assume condition code is 2#010#
alterbit 24, g4, g9  # g9 ← g4, with bit 24 set
```

Opcode: **alterbit** 58F REG

See Also: **checkbit**, **clearbit**, **notbit**, **setbit**

and, andnot

Mnemonics:

and	And
andnot	And Not

Format:

and	*src1*,	*src2*,	*dst*
	reg/lit	reg/lit	reg
andnot	*src1*,	*src2*,	*dst*
	reg/lit	reg/lit	reg

Description: Performs a bitwise AND (**and** instruction) or AND NOT (**andnot** instruction) operation on the *src2* and *src1* values and stores the result in *dst*. Note in the action expressions below, the *src2* operand comes first, so that with the **andnot** instruction the expression is evaluated as

{*src2* **andnot** (*src1*)}

rather than

{*src1* **andnot** (*src2*)}.

Action:

and: *dst* ← *src2* **and** *src1*;

andnot: *dst* ← *src2* **and not** (*src1*);

Faults: STANDARD

Example:

```
and 0x17, g8, g2     # g2 ← g8 AND 0x17
andnot r3, r12, r9   # r9 ← r12 AND NOT r3
```

Opcode:

and	581	REG
andnot	582	REG

See Also: **nand**, **nor**, **not**, **notand**, **notor**, **or**, **ornot**, **xnor**, **xor**

atadd

Mnemonic: **atadd** Atomic Add

Format:

atadd	*src/dst,*	*src,*	*dst*
	reg	reg/lit	reg
	addr		

Description: Adds the *src* value (full word) to the value in the memory location specified with the *src/dst* operand. The initial value from memory is stored in *dst*.

The read and write of memory are done atomically (i.e., other processors are prevented from accessing the word of memory specified with the *src/dst* operand until the operation has been completed).

The memory location in *src/dst* is the address of the first byte (least significant byte) of the word. The address is automatically aligned to a word boundary.

Action:

tempa ← *src/dst* **and not** (3); # force alignment to word boundary
temp ← atomic_read (tempa);
atomic_write (tempa) ← temp + *src*;
dst ← temp;

Faults: STANDARD

Example:

```
atadd r8, r2, r11    # r8 ← r2 + address r8,
                     # where r8 specifies the
                     # address of a word in
                     # memory; r11 ← initial
                     # value stored at address
                     # r8 in memory
```

Opcode: **atadd** 612 REG

See Also: **atmod**

atanr, atanrl

Mnemonics: **atanr** Arctangent Real
atanrl Arctangent Long Real

Format: **atanr*** *src1*, *src2*, *dst*
freg/flit freg/flit freg

Description: Calculates the arctangent of the quotient of *src2*/*src1* and stores the result in *dst*. The result is returned in radians and is in the range of -π to +π, inclusive. The sign of the result is always the sign of *src2*.

For the **atanrl** instruction, if the *src1*, *src2*, or *dst* operand references a global or local register, this register is the first (lowest numbered) of two successive registers. Also, this register must be even numbered (e.g., g0, g2, g4).

These instructions are commonly used as part of an algorithm to convert rectangular coordinates to polar coordinates. They can also be used to implement the FORTRAN intrinsic functions ATAN and ATAN2. If *src1* is the floating-point literal value +1.0, then these instructions return a result in the range of -π/2 to +π/2.

The following table gives the range of results for various values of *src2* and *src1*, assuming that neither overflow nor underflow occurs.

		Src1						
		-∞	**-F**	**-0**	**+0**	**+F**	**+∞**	**NaN**
	-∞	-3π/4	-π/2	-π/2	-π/2	-π/2	-π/4	NaN
	-F	-π	-π to -π/2	-π/2	-π/2	-π/2 to -0	-0	NaN
	-0	-π	-π	-π	-0	-0	-0	NaN
Src2	**+0**	+π	+π	+π	+0	+0	+0	NaN
	+F	+π	+π to +π/2	+π/2	+π/2	+π/2 to +0	+0	NaN
	+∞	+3π/4	+π/2	+π/2	+π/2	+π/2	+π/4	NaN
	NaN	NaN	NaN	NaN	NaN	NaN	NaN	NaN

Notes:

F Means finite-real number.

atanr, atanrl

Action: *dst* ← arctan (*src2*/*src1*);

Faults:

STANDARD — Refer to the discussion of faults at the beginning of this chapter.

Floating Reserved Encoding — One or more operands is an unnormalized (including denormalized) value and the normalizing-mode bit in the arithmetic controls is set.

The following floating-point exceptions can be raised. Whether or not an exception results in a fault being raised depends on the state of its associated mask bit in the arithmetic controls.

Floating Underflow — Result is too small for destination format.

Floating Invalid Operation — One or more operands are an SNaN value.

Floating Inexact — Result cannot be represented exactly in destination format.

Example:

```
atanrl g8, g10, fp3   # fp3 ←
                      # arctan (g10,g11/g8,g9)
atanrl 1.0, g0, g0    # g0,g1 ← arctan (g0,g1)
```

Opcode:

atanr	680	REG
atanrl	690	REG

See Also: **tanr**

atmod

Mnemonic: **atmod** Atomic Modify

Format:

atmod	*src*,	*mask*,	*src/dst*
	reg	reg/lit	reg
	addr		

Description: Copies the *src/dst* value into the memory location specified in *src*. The bits set in the *mask* operand select the bits to be modified in memory. The initial value from memory is stored in *src/dst*.

The read and write of memory are done atomically (i.e., other processors are prevented from accessing the word of memory specified with the *src/dst* operand until the operation has been completed).

The memory location in *src* is the address of the first byte (least significant byte) of the word to be modified. The address is automatically aligned to a word boundary.

Action:

tempa ← *src* **and not** (3); # force alignment to word boundary
temp ← atomic_read (tempa);
atomic_write (tempa) ← (*src/dst* **and** *mask*)
or (temp **and not**(*mask*));
src/dst ← temp;

Faults: STANDARD

Example:

```
atmod g5, g7, g10   # g5 ← g5 masked by g7,
                    # where g5 specifies the
                    # address of a word in
                    # memory;
                    # g10 ← initial value
                    # stored at address g5
                    # in memory
```

Opcode: **atmod** 610 REG

See Also: **atadd**

bal, balx

Mnemonic: **bal** Branch And Link
balx Branch And Link Extended

Format:

bal	*targ*	
	disp	
balx	*targ*,	*dst*
	mem	reg

Description: Stores the address of the next instruction (the instruction following the **bal** or **balx** instruction) and branches to the instruction specified with the *targ* operand.

With the **bal** instruction, the address of the next instruction is stored in register g14. The *targ* operand can be either a label or an absolute address that specifies the IP of the target instruction. This value can be no farther than -2^{23} to $(2^{23} - 4)$ from the current IP.

The **balx** instruction performs almost the same operation as the **bal** instruction except that the target instruction can be farther than -2^{23} to $(2^{23} - 4)$ from the current IP. With the **balx** instruction, the address of the next instruction is stored in **dst**. The *targ* operand is a memory type, which allows the full range of addressing modes to be used to specify the IP of the target instruction. Here, the "IP + displacement" addressing mode allows the instruction to be IP-relative. Indirect branching can be performed by placing the target address in a register and then using one of the register-indirect addressing modes.

Refer to Chapter 5 for a complete discussion of the addressing modes available with memory-type operands.

Note

At the machine level, the **bal** instruction uses the CTRL instruction format. With this format, the target instruction for the branch is specified by means of a word-displacement (represented by *displacement* in the following action statement for the **bal** instruction), which can range from -2^{21} to $(2^{21} - 1)$. To determine the IP of the target instruction, the processor converts this *displacement* value to a byte displacement (i.e., multiplies the value by 4). It then adds the resulting byte displacement to the current IP.

bal, balx

To allow labels or absolute addresses to be used in the assembly-language version of the **bal** instruction, the Intel 80960KB Assembler performs the following calculation to convert the *targ* value in an assembly-language instruction to the *displacement* value required by the machine instruction format:

displacement = (*targ*/4) - IP

For further information about the CTRL instruction format, refer to Appendix B.

Action:

bal: G14 ← IP + 4; # destination next IP is always g14
IP ← IP + *targ*; # resume execution at the new IP

balx: *dst* ← IP + inst length; # instruction length
is 4 or 8 bytes
IP ← *targ*; # resume execution at the new IP

Faults: STANDARD

Example:

```
bal xyz  # IP ← xyz;

balx (g2), g4  # IP ← (g2);
               # address of return instruction
               # is stored in g4; example of
               # indirect addressing.
```

Opcode:

bal	0B	CTRL
balx	85	MEM

See Also: **b, bx**

b, bx

Mnemonic: **b** Branch
bx Branch Extended

Format: **b** *targ*

bx *targ*
mem

Description: Branches to the instruction specified with the *targ* operand.

With the **b** instruction, the *targ* operand can be either a label or an absolute address that specifies the IP of the target instruction. This value can be no farther than -2^{23} to $(2^{23} - 4)$ from the current IP.

The **bx** instruction performs the same operation as the **b** instruction except that the target instruction can be farther than -2^{23} to $(2^{23} - 4)$ from the current IP. With the **bx** instruction, the *targ* operand is a memory type, which allows the full range of addressing modes to be used to specify the IP of the target instruction. Here, the "IP + displacement" addressing mode allows the instruction to be IP-relative. Indirect branching can be performed by placing the target address in a register and then using one of the register-indirect addressing modes.

Refer to Chapter 5 for a complete discussion of the addressing modes available with memory-type operands.

Note

At the machine level, the **b** instruction uses the CTRL instruction format. With this format, the target instruction for the branch is specified by means of a word-displacement (represented by *displacement* in the following action statement for the **b** instruction), which can range from -2^{21} to $(2^{21} - 1)$. To determine the IP of the target instruction, the processor converts this *displacement* value to a byte displacement (i.e., multiplies the value by 4). It then adds the resulting byte displacement to the current IP.

To allow labels or absolute addresses to be used in the assembly-language version of the **b** instruction, the Intel 80960KB Assembler performs the following calculation to convert the *targ* value in an assembly-language instruction to the *displacement* value required by the machine instruction format:

$$displacement = (targ/4) - IP$$

For further information about the CTRL instruction format, refer to Appendix B.

b, bx

Action:

b: IP ← IP + *displacement*; # resume execution at the new IP

bx: IP ← *targ*; # resume execution at the new IP

Faults: STANDARD

Example:

```
b xyz   # IP ← xyz;

bx 1332 (ip)   # IP ← IP + 1332;
               # this example uses ip-relative
               # addressing.
```

Opcode:

b	08	CTRL
bx	84	MEM

See Also: **bal**, **balx**, BRANCH IF, COMPARE INTEGER AND BRANCH, COMPARE ORDINAL AND BRANCH

bbc, bbs

Mnemonic: **bbc** Check Bit and Branch If Clear
bbs Check Bit and Branch If Set

Format: **bb*** *bitpos,* *src,* *targ*
reg/lit reg

Description: Checks the bit in *src* (designated by *bitpos*) and sets the condition code in the arithmetic controls according to the value found. The processor then performs a conditional branch based on the value of the condition code.

For the **bbc** instruction, if the selected bit in **src** is clear, the processor sets the condition code to 010_2 and branches to the instruction specified with the *targ* operand; otherwise, it sets the condition code to 000_2 and goes to the next instruction.

For the **bbs** instruction, if the selected bit is set, the processor sets the condition code to 010_2 and branches to *targ*; otherwise, it sets the condition code to 000_2 and goes to the next instruction.

When using the Intel 80960KB Assembler, the *targ* operand can be either a label or an absolute address that is no farther than -2^{12} to $(2^{12} - 4)$ from the current IP.

Note

At the machine level, the **bbc** and **bbs** instructions use the COBR instruction format. With this format, the target instruction for the branch is specified by means of a word-displacement (represented by *displacement* in the following action statement), which can range from -2^{10} to $(2^{10} - 1)$. To determine the IP of the target instruction, the processor converts this *displacement* value to a byte displacement (i.e., multiplies the value by 4). It then adds the resulting byte displacement to the IP of the next instruction.

To allow labels or absolute addresses to be used in the assembly-language versions of the **bbc** and **bbs** instructions, the Intel 80960KB Assembler performs the following calculation to convert the *targ* value in an assembly-language instruction to the *displacement* value required by the machine instruction format:

$$displacement = (targ/4) - (IP + 4)$$

For further information about the COBR instruction format, refer to Appendix B.

bbc, bbs

Action:

bbc:

if (*src* **and** 2^(*bitpos* **mod** 32)) = 0
  then AC.cc ← 2#010#;
    IP ← IP + 4 + (*displacement* * 4);
    # resume execution at the new IP
  else AC.cc ← 2#000#;
    IP ← IP + 4; # resume execution at the next IP
end if;

bbs:

if (*src* **and** 2^(*bitpos* **mod** 32)) = 1
  then AC.cc ← 2#010#;
    IP ← IP + 4 + (*displacement* * 4);
    # resume execution at the new IP
  else AC.cc ← 2#000#;
    IP ← IP + 4; # resume execution at the next IP
end if;

Faults: STANDARD

Example:

```
# assume bit 10 of r6 is clear
bbc 10, r6, xyz  # bit 10 of r6 is checked
                 # and found clear;
                 # AC.cc ← 2#010#
                 # IP ← xyz;
```

Opcode:

bbc	30	COBR
bbs	37	COBR

See Also: **chkbit**

BRANCH IF

Mnemonics:

be	Branch If Equal
bne	Branch If Not Equal
bl	Branch If Less
ble	Branch If Less Or Equal
bg	Branch If Greater
bge	Branch If Greater Or Equal
bo	Branch If Ordered
bno	Branch If Unordered

Format: **b*** *targ*
disp

Description: Branches to a new instruction according to the state of the condition code in the arithmetic controls.

For all branch-if instructions except the **bno** instruction, the processor branches to the instruction specified with the *targ* operand, if the logical AND of the condition code and the mask-part of the opcode is not zero. Otherwise, it goes to the next instruction.

For the **bno** instruction, the processor branches to the instruction specified with *targ*, if the logical AND of the condition code and the mask-part of the opcode is zero. Otherwise, it goes to the next instruction.

When using the Intel 80960KB Assembler, the *targ* operand can be either a label or an absolute address that specifies the IP of the target instruction. This value can be no farther than -2^{23} to $(2^{23} - 4)$ from the current IP.

Note

At the machine level, the branch-if instructions use the CTRL instruction format. With this format, the target instruction for the branch is specified by means of a word-displacement (represented by *displacement* in the following action statements), which can range from -2^{21} to $(2^{21} - 1)$. To determine the IP of the target instruction, the processor converts this *displacement* value to a byte displacement (i.e., multiplies the value by 4). It then adds the resulting byte displacement to the current IP.

BRANCH IF

To allow labels or absolute addresses to be used in the assembly-language version of the branch-if instructions, the Intel 80960KB Assembler performs the following calculation to convert the *targ* value in an assembly-language instruction to the *displacement* value required by the machine instruction format:

displacement = (*targ*/4) - IP

For further information about the CTRL instruction format, refer to Appendix B.

The following table shows the condition-code mask for each instruction:

Instruction	Mask	Condition
bno	000	Unordered
bg	001	Greater
be	010	Equal
bge	011	Greater or equal
bl	100	Less
bne	101	Not equal
ble	110	Less or equal
bo	111	Ordered

For the **bno** instruction (unordered), the branch is taken if the condition code is equal to 000_2.

The mask is in bits 0-2 of the opcode.

Action: For All Instructions Except **bno**:

if (mask **and** AC.cc) ≠ 2#000#
  then IP ← IP + *displacement*;   # resume execution at new IP
end if;

bno:

if AC.cc = 2#000#
  then IP ← IP + *displacement*;   # resume execution at new IP
end if;

BRANCH IF

Faults: STANDARD

Example:

```
# assume AC.cc AND 2#100# are ≠ 0
bl xyz  # IP ← xyz;
```

Opcode:

be	12	CTRL
bne	15	CTRL
bl	14	CTRL
ble	16	CTRL
bg	11	CTRL
bge	13	CTRL
bo	17	CTRL
bno	10	CTRL

See Also: **b**, **bx**

call

Mnemonic: **call** Call

Format: **call** *targ*

Description: Calls a new procedure. The processor performs a local call operation as described in Chapter 4 in the section titled "Local Calls." As part of this operation, the processor allocates a new set of local registers and a new stack frame for the called procedure. The processor then goes to the instruction specified with the *targ* argument and begins execution of the new procedure.

When using the Intel 80960KB Assembler, the *targ* operand can be either a label or an absolute address that specifies the IP of the first instruction in the called procedure. This value can be no farther than -2^{23} to $(2^{23} - 4)$ from the current IP.

Note

At the machine level, the **call** instruction uses the CTRL instruction format. With this format, the first instruction of the called procedure is specified by means of a word-displacement (represented by *displacement* in the following action statement), which can range from -2^{21} to $(2^{21} - 1)$. To determine the IP of the target instruction, the processor converts this *displacement* value to a byte displacement (i.e., multiplies the value by 4). It then adds the resulting byte displacement to the current IP.

To allow labels or absolute addresses to be used in the assembly-language version of the **call** instruction, the Intel 80960KB Assembler performs the following calculation to convert the *targ* value in an assembly-language instruction to the *displacement* value required by the machine instruction format:

displacement = (*targ*/4) - IP

For further information about the CTRL instruction format, refer to Appendix B.

call

Action:

wait for any uncompleted instructions to finish;
temp ← (SP + 63) **and not** (63); # round to next boundary
RIP ← IP;
if register_set_available
  then allocate as new frame;
  else save a register_set in memory at its FP;
    allocate as new frame;
local register references now refer to new frame
IP ← IP + *displacement*;
PFP ← FP;
FP ← temp;
SP ← temp + 64;

Faults: STANDARD

Example:

```
call xyz   # IP ← xyz
```

Opcode: **call** 09 CTRL

See Also: **bal, calls, callx**

calls

Mnemonic: **calls** Call System

Format: **calls** *targ*
reg/lit

Description: Calls a system procedure. The **targ** operand gives the number of the procedure being called.

For this instruction, the processor performs the system call operation described in Chapter 4 in the section titled "System Calls." The **targ** operand provides an index to an entry in the system procedure table. From this entry, the processor gets the IP of the called procedure.

The procedure called can be either a local procedure or a supervisor procedure, depending on the entry type in the procedure table. If it is a supervisor procedure, the processor also switches to supervisor mode (if it is not already in this mode).

As part of this operation, the processor allocates a new set of local registers and a new stack frame for the called procedure. If the processor switches to the supervisor mode, the new stack frame is created on the supervisor stack.

calls

Action:

if *targ* > 259 then raise Protection Length Fault;
wait for any uncompleted instructions to finish;
temp_p_e ← memory (SPT, 48 + (4 * *targ*));
SPT is pointer to system procedure table from IMI
RIP ← IP;
IP ← temp_p_e.address; **if** (temp_p_e.type = local) **or**
execution_mode = supervisor
  then temp ← (SP + 63) and not(63);
    tempRRR ← 2#000#;
  else temp ← memory (SPTSS, 12);   # supervisor call
    tempRRR ← 2#01T#;   # T is process_controls.T
    execution_mode ← supervisor;
    process_controls.T ← temp.T;
endif;
if frame_available
  then allocate as new frame;
  else save a frame in memory at its FP;
    allocate as new frame;
# local register references now refer to new frame
endif;
PFP ← FP;
L0.RRR ← tempRRR;
FP ← temp;
SP ← temp + 64;

Faults: STANDARD

Example:

```
calls r12  # IP ← value obtained from
           # procedure table for procedure
           # number given in r12
```

Opcode: **calls** 660 REG

See Also: **bal, call, callx**

callx

Mnemonic: **callx** Call Extended

Format: **callx** *targ*
mem

Description: Calls a new procedure. The processor performs a local call operation as described in Chapter 4 in the section titled "Local Calls." As part of this operation, the processor allocates a new set of local registers and a new stack frame for the called procedure. The processor then goes to the instruction specified with the *targ* argument and begins execution of the new procedure.

This instruction performs the same operation as the **call** instruction except that the target instruction can be farther than -2^{23} to $(2^{23} - 4)$ from the current IP.

The *targ* operand is a memory type, which allows the full range of addressing modes to be used to specify the IP of the target instruction. The "IP + displacement" addressing mode allows the instruction to be IP-relative. Indirect calls can be performed by placing the target address in a register and then using one of the register-indirect addressing modes.

Refer to Chapter 5 for a complete discussion of the addressing modes available with memory-type operands.

Action:

wait for any uncompleted instructions to finish;
temp ← (SP + 63) **and not** (63); # round to next boundary
RIP ← IP;
if register_set_available
  then allocate as new frame;
  else save a register_set in memory at its FP;
    allocate as new frame;
# local register references now refer to new frame
endif;
IP ← *targ*;
PFP ← FP;
FP ← temp;
SP ← temp + 64;

callx

Faults: STANDARD

Example:

```
callx (g5)   # IP ← (g5), where the address
             # in g5 is the address of the new
             # procedure
```

Opcode: **bal, callx** 86 MEM

See Also: **call, calls**

chkbit

Mnemonic: **chkbit** Check Bit

Format:

chkbit	*bitpos*,	*src*
	reg/lit	reg/lit

Description: Checks the bit in *src* designated by *bitpos* and sets the condition code according to the value found. If the bit is set, the condition code is set to 010_2; if the bit is clear, the condition code is set to 000_2.

Action:

if (*src* **and** 2^(*bitpos* **mod** 32)) = 0
  then AC.cc ← 2#000#;
  else AC.cc ← 2#010#;
end if;

Faults: STANDARD

Example:

```
chkbit 13, g8   # checks bit 13 in g8
```

Opcode: **chkbit** 5AE REG

See Also: **alterbit**, **clrbit**, **notbit**, **setbit**

classr, classrl

Mnemonic: **classr** Classify Real
classrl Classify Long Real

Format: **classr*** *src*
freg/flit

Description: Checks the classification of the real number in *src* and stores the class in arithmetic-status bits (3 through 6) of the arithmetic controls.

For the **classrl** instruction, if the *src* operand references a global or local register, this register is the first (lowest numbered) of two successive registers. Also, this register must be even numbered (e.g., g0, g2, g4).

The following table shows the setting of the arithmetic-status bits depending on the classification of the operand.

AStatus	Classification
s000	Zero
s001	Denormalized number
s010	Normal finite number
s011	Infinity
s100	Quiet NaN
s101	Signaling NaN
s110	Reserved operand

The "s" bit is set to the sign of the *src* operand.

Refer to Chapter 7 for a discussion of the different real number classifications.

classr, classrl

Action:

s ← sign_of(*src*)
if *src* = 0
    then arithmetic_status ← s000;
elseif *src* = denormalized
    then arithmetic_status ← s001;
elseif *src* = normal finite
    then arithmetic_status ← s010;
elseif *src* = ∞
    then arithmetic_status ← s011;
elseif *src* = QNaN
    then arithmetic_status ← s100;
elseif *src* = SNaN
    then arithmetic_status ← s101;
elseif *src* = reserved operand
    then arithmetic_status ← s110;
end if

Faults:

STANDARD — Refer to the discussion of faults at the beginning of this chapter.

None of the floating-point exceptions can be raised.

Example:

```
classrl g12   # classifies long real in g12,g13
```

Opcode:

classr	68F	REG
classrl	69F	REG

clrbit

Mnemonic: **clrbit** Clear Bit

Format: **clrbit** *bitpos*, reg/lit *src*, reg/lit *dst* reg

Description: Copies the *src* value to *dst* with one bit cleared. The *bitpos* operand specifies the bit to be cleared.

Action: *dst* ← *src* **and not**(2^(*bitpos* **mod** 32));

Faults: STANDARD

Example:

```
clrbit 23, g3, g6   # g6 ← g3 with bit 23
                    # cleared
```

Opcode: **clrbit** 58C REG

See Also: **alterbit, chkbit, notbit, setbit**

cmpi, cmpo

Mnemonics: **cmpi** Compare Integer
cmpo Compare Ordinal

Format: **cmp*** *src1*, *src2*
reg/lit reg/lit

Description: Compares the *src2* and *src1* values and sets the condition code according to the results of the comparison. The following table shows the setting of the condition code for the three possible results of the comparison.

Condition Code	Comparison
100	*src1* < *src2*
010	*src1* = *src2*
001	*src1* > *src2*

The **cmpi** instruction followed by one of the branch-if instructions is equivalent to one of the compare-integer-and-branch instructions. The latter method of comparing and branching produces more compact code; however, the former method can result in faster running code because it takes advantage of the processor's pipelined architecture. The same is true for the **comp** instruction and the compare-ordinal-and-branch instructions.

Action: **if** *src1* < *src2* **then** AC.cc ← 2#100#;
elseif *src1* = *src2* **then** AC.cc ← 2#010#;
else AC.cc ← 2#001#;
end if;

Faults: STANDARD

Example:

```
cmpo 0x10, r9    # compare values in r9 and 0x10
                 # and set condition code
```

Opcode: **cmpi** 5A1 REG
cmpo 5A0 REG

See Also: **cmpibe, cmpr, cmpdeci, cmpdeco**

cmpdeci, cmpdeco

Mnemonics: **cmpdeci** Compare and Decrement Integer
cmpdeco Compare and Decrement Ordinal

Format: **cmpdec*** *src1*, reg/lit *src2*, reg/lit *dst* reg

Description: Compares the *src2* and *src1* values and sets the condition code according to the results of the comparison. The *src2* operand is then decremented by one and the result is stored in *dst*.

The following table shows the setting of the condition code for the three possible results of the comparison.

Condition Code	Comparison
100	*src1* < *src2*
010	*src1* = *src2*
001	*src1* > *src2*

These instructions are intended for use in ending iterative loops. For the **cmpdeci** instruction, interger overflow is ignored to allow looping down through the minimum integer values.

Action:

if *src1* < *src2* **then** AC.cc ← 2#100#;
elseif *src1* = *src2* **then** AC.cc ← 2#010#;
elseif *src1* > *src2* **then** AC.cc ← 2#001#;
end if;
dst ← *src2* - 1; #overflow suppressed for **cmpdeci**
instruction

Faults: STANDARD

Example:

```
cmpdeci 12, g7, g1    # g7 and 12 are compared;
                      # g1 ← g7 - 1
```

Opcode:

cmpdeci	5A7	REG
cmpdeco	5A6	REG

See Also: **cmpinco**, **cmpo**

cmpinci, cmpinco

Mnemonics: **cmpinci** Compare and Increment Integer
cmpinco Compare and Increment Ordinal

Format: **cmpinc*** *src1*, reg/lit *src2*, reg/lit *dst* reg

Description: Compares the *src2* and *src1* values and sets the condition code according to the results of the comparison. The *src2* operand is then incremented by one and the result is stored in *dst*.

The following table shows the setting of the condition code for the three possible results of the comparison.

Condition Code	Comparison
100	*src1* < *src2*
010	*src1* = *src2*
001	*src1* > *src2*

These instructions are intended for use in ending iterative loops. For the **cmpinci** instruction, integer overflow is ignored to allow looping up through the maximum integer values.

Action:

if *src1* < *src2* **then** AC.cc ← 2#100#;
elseif *src1* = *src2* **then** AC.cc ← 2#010#;
elseif *src1* > *src2* **then** AC.cc ← 2#001#;
end if;
dst ← *src2* + 1; # overflow suppressed for **cmpinci**
instruction

Faults: STANDARD

Example:

```
cmpinco r8, g2, g9    # g2 and r8 are compared;
                      # g9 ← g2 + 1
```

Opcode:

cmpinci	5A5	REG
cmpinco	5A4	REG

See Also: **cmpdeco**, **cmpo**

cmpor, cmporl

Mnemonics: **cmpor** Compare Ordered Real
cmporl Compare Ordered Long Real

Format: **cmpor*** *src1*, *src2*
freg/flit freg/flit

Description: Compares the *src2* and *src1* values and sets the condition code according to the results of the comparison.

For the **cmporl** instruction, if the *src1* or *src2* operand references a global or local register, this register is the first (lowest numbered) of two successive registers. Also, this register must be even numbered (e.g., g0, g2, g4).

The following table shows the setting of the condition code for the four possible results of the comparison.

Condition Code	Comparison
100	*src1* < *src2*
010	*src1* = *src2*
001	*src1* > *src2*
000	if either *src1* or *src2* is a NaN

The algorithm for these instructions checks the classification of the operands. If either is in the NaN class, the condition code is set to 000_2 and a floating invalid-operation exception is raised. The **cmpor** and **cmporl** instructions operate the same as the **cmpr** and **cmprl** instructions, except that the latter instructions do not signal an exception if a NaN value is detected.

If a floating-reserved-encoding fault occurs, the condition code results are undefined.

Action:

if *src1* < *src2*
  then AC.cc ← 2#100#;
    elseif *src1* = *src2*
      then AC.cc ← 2#010#;
        elseif *src1* > *src2*
          then AC.cc ← 2#001#;
  else AC.cc ← 2#000#; # indicates one number is a NaN
  raise floating invalid operation fault
end if;

cmpor, cmporl

Faults:

STANDARD	Refer to the discussion of faults at the beginning of this chapter.
Floating Reserved Encoding	One or more operands is an unnormalized (including denormalized) value and the normalizing-mode bit in the arithmetic controls is set.

The following floating-point exception can be raised. Whether or not the exception results in a fault being raised depends on the state of its associated mask bit in the arithmetic controls.

Floating Invalid Operation	One or more operands are a NaN value.

Example:

```
cmporl g6, g12    # compare value in g12,g13
                  # with value in g6,g7
```

Opcode:

cmpor	684	REG
cmporl	694	REG

See Also: **cmpr, cmpi, BRANCH IF**

cmpr, cmprl

Mnemonics: **cmpr** Compare Real
cmprl Compare Long Real

Format: **cmpr*** *src1*, *src2*
freg/flit freg/flit

Description: Compares the *src2* and *src1* values and sets the condition code according to the results of the comparison. For the **cmprl** instruction, if the *src1* or *src2* operand references a global or local register, this register is the first (lowest numbered) of two successive registers.

The following table shows the setting of the condition code for the four possible results of the comparison.

Condition Code	Comparison
100	*src1* < *src2*
010	*src1* = *src2*
001	*src1* > *src2*
000	if either *src1* or *src2* is a NaN

The algorithm for these instructions checks the classification of the operands. If either is in the NaN class, the condition code is set to 000_2, but no fault is raised. The **cmpr** and **cmprl** instructions operate the same as the **cmpor** and **cmporl** instructions, except that the latter instructions raise an invalid-operand exception if a NaN value is detected.

If a floating-reserved-encoding fault occurs, the condition code results are undefined.

Action:

if *src1* < *src2*
  then AC.cc ← 2#100#;
    elseif *src1* = *src2*
      then AC.cc ← 2#010#;
        elseif *src1* > *src2*
          then AC.cc ← 2#001#;
  else AC.cc ← 2#000#; # indicates one number is a NaN
end if;

cmpr, cmprl

Faults:

STANDARD	Refer to the discussion of faults at the beginning of this chapter.
Floating Reserved Encoding	One or more operands is an unnormalized (including denormalized) value and the normalizing-mode bit in the arithmetic controls is set.

The following floating-point exception can be raised. Whether or not the exception results in a fault being raised depends on the state of its associated mask bit in the arithmetic controls.

Floating Invalid Operation	One or more operands are an SNaN value.

Example:

```
cmprl g2, g6  # compare values in g6,g7
              # and g2,g3
```

Opcode:

cmpr	685	REG
cmprl	695	REG

See Also: **cmpor, cmpi, BRANCH IF**

COMPARE AND BRANCH

Mnemonics:

cmpibe	Compare Integer And Branch If Equal
cmpibne	Compare Integer And Branch If Not Equal
cmpibl	Compare Integer And Branch If Less
cmpible	Compare Integer And Branch If Less Or Equal
cmpibg	Compare Integer And Branch If Greater
cmpibge	Compare Integer And Branch If Greater Or Equal
cmpibo	Compare Integer And Branch If Ordered
cmpibno	Compare Integer And Branch If Unordered
cmpobe	Compare Ordinal And Branch If Equal
cmpobne	Compare Ordinal And Branch If Not Equal
cmpobl	Compare Ordinal And Branch If Less
cmpoble	Compare Ordinal And Branch If Less Or Equal
cmpobg	Compare Ordinal And Branch If Greater
cmpobge	Compare Ordinal And Branch If Greater Or Equal

Format:

cmpib*	*src1*,	*src2*,	*targ*
	reg/lit	reg	
cmpob*	*src1*,	*src2*,	*targ*
	reg/lit	reg	disp

Description: Compares the *src2* and *src1* values and sets the condition code according to the results of the comparison. If the logical AND of the condition code and the mask-part of the opcode is not zero, the processor branches to the instruction specified with the *targ* operand; otherwise, the processor goes to the next instruction.

When using the Intel 80960KB Assembler, the *targ* operand can be either a label or an absolute address that is no farther than -2^{12} to $(2^{12} - 4)$ from the current IP.

Note

At the machine level, the compare-and-branch instructions use the COBR instruction format. With this format, the target instruction for the branch is specified by means of a word-displacement (represented by *displacement* in the following action statement), which can range from -2^{10} to $(2^{10} - 1)$. To determine the IP of the target instruction, the processor converts this *displacement* value to a byte displacement (i.e., multiplies the value by 4). It then adds the resulting byte displacement to the IP of the next instruction.

COMPARE AND BRANCH

To allow labels or absolute addresses to be used in the assembly-language versions of these instructions, the Intel 80960KB Assembler performs the following calculation to convert the *targ* value in an assembly-language instruction to the *displacement* value required by the machine instruction format:

displacement = (*targ*/4) - (IP + 4)

For further information about the COBR instruction format, refer to Appendix B.

The following table shows the condition-code mask for each instruction:

Instruction	Mask	Branch Condition
cmpibno	000	No Condition
cmpibg	001	*src1* > *src2*
cmpibe	010	*src1* = *src2*
cmpibge	011	*src1* ≥ *src2*
cmpibl	100	*src1* < *src2*
cmpibne	101	*src1* ≠ *src2*
cmpible	110	*src1* ≤ *src2*
cmpibo	111	Any Condition
cmpobg	001	*src1* > *src2*
cmpobe	010	*src1* = *src2*
cmpobge	011	*src1* ≥ *src2*
cmpobl	100	*src1* < *src2*
cmpobne	101	*src1* ≠ *src2*
cmpoble	110	*src1* ≤ *src2*

The **cmpibo** instruction always branches; the **cmpibno** instruction never branches.

The functions that these instructions perform can be duplicated with a **cmpi** instruction followed by a branch-if instruction, as described in the description of the **cmpi** instruction in this chapter.

COMPARE AND BRANCH

Action:

if *src1* < *src2* **then** AC.cc ← 2#100#;
elseif *src1* = *src2* **then** AC.cc ← 2#010#;
else AC.cc ← 2#001#;
end if;
if mask **and** AC.cc ≠ 2#000#
  then IP ← IP + 4 + (*displacement* * 4);
  # resume execution at the new IP
  else IP ← IP + 4;
# resume execution at the next IP
end if;

Faults: STANDARD

Example:

```
# assume g3 < g9
cmpibl g3, g9, xyz   # g9 is compared with g3;
                     # IP ← xyz.

# assume r7 ≥ 19
cmpobge r7, 19, xyz   # 19 is compared with r7
                      # IP ← xyz.
```

Opcode:

cmpibe	3A	COBR
cmpibne	3D	COBR
cmpibl	3C	COBR
cmpible	3E	COBR
cmpibg	39	COBR
cmpibge	3B	COBR
cmpibo	3F	COBR
cmpibno	38	COBR
cmpobe	32	COBR
cmpobne	35	COBR
cmpobl	34	COBR
cmpoble	36	COBR
cmpobg	31	COBR
cmpobge	33	COBR

See Also: **BRANCH IF**, cmpi

concmpi, concmpo

Mnemonics: **concmpi** Conditional Compare Integer
concmpo Conditional Compare Ordinal

Format: **concmp*** *src1*, *src2*
reg/lit reg/lit

Description: Compares the *src2* and *src1* values if bit 2 of the condition code is not set. If the comparison is performed, the condition code is set according to the results of the comparison.

These instructions are provided to facilitate bounds checking by means of two-sided range comparisons (e.g., is A between B and C?). They are generally used after a compare instruction to test whether a value is inclusively between two other values.

The example below illustrates this application by testing whether the value in g3 is between the values in g5 and g6, where g5 is assumed to be less than g6. First a comparison (**cmpo**) of g3 and g6 is performed. If g3 is less than or equal to g6 (i.e., condition code is either 010_2 or 001), a conditional comparison (**concmpo**) of g3 and g5 is then performed. If g3 is greater than or equal to g5 (indicating that g3 is within the bounds of g5 and g6), the condition code is set to 010_2; otherwise, it is set to 001_2.

Action:

if (AC.cc **and** 2#100#) = 0 **then**
  if *src1* ≤ *src2*
    then AC.cc ← 2#010;
    else AC.cc ← 2#001;
  endif;
endif;

Faults: STANDARD

Example:

```
cmpo g6, g3      # compares g6 and g3 and sets
                 # condition code
concmpo g5, g3   # if condition code is not
                 # 2#1xx#, g5 is compared
                 # with g3
```

Opcode:

concmpi	5A3	REG
concmpo	5A2	REG

See Also: **cmpo**, **cmpi**

cosr, cosrl

Mnemonics: **cosr** Cosine Real
cosrl Cosine Long Real

Format: **cosr*** *src*, *dst*
freg/flit freg

Description: Calculates the cosine of the value in *src* and stores the result in *dst*. The *src* value is an angle given in radians. The resulting *dst* value is in the range -1 to +1, inclusive.

For the **cosrl** instruction, if the *src* or *dst* operand references a global or local register, this register is the first (lowest numbered) of two successive registers. Also, this register must be even numbered (e.g., g0, g2, g4).

The following table shows the results obtained when taking the cosine of various classes of numbers with neither overflow nor underflow.

Src	Dst
-∞	*
-F	-1 to +1
-0	+1
+0	+1
+F	-1 to +1
+∞	*
NaN	NaN

Notes:
F Means finite-real number
***** Indicates floating invalid-operation exception

In the trigonometric instructions, the 80960KB uses a value for π with a 66-bit mantissa which is 2 bits more than are available in the extended-real format. The section in Chapter 12 titled "Pi" gives this π value, along with some suggestions for representing this value in a program.

Action: *dst* ← **cosine** (*src*);

cosr, cosrl

Faults:

STANDARD	Refer to the discussion of faults at the beginning of this chapter.
Floating Reserved Encoding	One or more operands is an unnormalized (including denormalized) value and the normalizing-mode bit in the arithmetic controls is set.

The following floating-point exceptions can be raised. Whether or not an exception results in a fault being raised depends on the state of its associated mask bit in the arithmetic controls.

Floating Invalid Operation	The *src* operand is ∞.
	One or more operands are an SNaN value.
Floating Inexact	Result cannot be represented exactly in destination format.

Example:

```
cosrl r8, g2    # cosine of value in r8,r9 is
                # stored in g2,g3
```

Opcode:

cosr	68D	REG
cosrl	69D	REG

See Also: **sinr**, **sinrl**, **tanr**, **tanrl**

cpyrsre, cpysre

Mnemonics: **cpysre** Copy Sign Real Extended
cpyrsre Copy Reversed Sign Real Extended

Format:

cpy*	*src1*,	*src2*,	*dst*
	freg/flit	freg/flit	freg

Description: Copies the absolute value of *src1* into *dst*. For the **cpysre** instruction, the sign of *src2* is copied to *dst*; for the **cpyrsre** instruction, the opposite of the sign of *src2* is copied to *dst*.

If the *src1*, *src2*, or *dst* operand references a global or local register, this register is the first (lowest numbered) of three successive registers. Also, the number of this register must be a multiple of four (e.g., g0, g4, g8).

These instructions only operate on values in the extended-real format. The same operations can be performed on real- and long-real values using the **setbit** and **clearbit** instructions, or a combination of the **chkbit** and **alterbit** instructions.

Action:

cpysre **if** *src2* is positive
  then *dst* ← abs (*src1*)
  else *dst* ← -abs (*src1*)

cpyrsre **if** *src2* is negative
  then *dst* ← abs (*src1*)
  else *dst* ← -abs (*src1*)

Faults:

STANDARD	Refer to the discussion of faults at the beginning of this chapter.
Floating Reserved Encoding	One or more operands is a denormalized value and the normalizing-mode bit in the arithmetic controls is set.

Example:

```
cpysre fp0, fp1, fp2
# absolute value from fp0 is copied to
# fp2; sign from fp1 is copied to fp2
```

Opcode:

cpysre	6E2	REG
cpyrsre	6E3	REG

cvtilr, cvtir

Mnemonics: **cvtilr** Convert Long Integer to Real
cvtir Convert Integer to Real

Format: **cvti*** *src*, *dst*
reg/lit freg

Description: Converts the integer in *src* to a real and stores the result in *dst*. For the **cvtilr** instruction, the *src* operand references the first (lowest numbered) of two successive registers. Also, this register must be even numbered (e.g., g0, g2, g4).

Converting an integer to long real format requires two instructions. First, the integer is converted to extended real format by using the **cvtir** or **cvtilr** instruction with a floating-point register as a destination. Then the **movrl** instruction is used to move the value from the floating-point register to two global or local registers, causing an explicit conversion to long real format. (Note that this conversion is always exact.) The example section below illustrates this conversion.

Action: *dst* ← **real** (*src*);

Faults: STANDARD — Refer to the discussion of faults at the beginning of this chapter.

The following floating-point exception can be raised. Whether or not the exception results in a fault being raised depends on the state of its associated mask bit in the arithmetic controls.

Floating Inexact — Can only be signaled when converting an integer to real (32-bit) format

Example:

```
# Conversion of an integer to a long real value
cvtir g6, fp3
movrl fp3, g8  # result stored in g8,g9
```

Opcode:

cvtir	674	REG
cvtilr	675	REG

See Also: **cvtri**, **movr**

cvtri, cvtril, cvtzri, cvtzril

Mnemonics:

cvtri	Convert Real To Integer
cvtril	Convert Real To Integer Long
cvtzri	Convert Truncated Real To Integer
cvtzril	Convert Truncated Real To Long Integer

Format:

cvtri*	*src*,	*dst*
	freg/flit	reg

Description: Converts the real value in *src* to an integer and stores the result in *dst*.

For the **cvtril** and **cvtzril** instructions, the *dst* operand references the first (lowest numbered) of two successive registers. Also, this register must be even numbered (e.g., g0, g2, g4).

The nontruncated versions of these instructions round according to the current rounding mode in the Arithmetic Controls register. The truncated versions always round toward zero.

Converting a long real value to an integer requires two instructions. First, the long real value is converted to extended real format by using the **movrl** instruction with a floating-point register as a destination. (Note that this operation is always exact.) Then one of the convert real-to-integer instructions is used to move the value from the floating-point register to one or two global or local registers. The example section below illustrates this conversion.

If the magnitude of the result cannot be represented in the destination, an integer-overflow fault is raised, and the maximum positive or maximum negative value is stored in the destination (depending on whether the real value was positive or negative, respectively).

Action: *dst* ← **integer** (*src*1);
src1 is rounded to integer value

cvtri, cvtril, cvtzri, cvtzril

Faults: STANDARD — Refer to the discussion of faults at the beginning of this chapter.

The following exception can be raised. Whether or not the exception results in a fault being raised depends on the state of its associated mask bit in the arithmetic controls register.

Integer Overflow — Result is too large for destination format.

Example:

```
# Conversion of long real value to an integer
movrl g4, fp2      # long-real source is
                   # converted to extended-real
                   # format and moved to fp2

cvtril fp2, g12    # extended-real value is
                   # converted to long integer
```

Opcode:

cvtri	6C0	REG
cvtril	6C1	REG
cvtzri	6C2	REG
cvtzril	6C3	REG

See Also: **cvtir**, **movr**

daddc

Mnemonic: **daddc** Decimal Add With Carry

Format: **daddc** *src1*, *src2*, *dst*
reg reg reg

Description: Adds bits 0 through 3 of *src2* and *src1* and bit 1 of the condition code (used here as a carry bit). The result is stored in bits 0 through 3 of *dst*. If the addition results in a carry, bit 1 of the condition code is set. Bits 4 through 31 of *src* are copied to *dst* unchanged.

This instruction is intended to be used iteratively to add binary-coded-decimal (BCD) values in which the least-significant four bits of the operands represent the decimal numbers 0 to 9. The instruction asssumes that the least significant 4 bits of both operands are valid BCD numbers. If these bits are not valid BCD numbers, the resulting value in *dst* is unpredictable.

Action:

Let the value of the condition code be xCx.
dst ← *src2* + *src1* + C;
AC.cc ← 2#0C0#;
C is carry from addition of bits 0 through 4 of operands
Bits 4 - 31 of *dst* are same as bits 4 - 31 of *src2*

Faults: STANDARD

Example:

```
daddc g5, g9, g10  # g10 ← g9 + g5 + Carry Bit,
                   # where arithmetic is
                   # carried out only on bits 0
                   # through 3 of the operands
```

Opcode: **daddc** 642 REG

See Also: **dsubc, dmovt**

divi, divo

Mnemonic:	**divi**	Divide Integer
	divo	Divide Ordinal

Format: **div*** *src1*, reg/lit *src2*, reg/lit *dst* reg

Description: Divides the *src2* value by the *src1* value and stores the result in *dst*.

For the **divi** instruction, and integer-overflow fault can be signaled.

Action: *dst* ← *src2* / *src1*;

Faults:

STANDARD	Refer to discussion of faults at the beginning of this chapter.
Arithmetic Zero Divide	The *src1* operand is 0.

The following fault condition can be raised with the **divi** instruction. Whether or not a fault is raised depends on the state of its associated mask bit in the arithmetic-controls register.

Integer Overflow	Result is too large for destination format.

Example:

```
divo r3, r8, r13 # r13 ← r8/r3
```

Opcode:

divi	74B	REG
divo	70B	REG

See Also: **ediv, mulo**

divr, divrl

Mnemonic: **divr** Divide Real
divrl Divide Long Real

Format: **divr*** *src1*, freg/flit *src2*, freg/flit *dst* freg

Description: Divides the *src2* value by the *src1* value and stores the result in *dst*.

For the **divrl** instruction, if the *src1*, *src2*, or *dst* operand references a global or local register, this register is the first (lowest numbered) of two successive registers. Also, this register must be even numbered (e.g., g0, g2, g4).

The sign of the result is always the exclusive-OR of the source signs, even if one or more of the source values is 0, ∞, or a NaN.

The following table shows the results obtained when dividing various classes of numbers, assuming that neither overflow nor underflow occurs.

Src2 \ Src1	-∞	-F	-0	+0	+F	+∞	NaN
-∞	*	+∞	+∞	-∞	-∞	*	NaN
-F	+0	+F	**	**	-F	-0	NaN
-0	+0	+0	*	*	-0	-0	NaN
+0	-0	-0	*	*	+0	+0	NaN
+F	-0	-F	**	**	+F	+0	NaN
+∞	*	-∞	-∞	+∞	+∞	*	NaN
NaN	NaN	NaN	NaN	NaN	NaN	NaN	NaN

Notes:

F Means finite-real number.
* Indicates floating invalid-operation exception.
** Indicates floating zero-divide exception.

Action: *dst* ← *src2* / *src1*;

divr, divrl

Faults:

STANDARD	Refer to the discussion of faults at the beginning of this chapter.
Floating Reserved Encoding	One or more operands is an unnormalized (including denormalized) value and the normalizing-mode bit in the arithmetic controls is set.

The following floating-point exceptions can be raised. Whether or not an exception results in a fault being raised depends on the state of its associated mask bit in the arithmetic controls.

Floating Overflow	Result is too large for destination format.
Floating Underflow	Result is too small for destination format.
Floating Zero Divide	The *src1* operand is 0 and the *src2* operand is numeric and finite.
Floating Invalid Operation	Both source operands are 0 or both are ∞.
	One or more operands are an SNaN value.
Floating Inexact	Result cannot be represented exactly in destination format.

Example:

```
divrl g10, g0, fp1 # fp1 ← g0,g1 / g10,g11
```

Opcode:

divr	78B	REG
divrl	79B	REG

See Also: **ediv**, **mulr**, **mulrl**

dmovt

Mnemonic: **dmovt** Decimal Move And Test

Format: **dmovt** *src*, *dst*
reg reg

Description: Copies the *src* value into *dst*. The least-significant eight bits of the *src* value are tested to determine whether or not they constitute a valid ASCII decimal (00110000_2 .. 00111001_2), and the condition code is set accordingly. If the value is a valid ASCII decimal, the condition code is set to 000_2; otherwise, it is set to 010_2.

This instruction is intended to be used iteratively to validate decimal strings.

Action:

dst ← *src*;
if *src* = 2#0011000# .. 2#00111001#
  then AC.cc ← 2#000#;
  else AC.cc ← 2#010#;
end if;

Faults: STANDARD

Example:

```
dmovt g1, g6 # g6 ← g1;
             # g1 tested for decimal value
```

Opcode: **dmovt** 644 REG

See Also: **daddc**, **dsubc**

dsubc

Mnemonic: **dsubc** Decimal Subtract With Carry

Format: **dsubc** *src1*, *src2*, *dst*
reg reg reg

Description: Subtracts bits 0 through 3 of *src2* and *src1* and bit 1 of the condition code (used here as a carry bit). The result is stored in bits 0 through 3 of *dst*. If the subtraction results in a carry, bit 1 of the condition code is set. Bits 4 through 31 of *src* are copied to *dst* unchanged.

This instruction is intended to be used iteratively to subtract binary-coded-decimal (BCD) values in which the least-significant four bits of the operands represent the decimal numbers 0 to 9. The instruction asssumes that the least significant 4 bits of both operands are valid BCD numbers. If these bits are not valid BCD numbers, the resulting value in *dst* is unpredictable.

Action:

Let the value of the condition code be xCx.
dst ← *src2* - *src1* - 1 + C;
AC.cc ← 2#0C0#;
C is carry from subtraction of bits 0 through 4 of operands
Bits 4 - 31 of *dst* are same as bits 4 - 31 of *src2*

Faults: STANDARD

Example:

```
dsubc r1, r2, r12 # r12 ← r2 - r1 -1 + Carry
                  # Bit, where arithmetic is
                  # carried out only on bits 0
                  # through 3 of the operands
```

Opcode: **dsubc** 643 REG

See Also: **daddc**, **dmovt**

ediv

Mnemonic: **ediv** Extended Divide

Format:

ediv	*src1*,	*src2*,	*dst*
	reg/lit	reg/lit	reg

Description: Divides *src2* by *src1* and stores the result in *dst*. The *src2* value is a long ordinal (i.e., 64 bits), which is contained in two adjacent registers. The *src2* operand specifies the lower numbered register, which contains the least significant bits of the operand. The *src2* operand must be an even numbered register (i.e., r0, r2, r4, ... or g0, g2, ...). The *src1* value is a normal ordinal (i.e., 32 bits).

The remainder is stored in the register designated by *dst* and the quotient is stored in the next highest numbered register. The *dst* operand must be an even numbered register (i.e., r0, r2, r4, ... or g0, g2, ...).

This instruction performs ordinal arithmetic.

If this operation overflows (i.e., the quotient or remainder do not fit in 32-bits), no fault is raised and the result is undefined.

Action:

dst ← (*src2* - (*src2* / *src1*) ∗ *src1*); # remainder
dst + 1 ← (*src2* / *src1*); # quotient

Faults: STANDARD, Arithmetic Integer Divide

Example:

```
ediv g3, g4, g10 # g10 ← remainder of g4,g5/g3
                 # g11 ← quotient of g4,g5/g3
```

Opcode: **ediv** 671 REG

See Also: **emul**

emul

Mnemonic: **emul** Extended Multiply

Format: **emul** *src1*, *src2*, *dst*
reg/lit reg/lit reg

Description: Multiplies *src2* by *src1* and stores the result in *dst*. The result is a long ordinal (i.e., 64 bits), which is stored in two adjacent registers. The *dst* operand specifies the lower numbered register, which receives the least significant bits of the result. The *dst* operand must be an even numbered register (i.e., r0, r2, r4, ... or g0, g2, ...).

This instruction performs ordinal arithmetic.

Action: *dst* ← (*src1* * *src2*) mod 2^32;
dst + 1 ← (*src* * *src2*)/mod 2^32;

Faults: STANDARD

Example:

```
emul r4, r5, g2  # g2,g3 ← r4 * r5
```

Opcode: **emul** 670 REG

See Also: **ediv**

expr, exprl

Mnemonic: **expr** Exponent Real
exprl Exponent Long Real

Format: **exp*** *src*, *dst*
freg/flit freg

Description: Calculates an approximation of the exponential value of 2 to the *src* power, minus 1, and stores the result in *dst*. The *src* value must be within the range of -0.5 to +0.5, inclusive. If the *src* value is outside this range, the result is undefined.

For the **exprl** instruction, if the *src* or *dst* operand references a global or local register, this register is the first (lowest numbered) of two successive registers. Also, this register must be even numbered (e.g., g0, g2, g4).

The following table shows the results obtained when computing the exponent of various classes of numbers.

Src	Dst
-0.5 to -0	$-(1/\sqrt{2})-1$ to -0
-0	-0
+0	+0
+0 to +0.5	+0 to $\sqrt{2}-1$

Notes:
*** Results are unpredictable

Action: $dst \leftarrow (2\hat{}src) - 1;$

expr, exprl

Faults:

STANDARD	Refer to the discussion of faults at the beginning of this chapter.
Floating Reserved Encoding	One or more operands is an unnormalized (including denormalized) value and the normalizing-mode bit in the arithmetic controls is set.

The following floating-point exceptions can be raised. Whether or not an exception results in a fault being raised depends on the state of its associated mask bit in the arithmetic controls.

Floating Underflow	Result is too small for destination format.
Floating Invalid Operation	One or more operands are an SNaN value.
Floating Inexact	Result cannot be represented exactly in destination format.

Example:

```
# y = 2^x    (y and x in g0)
# uses identity
#     2^x = 2^(I+f)
#         = 2^I * ((2^f - 1)+1)
# where:  I integer, -0.5 <= f <= +0.5
# assumes round-to-nearest
# does not handle infinities or NaNs
_pow2x:
        roundr  g0,fp0          # I in fp0
        subr    fp0,g0,g0       # f in g0
        expr    g0,g0
        addr    0f1.0,g0,g0
        cvtri   fp0,g1
        scaler  g1,fp0,g0
```

Opcode:

expr	689	REG
exprl	699	REG

See Also: **scaler**, **logr**

extract

Mnemonic: **extract** Extract

Format:

extract	*bitpos*,	*len*,	*src/dst*
	reg/lit	reg/lit	reg

Description: Shifts a specified bit field in *src/dst* right and fills the bits to the left of the shifted bit field with zeros. The *bitpos* value specifies the least significant bit of the bit field to be shifted, and the *len* value specifies the length of the bit field.

Action: *src/dst* ← (*src/dst* / 2^(*bitpos* **mod** 32))
and (2^*len* - 1);

Faults: STANDARD

Example:

```
extract 5, 12, g4 # g4 ← g4 with bits 5
                  # through 16 shifted right
```

Opcode: **extract** 651 REG

See Also: **modify**

FAULT IF

Mnemonic:

faulte	Fault If Equal
faultne	Fault If Not Equal
faultl	Fault If Less
faultle	Fault If Less Or Equal
faultg	Fault If Greater
faultge	Fault If Greater Or Equal
faulto	Fault If Ordered
faultno	Fault If Unordered

Format: **fault***

Description: Raises a constraint-range fault if the logical AND of the condition code and the mask-part of the opcode is not zero.

The following table shows the condition-code mask for each instruction:

Instruction	Mask	Condition
faultno	000	Unordered
faultg	001	Greater
faulte	010	Equal
faultge	011	Greater or equal
faultl	100	Less
faultne	101	Not equal
faultle	110	Less or equal
faulto	111	Ordered

For the **faultno** instruction (unordered), the fault is raised if the condition code is equal to 2#000#.

Action: For all instructions except **faultno**:

if (mask **and** AC.cc) ≠ 2#000#
    then raise constraint-range fault;
end if;

faultno:

if AC.cc = 2#000#
    then raise constraint-range fault;
end if;

FAULT IF

Faults: STANDARD, Constraint Range

Example:

```
# assume 2#110# AND AC.cc ≠ 2#000#
faultle # raises Constraint Range Fault
```

Opcode:

faulte	1A	CTRL
faultne	1D	CTRL
faultl	1C	CTRL
faultle	1E	CTRL
faultg	19	CTRL
faultge	1B	CTRL
faulto	1F	CTRL
faultno	18	CTRL

See Also: **be, teste**

flushreg

Mnemonic: **flushreg** Flush Local Registers

Format: **flushreg**

Description: Copies the contents of all the cached local-register sets into their associated register-save areas in the procedure stack. The contents of all the local-register sets except for the current set are then marked as invalid. On a return, the local registers for the frame being returned to are then loaded from the stack.

The **flushreg** instruction is provided to allow a compiler or applications program to circumvent the normal call/return mechanism of the processor. For example, a compiler may need to back up several frames in the stack on the next return, rather than using the normal return mechansim that returns one frame at a time. Here, the compiler uses the **flushreg** instruction to update the stack with the current states of the saved register sets. The compiler can then return to any frame in the stack without losing the contents of the saved local-register sets. To return to a frame other than the frame directly below the current frame, the complier merely modifies the PFP in register r0 of the current frame to point to the frame that it wishes to return to.

Action: Each register set except the current set is flushed to its associated stack frame in memory and marked as purged, meaning that they will be reloaded from memory if and when they become the current local register set.

Faults: STANDARD

Example: `flushreg`

Opcode: **flushreg** 66D REG

fmark

Mnemonic: **fmark** Force Mark

Format: **fmark**

Description: Generates a breakpoint trace-event, regardless of the setting of the breakpoint trace mode flag.

When a breakpoint trace event is detected, the trace-fault-pending flag (bit 10) of the process controls word and the breakpoint-trace-event flag (bit 23) of the trace controls are set. Before the next instruction is executed, a trace fault is generated.

For more information on trace-fault generation, refer to Chapter 12.

Action:

if process.trace_controls **and** breakpoint_trace_flag
  then
    raise trace breakpoint fault
endif

Faults: STANDARD, Breakpoint Trace

Example:

```
ld xyz, r4
addi r4, r5, r6
fmark
# Breakpoint trace event is generated at
# this point in the instruction stream.
```

Opcode: **fmark** 66C REG

See Also: **mark**

LOAD

Mnemonic:

ld	Load
ldob	Load Ordinal Byte
ldos	Load Ordinal Short
ldib	Load Integer Byte
ldis	Load Integer Short
ldl	Load Long
ldt	Load Triple
ldq	Load Quad

Format:

ld*	*src*,	*dst*
	mem	reg

Description: Copies a byte or string of bytes from memory into a register or group of successive registers. The *src* operand specifies the address of the first byte to be loaded. The full range of addressing modes may be used in specifying *src*. (Refer to Chapter 5 for a complete discussion of the addressing modes available with memory-type operands.)

The *dst* operand specifies a register or the first (lowest numbered) register of successive registers.

The **ldob** and **ldib**, and **ldos** and **ldis** instructions load a byte and half word, respectively, and convert it to a full 32-bit word. The **ld**, **ldl**, **ldt**, and **ldq** instructions copy 4, 8, 12, and 16 bytes, respectively, from memory into successive registers.

For the **ldl** instruction, **dst** must specify an even numbered register (e.g., g0, g2, ..., g12). For the **ldt** and **ldq** instructions, **dst** must specify a register number that is a multiple of four (e.g., g0, g4, g8). If the data extends beyond register g15 or r15 for the **ldl**, **ldt**, or **ldq** instruction, the results are unpredictable.

Action: *dst* ← memory (*src*);

Faults: STANDARD

Example:

```
ldl 2456 (r3), r10  # r10, r11 ← value of two
                    # words beginning at offset
                    # 2456 plus the address in
                    # r3 in memory
```

LOAD

Opcode:

ld	90	MEM
ldob	80	MEM
ldos	88	MEM
ldib	C0	MEM
ldis	C8	MEM
ldl	98	MEM
ldt	A0	MEM
ldq	B0	MEM

See Also: MOVE, STORE

lda

Mnemonic: **lda** Load Address

Format: **lda** *src* *dst*
mem reg
efa

Description: Computes the effective address specified with *src* and stores it in *dst*. The *src* address is not checked for validity.

An important application of this instruction is to load a constant longer than 5 bits into a register. (To load a register with a constant of 5 bits or less, the move instruction (**mov**) can be used with a literal as the *src* operand.)

Action: *dst* ← efa (*src*);

Faults: STANDARD

Example:

```
lda 58 (g9), g1   # Computes the effective
                  # address specified with
                  # 58 (g9) and stores it in g1

lda 0x749, r8     # loads the constant 16#749#
                  # in r8
```

Opcode: **lda** 8C MEM

logbnr, logbnrl

Mnemonic: **logbnr** Log Binary Real
logbnrl Log Binary Long Real

Format: **logbnr*** *src*, *dst*
freg/flit freg

Description: Calculates the $\log_2$ (*src*) and stores the integral part of this value (i.e., the part to the left of the binary point) as a real number in *dst*. The result of this operation is an unbiased exponent. When *src* is a denormalized number, *dst* is the unbiased exponent that *src* would have if the format had unlimited exponent range.

(The fractional part of $\log_2$ (*src*) is ignored. If the fractional part is needed, use the **logr** or **logrl** instruction.)

This instruction implements the IEEE recommended function *logb*. It is useful for calculating the order of magnitude of a number.

For the **logbnrl** instruction, if the *src2* or *dst* operand references a global or local register, this register is the first (lowest numbered) of two successive registers. Also, this register must be even numbered (e.g., g0, g2, g4).

The following table shows the results obtained when taking the log binary of various classes of numbers, assuming that neither overflow nor underflow occurs.

Src	**Dst**
-∞	+∞
-F	±F
-0	**
+0	**
+F	±F
+∞	+∞
NaN	NaN

Notes:
F Means finite-real number
** Indicates floating zero-divide exception

logbnr, logbnrl

Note that the significand of the *src* operand can be extracted by using the **scaler** or **scalerl** instruction.

Action:

dst ← ($\mathbf{log_2}$ (unbiased exponent (*src*)) - fraction);
\# the integral part of the unbiased exponent of *src*
\# is stored in *dst* as a biased real

Faults:

STANDARD	Refer to the discussion of faults at the beginning of this chapter.
Floating Reserved Encoding	One or more operands is an unnormalized (including denormalized) value and the normalizing-mode bit in the arithmetic controls is set.

The following floating-point exceptions can be raised. Whether or not an exception results in a fault being raised depends on the state of its associated mask bit in the arithmetic controls.

Floating Underflow	Result is too small for destination format.
Floating Invalid Operation	One or more operands are an SNaN value.
Floating Inexact	Result cannot be represented exactly in destination format.
Floating Zero Divide	The *src* operand is 0.

Example:

```
logbnrl g12, fp3     # fp3 ← integral part
                     # of log2 (g12,g13)
```

Opcode:

logbnr	68A	REG
logbnrl	69A	REG

See Also: **logr**, **scaler**

logepr, logeprl

Mnemonic: **logepr** Log Epsilon Real
logeprl Log Epsilon Long Real

Format: **logepr*** *src1*, *src2*, *dst*
freg/flit freg/flit freg

Description: Calculates (*src2* * $\log_2$ (*src1* + 1)), and stores the result in *dst*.

For the **logeprl** instruction, if the *src1*, *src2*, or *dst* operand references a global or local register, this register is the first (lowest numbered) of two successive registers. Also, this register must be even numbered (e.g., g0, g2, g4).

The following table shows the results obtained when taking the log epsilon of various classes of numbers, assuming that neither overflow nor underflow occurs.

		Src1					
		(1/√2) -1 to -0	-0	+0	+0 to √2 -1	NaN
	-∞	-∞	*	*	-∞	NaN
	-F	+F	+0	-0	-F	NaN
	-0	+0	+0	-0	-0	NaN
Src2	+0	-0	-0	+0	+0	NaN
	+F	-F	-0	+0	+F	NaN
	+∞	+∞	*	*	+∞	NaN
	NaN	NaN	NaN	NaN	NaN	NaN

Notes:

F Means finite-real number.

* Indicates floating invalid-operation exception.

This instruction offers optimal accuracy for values of *src1* + 1 close to 1 (i.e., for values of *src1* close to 0). This expression is commonly found in compound interest and annuity calculations. The result can be simply converted into a value in another logarithm base by including a scale factor in *src2*.

logepr, logeprl

The following equation is used to calculate the scale factor for a particular logarithm base, where n is the logarithm base desired for the result stored in *dst*:

$$\text{scale factor} = \log_n 2$$

The range of *src1* is restricted to the following:

$$1/\text{sqrt}(2) \le src1 + 1 \le \text{sqrt}(2)$$

When the *src1* operand is outside this range, the **logr** or **logrl** instruction can be used with very insignificant loss of accuracy by adding 1.0 to *src1*.

Action: $dst \leftarrow src2 * \mathbf{log_2}(src1 + 1);$

Faults:

STANDARD	Refer to the discussion of faults at the beginning of this chapter.
Floating Reserved Encoding	One or more operands is an unnormalized (including denormalized) value and the normalizing-mode bit in the arithmetic controls is set.

The following floating-point exceptions can be raised. Whether or not an exception results in a fault being raised depends on the state of its associated mask bit in the arithmetic controls.

Floating Overflow	Result is too large for destination format.
Floating Underflow	Result is too small for destination format.
Floating Invalid Operation	The *src1* operand is 0 and the *src2* operand is ∞.
	The *src1* operand does not fall within the range defined in the above description section.
	One or more operands are an SNaN value.
Floating Inexact	Result cannot be represented exactly in destination format.

logepr, logeprl

Example:

```
logepr g8, g4, fp2
# fp2 ← g4,g5 * log2 (g8,g9 + 1)
```

Opcode:

logepr	681	REG
logeprl	691	REG

See Also: **logr**

logr, logrl

Mnemonic: **logr** Log Real
logrl Log Long Real

Format: **logr*** *src1*, *src2*, *dst*
freg/flit freg/flit freg

Description: Calculates (*src2* * $\log_2$ (*src1*)), and stores the result in *dst*. (The **logbnr** and **logbnrl** instructions perform this function more efficiently, if only an estimate is needed.)

For the **logrl** instruction, if the *src1*, *src2*, or *dst* operand references a global or local register, this register is the first (lowest numbered) of two successive registers. Also, this register must be even numbered (e.g., g0, g2, g4).

The following table shows the results obtained when taking the log of various classes of numbers, assuming that neither overflow nor underflow occurs.

Src2 \ Src1	-∞	-F	-0	+0	+F	+∞	NaN
-∞	*	*	**	**	±∞	-∞	NaN
-F	*	*	**	**	±F	-∞	NaN
-0	*	*	*	*	±0	*	NaN
+0	*	*	*	*	±0	*	NaN
+F	*	*	**	**	±F	+∞	NaN
+∞	*	*	**	**	±∞	+∞	NaN
NaN	NaN	NaN	NaN	NaN	NaN	NaN	NaN

Notes:

F Means finite-real number.
* Indicates floating invalid-operation exception.
** Indicates floating zero-divide exception.

The **logr** instruction combined with the **expr** instruction forms the basis for the power function x^y.

logr, logrl

Adding 1.0 to a number to be used as the *src1* operand will cause information to be lost. To perform this function, use the **logepr** or **logeprl** instruction.

These instructions provide a simple method of converting the result of the $\log_2$ arithmetic into a value in another logarithm base by including a scale factor in *src2*. The following equation is used to calculate the scale factor for a particular logarithm base, where n is the logarithm base desired for the result stored in *dst*;

$$\text{scale factor} = \log_n 2$$

Action: $dst \leftarrow src2 * \mathbf{log_2}\,(src1);$

Faults:

STANDARD	Refer to the discussion of faults at the beginning of this chapter.
Floating Reserved Encoding	One or more operands is an unnormalized (including denormalized) value and the normalizing-mode bit in the arithmetic controls is set.

The following floating-point exceptions can be raised. Whether or not an exception results in a fault being raised depends on the state of its associated mask bit in the arithmetic controls.

Floating Overflow	Result is too large for destination format.
Floating Underflow	Result is too small for destination format.
Floating Zero Divide	The *src1* operand is 0 and *src2* is non-zero.
Floating Invalid Operation	The *src1* and *src2* operands are both 0.
	The *src1* operand is ∞ and the *src2* operand is 0.
	The *src1* operand is 1 and the *src2* operand is ∞.
	The *src1* operand is negative and non-zero.
	One or more operands are an SNaN value.
Floating Inexact	Result cannot be represented exactly in destination format.

logr, logrl

Example:

```
logrl r2, g8, g2  # g2,g3 ← g8,g9 * log2(r2,r3)
```

Opcode:

logr	682	REG
logrl	692	REG

See Also: **expr**, **logepr**

mark

Mnemonic: **mark** Mark

Format: **mark**

Description: Generates a breakpoint trace event if the breakpoint trace mode has been enabled. The breakpoint trace mode is enabled if the trace-enable bit (bit 0) of the process controls and the breakpoint-trace mode bit (bit 7) of the trace controls have been set. Both these words are located in the PCB.

When a breakpoint trace event is detected, the trace-fault-pending flag (bit 10) of the process controls and the breakpoint-trace-event flag (bit 23) of the trace controls are set. Before the next instruction is executed, a trace fault is generated.

If the breakpoint-trace mode has not been enabled, the **mark** instruction behaves like a no-op.

For more information on trace-fault generation, refer to Chapter 12.

Action: raise trace breakpoint fault

Faults: STANDARD, Breakpoint Trace

Example:

```
# Assume that the breakpoint trace mode is
# enabled.
ld xyz, r4
addi r4, r5, r6
mark
# Breakpoint trace event is generated at
# this point in the instruction stream.
```

Opcode: **mark** 66B REG

See Also: **fmark, modpc, modtc**

modac

Mnemonic: **modac** Modify AC

Format: **modac** *mask*, *src*, *dst*
reg/lit reg/lit reg

Description: Reads and modifies the arithmetic controls. The *src* operand contains the value to be placed in the arithmetic controls and the *mask* operand specifies the bits that may be changed. Only the bits set in *mask* are modified in the arithmetic controls. Once the arithmetic controls have been changed, their initial state is copied into *dst*.

Action:

temp ← AC
AC ← (*src* **and** *mask*) **or**
(AC **and not** (*mask*));
dst ← temp;

Faults: STANDARD

Example:

```
g1, g9, g12    # AC ← g9, masked by g1
               # g12 ← initial value of AC
```

Opcode: **modac** 645 REG

See Also: **modpc**, **modtc**

modi

Mnemonic: **modi** Modulo Integer

Format: **modi** *src1*, *src2*, *dst*
reg/lit reg/lit reg

Description: Divides *src2* by *src1*, where both are integers, and stores the modulo remainder of the result in *dst*. If the result is nonzero, *dst* is given the same sign as *src1*.

Action:

dst ← *src2* - ((*src2*/*src1*) * *src1*);
if *src2* * *src1* < 0
  then *dst* ← *dst* + *src1*;
end if;

Faults: STANDARD, Arithmetic Zero Divide

Example:

```
modi r9, r2, r5,    # r5 ← modulo (r2/r9)
```

Opcode: **modi** 749 REG

See Also: **div**, **remi**

modify

Mnemonic: **modify** Modify

Format: **modify** *mask*, *src*, *src/dst*
reg/lit reg/lit reg

Description: Modifies selected bits in *src/dst* with bits from *src*. The *mask* operand selects the bits to be modified: only the bits set in the mask are modified in *src/dst*.

Action: *src/dst* ← (*src* **and** *mask*) **or** (*src/dst* **and not** (*mask*));

Faults: STANDARD

Example:
```
modify g8, g10, r4    # r4 ← g10 masked by g8
```

Opcode: **modify** 650 REG

See Also: **alterbit**, **extract**

modpc

Mnemonic: **modpc** Modify Process Controls

Format: **modpc** *src*, *mask*, *src/dst*
reg/lit reg/lit reg

Description: Reads and modifies the processor's internally cached process controls as specified with *mask* and *src/dst*. The *src/dst* operand contains the value to be placed in the process controls and the *mask* operand specifies the bits that may be changed. Only the bits set in the mask are modified in the process controls. Once the process controls have been changed, their initial value is copied into *src/dst*. The *src* operand is a dummy operand that should be set equal to the *mask* operand.

The processor must be in the supervisor mode to modify the process controls using this instruction. If the *mask* operand is set to 0, this instruction can be used to read the process controls, without the processor being in the supervisor mode.

If the action of this instruction results in the priority of the processor being lowered, the interrupt table is checked for pending interrupts.

Changing the state, resume, internal state, and trace enable fields of the process controls can lead to unpredictable behavior, as described in Chapter 7 in the section titled "Changing the Process-Controls Word."

Action:

```
if mask ≠ 0
  then if process.process_controls.execution_mode ≠ supervisor
    then raise type-mismatch fault;
    end if;
    temp ← process.process_controls;
    process.process_controls ←
      (mask and src/dst) or
      (process.process_controls and not (mask));
    src/dst ← temp;
    if (temp.priority > process.process_controls.priority
      then check_pending_interrupts;
      # if continue here, no interrupt to do
    end if;
  else src/dst ← process.process_controls;
end if;
```

modpc

Faults: STANDARD, Type Mismatch

Example:

```
modpc g9, g9, g8    # process controls ← g8
                    # masked by g9
```

Opcode: **modpc** 655 REG

See Also: **modac**, **modtc**

modtc

Mnemonic: **modtc** Modify Trace Controls

Format: **modtc** *mask*, *src*, *dst*
reg/lit reg/lit reg

Description: Reads and modifies the trace controls for the current process. The processor changes its internally cached trace controls as specified with *mask* and *src*. The *src* operand contains the value to be placed in the trace controls and the *mask* operand specifies the bits that may be changed. Only the bits set in the mask are modified in the trace controls. Once the trace controls have been changed, their initial state is copied into *dst*.

This instruction only affects the trace controls cached in processor. The trace controls in the PCB for the current process are not affected.

Since bits 8 through 15 and 24 through 31 of the trace-controls word are reserved, the *mask* operand is ANDed with $00FF00FF_{16}$ to insure that these bits are not set in the mask.

The changed trace controls take effect on the first non-branching instruction fetched from memory. Since instructions are prefetched four at a time, the trace controls may not take effect for up to the next four instructions executed.

For more information on the trace controls, refer to Chapters 12 and 16.

Action:

temp ← process.trace_controls;
temp1 ← 16#00FF00FF# and *mask*;
process.trace_controls ←
(temp1 and *src*) **or**
(process.trace_controls **and** not(temp1));
dst ← temp;

Faults: STANDARD

Example:

```
modtc g12, g10, g2
# trace controls ← g10 masked by g12;
# previous trace controls stored in g2
```

Opcode: **modtc** 654 REG

See Also: **modac**, **modpc**

MOVE

Mnemonic:	**mov**	Move	
	movl	Move Long	
	movt	Move Triple	
	movq	Move Quad	
Format:	**mov***	*src*,	*dst*
		reg/lit	reg

Description: Copies the content of one or more source registers (specified with the *src* operand) to one or more destination registers (specified with the *dst* operand).

For the **movl**, **movt**, and **movq** instructions, the *src* and *dst* operands specify the first (lowest numbered) register of several successive registers. The *src* and *dst* registers must be even numbered (e.g., g0, g2) for the **movl** instruction and an integral multiple of four (e.g., g0, g4) for the **movt** and **movq** instructions.

When the *src* and *dst* operands overlap, the value moved is unpredictable.

Action: *dst* ← *src*;

Faults: STANDARD

Example:

```
movt g8, r4    # r4, r5, r6 ← g8, g9, g10
```

Opcode:		
mov	5CC	REG
movl	5DC	REG
movt	5EC	REG
movq	5FC	REG

See Also: **ld, movr, st**

movr, movre, movrl

Mnemonic:

movr	Move Real
movrl	Move Long Real
movre	Move Extended Real

Format:

movr*	*src,*	*dst*
	freg/flit	freg

Description: Copies a real value from one or more source registers (specified with the *src* operand) to one or more destination registers (specified with the *dst* operand).

For the **movrl** instruction, if the *src* or *dst* operand references a global or local register, this register is the first (lowest numbered) of two successive registers. For the **movre** instruction, if the *src* or *dst* operand references a global or local register, this register is the first (lowest numbered) of three successive registers.

When copying real numbers between global or local registers and floating-point registers, conversion between real or long-real format to extended-real format is performed implicitly. Conversion between real and long-real formats must be done through floating-point registers and requires two instructions, as illustrated in the example below.

When the **movre** instruction moves an operand from global or local registers to a floating-point register, it automatically truncates the most-significant 16 bits of the word in the third register (refer to Figure 12-5). Likewise, when this instruction is used to move an operand from a floating-point register to global or local registers, it adds 16 zeros to the third word. The **movre** instruction is not a numeric instruction; it merely manipulates bits.

The **movr** and **movrl** instructions can cause a floating-point exception to be raised, which might result in a fault being raised, as is explained in the section below on faults. The **movre** instruction can never raise an exception and thus never faults.

Action: *dst* ← *src*;

movr, movre, movrl

Faults:

STANDARD	Refer to the discussion of faults at the beginning of this chapter.
Floating Reserved Encoding	One or more operands is an unnormalized (including denormalized) value and the normalizing-mode bit in the arithmetic controls is set.

The following floating-point exceptions can be raised. Whether or not an exception results in a fault being raised depends on the state of its associated mask bit in the arithmetic controls.

Floating Overflow	Result is too large for destination format.
Floating Underflow	Result is too small for destination format.
Floating Invalid Operation	Source operand is an SNaN value.
Floating Inexact	Result cannot be represented exactly in destination format.

Example:

```
# Conversion of real value in g3 to a
# to a long real value, which is stored
# in g4,g5
movr g3, fp2
movrl fp2, g4
```

Opcode:

movr	6C9	REG
movrl	6D9	REG
movre	6E9	REG

See Also: **mov**

muli, mulo

Mnemonic:	**muli**	Multiply Integer
	mulo	Multiply Ordinal

Format:	**mul***	*src1*,	*src2*,	*dst*
		reg/lit	reg/lit	reg

Description: Multiplies the *src2* value by the *src1* value and stores the result in *dst*.

Action: *dst* ← *src2* * *src1*;

Faults: STANDARD, Integer Overflow

Example:

```
muli r3, r4, r9    # r9 ← r4 TIMES r3
```

Opcode:	**muli**	741	REG
	mulo	701	REG

See Also: **emul, mulr**

mulr, mulrl

Mnemonic: **mulr** Multiply Real
mulrl Multiply Long Real

Format: **mulr*** *src1*, *src2*, *dst*
freg/flit freg/flit freg

Description: Multiplies the *src2* value by the *src1* value and stores the result in *dst*.

For the **mulrl** instruction, if the *src1*, *src2*, or *dst* operand references a global or local register, this register is the first (lowest numbered) of two successive registers. Also, this register must be even numbered (e.g., g0, g2, g4).

The sign of the result is always the exclusive-OR of the source signs, even if one or more of the source values is 0, ∞, or a NaN.

The following table shows the results obtained when multiplying various classes of numbers together, assuming that neither overflow nor underflow occurs.

		Src1							
		-∞	**-F**	**-0**	**+0**	**+F**	**+∞**	**NaN**
	-∞	+∞	+∞	*	*	-∞	-∞	NaN
	-F	+∞	+F	+0	-0	-F	-∞	NaN
	-0	*	+0	+0	-0	-0	*	NaN
Src2	**+0**	*	-0	-0	+0	+0	*	NaN
	+F	-∞	-F	-0	+0	+F	+∞	NaN
	+∞	-∞	-∞	*	*	+∞	+∞	NaN
	NaN	NaN	NaN	NaN	NaN	NaN	NaN	NaN

Notes:

F Means finite-real number.

* Indicates floating invalid-operation exception.

When you need to multiply by the power of 2, the **scaler** and **scalerl** instructions can also be used.

Action: *dst* ← *src2* * *src1*;

mulr, mulrl

Faults:

STANDARD	Refer to the discussion of faults at the beginning of this chapter.
Floating Reserved Encoding	One or more operands is an unnormalized (including denormalized) value and the normalizing-mode bit in the arithmetic controls is set.

The following floating-point exceptions can be raised. Whether or not an exception results in a fault being raised depends on the state of its associated mask bit in the arithmetic controls.

Floating Overflow	Result is too large for destination format.
Floating Underflow	Result is too small for destination format.
Floating Invalid Operation	One source operand is 0 and the other is ∞.
	One or more operands are an SNaN value.
Floating Inexact	Result cannot be represented exactly in destination format.

Example:

```
mulrl g12, g4, fp2    # fp2 ← g4,g5 * g12,g13
```

Opcode:

mulr	78C	REG
mulrl	79C	REG

See Also: **emul, muli, scaler**

nand

Mnemonic: **nand** Nand

Format: **nand** *src1*, reg/lit *src2*, reg/lit *dst* reg

nand	*src1*,	*src2*,	*dst*
	reg/lit	reg/lit	reg

Description: Performs a bitwise NAND operation on the *src2* and *src1* values and stores the result in *dst*.

Action: *dst* ← (**not** (*src2*)) **or not** (*src1*);

Faults: STANDARD

Example:

```
nand g5, r3, r7    # r7 ← r3 NAND g5
```

Opcode: **nand** 58E REG

See Also: **and**, **andnot**, **nor**, **not**, **notand**, **notor**, **or**, **ornot**, **xnor**, **xor**

nor

Mnemonic:	**nor**	Nor		
Format:	**nor**	*src1*, reg/lit	*src2*, reg/lit	*dst* reg

Description: Performs a bitwise NOR operation on the *src2* and *src1* values and stores the result in *dst*.

Action: *dst* ← **not** (*src2*) **and not** (*src1*);

Faults: STANDARD

Example:

```
nor g8, 28, r5    # r5 ← 28 NOR g8
```

Opcode: **nor** 588 REG

See Also: **and, andnot, nand, not, notand, notor, or, ornot, xnor, xor**

not, notand

Mnemonic:

not	Not
notand	Not And

Format:

not	*src*,	*dst*	
	reg/lit	reg	
notand	*src1*,	*src2*,	*dst*
	reg/lit	reg/lit	reg

Description: Performs a bitwise NOT (**not** instruction) or NOT AND (**notand** instruction) operation on the *src2* and *src1* values and stores the result in *dst*.

Action:

not: *dst* ← **not** (*src1*);

notand: *dst* ← (**not** (*src2*)) **and** *src1*;

Faults: STANDARD

Example:

```
not g2, g4            # g4 ← NOT g2
notand r5, r6, r7     # r7 ← NOT r6 AND r5
```

Opcode:

not	58A	REG
notand	584	REG

See Also: **and**, **andnot**, **nand**, **nor**, **notor**, **or**, **ornot**, **xnor**, **xor**

notbit

Mnemonic: **notbit** Not Bit

Format:

notbit	*bitpos*,	*src*,	*dst*
	reg/lit	reg/lit	reg

Description: Copies the *src* value to *dst* with one bit toggled. The *bitpos* operand specifies the bit to be toggled.

Action: *dst* ← *src* **xor** 2^(*bitpos* **mod** 32);

Faults: STANDARD

Example:

```
notbit r3, r12, r7    # r7 ← r12 with the bit
                      # specified in r3 toggled
```

Opcode: **notbit** 580 REG

See Also: **alterbit, chkbit, clrbit, setbit**

notor

Mnemonic:	**notor**	Not Or		
Format:	**notor**	*src1*, reg/lit	*src2*, reg/lit	*dst* reg

Description: Performs a bitwise NOT OR operation on the *src2* and *src1* values and stores the result in *dst*.

Action: *dst* ← (**not** (*src2*)) **or** *src1*;

Faults: STANDARD

Example:

```
notor g12, g3, g6    # g6 ← NOT g3 OR g12
```

Opcode: **notor** 58D REG

See Also: **and, andnot, nand, nor, not, notand, or, ornot, xnor, xor**

or, ornot

Mnemonic: **or** Or
ornot Or Not

Format:

or	*src1*,	*src2*,	*dst*
	reg/lit	reg/lit	reg
ornot	*src1*,	*src2*,	*dst*
	reg/lit	reg/lit	reg

Description: Performs a bitwise OR (**or** instruction) or ORNOT (**ornot** instruction) operation on the *src2* and *src1* values and stores the result in *dst*.

Action:

or: *dst* ← *src2* **or** *src1*;

ornot: *dst* ← *src2* **or not** (*src1*);

Faults: STANDARD

Example:

```
or 14, g9, g3          # g3 ← g9 OR 14
ornot r3, r8, r11      # r11 ← r8 OR NOT r3
```

Opcode:

or	587	REG
ornot	58B	REG

See Also: **and**, **andnot**, **nand**, **nor**, **not**, **notand**, **notor**, **xnor**, **xor**

remi, remo

Mnemonic: **remi** Remainder Integer
remo Remainder Ordinal

Format: **rem*** *src1*, *src2*, *dst*
reg/lit reg/lit reg

Description: Divides *src2* by *src1* and stores the remainder in *dst*. The sign of the result (if nonzero) is the same as the sign of *src2*.

Action: *dst* ← *src2* - ((*src2* / *src1*) * *src1*);

Faults:

STANDARD	Refer to discussion of faults at the beginning of this chapter.
Integer Overflow	Result is too large for destination format. This fault is signaled only when executing the **remi** instruction and if both of the following conditions are met: (1) the integer-overflow mask in the arithmetic-controls registers is clear and (2) the source operands have like signs and the sign of the result operand is different than the signs of the source operands.

Example:

```
remo r4, r5, r6    # r6 ← r5 rem r4
```

Opcode:

remi	748	REG
remo	708	REG

See Also: **remr, modi**

remr, remrl

Mnemonic: **remr** Remainder Real
remrl Remainder Long Real

Format: **remr*** *src1*, *src2*, *dst*
freg/flit freg/flit freg

Description: Divides *src2* by *src1* and stores the remainder in *dst*. The sign of the result (if nonzero) is the same as the sign of *src2*.

For the **remrl** instruction, if the *src1*, *src2*, or *dst* operand references a global or local register, this register is the first (lowest numbered) of two successive registers. Also, this register must be even numbered (e.g., g0, g2, g4).

The following table shows the results obtained when computing the remainder of various classes of numbers, assuming that neither overflow nor underflow occurs.

Src2 \ Src1	-∞	-F	-0	+0	+F	+∞	NaN
-∞	*	*	*	*	*	*	NaN
-F	src2	-F or -0	**	**	-F or -0	src2	NaN
-0	-0	-0	*	*	-0	-0	NaN
+0	+0	+0	*	*	+0	+0	NaN
+F	src2	+F or +0	**	**	+F or +0	src2	NaN
+∞	*	*	*	*	*	*	NaN
NaN	NaN	NaN	NaN	NaN	NaN	NaN	NaN

Notes:

F Means finite-real number.
* Indicates floating invalid-operation exception.
** Indicates floating zero-divide exception.

When the result is 0, its sign is the same as that of *src2*. When the *src1* is ∞, the result is equal to the *src2*.

The result of this operation is always exact if the destination format is at least as wide as the *src2* and *src1*.

remr, remrl

The remainder provided with the **remr** and **remrl** instructions is different from the remainder described in the IEEE floating-point standard. The difference is related to how the quotient (N) of the expression (*src2*/*src1*) is determined.

As shown below in the action statement, N for the **remr** and **remrl** instructions is the nearest integer value obtained when the exact result (E) of the expression (*src2*/*src1*) is truncated toward zero. N will always be less than or equal to the absolute value of E.

For the IEEE standard, N is simply the nearest integer value to E. Here, N may be less than, equal to, or greater than the absolute value of E.

To help determine the IEEE remainder from the result given by the **remr** and **remrl** instructions, the following information about the quotient is given in the arithmetic-status field in the arithmetic:

Arithmetic Status Bit	Meaning
6	Q1, the next-to-last quotient bit
5	Q0, the last quotient bit
4	QR, the value the next quotient bit would have if one more reduction were performed (the "round" bit of the quotient)
3	QS, set if the remainder after the QR reduction would be nonzero (the "sticky" bit of the quotient)

The information can then be used to determine the IEEE standard remainder, as shown in the example below.

Action:

dst ← *src2* - (N ∗ *src1*);
where N = truncate (*src2*/*src1*.
Here, (*src2*/*src1*) is truncated
toward zero to the nearest integer.

remr, remrl

Faults:	STANDARD	Refer to the discussion of faults at the beginning of this chapter.
	Floating Reserved Encoding	One or more operands is an unnormalized (including denormalized) value and the normalizing-mode bit in the arithmetic controls is set.

The following floating-point exceptions can be raised. Whether or not an exception results in a fault being raised depends on the state of its associated mask bit in the arithmetic controls.

Floating Overflow	Result is too large for destination format.
Floating Underflow	Result is too small for destination format.
Floating Zero Divide	The *src1* operand is 0.
Floating Invalid Operation	The *src2* operand is ∞.
	The *src1* operand is 0.
	One or more operands are an SNaN value.
Floating Inexact	Result cannot be represented exactly in destination format.

Example:

```
remrl g6, g8, fp1
# fp1 ← g8,g9 rem g6,g7
```

Opcode:

remr	683	REG
remrl	693	REG

See Also: **remi**, **modi**

ret

Mnemonic: **ret** Return

Format: **ret**

Description: Returns process control to the calling procedure. The current stack frame (i.e., that of the called procedure) is deallocated and the FP is changed to point to the stack frame of the calling procedure. Instruction execution is continued at the instruction pointed to by the RIP in the calling procedure's stack frame, which is the instruction immediately following the call instruction.

As shown in the action statement below, the action that the processor takes on the return is determined by the return status and prereturn trace bits. These bits are contained in bits 0, through 3 of register r0 of the current set of local registers.

Refer to Chapter 4 for further discussion of the **return** instruction.

Action:

```
wait for any uncompleted instructions to finish;
case frame_status is

2#000#:  FP ← PFP;
         free current register_set;
         if register_set (FP) not allocated
           then retrieve from memory(FP);
         end if;
         IP ← RIP;

2#001#:  x ← memory(FP-16);
         y ← memory(FP-12);
         do case 000 action;
         arithmetic_controls ← y;
         if execution_mode = supervisor
           then process_controls ← x;
         end if;

2#010#:  if execution_mode ≠ supervisor
         then go to case 000;
         else process_controls.T ← 0;
           execution_mode ← user;
           go to case 000;
         end if;
```

ret

```
2#011#:  if execution_mode ≠ supervisor
             then go to case 000;
             else process_controls.T ← 1;
               execution_mode ← user;
               go to case 000;
             end if;

2#100#:  undefined

2#101#:  undefined

2#110#:  if execution_mode = supervisor
             then free current register set;
               check_pending_interrupts;
               # if continue here, no interrupt to do
               do case 000 action;
             end if;

2#111#:  x ← memory(FP-16);
             y ← memory(FP-12);
             do case 000 action;
             arithmetic_controls ← y;
             if execution_mode = supervisor
               then process_controls ← x;
                 check_pending_interrupts;
             end if;
```

Faults: STANDARD

Example:

```
ret    # process control returns to
       # calling procedure
       # environment
```

Opcode: **ret** 0A CTRL

See Also: **call**, **calls**, **callx**

rotate

Mnemonic: **rotate** Rotate

Format: **rotate** *len*, *src*, *dst*
reg/lit reg/lit reg

Description: Copies *src* to *dst* and rotates the bits in the resulting *dst* operand to the left (toward higher significance). (The bits shifted off the left end of the word are inserted at the right end of the word.) The *len* operand specifies the number of bits that the *dst* operand is rotated. The **len** operand can range from 0 to 31.

This instruction can also be used to rotate bits to the right. Here, the number of bits the word is to be rotated right is subtracted from 32 to get the *len* operand.

Action: *dst* ← rotate (*len* mod 32 (*src*))

Faults: STANDARD

Example:

```
rotate r4, r8, r12    # r12 ← r8
                      # with bits rotated
                      # r4 bits to left
```

Opcode: **rotate** 59D REG

See Also: **SHIFT**

roundr, roundrl

Mnemonic: **roundr** Round Real
roundrl Round Long Real

Format: **roundr*** *src*, *dst*
freg/flit freg

Description: Rounds *src* to the nearest integral value, depending on the rounding mode, and stores the result in *dst*.

For the **roundrl** instruction, if the *src* or *dst* operand references a global or local register, this register is the first (lowest numbered) of two successive registers. Also, this register must be even numbered (e.g., g0, g2, g4).

If the *src* operand is ∞ the result is *src*. If the *src* operand is not an integral value, a floating-inexact exception is raised.

Action: *dst* ← round_to_integral_value (*src1*);

Faults:

STANDARD	Refer to the discussion of faults at the beginning of this chapter.
Floating Reserved Encoding	One or more operands is an unnormalized (including denormalized) value and the normalizing-mode bit in the arithmetic controls is set.

The following floating-point exceptions can be raised. Whether or not an exception results in a fault being raised depends on the state of its associated mask bit in the arithmetic controls.

Floating Overflow	Result is too large for destination format.
Floating Underflow	Result is too small for destination format.
Floating Invalid Operation	One or more operands are an SNaN value.
Floating Inexact	Result cannot be represented exactly in destination format.

Example:

```
roundrl r4, r10
# r10,r11  ← r4,r5 rounded
```

Opcode:

roundr	68B	REG
roundrl	69B	REG

scaler, scalerl

Mnemonic: scaler — Scale Real
scalerl — Scale Long Real

Format: **scaler*** *src1*, *src2*, *dst*
reg/lit freg/flit freg

Description: Multiplies *src2* by 2 to the power of *src1* and stores the result in *dst*. The *src1* operand is an integer; whereas, *src2* and *dst* are reals.

For the **scalerl** instruction, if the *src2* or *dst* operand references a global or local register, this register is the first (lowest numbered) of two successive registers. Also, this register must be even numbered (e.g., g0, g2, g4).

The following table shows the results obtained when scaling various classes of numbers, assuming that neither overflow nor underflow occurs.

Src2 \ Src1	-N	0	+N
-∞	-∞	-∞	-∞
-F	-F	-F	-F
-0	-0	-0	-0
+0	+0	+0	+0
+F	+F	+F	+F
+∞	+∞	+∞	+∞
NaN	NaN	NaN	NaN

Notes:

F Means finite-real number.

N Means integer.

In most cases, only the exponent is changed and the mantissa (fraction) remains unchanged. However, when the *src1* operand is a denormalized value, the mantissa is also changed and the result may turn out to be a normalized number. Similarly, if overflow or underflow results from a scale operation, the resulting mantissa will differ from the source's mantissa.

scaler, scalerl

Refer to the sections titled "Floating Overflow Exception" and "Floating Underflow Exception" in Chapter 12 for further discussion of how overflow and underflow are handled.

Action: *dst* ← *src2* ∗ (2^*src1*)

Faults:

STANDARD	Refer to the discussion of faults at the beginning of this chapter.
Floating Reserved Encoding	One or more operands is an unnormalized (including denormalized) value and the normalizing-mode bit in the arithmetic controls is set.

The following floating-point exceptions can be raised. Whether or not an exception results in a fault being raised depends on the state of its associated mask bit in the arithmetic controls.

Floating Overflow	Result is too large for destination format.
Floating Underflow	Result is too small for destination format.
Floating Zero Divide	The *src1* operand is 0.
Floating Invalid Operation	One or more operands are an SNaN value.
Floating Inexact	Result cannot be represented exactly in destination format.

Example:

```
scalerl g6, g2, fp0
# fp0 ← g2,g3 * 2^g6
```

Opcode:

scaler	677	REG
scalerl	676	REG

See Also: **mulr**

scanbit

Mnemonic: **scanbit** Scan For Bit

Format: **scanbit** *src*, *dst*
reg/lit reg

Description: Searches the *src* value for the most-significant set bit (1 bit). If a most-significant 1 bit is found, its bit number is stored in *dst* and the condition code is set to 010_2. If the *src* value is zero, all 1's are stored in *dst* and the condition code is set to 000_2.

Action:

dst ← 16#FFFFFFFF#;
AC.cc ← 2#000#;
for i in 31..0 **reverse loop**
    if (*src* **and** 2^i) ≠ 0
    then
        dst ← i;
        AC.cc ← 2#010#;
        exit;
    end if;
end loop;

Faults: STANDARD

Example:

```
# assume g8 is nonzero
scanbit g8, g10
# g10 ← bit number of
# most-significant set bit
# in g8; AC.cc ← 2#010#
```

Opcode: **scanbit** 641 REG

See Also: **spanbit**

scanbyte

Mnemonic: **scanbyte** Scan Byte Equal

Format: **scanbyte** *src1*, *src2*
reg/lit reg/lit

Description: Performs a byte-by-byte comparison of *src1* and *src2* and sets the condition code to 2#010# if any two corresponding bytes are equal. If no corresponding bytes are equal, the condition code is set to 000_2.

Action:

if (*src1* **and** 16#000000FF#) = (*src2* **and** 16#000000FF#) **or**
(*src1* **and** 16#0000FF00#) = (*src2* **and** 16#0000FF00#) **or**
(*src1* **and** 16#00FF0000#) = (*src2* **and** 16#00FF0000#) **or**
(*src1* **and** 16#FF000000#) = (*src2* **and** 16#FF000000#)
then AC.cc ← 2#010#;
else AC.cc ← 2#000#;
endif;

Faults: STANDARD

Example:

```
# assume r9 = 0x11AB1100
scanbyte 0x00AB0011, r9
# AC.cc ← 2#010#
```

Opcode: **scanbyte** 5AC REG

setbit

Mnemonic: **setbit** Set Bit

Format: **setbit** *bitpos*, *src*, *dst*
reg/lit reg/lit reg

Description: Copies the *src* value to *dst* with one bit set. The *bitpos* operand specifies the bit to be set.

Action: *dst* ← *src* **or** 2^(*bitpos* **mod** 32);

Faults: STANDARD

Example:

```
setbit 15, r9, r1
# r1 ← r9 with bit 15 set
```

Opcode: **setbit** 583 REG

See Also: **alterbit, chkbit, clrbit, notbit,**

SHIFT

Mnemonic:

shlo	Shift Left Ordinal
shro	Shift Right Ordinal
shli	Shift Left Integer
shri	Shift Right Integer
shrdi	Shift Right Dividing Integer

Format:

sh*	*len*,	*src*,	*dst*
	reg/lit	reg/lit	reg

Description: Shifts *src* left or right by the number of digits indicated with the *len* operand and stores the result in *dst*. This operation (with the exception of the **shri** instruction, as described below) is equivalent to multiplying (shift left) or dividing (shift right) the *src* value by 2^{len}.

The **shri** instruction performs a conventional arithmetic right shift, which, when used as a divide, produces an incorrect quotient for negative *src* values. To get a correct quotient for a negative *src* value, use the **shrdi** instruction, which performs correct rounding of negative results.

Action:

shlo:

```
if len < 32
then dst ← src* 2^len
else dst ← 0;
end if;
```

shro:

```
if len < 32
then dst ← src/2^len
else dst ← 0;
end if;
```

shli:

```
dst ← src* 2^len
```

shri:

```
if src ≥ 0
then if len < 32
  then dst ← src/2^len
  else dst ← 0;
else if len < 32
  then dst ← (src - 2^len + 1)/2^len
  else dst ← -1;
  end if;
end if;
```

shrdi:

```
dst ← src/2^len
```

SHIFT

Faults: STANDARD, Integer Overflow

Example:

```
shli 13, g4, r6
# g6 ← g4 shifted left 13 bits
```

Opcode:

shlo	59C	REG
shro	598	REG
shli	59E	REG
shri	59B	REG
shrdi	59A	REG

See Also: **divi, muli, rotate**

sinr, sinrl

Mnemonics:

sinr	Sine Real
sinrl	Sine Long Real

Format:

sinr*	*src*,	*dst*
	freg/flit	freg

Description: Calculates the sine of *src* and stores the result in *dst*. The *src* value is an angle given in radians. The resulting *dst* value is in the range -1 to +1, inclusive.

For the **sinrl** instruction, if the *src* or *dst* operand references a global or local register, this register is the first (lowest numbered) of two successive registers. Also, this register must be even numbered (e.g., g0, g2, g4).

The following table shows the results obtained when taking the sine of various classes of numbers, assuming that neither overflow nor underflow occurs.

Src	Dst
-∞	*
-F	-1 to +1
-0	-0
+0	+0
+F	-1 to +1
+∞	*
NaN	NaN

Notes:
- F Means finite-real number
- * Indicates floating invalid-operation exception

In the trigonmetic instructions, the 80960KB uses a value for π with a 66-bit mantissa which is 2 bits more than are available in the extended-real format. The section in Chapter 12 titled "Pi" gives this π value, along with some suggestions for representing this value in a program.

Action: *dst* ← **sin** (*src*);

sinr, sinrl

Faults:

STANDARD	Refer to the discussion of faults at the beginning of this chapter.
Floating Reserved Encoding	One or more operands is an unnormalized (including denormalized) value and the normalizing-mode bit in the arithmetic controls is set.

The following floating-point exceptions can be raised. Whether or not an exception results in a fault being raised depends on the state of its associated mask bit in the arithmetic controls.

Floating Underflow	Result is too small for destination format.
Floating Invalid Operation	The *src* operand is ∞.
	One or more operands is an SNaN value.
Floating Inexact	Result cannot be represented exactly in destination format.

Example:

```
sinrl g6, g0
# sine of value in g6,g7
# is stored in g0,g1
```

Opcode:

sinr	68C	REG
sinrl	69C	REG

See Also: **cosr**, **tanr**

spanbit

Mnemonic: **spanbit** Span Over Bit

Format: **spanbit** *src*, *dst*
reg/lit reg

Description: Searches the *src* value for the most-significant clear bit (0 bit). If a most-significant 0 bit is found, its bit number is stored in *dst* and the condition code is set to 010_2. If the *src* value is all 1's, all 1's are stored in **dst** and the condition code is set to 000_2.

Action:

```
dst ← 16#FFFFFFFF#;
AC.cc ← 2#000#;
for i in 31..0 reverse loop
  if (src and 2^i) = 0
  then
    dst ← i;
    AC.cc ← 2#010#;
    exit;
  end if;
end loop;
```

Faults: STANDARD

Example:

```
# assume r2 is not 16#FFFFFFFF#
spanbit r2 r9
# r9 ← bit number of
# most-significant clear bit
# in r2; AC.cc ← 2#010#
```

Opcode: **spanbit** 640 REG

See Also: **scanbit**

sqrtr, sqrtrl

Mnemonic: **sqrtr** Square Root Real
sqrtrl Square Root Long Real

Format: **sqrtr*** *src*, *dst*
freg/flit freg

Description: Calculates the square root of *src* and stores it in *dst*.

For the **sqrtrl** instruction, if the *src* or *dst* operand references a global or local register, this register is the first (lowest numbered) of two successive registers. Also, this register must be even numbered (e.g., g0, g2, g4).

The following table shows the results obtained when taking the square root of various classes of numbers, assuming that neither overflow nor underflow occurs.

Src	Dst
-∞	*
-F	*
-0	-0
+0	+0
+F	+F
+∞	+∞
NaN	NaN

Notes:
F Means finite-real number
* Indicates floating invalid-operation exception

With these instructions, it is not possible to raise a floating overflow or floating underflow fault unless the *src* operand is in a floating-point register and the *dst* operand is not.

Action: *dst* ← sqrt (*src*);

sqrtr, sqrtrl

Faults:

STANDARD	Refer to the discussion of faults at the beginning of this chapter.
Floating Reserved Encoding	One or more operands is an unnormalized (including denormalized) value and the normalizing-mode bit in the arithmetic controls is set.

The following floating-point exceptions can be raised. Whether or not an exception results in a fault being raised depends on the state of its associated mask bit in the arithmetic controls.

Floating Overflow	Result is too large for destination format.
Floating Underflow	Result is too small for destination format.
Floating Invalid Operation	The *src* operand is less than -0.
	The *src* operand is an SNaN value.
Floating Inexact	Result cannot be represented exactly in destination format.

Example:

```
sqrtrl g6, fp0
# fp0 ← sqrt of g6,g7
```

Opcode:

sqrtr	688	REG
sqrtrl	698	REG

STORE

Mnemonic:

st	Store
stob	Store Ordinal Byte
stos	Store Ordinal Short
stib	Store Integer Byte
stis	Store Integer Short
stl	Store Long
stt	Store Triple
stq	Store Quad

Format:

st*	*src,*	*dst*
	reg/lit	mem

Description:

Copies a byte or string of bytes from a register or group of registers to memory. The *src* operand specifies a register or the first (lowest numbered) register of successive registers.

The *dst* operand specifies the address of the memory location where the byte or the first byte of a string of bytes is to be stored. The full range of addressing modes may be used in specifying *dst*. (Refer to Chapter 5 for a complete discussion of the addressing modes available with memory-type operands.)

The **stob** and **stib**, and **stos** and **stis** instructions store a byte and half word, respectively, from the low order bytes of the *src* register. The **st**, **stl**, **stt**, and **stq** instructions copy 4, 8, 12, and 16 bytes, respectively, from successive registers to memory.

For the **stl** instruction, **dst** must specify an even numbered register (e.g., g0, g2, ..., g12). For the **stt** and **stq** instructions, **dst** must specify a register number that is a multiple of four (e.g., g0, g4, g8).

Action:

memory (*dst*) ← *src*;

Faults:

STANDARD, Integer Overflow Fault (**stib** and **stis** instructions only)

Example:

```
st g2, 1256 (g6)
# word beginning at offset
# 1256 + (g6) ← g2
```

STORE

Opcode:

st	92	MEM
stob	82	MEM
stos	8A	MEM
stib	C2	MEM
stis	CA	MEM
stl	9A	MEM
stt	A2	MEM
stq	B2	MEM

See Also: **LOAD, MOVE**

subc

Mnemonic: **subc** Subtract Ordinal With Carry

Format: **subc** *src1*, *src2*, *dst*
reg/lit reg/lit reg

Description: Subtracts (*src1* - 1) from *src2*, adds bit 1 of the condition code (used here as a carry bit), and stores the result in *dst*. If the ordinal subtraction results in a carry, bit 1 of the condition code is set.

This instruction can also be used for integer subtraction. Here, if integer subtraction results in an overflow, bit 0 of the condition code is set.

The *subc* instruction does not distinguish between ordinals and integers: it sets bits 0 and 1 of the condition code regardless of the data type.

Action:

```
# Let the value of the condition code be xCx.
dst ← src2 - (src1 - 1) + C;
AC.cc ← 2#0CV#;
# C is carry from ordinal subtraction.
# V is 1 if integer subtraction would have generated
# an overflow.
```

Faults: STANDARD

Example:

```
subc g5, g6, g7
# g7 ← g6 - (g5 - 1)
# + Carry Bit
```

Opcode: **subc** 5B2 REG

See Also: **addc**

subi, subo

Mnemonic:	**subi**	Subtract Integer		
	subo	Subtract Ordinal		
Format:	**sub***	*src1*,	*src2*,	*dst*
		reg/lit	reg/lit	reg

Description: Subtracts *src1* from *src2* and stores the result in *dst*. The binary results from these two instructions are identical. The only difference is that **subi** can signal an integer overflow.

Action: *dst* ← *src2* - *src1*;

Faults: STANDARD, Integer Overflow (**subi** instruction only)

Example:

```
subi g6, g9, g12    # g12 ← g9 - g6
```

Opcode:	**subi**	593	REG
	subo	592	REG

See Also: **addi**, **addr**, **subc**, **subr**

subr, subrl

Mnemonic: **subr** Subtract Real
subrl Subtract Long Real

Format: **subr*** *src1*, freg/flit *src2*, freg/flit *dst* freg

Description: Subtracts *src1* from *src2* and stores the result in *dst*.

For the **subrl** instruction, if the *src1*, *src2*, or *dst* operand references a global or local register, this register is the first (lowest numbered) of two successive registers. Also, this register must be even numbered (e.g., g0, g2, g4).

The following table shows the results obtained when subtracting various classes of numbers, assuming that neither overflow nor underflow occurs.

		Src1							
		-∞	**-F**	**-0**	**+0**	**+F**	**+∞**	**NaN**
	-∞	*	-∞	-∞	-∞	-∞	-∞	NaN
	-F	+∞	±F or ±0	src2	src2	-F	-∞	NaN
	-0	+∞	src1	±0	-0	src1	-∞	NaN
Src2	**+0**	+∞	src1	+0	±0	src1	-∞	NaN
	+F	+∞	+F	src2	src2	±F or ± 0	-∞	NaN
	+∞	+∞	+∞	+∞	+∞	+∞	*	NaN
	NaN	NaN	NaN	NaN	NaN	NaN	NaN	NaN

Notes:

F Means finite-real number.

***** Indicates floating invalid-operation exception.

When the difference between two operands of like sign is zero, the result is +0, except for the round toward -∞ mode, in which case the result is -0. This instruction also guarantees that +0 - (-0) = +0, and that -0 - (+0) = -0.

When one source operand is ∞, the result is ∞ of the expected sign. If both source operands are ∞ of the same sign, an invalid-operation exception is raised.

subr, subrl

Action: *dst* ← *src2* - *src1*;

Faults:

STANDARD	Refer to the discussion of faults at the beginning of this chapter.
Floating Reserved Encoding	One or more operands is an unnormalized (including denormalized) value and the normalizing-mode bit in the arithmetic controls is set.

The following floating-point exceptions can be raised. Whether or not an exception results in a fault being raised depends on the state of its associated mask bit in the arithmetic controls.

Floating Overflow	Result is too large for destination format.
Floating Underflow	Result is too small for destination format.
Floating Invalid Operation	Source operands are infinities of like sign.
	One or more operands are an SNaN value.
Floating Inexact	Result cannot be represented exactly in destination format.

Example:

```
subrl g6, fp0, fp1
# fp1 ← fp0 - g6,g7
```

Opcode:

subr	78D	REG
subrl	79D	REG

See Also: **subi**, **subc**, **addr**

syncf

Mnemonic: syncf Synchronize Faults

Format: syncf

Description: Waits for any faults to be generated associated with any prior uncompleted instructions.

Action:

if arithmetic_controls.nif
  then;
  else wait until no imprecise faults can occur
    associated with any uncompleted instructions;
end if;

Faults: STANDARD

Example:

```
ld xyz, g6
addi r6, r8, r8
syncf
and g6, 0xFFFF, g8
# the syncf instruction insures that any faults
# that may occur during the execution of the
# ld and addi instructions occur before the
# and instruction is executed
```

Opcode: syncf 66F REG

See Also: mark, fmark

synld

Mnemonic: **synld** Synchronous Load

Format:

synld	*src*,	*dst*
	reg	reg
	addr	addr

Description: Copies a word from the memory location specified with *src* into *dst* and waits for the completion of all memory operations, including those initiated prior to the **synld** instruction. When the load has been successfully completed, the condition code is set to 2#010#.

The primary function of this instruction is for reading IAC messages, the IAC Message Control word, or the IAC Interrupt Control Register. However, this instruction is not restricted to IAC applications. It may be used when it is important to guarantee the completion of the load operation before proceeding or to avoid a bad-access fault.

The setting of the condition code indicates whether or not the load was completed successfully. If the load operation results in a bad access condition (e.g., reading an AP-bus interconnect register), the condition code is set to 000_2, but the bad-access fault is not raised.

Action:

```
if PRCB.addressing_mode = physical
  then tempa ← src;
  else tempa ← physical_address (src);
end if;
tempa ← tempa and 16#FFFFFFFC#; # force alignment
if tempa = 16#FF000004#
  then dst ← interrupt_control_reg;
    AC.cc ← 2#010#;
  else dst ← memory (tempa);
    if bad_access
      then AC.cc ← 2#000#;
      else AC.cc ← 2#010#;
    end if;
end if;
```

Faults: STANDARD

synld

Example:

```
lda 16#FF000010#, g8
synld g8, g9   # g9 ← word from IAC
               # message buffer;
               # AC.cc = 2#010#
```

Opcode: **synld** 615 REG

See Also: **synmov**

synmov, synmovl, synmovq

Mnemonic:

synmov	Synchronous Move
synmovl	Synchronous Move Long
synmovq	Synchronous Move Quad

Format:

synmov*	*dst,*	*src*
	reg	reg
	addr	addr

Description: Copies 1 (**synmov**), 2 (**synmovl**), or 4 (**synmovq**) words from the memory location specified with *src* to the memory location specified with *dst* and waits for the completion of all memory operations, including those initiated prior to this instruction. When the move has been successfully completed, the condition code is set to 010_2.

The *src* and *dst* operands specify the address of the first (lowest address) word. These addresses should be for word boundaries (**synmov**), double-word boundaries (**synmovl**), or quad-word boundaries (**synmovq**). If not, the processor forces alignment to these boundaries.

The primary function of these instructions is for sending IAC messages. However, this instruction is not restricted to IAC applications. It may be used when it is important to guarantee the completion of the move operation before proceeding or to avoid a Bad Access Fault.

The setting of the condition code indicates whether or not the move was completed successfully. If the move operation results in a bad access condition (e.g., sending an IAC message to a non-existent agent on the AP-bus), the condition code is set to 000_2, but the Bad Access Fault is not raised.

Address $FF000010_{16}$ is used to send an IAC message to the processor upon which the instruction is executed. Refer to Chapter 11 for further information about sending internal IAC messages.

synmov, synmovl, synmovq

Action: **synmov**:

```
if PRCB.addressing_mode = physical
   then tempa ← dst;
   # dst is used as a physical address
   else tempa ← physical_address (dst);
   # dst translated into a physical address
end if;
tempa ← tempa and 16#FFFFFFFC#;
# force alignment
if tempa = 16#FF000004#
   then interrupt_control_reg ← memory (src)
      AC.cc ← 2#010#;
   else temp ← memory (src);
      memory (tempa) ← temp;
      # write operations into memory (tempa) are
      # interpreted as noncacheable
      wait for completion;
      if bad_access
         then AC.cc ← 2#000#;
         else AC.cc ← 2#010#;
      end if;
end if;
```

synmovl:

```
if PRCB.addressing_mode = physical
   then tempa ← dst;
   # dst is used as a physical address
   else tempa ← physical_address (dst);
   # dst is translated into as a physical address
end if;
tempa ← tempa and 16#FFFFFFF8#; # force alignment
temp ← memory (src);
memory (tempa) ← temp;
# write operations into memory (tempa) are interpreted
# as noncacheable
wait for completion;
if bad_access
   then AC.cc ← 2#000#;
   else AC.cc ← 2#010#;
end if;
```

synmov, synmovl, synmovq

synmovq:

if PRCB.addressing_mode = physical
  then tempa ← *dst*;
  # *dst* is used as a physical address
  else tempa ← physical_address (*dst*);
  # *dst* is translated into as a physical address
end if;
tempa ← tempa **and** 16#FFFFFFF0#; # force alignment
temp ← memory (*src*);
if tempa = 16#FF000010#
  then AC.cc ← 2#010#;
  use temp as a received iac message;
  else memory (tempa) ← temp;
  # write operations into memory (tempa) are interpreted
  # as noncacheable
    wait for completion;
    if bad_access
      then AC.cc ← 2#000#;
      else AC.cc ← 2#010#;
    end if;
end if;

Faults: STANDARD

Example:

```
lda 16#FF000010#, g7
# g7 ← 16#FF000010
synmovq g7, g8
# g7 ← IAC message from g8
```

Opcode:

synmov	600	REG
synmovl	601	REG
synmovq	602	REG

See Also: **synld**

tanr, tanrl

Mnemonics: **tanr** Tangent Real
tanrl Tangent Long Real

Format: **tanr*** *src*, *dst*
freg/flit freg

Description: Calculates the tangent of *src* and stores the result in *dst*. The *src* value is an angle given in radians. The resulting *dst* value is in the range of -∞ to +∞, inclusive; a result of -∞ or +∞ will result in a floating invalid-operation exception being signaled.

For the **tanrl** instruction, if the *src* or *dst* operand references a global or local register, this register is the first (lowest numbered) of two successive registers. Also, this register must be even numbered (e.g., g0, g2, g4).

The following table shows the results obtained when taking the tangent of various classes of numbers, assuming that neither overflow nor underflow occurs.

Src	Dst
-∞	*
-F	-F to +F
-0	-0
+0	+0
+F	-F to +F
+∞	*
NaN	NaN

Notes:
F Means finite-real number
* Indicates floating invalid-operation exception

If the source operand is a finite value, the result will be finite, unless the *src* operand is in a floating-point register and the *dst* operand is not.

In the trigonmetic instructions, the 80960KB uses a value for π with a 66-bit mantissa which is 2 bits more than are available in the extended-real format. The section in Chapter 12 titled "Pi" gives this π value, along with some suggestions for representing this value in a program.

tanr, tanrl

Action: *dst* ← tangent (*src*);

Faults:

STANDARD	Refer to the discussion of faults at the beginning of this chapter.
Floating Reserved Encoding	One or more operands is an unnormalized (including denormalized) value and the normalizing-mode bit in the arithmetic controls is set.

The following floating-point exceptions can be raised. Whether or not an exception results in a fault being raised depends on the state of its associated mask bit in the arithmetic controls.

Floating Overflow	Result is too large for destination format.
Floating Underflow	Result is too small for destination format.
Floating Invalid Operation	The *src* operand is ∞.
	One or more operands are an SNaN value.
Floating Inexact	Result cannot be represented exactly in destination format.

Example:

```
tanrl g4, fp0    # tangent of value in g4,g5 is
                 # stored in fp0
```

Opcode:

tanr	68E	REG
tanrl	69E	REG

See Also: **cosr**, **sinr**

TEST

Mnemonic:

teste	Test For Equal
testne	Test For Not Equal
testl	Test For Less
testle	Test For Less or Equal
testg	Test For Greater
testge	Test For Greater or Equal
testo	Test For Ordered
testno	Test For Unordered

Format: **test*** *dst*
reg

Description: Stores a true (1) in *dst* if the logical AND of the condition code and the mask-part of the opcode is not zero. Otherwise, the instruction stores a false (0) in *dst*.

The following table shows the condition-code mask for each instruction:

Instruction	Mask	Condition
testno	000	Unordered
testg	001	Greater
teste	010	Equal
testge	011	Greater or equal
testl	100	Less
testne	101	Not equal
testle	110	Less or equal
testo	111	Ordered

For the **testno** instruction (Unordered), a true is stored if the condition code is 2#000#; otherwise a false is stored.

TEST

Action: For All Instructions Except **testno**:

```
if (mask and AC.cc) ≠ 2#000#
        then dst ← 1;  # dst set for true
        else dst ← 0;  # dst set for false
end if;
```

testno:

```
if AC.cc = 2#000#
        then dst ← 1;  # dst set for true
        else dst ← 0;  # dst set for false
end if;
```

Faults: STANDARD

Example:

```
# assume AC.cc = 2#100#
testl g9   # g9 ← 16#00000001#
```

Opcode:

teste	22	COBR
testne	25	COBR
testl	24	COBR
testle	26	COBR
testg	21	COBR
testge	23	COBR
testo	27	COBR
testno	20	COBR

See Also: **cmpi, cmpdeci, cmpinci**

xnor, xor

Mnemonic: **xnor** Exclusive Nor
xor Exclusive Or

Format:

xnor	*src1*,	*src2*,	*dst*
	reg/lit	reg/lit	reg
xor	*src1*,	*src2*,	*dst*
	reg/lit	reg/lit	reg

Description: Performs a bitwise XNOR (**xnor** instruction) or XOR (**xor** instruction) operation on the *src2* and *src1* values and stores the result in *dst*.

Action:

xnor: *dst* ← **not** (*src2* **or** *src1*) **or** (*src2* **and** *src1*);

xor: *dst* ← (*src2* **or** *src1*) **and** **not** (*src2* **and** *src1*);

Faults: STANDARD

Example:

```
xnor r3, r9, r12      # r12 ← r9 XNOR r3
xor g1, g7, g4        # g4 ← g7 XOR g1)
```

Opcode:

xnor	589	REG
xor	586	REG

See Also: **and**, **andnot**, **nand**, **nor**, **not**, **notand**, **notor**, **or**, **ornot**

Floating-Point Operation **12**

CHAPTER 12
FLOATING-POINT OPERATION

This chapter describes the floating-point processing capabilities of the 80960KB processor. The subjects discussed include the real number data types, the execution environment for floating-point operations, the floating-point instructions, and fault and exception handling.

INTRODUCING THE 80960KB FLOATING-POINT ARCHITECTURE

The floating-point architecture used in the 80960KB processor is designed to allow a convenient implementation of the IEEE Standard 754-1985 for Binary Floating-Point Arithmetic. This hardware architecture, along with a small amount of software support, conforms to the IEEE standard and provides support for the following data structures and operations:

- Real (32-bit), long real (64-bit), and extended real (80-bit) floating-point number formats.
- Add, subtract, multiply, divide, square root, remainder, and compare operations
- Conversion between integer and floating-point formats
- Conversion between different floating-point formats
- Handling of floating-point exceptions, including non-numbers (NaNs)

The software to support the 80960KB floating-point architecture is needed primarily to handle conversions between real numbers and decimal strings.

In addition, the 80960KB floating-point architecture supports several functions that go beyond the IEEE standard. These functions fall into two categories:

- functions recommended in the appendix to the IEEE standard, such as copy sign and classify, and
- commonly used transcendental functions, including trigonometric, logarithmic, and exponential functions.

REAL NUMBERS AND FLOATING-POINT FORMAT

This section provides an introduction to real numbers and how they are represented in floating-point format. Readers who are already familiar with numeric processing techniques and the IEEE standard may wish to skip this section.

Real Number System

As shown at the top of Figure 12-1, the real-number system comprises the continuum of real numbers from minus infinity (-∞) to plus infinity (+∞).

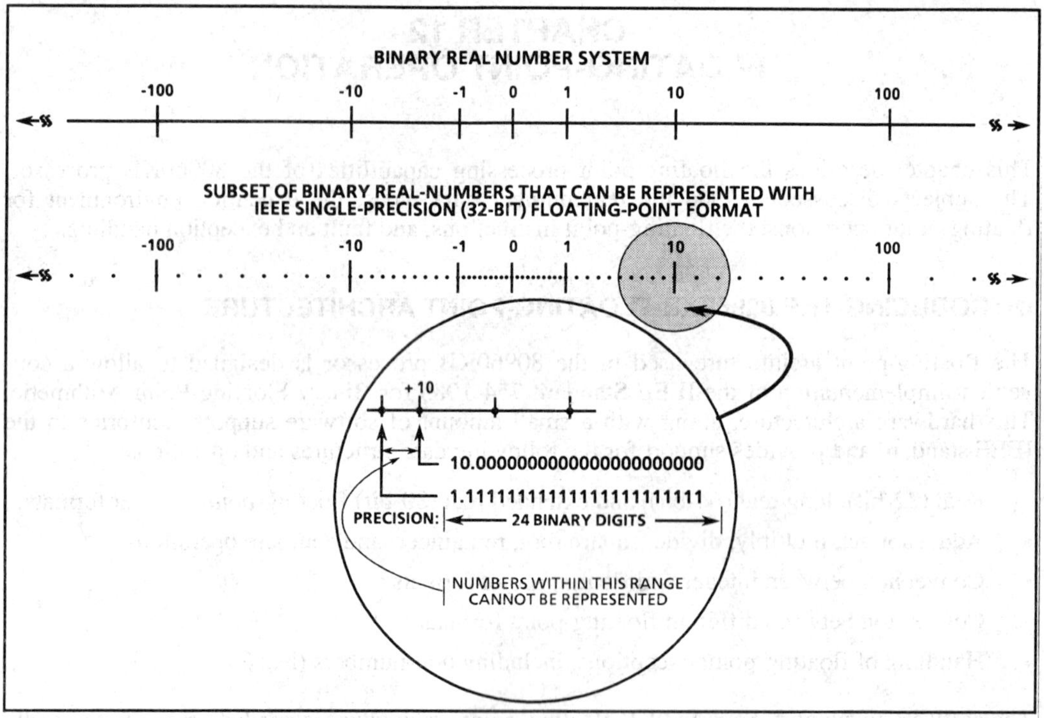

Figure 12-1: Binary Number System

Because the size and number of registers that any computer can have is limited, only a subset of the real-number continuum can be used in real-number calculations. As shown at the bottom of Figure 12-1, the subset of real numbers that a particular processor supports represents an approximation of the real number system. The range and precision of this real-number subset is determined by the format that the processor uses to represent real numbers.

Floating-Point Format

To increase the speed and efficiency of real number computations, computers or numeric processors typically represent real numbers in a binary floating-point format. In this format, a real number has three parts: a sign, a significand, and an exponent. Figure 12-2 shows the binary floating-point format that the processor uses. This format conforms to the IEEE standard.

The sign is a binary value that indicates whether the number is positive (0) or negative (1). The significand has two parts: a one-bit binary integer (also referred to as the j-bit) and a binary fraction. The j-bit is often not represented, but instead is an implied value. The exponent is a binary integer that represents the base-2 power that the significand is raised to.

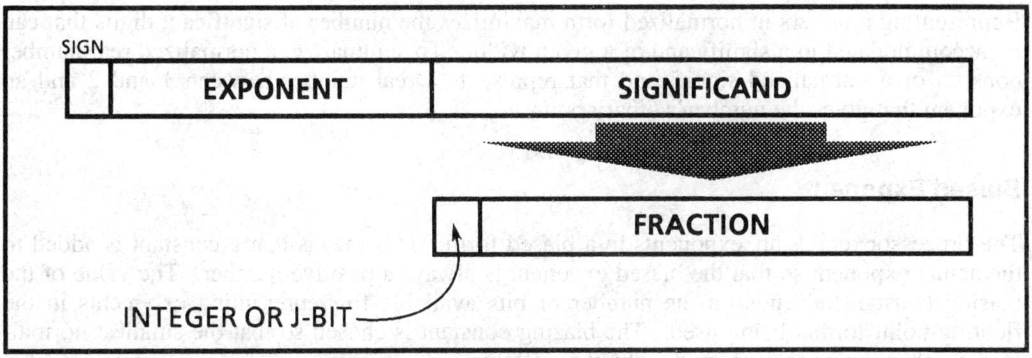

Figure 12-2: Binary Floating-Point Format

Table 12-1 shows how the real number 201.187 (in ordinary decimal format) is stored in floating-point format. The table lists a progression of real number notations that leads to the format that the 80960KB processor uses. In this format, the binary real number is normalized and the exponent is biased.

Table 12-1: Real Number Notation

NOTATION	VALUE		
ORDINARY DECIMAL	201.187		
SCIENTIFIC DECIMAL	$2.01187E_{10}2$		
SCIENTIFIC BINARY	$1.1001001001011111E_{2}111$		
SCIENTIFIC BINARY (BIASED EXPONENT)	$1.1001001001011111E_{2}10000110$		
32-BIT FLOATING-POINT FORMAT (NORMALIZED)	SIGN	BIASED EXPONENT	SIGNIFICAND
	0	10000110	1001001001011111 ← 1. (IMPLIED)

Normalized Numbers

In most cases, the processor represents real numbers in normalized form. This means that except for zero, the significand is always made up of an integer of 1 and a fraction as follows:

1.fff...ff

For values less than 1, leading zeros are eliminated. (For each leading zero eliminated, the exponent is decremented by one.)

Representing numbers in normalized form maximizes the number of significant digits that can be accommodated in a significand of a given width. To summarize, a normalized real number consists of a normalized significand that represents a real number between 1 and 2 and an exponent that gives the number's binary point.

Biased Exponent

The processor represents exponents in a biased form. This means that a constant is added to the actual exponent so that the biased exponent is always a positive number. The value of the biasing constant depends on the number of bits available for representing exponents in the floating-point format being used. The biasing constant is chosen so that the smallest normalized number can be reciprocated without overflow.

Real Number and Non-Number Encodings

The real numbers that are encoded in the floating-point format described above are generally divided into three classes: ± 0, ± nonzero-finite numbers, and ± ∞. Encodings for non-numbers (NaNs) are also defined. The term NaN stands for "Not a Number."

Figure 12-3 shows how the encodings for these numbers and non-numbers fit into the real number continuum. The encodings shown here are for the IEEE single-precision (32-bit) format, where the term "s" indicates the sign bit, "e" the biased exponent, and "f" the fraction. (The exponent values are given in decimal.)

Signed Zeros

Zero can be represented as a +0 or a -0 depending on the sign bit. Both encodings are equal in value. The sign of a zero result depends on the operation being performed and the rounding mode being used. Signed zeros have been provided to aid in implementing interval arithmetic. The sign of a zero may indicate the direction from which underflow occurred, or it may indicate the sign of an ∞ that has been reciprocated.

Signed, Nonzero, Finite Values

The class of signed, nonzero, finite values is divided into two groups: normalized and denormalized. The normalized finite numbers comprise all the nonzero finite values that can be encoded in a normalized real number format from zero to ∞. In the 32-bit form shown in Figure 12-3, this group of numbers includes all the numbers with biased exponents ranging from 1 to 254_{10} (unbiased, the exponent range is from -126_{10} to $+127_{10}$).

Denormalized Numbers

When real numbers become very close to zero, the normalized-number format can no longer be used to represent the numbers. This is because the range of the exponent is not large enough to compensate for shifting the binary point to the right to eliminate leading zeros.

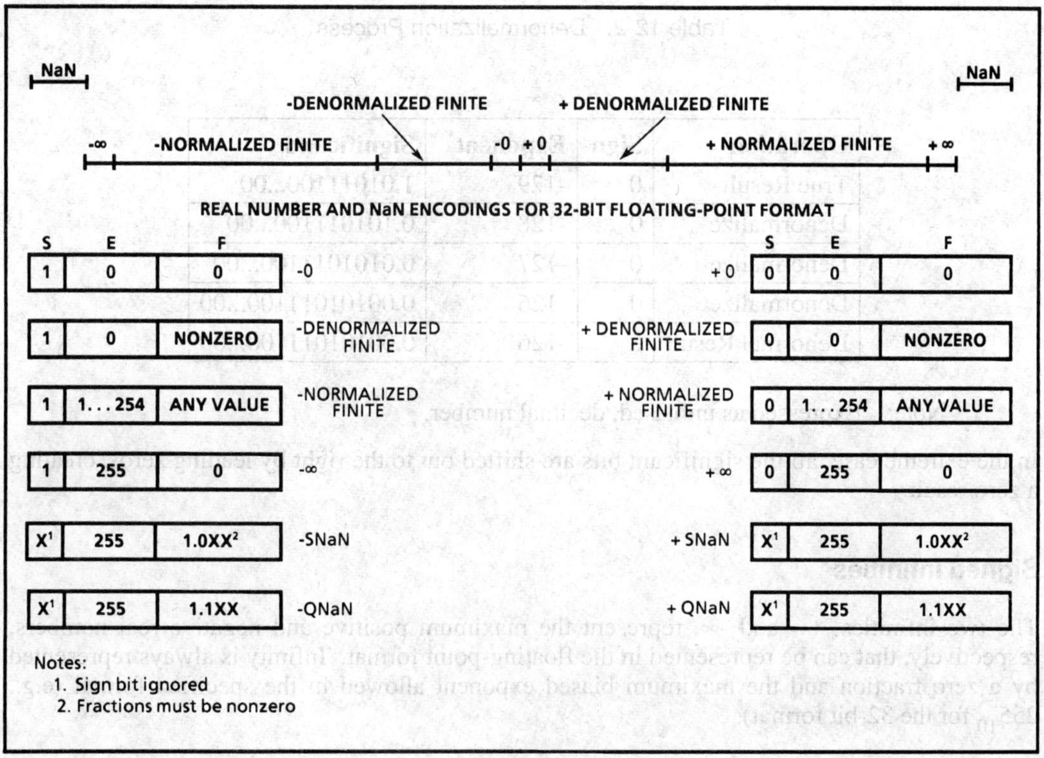

Figure 12-3: Real Numbers and NaNs

When the biased exponent is zero, smaller numbers can only be represented by making the integer bit (and perhaps other leading bits) of the significand zero. The numbers in this range are called denormalized numbers. The use of leading zeros with denormalized numbers allows smaller numbers to be represented. However, this denormalization causes a loss of precision (the number of significant bits in the fraction is reduced by the leading zeros).

When performing normalized floating-point computations, a processor normally operates on normalized numbers and produces normalized numbers as results. Denormalized numbers represent an underflow condition.

A denormalized number is computed through a technique called gradual underflow. Table 12-2 gives an example of gradual underflow in the denormalization process. Here the 32-bit format is being used, so the minimum exponent (unbiased) is -126_{10}. The true result in this example requires an exponent of -129_{10} in order to have a normalized number. Since -129_{10} is beyond the allowable exponent range, the result is denormalized by inserting leading zeros until the minimum exponent of -126_{10} is reached.

Table 12-2: Denormalization Process

Operation	Sign	Exponent*	Significand
True Result	0	-129	1.01011100...00
Denormalize	0	-128	0.101011100...00
Denormalize	0	-127	0.0101011100...00
Denormalize	0	-126	0.00101011100...00
Denormal Result	0	-126	0.00101011100...00

Note: *Expressed as unbiased, decimal number.

In the extreme case, all the significant bits are shifted out to the right by leading zeros, creating a zero result.

Signed Infinities

The two infinities, +∞ and -∞, represent the maximum positive and negative real numbers, respectively, that can be represented in the floating-point format. Infinity is always represented by a zero fraction and the maximum biased exponent allowed in the specified format (e.g., 255_{10} for the 32-bit format).

Whereas denormalized numbers represent an underflow condition, the two infinity numbers represent the result of an overflow condition. Here, the normalized result of a computation has a biased exponent greater than the largest allowable exponent for the selected result format.

NaNs

Since NaNs are non-numbers, they are not part of the real number line. In Figure 12-3, the encoding space for NaNs in the 80960KB floating-point formats is shown above the ends of the real number line. This space includes any value with the maximum allowable biased exponent and a non-zero fraction. (The sign bit is ignored for NaNs.)

The IEEE standard defines two specific NaN values: a quiet NaN (QNaN) and a signaling NaN (SNaN). A QNaN is a NaN with the most significant fraction bit set; an SNaN is a NaN with the most significant fraction bit clear. QNaNs are allowed to propagate through most arithmetic operations without signaling an exception. SNaNs signal an invalid-operation exception whenever they appear as operands in arithmetic operations. Exceptions are discussed later in this chapter in the section titled "Exceptions and Fault Handling."

The section at the end of this chapter titled "Operations on NaNs" provides detailed information on how the processor handles NaNs.

REAL DATA TYPES

The processor supports three real-number data formats: real, long real, and extended real. These formats correspond directly to the single-precision, double-precision, and double-extended precision formats in the IEEE standard. Figure 12-4 shows these data formats and gives the resolution that each provides.

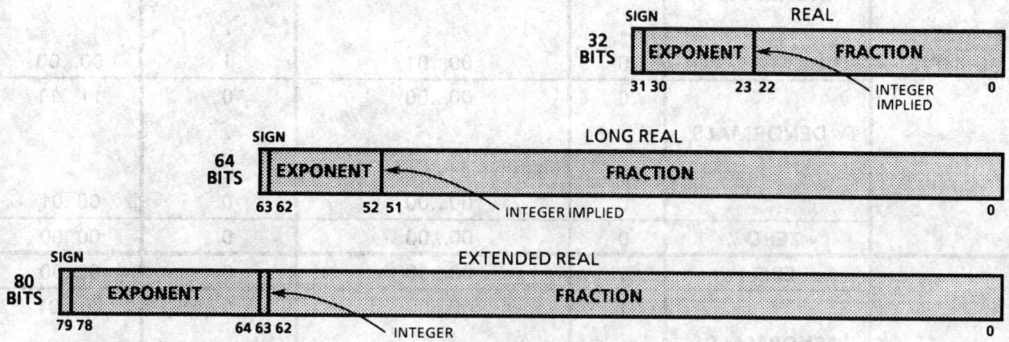

DATA TYPE	RANGE
Real	2^{-126} to 2^{127} ($\sim 10^{-45}$ to $\sim 10^{38}$)
Long Real	2^{-1022} to 2^{1023} ($\sim 10^{-324}$ to $\sim 10^{308}$)
Extended Real	2^{-16382} to 2^{16383} ($\sim 10^{-4950}$ to $\sim 10^{+4932}$)

Figure 12-4: Real Number Formats

For the real and long-real formats, only the fraction is given for the significand. The integer is assumed to be 1 for all numbers except 0 and denormalized finite numbers.

For the extended-real format, the integer is contained in bit 63, and the most-significant fraction bit is bit 62. Here, the integer is explicitly set to 1 for normalized numbers, infinities, and NaNs, and to 0 for zero and denormalized numbers.

Table 12-3 shows the encodings for all the classes of real numbers (i.e., zero, denormalized finite, normalized finite, and ∞) and NaNs, for each of the three real data-types.

EXECUTION ENVIRONMENT FOR FLOATING-POINT OPERATIONS

An important feature of the 80960KB processor is that the floating-point processing capabilities have been integrated into the execution environment of the processor. Operations on floating-point numbers are carried out using the same registers that are used for ordinals and integers. In addition, four floating-point registers have been provided for extended-precision floating-point arithmetic.

The following sections describe how floating-point operations are handled in the processor's execution environment.

Table 12-3: Real Numbers and NaN Encodings

CLASS		SIGN	BIASED EXPONENT	INTEGER[1]	FRACTION
POSITIVE	+ ∞	0	11...11	1	00...00
	+ NORMALS	0	11...10	1	11...11
		.	.	.	
		.	.	.	
		0	00...01	1	00...00
	+ DENORMALS	0	00...00	0	11...11
		.	.	.	.
		.	.	.	.
		0	00...00	0	00..01
	+ ZERO	0	00...00	0	00..00
NEGATIVE	-ZERO	1	00...00	0	00..00
	-DENORMALS	1	00...00	0	00...01
		.	.	.	.
		.	.	.	
		1	00...00	0	11...11
	-NORMALS	1	00...01	1	00...00
		.	.	.	
		.	.	.	
		.	.	.	
		1	11...10	1	11...11
	-∞	1	11...11	1	00...00
NaN	SNaN	X	11...11	1	0X...XX[2]
	QNaN	X	11...11	1	1X...XX

	BIASED EXPONENT	FRACTION
REAL:	8 BITS	23 BITS
LONG REAL:	11 BITS	52 BITS
EXTENDED REAL:	15 BITS	63 BITS

Notes:

1. Integer is implied for real and long real formats and is not stored.
2. Fraction for SNaN must be non-zero.

Registers

All of the registers in the processor's execution environment, (i.e., global, local, and floating point) can be used for floating-point operations. When using global or local registers, real values (i.e., 32 bits) are contained in one register; long-real values (i.e., 64 bits) are contained in two successive registers; and extended-real values (i.e., 80 bits) are contained in three successive registers.

Figure 12-5 shows how the three forms of the real data type are encoded when stored in global and local registers. Note that long-real values must be aligned on even-numbered register boundaries (e.g., g0, g2, ...). Extended-real values must be aligned on register boundaries that are an integral multiple of four (e.g., g0, g4, ...).

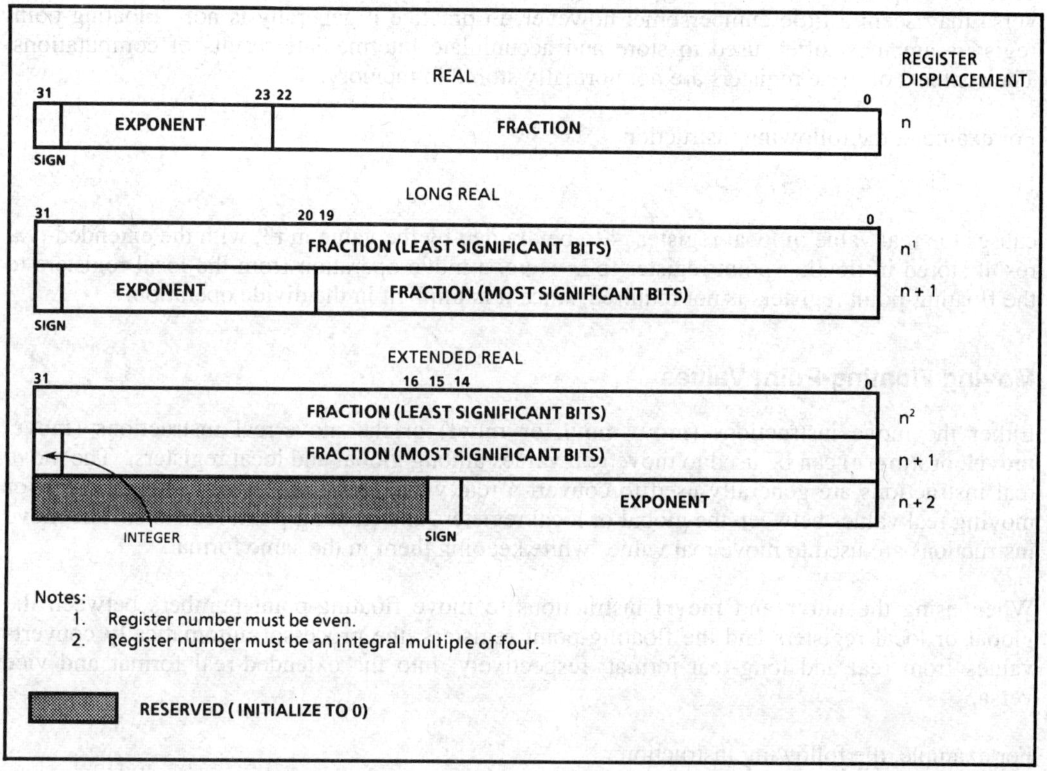

Figure 12-5: Storage of Real Values in Global and Local Registers

Real values in the floating-point registers are always in the extended-real format. When a real or long-real value is moved from global or local registers to a floating-point register, the processor automatically reformats it for the extended-real format.

Loading and Storing Floating-Point Values

Floating-point values are loaded from memory into global or local registers using the load (**ld**), load long (**ldl**), and load triple (**ldt**) instructions. Likewise, floating-point values in global or local registers are stored in memory using the store (**st**), store long (**stl**), and store triple (**stt**) instructions.

Loading a floating-point value into a floating-point register requires two steps (two instructions). First, a floating-point value must be loaded from memory into one or more global or local registers. Then, the value must be moved to the floating-point register using a move real (**movr**), move long-real (**movrl**), or move extended-real (**movre**) instruction.

A similar two-step procedure is required to store a value from a floating-point register into memory. The value must first be moved into one or more global or local registers (using a **movr**, **movrl**, or **movre** instruction), then stored in memory.

This two-step method for moving values from memory into floating-point registers and vice versa may seem a little cumbersome; however, in practice it generally is not. Floating-point registers are most often used to store and accumulate intermediate results of computations. The contents of these registers are not normally stored in memory.

For example, the following instruction

```
divr r3, r4, fp2
```

causes the real value in local register r4 to be divided by the value in r3, with the extended-real result stored in floating-point register fp2. Here, a move operation from the local registers to the floating-point registers is not required, since it is implicit in the divide operation.

Moving Floating-Point Values

Either the move instructions (**mov**, **movl**, or **movt**) or the move-real instructions (**movr**, **movrl**, or **movre**) can be used to move real values among global and local registers. The move real instructions are generally used to convert a real value from one format to another or for moving real values between the global or local registers and floating-point registers. The move instructions are used to move real values while keeping them in the same format.

When using the **movr** and **movrl** instructions to move floating-point numbers between the global or local registers and the floating-point registers, the processor automatically converts values from real and long-real format, respectively, into the extended-real format and vice versa.

For example, the following instruction

```
movr g3, fp1
```

causes a 32-bit, real value in global register g3 to be converted to 80-bit, extended-real format and placed in floating-point register fp1.

Going the opposite direction, the instruction

```
movrl fp0, r4
```

causes an extended-real value in floating-point register fp0 to be converted to 64-bit, long-real format and placed in local registers r4 and r5.

The **movre** instruction moves 80-bit, extended-real values between registers, without format conversion. When this instruction is used to move a value from three global or local registers to a floating-point register, the processor extracts the 80-bit value from the three word extended-real format. When moving a value from a floating-point register to global or local registers, the processor inserts the 80-bit value into the three registers in the three-word format.

Arithmetic Controls

The arithmetic controls are used extensively to control the arithmetic and faulting properties of floating-point operations. Table 12-4 shows the bits in the arithmetic controls that are used in floating-point operations.

Table 12-4: Arithmetic Controls Used in Floating-Point Operations

Arithmetic Control Bits	Function
0 - 2	Condition code
3 - 6	Arithmetic status field
8	Integer overflow flag
12	Integer overflow mask
16	Floating overflow flag
17	Floating underflow flag
18	Floating invalid-operation flag
19	Floating zero-divide flag
20	Floating inexact flag
24	Floating overflow mask
25	Floating underflow mask
26	Floating invalid-operation mask
27	Floating zero-divide mask
28	Floating inexact mask
29	Normalizing mode flag
30 - 31	Rounding control

The condition code flags are used to indicate the results of comparisons of real numbers, just as they are for integers and ordinals.

The arithmetic status field is used to record results from the classify real (**classr** and **classrl**) and remainder real (**remr** and **remrl**) instructions. These instructions are discussed later in this chapter.

The floating-point flags indicate exceptions to floating-point operations. Here, the term exception refers to a potentially undesirable operation (such as dividing a number by zero) or an undesirable result (such as underflow). The flags provide a means of recording the occurrence of specific exceptions.

The floating-point masks provide a method of inhibiting the processor from invoking a fault handler when an exception is detected.

Use of the floating-point flag and mask bits are discussed later in this chapter in the section titled "Exceptions and Fault Handling."

Normalizing Mode

The normalizing-mode flag specifies whether the processor operates in normalizing mode (set) or not (clear).

Normalizing mode is the most common mode of operation. Here, the processor operates on valid floating-point operands, regardless of whether they are normalized or denormalized values.

When the processor is not operating in normalizing mode, it signals a reserved-encoding exception whenever it encounters a denormalized floating-point value as a source operand. In either mode, denormalized numbers are be produced if the underflow exception is masked.

There are no flag or mask bits in the arithmetic controls for this exception. When a reserved-encoding exception is detected, the processor generates a floating reserved-encoding fault and leaves the destination operand unchanged (i.e., no result is stored).

The unnormalized mode of operation is provided to allow unnormalized arithmetic to be simulated with software. Here, a fault handler routine can be used to perform unnormalized arithmetic whenever a reserved-encoding exception is signaled.

Rounding Control

Often the infinitely precise result of an arithmetic operation cannot be encoded exactly in the format of the destination operand. For example, the following value has a 24-bit fraction. The least-significant bit of this fraction (the underlined bit) cannot be encoded exactly in the real (32-bit) format:

$$1.0001\ 0000\ 1000\ 0011\ 1001\ 011\underline{1}E_2\ 101$$

The processor must then round the result to one of the following two values:

$$1.0001\ 0000\ 1000\ 0011\ 1001\ 011E_2\ 101$$

$$1.0001\ 0000\ 1000\ 0011\ 1001\ 100E_2\ 101$$

A rounded result is called an inexact result. When an inexact result is produced, the floating-point inexact flag bit in the arithmetic controls is set.

The processor rounds results according to the destination format (real, long real, or extended real) and the setting of the rounding-mode flags of the arithmetic controls. Four types of rounding are allowed, as described in Table 12-5.

Table 12-5: Rounding Methods

Rounding Mode	Description
Round up (toward +∞)	Rounded result is close to but no less than the infinitely precise result
Round down (toward -∞)	Rounded result is close to but no greater than the infinitely precise result
Round toward zero (Truncate)	Rounded result is close to but no greater in absolute value than the infinitely precise result
Round to nearest (even)	Rounded result is close to the infinitely precise result. If two values are equally close, the result is the even value (i.e., the one with the least-significant bit of zero).

When the infinitely precise result is between the largest positive finite value allowed in a particular format and +∞, the processor rounds the result as shown in Table 12-6.

Table 12-6: Rounding of Positive Numbers

Rounding Mode	Description
Round up (toward +∞)	+∞
Round down (toward -∞)	Maximum, positive finite value
Round toward zero (Truncate)	Maximum, positive finite value
Round to nearest (even)	+∞

When the infinitely precise result is between the largest negative finite value allowed in a particular format and -∞, the processor rounds the result as shown in Table 12-7.

Table 12-7: Rounding of Negative Numbers

Rounding Mode	Description
Round up (toward +∞)	Maximum, negative finite value
Round down (toward -∞)	-∞
Round toward zero (Truncate)	Maximum, negative finite value
Round to nearest (even)	-∞

The rounding modes have no effect on comparison operations, operations that produce exact results, or operations that produce NaN results.

The floating-point instructions allow a result to be stored in a shorter destination than the source operands. For example, the instruction

```
addr fp1, fp2, g5
```

produces a real (32-bit) result from two extended-real (80-bit) source operands. In all such operations, only one rounding error occurs: the error that occurs when rounding the infinitely precise result to the size of the destination format.

Technically, an operation which computes a narrow result from wide operands is in violation of the IEEE standard. However, systems that are designed to conform to the IEEE standard do not need to use this capability of the processor.

INSTRUCTION FORMAT

The instruction format for floating-point instructions is the same as for the other processor instructions. When programming in assembly language, an assembly language statement begins with an instruction mnemonic and is followed by from one to three operands. For example, the multiply-real instruction **mulr** might be used as follows:

```
mulr r8, r9, fp3
```

Here, real operands in local registers r8 and r9 are multiplied together and the result is stored in floating-point register fp3.

From the machine level point of view, all floating-point instructions use the REG format. Refer to Appendix B for details on the REG format instructions.

INSTRUCTION OPERANDS

Operands for floating-point instructions can be either floating-point literals or registers. The processor recognizes two encodings for floating-point literals: +0.0 and +1.0.

All of the registers in the processor's execution environment (global registers g0 through g15, local registers r0 through r15, and floating-point registers fp0 through fp3) can be used as operands in floating-point instructions. (Of course, registers g15, r0, r1, and r2 would generally not be used for storing floating-point numbers, since they are reserved for stack management functions.)

When global or local registers are specified as operands, the instruction mnemonic (or opcode) determines how the values in these registers are interpreted. For example, there are two floating-point divide instructions: divide real (**divr**) and divide long real (**divrl**). When using the **divr** instruction, the processor assumes that global- or local-register operands contain real (32-bit) values. When using the **divrl** instruction, global- or local-register operands are assumed to contain long-real (64-bit) values.

With either instruction, floating-point registers (containing extended-real values) can also be used as operands.

Using floating-point registers as operands allows mixed format or mixed precision arithmetic to be performed with either real and extended-real values or long-real and extended-real values. Mixed-format operations with real and long-real values are not supported.

SUMMARY OF FLOATING-POINT INSTRUCTIONS

The processor's floating-point instructions consist of all instructions for which as least one operand is a real data type.

These instructions can be divided into the following groups:

- Data Movement
- Data Type Conversion
- Basic Arithmetic
- Comparison and Classification
- Trigonometric
- Logarithmic and Exponential

The following sections give a brief overview of the instructions in each group. Detailed descriptions of the operations of these instructions are given in Chapter 11.

Data Movement

As has been described earlier in this chapter, the non-floating-point load and store instructions are used to move real values between registers and memory. Once in registers, the non-floating-point move instructions (**mov**, **movl**, and **movt**) are used to move real values between global and local registers without format conversion; whereas, the floating-point move instructions (**movr**, **movrl**, and **movre**) are used to move real values between global and local registers and floating-point registers.

The copy-sign-real extended (**cpysre**) and copy-reverse-sign real-extended (**cpyrsre**) instructions provide a means of copying the sign of one extended-real value to another, if one of the values is in a floating-point register. This operation is best performed on real and long-real values using the bit instructions **chkbit** and **alterbit**.

Data Type Conversion

Two types of data type conversions are provided: conversion from one floating-point format to another (e.g., real to extended real) and conversion between integer and real.

Conversion between floating-point formats is handled in either of two ways: explicitly by move instructions or implicitly by using the floating-point registers as operands in instructions.

As described earlier in this chapter, the **movr** instruction implicitly converts values from real to extended real, and vice versa, when moving values between global or local registers and floating-point registers. Likewise, the **movrl** instruction implicitly converts values from long real to extended real, and vice versa.

Conversion between real and long-real formats requires the use of both instructions. For example, the following two instructions convert a real value in global register g6 to a long-real value contained in g6 and g7, using a floating-point register for intermediate storage of the value:

```
movr g6, fp1
movrl fp1, g6
```

Implicit format conversion is also provided through the arithmetic, trigonometric, logarithmic, and exponential instructions. For example, the instruction

```
addr r4, r5, fp2
```

adds two real values together and produces an extended-real result.

The following six instructions allow conversion between integers and reals:

cvtir	convert integer to real
cvtilr	convert long integer to long real
cvtri	convert real to integer
cvtril	convert real to long integer
cvtzri	convert truncated real to integer
cvtzril	convert truncated real to long integer

Both the **cvtir** and **cvtilr** instructions can be used to convert an integer to an extended-real value by specifying that the result be placed in a floating-point register.

The convert real-to-integer instructions round off the real value to the nearest integer or long-integer value. For the **cvtri** and **cvtril** instructions, the rounding mode determines the direction the real number is rounded. For the convert truncated real-to-integer instructions (**cvtzri** and **cvtzril**), rounding is always toward zero. The latter two instructions are provided to allow efficient implementation of FORTRAN-like truncation semantics.

Extended-real values can be converted to integers by using a floating-point register as a source operand in either of the convert real-to-integer instructions.

Converting long-real values to integers requires two instructions, as in the following example:

```
movrl g6, fp3
cvtzri fp3, g6
```

The first instruction moves the long-real value to a floating-point register. The second instruction converts the extended-real value to an integer.

Basic Arithmetic

The following instructions perform the basic arithmetic operations specified in the IEEE standard:

addr	add real
addrl	add long real
subr	subtract real
subrl	subtract long real
mulr	multiply real
mulrl	multiply long real
divr	divide real
divrl	divide long real
remr	remainder real
remrl	remainder long real
roundr	round real
roundrl	round long real
sqrtr	square root real
sqrtrl	square root long real

The round instructions round the floating-point operand to its nearest integral (i.e., integer) value, based on the current rounding mode. These instructions perform a function similar to the convert real-to-integer instructions except that the result is in floating-point format.

Comparison, Branching, and Classification

Comparison of floating-point values differs from comparison of integers or ordinals because with floating-point values there are four, rather than the usual three, mutually exclusive relationships: less than, equal to, greater than, and unordered.

The unordered relationship is true when at least one of the two values being compared is a NaN. This additional relationship is required because, by definition, NaNs are not numbers, so they cannot have greater than, equal, or less than relationships with other floating-point values.

The following instructions are provided for comparing floating-point values:

cmpr	compare real
cmprl	compare long real
cmpor	compare ordered real
cmporl	compare ordered long real

All of these instructions set the condition code flags in the arithmetic controls to indicate the results of the comparison. With the compare instructions (**cmpr** and **cmprl**), the condition code flags are set to 000_2 for the unordered condition. With the compare ordered instructions (**cmpor** and **cmporl**), the condition code flags are set to 000_2 and an invalid-operation exception is signaled for the unordered condition.

Two branch instructions (**bo** and **bno**) allow conditional branching to be performed on an ordered or unordered condition, respectively. With these instructions, the processor checks the condition code flags for unordered (000_2) or ordered (111_2) and branches accordingly.

The classify-real instructions (**classr** and **classrl**) provide a means of determining the class of a floating-point value (i.e., zero, denormalized finite, normalized finite, ∞, SNaN, or QNaN). The result of this operation is stored in the arithmetic status field of the arithmetic controls.

Trigonometric

The following instructions provide four common trigonometric functions:

sin	sine real
sinrl	sine long real
cosr	cosine real
cosrl	cosine long real
tanr	tangent real
tanrl	tangent long real
atanr	arctangent real
atanrl	arctangent long real

The arctangent instructions facilitate conversion from rectangular to polar coordinates.

Pi

The processor uses the following value for π in its computations:

$$\pi = 0.f * 2^e$$

where:

f = C90FDAA2 2168C234 C_{16}

e = 2 if significand is 0.f

(The spaces in the fraction above indicate 32-bit boundaries.)

This value has a 66-bit mantissa, which is 2 bits more than is allowed in the significand of an extended-real value. (Since 66 bits is not an even number of hex digits, two additional zeros have been added to the value so that it can be represented in a hexadecimal format. The least-significant hex digit (C_{16}) is thus 1100_2, where the two least significant bits represent bits 67 and 68 of the mantissa.)

If the results of computations that explicitly use π are to be used in the sine, cosine, or tangent instructions, the full 66-bit fraction for π should be used. This insures that the results are consistent with the argument reduction algorithms that these instructions use. Using a rounded version of π can cause inaccuracies in result values, which if propagated through several calculations, might result in meaningless results.

A common method of representing the full 66-bit fraction of π is to separate the value into two numbers. For example, the following two long-real values added together give the value for π shown above with the full 66-bit fraction:

$$\pi = \text{high}\pi + \text{low}\pi$$

where:

$$\text{high}\pi = 400921\text{FB}\ \ 54400000_{16}$$

$$\text{low}\pi = 3\text{DD}0\text{B}461\ \ 1\text{A}600000_{16}$$

Here *highπ* gives the most significant 33 bits of π and *lowπ* gives the least significant 33 bits. Similar versions of π can also be written in the extended-real format.

When using this two-part π value in an algorithm, parallel computations should be performed on each part, with the results kept separate. When all the computations are complete, the two results can be added together to form the final result.

Logarithmic, Exponential, and Scale

The following instructions provide three different logarithmic functions, an exponential function, and a scale function:

logbnr	log binary real
logbnrl	log binary long real
logr	log real
logrl	log long real
logepr	log epsilon real
logeprl	log epsilon long real
expr	exponent real
exprl	exponent long real
scaler	scale real
scalerl	scale long real

These instructions are described in detail in Chapter 11. The following is a brief description of their functions.

The log binary instructions compute the IEEE recommended function *logb (X)*. The result is an integral value that is the binary log of X.

The log instructions compute the function *Y * log (X)*, where the log of X is the base-2 logarithm.

The log epsilon instructions compute the function *Y * log (X + 1)*, where the log of X + 1 is a base-2 logarithm.

The exponent instructions compute the value $2^X - 1$.

The scale instructions perform a multiplication of a floating-point value by a power of 2.

Arithmetic Versus Nonarithmetic Instructions

The floating-point instructions can be divided into two groups: arithmetic and nonarithmetic. Arithmetic instructions are those that are sensitive to real values, meaning that they distinguish among NaN, ∞, normalized finite, denormalized finite, and zero values.

All but five of the floating-point instructions are arithmetic. The five nonarithmetic instructions are move-real extended (**movre**), copy-sign real extended (**cpysre**), copy-reversed-sign real extended (**cpyrsre**), and classify real (**classr** and **classrl**). These nonarithmetic instructions are insensitive to real values and cannot generate floating-point exceptions or faults.

This distinction between arithmetic and nonarithmetic instructions is important because floating-point exceptions and faults can be signaled only during the execution of arithmetic instructions.

OPERATIONS ON NANS

As was described earlier in this chapter, the processor supports two types of NaNs: QNaN and SNaN. An SNaN is any NaN value with its most-significant fraction bit set to 0 and at least one other fraction bit set to 1. (If all the fraction bits are set to 0, the value is an ∞.) A QNaN is any NaN value with the most-significant fraction bit set to 1. The sign bit of a NaN is not interpreted.

In general, when a QNaN is used in one or more arithmetic floating-point instructions, it is allowed to propagate through a computation. An SNaN on the other hand causes a floating invalid-operation exception to be signaled.

The floating invalid-operation exception has a flag and a mask bit associated with it in the arithmetic controls. The mask bit determines how the processor handles an SNaN value. If the floating invalid-operation mask bit is set, the SNaN is converted to a QNaN by setting the most significant fraction bit of the value to a 0. The result is then stored in the destination and the floating invalid-operation flag is set. If the invalid operation mask is clear, a floating invalid-operation fault is signaled and no result is stored in the destination.

When the result is a QNaN, the format of the result is as shown in Table 12-8, depending on the form of the source operands.

Table 12-8: Format of QNaN Results

Source Operands	QNaN Result
Only one operand is NaN, destination is same width	QNaN version of NaN source
Only one operand is NaN, destination is longer	QNaN version of NaN source, with fraction extended with zeros
Only one operand is NaN, destination is shorter	QNaN version of NaN source, with fraction truncated
Both operands are NaNs	QNaN version of source whose fraction field has greatest magnitude, with fraction extended or truncated as described above

In some cases, a QNaN result is returned when none of the source operands are NaNs. Here, a standard QNaN is returned. The significand for the standard QNaN is as follows:

1.1000...00

(For real and long-real destinations, the integer bit will be an implied 1.)

Other than the rules specified above, software is free to use the other bits of a NaN for any purpose.

EXCEPTIONS AND FAULT HANDLING

Occasionally, a floating-point instruction can result in an exception being signaled. The processor recognizes six floating-point exceptions:

- Floating Reserved Encoding
- Floating Invalid Operation
- Floating Zero Divide
- Floating Overflow
- Floating Underflow
- Floating Inexact

These exceptions can be divided into two categories:

1. Situations in which one or more source operands are inappropriate for an operation and would cause an exception to be signaled.
2. Situations in which the result of an operation is exceptional.

The reserved encoding, invalid operation, and division-by-zero exceptions fall in the first category; the overflow, underflow, and inexact exceptions fall in the second category.

Except for the floating reserved-encoding exception, each of these exceptions has a flag and a mask bit associated with it in the arithmetic controls. When an exception condition occurs, the processor performs one of the following operations:

- If the mask bit for the exception is set, the flag for the exception is set and instruction execution continues, substituting a default value in place of the result.
- If the mask bit for the exception is clear, the flag for the exception is not set and a floating-point arithmetic fault is raised. The processor then stores diagnostic information in the fault information area and diverts instruction execution to a fault handler.

Since the floating reserved-encoding exception does not have a flag or mask bit, it always results in a fault.

Note

The floating-point exception flags are "sticky," which means that the processor does not implicitly clear them while carrying out floating-point operations. They may be cleared by software.

Fault Handler

As is described in Chapter 9, when a floating-point fault is signaled, the processor calls a single fault handler. This fault handler determines how to handle the specific fault subtype by interpreting the floating-point exception flags and the information in the fault record.

Floating Reserved-Encoding Exception

A reserved encoding exception occurs as a result of either of the following two conditions:

- When a reserved encoding is used as an operand in a floating-point instruction, or
- When a denormalized value is used as an operand in a floating-point instruction and the normalizing-mode bit in the arithmetic controls is clear.

The first condition is rare. It can only occur if a program presents an extended-real value to the processor that has a zero j-bit (integer part) and a non-zero biased exponent.

The second condition was discussed earlier in this chapter in the section titled "Normalizing Mode." This condition is also rare, since the vast majority of programs run with the normalizing mode enabled.

There is neither a flag nor a mask bit for this exception. When a reserved-encoding exception occurs, the processor raises a floating reserved-encoding fault and does not store a result.

Floating Invalid-Operation Exception

The invalid-operation exception indicates that one of the source operands is inappropriate for the type of operation being performed. The following conditions cause this exception to be signaled:

- Any arithmetic operation on an SNaN
- Addition of infinities of unlike sign
- Subtraction of infinities of like sign
- Multiplication of zero by ∞
- Division of zero by zero or ∞ by ∞
- Remainder of x by y, if y is zero or x is ∞
- Square root of a negative, nonzero value
- Conversion of a NaN from floating-point format to integer format
- Sine, cosine, or tangent of ∞
- y * log (x), if:
  - x is negative and nonzero,
  - y is zero and x is ∞,
  - y and x are zero, or
  - y is ∞ and x is 1
- Log epsilon of (y, x), if y is ∞ and x is 0
- Compare ordered, if a source operand is a NaN

When a floating invalid-operation exception occurs and its mask is set, the following occurs:

- When the result is a floating-point value, the standard QNaN value is stored in the destination and the floating invalid-operation flag is set. (A discussion of how the processor handles NaNs was provided earlier in this chapter in the section titled "Operations on NaNs.")
- When the result is an integer, the maximum negative integer is stored in the destination and the floating invalid-operation flag is set.

When the mask is clear, no result is stored; the floating invalid-operation flag is not set; and the floating invalid-operation fault is signaled.

Floating Zero-Divide Exception

The floating zero-divide exception is signaled when an exact non-finite result would be produced from finite operands. (Note that a different exception, overflow, is signaled when an infinite result is produced inexactly from finite operands.) The most common example of this exception is a division operation, where the divisor is zero and the dividend is a nonzero, finite value.

When the floating zero-divide mask is set: a correctly signed ∞ is stored in the destination and the floating zero-divide flag is set. When the mask is clear, no result is stored; the floating zero-divide flag is not set; and a floating zero-divide fault is signaled.

Floating Overflow Exception

The overflow exception occurs when the infinitely precise result of a floating-point instruction exceeds the largest allowable finite value for the specified destination format. For example, if the destination format is real (32 bits), overflow occurs when the infinitely precise result falls outside the range $-1.0 * 2^{126}$ to $1.0 * 2^{126}$ (exclusive), where 126 is the unbiased exponent of the result.

When the floating overflow mask is set, a rounded result is stored in the destination and the floating overflow flag is set. The current rounding mode determines the method used to round the result.

When the mask is clear: no result is stored in the destination and the floating overflow flag is not set. Instead, the processor stores the result in extended-real format in the fault information area. The fraction of the extended-real value is rounded to the instruction's destination precision. For example, if the destination operand's format is real (32 bits), the extended-real fraction is rounded to 23 bits, with the 40 least-significant bits filled with zeros.

If the exponent exceeds the range of the extended-real format (16383 unbiased), then the exponent is divided by 2^{24576} and a flag (bit 1 of the fault flags byte or override flags byte) is set in the fault information area to indicate that the exponent has been bias adjusted. After this fault information is stored, a floating overflow fault is signaled.

When using the scale instructions (**scaler** or **scalerl**), massive overflow can occur, where the infinitely precise result is too large to be represented, even with a bias adjusted exponent. Here, a properly signed ∞ is stored in the fault record.

The floating overflow exception cannot occur on a conversion from floating-point format to integer format (although an integer overflow exception can occur).

Floating Underflow Exception

An underflow condition occurs when the infinitely precise result of a floating-point instruction is less than the smallest possible normalized, finite value for the specified destination format. For example, for the real (32-bit) format, underflow occurs when an infinitely precise result falls in the range $-1.0 * 2^{-126}$ to $1.0 * 2^{-126}$ (exclusive), where -126 is the unbiased exponent.

When a floating underflow condition occurs, the setting of the floating underflow mask determines how the processor handles the condition.

If the mask is set when an underflow condition occurs, the processor goes ahead and denormalizes the result. Then if the result is exact, it is stored in the destination and the floating underflow exception is not signaled, nor is the floating underflow flag set. If, on the other hand, the denormalized result is inexact, the floating underflow flag is set and the processor goes on to handle the inexact condition as described in the next section.

If the floating underflow mask is clear when an underflow-condition occurs, no result is stored in the destination and the floating underflow flag is not set. Instead, the processor stores the result in extended-real format in the fault information area, with the fraction of the extended-real value rounded to the instruction's destination precision. For example, if the destination precision is real (23-bit fraction) the 40 least-significant bits of the fraction are set to 0.

If the exponent of the value stored is less than the minimum allowable value in the extended-real format (-16,382 unbiased), then the exponent is multiplied by 2^{24576} and a flag (bit 1 of the fault or override flags byte) is set in the fault information area to indicate that the exponent has been bias adjusted. After this information is stored, a floating underflow fault is signaled.

The scale instructions can cause massive underflow to occur, where the infinitely precise result is too small to be represented, even with a bias adjusted exponent. Here, a properly signed zero is stored in the fault record.

Refer to the section later in this chapter titled "Floating-Point Underflow Condition" for more information on the interaction of the floating underflow and inexact exceptions.

Floating Inexact Exception

The floating inexact exception occurs when an infinitely precise result cannot be encoded in the format specified for the destination operand. Either of the following two conditions can cause an inexact exception to be signaled:

- When a result is rounded and the result is not exact
- When overflow occurs and the floating overflow mask is set

If the floating inexact mask is set when an inexact condition occurs and an unmasked overflow or underflow condition does not occur, the rounded result is stored in the destination and the floating-point inexact flag is set. The current rounding mode determines the method used to round the result.

If the floating inexact mask is clear when an inexact condition occurs, the floating inexact flag is not set and one of the following operations is carried out:

- If only the inexact condition has occurred, the processor stores the rounded result in the specified destination, then raises a floating-inexact fault.
- If the inexact condition occurs along with overflow or underflow, no result is stored in the destination. Instead, the processor stores the result in extended-real format in the fault information area, as described for the floating overflow and underflow exceptions, then raises a floating inexact fault.

Refer to the following section for more information on the interaction of the floating underflow and inexact exceptions.

Floating-Point Underflow Condition

Two aspects of underflow are important in numeric processings: the "tininess" of a number and "loss of accuracy." A result is tiny when it is nonzero and its exponent is between $\pm 2^{Emin}$, where E_{min} is the smallest unbiased exponent allowed in the destination format. For example, if the destination format is long-real (64-bit format), a result is tiny if it is nonzero and in the range of $+1 * 2^{-1022}$ to $-1 * 2^{-1022}$. The ability to detect a tiny result is important because such a result may cause an exception to be signaled in a later operation (e.g., overflow on a division).

Loss of accuracy occurs when a tiny result is approximated as part of the denormalization process so that it will fit into the destination format.

In the 80960KB processor, tininess is detected after rounding as an underflow condition. Loss of accuracy is detected as an inexact condition.

The algorithm in Figure 12-6 shows how the processor responds to these two conditions, when a floating-point operation produces a tiny result.

An important point to note in this algorithm is that if the underflow mask is set, an underflow exception is signaled only if the denormalized result is inexact. If the denormalized number is exact, no flags are set and no faults are signaled.

```
generate infinitely precise result  # exponent and significand;
if exponent < underflow threshold
   then
      if underflow fault mask clear
         then
            goto underflow fault handler;
            exit algorithm;
         else generate denormalized number
            if denormalized significand equals infinitely precise significand
               then
                  store denormalized result in destination;
                  # no underflow is signaled;
               else
                  set underflow flag in AC;
                  if inexact fault mask is clear
                     then
                        goto inexact fault handler;
                        exit algorithm;
                     else
                        set inexact flag in AC;
                        store denormalized result in destination;
                  end if;
            end if;
      end if;
   else
      if infinitely precise result is inexact
         then
            if inexact fault mask is clear
               then
                  goto inexact fault handler;
                  exit algorithm;
               else
                  set inexact flag in AC;
                  store normalized result in destination;
            end if;
         else
            store normalized result in destination;
      end if;
end if;
exit algorithm
```

Figure 12-6: Interaction of Floating Underflow and Inexact Exceptions

Interagent Communication 13

CHAPTER 13
INTERAGENT COMMUNICATION

This chapter describes the interagent communication (IAC) mechanism of the 80960KB processor. Included is a description of the IAC message structure, the IAC message sending and receiving mechanism, and reference information on the available IAC messages.

Note

The 80960KB processor's interagent communication mechanism is an extension to the 80960 architecture and may not be supported in other processors based on this architecture.

INTRODUCTION TO IAC MESSAGES

The IAC facilities provide a mechanism for agents connected to the processor's bus to communicate with the processor by means of messages. The agents that use these facilities may be other 80960KB processors, I/O processors, or special purpose hardware. Programs running on the 80960KB processor can also use this message-passing mechanism to send messages internally to the processor.

The primary function of these facilities is to provide an alternative to the interrupt mechanism for external hardware to communicate with the processor. Also, certain processor functions like reinitialization, purging the instruction cache, and setting breakpoint registers can only be carried out with this mechanism.

IAC messages (referred to here as IACs) are four words in length and are exchanged by means of message buffers that are mapped to memory. All the usable IACs are predefined. The processor handles an IAC in much the same way as it handles an instruction.

The processor provides two mechanisms for exchanging IACs: external and internal. The external IAC mechanism is used to pass IACs between two agents on the processor's bus. A processor uses the internal IAC mechanism to pass an IAC to itself.

IAC MESSAGE FORMAT

Figure 13-1 shows the format for an IAC message. Each message consists of a message-type field and up to five parameter fields.

The message type is an 8-bit binary code. Each IAC has a unique message type.

The parameters can be 8, 16, or 32-bits in length, depending on the specified field. Many of the IACs do not require parameters. When a message type does require one or more parameters, the processor only looks at the required parameter fields. Those fields not used are ignored.

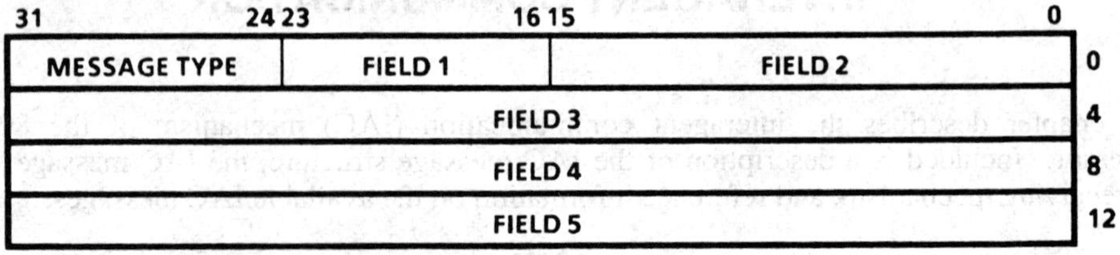

Figure 13-1: IAC Message Format

SOFTWARE REQUIREMENTS FOR HANDLING IACS

No special software, such as dedicated data structures or stacks, are required to handle IACs. An IAC is sent with a quad synchronous move instruction (**synmovq**). When the processor receives an IAC, it handles it independently from the program execution environment. It does not use the instruction execution unit, the registers (global or local), the stack, or memory. Thus, the state of the processor when the IAC is received does not need to be saved.

Some IACs, such as the purge instruction cache IAC, do not affect the processor's state. The processor treats these IACs as if they were an instruction inserted in the control flow of the process. When the IAC action is complete, the processor resumes work on the program it is currently running.

Other IACs, such as the reinitialize processor IAC, cause the state of the processor or the control of the currently running program to be permanently changed. In these instances, the processor resumes activity in its new processor state, following the execution of the IAC.

All IACs are assumed to have a priority of 31, so the processor executes the action requested in the IAC message immediately, even if the processor's current priority is 31. While the processor is handling an IAC, it will not respond to interrupts signaled on the interrupt pins.

INTERNAL IACS

Internal IACs are used for functions such as setting breakpoint registers, purging the instruction cache, or sending software initiated interrupts.

To send an internal IAC, software must perform the following steps:

1. Load the message into four consecutive words in memory, with the first word aligned on a word boundary.
2. Execute a **synmovq** instruction to move the message from its source address to destination address $FF000010_{16}$.

When the destination operand of a **synmovq** instruction is $FF000010_{16}$, the processor interprets the instruction as a send internal-IAC instruction. The processor then receives the IAC by moving the message from memory into an internal message buffer.

The action of the **synmovq** move instruction insures that the loading of the message into the processor is completed before the processor is allowed to perform any other chores.

Note

The address range of $FF000000_{16}$ through $FFFFFFFF_{16}$ is reserved for interrupt handling and IAC message passing.

EXTERNAL IACS

External IACs are used by agents external to the processor to initiate processor actions such as testing for pending interrupts or freezing the processor. External IACs can be sent between two 80960KB processors that are connected to the same bus or by external logic that duplicates the external IAC sending mechanism. The following sections describe how one processor sends an IAC to another processor. The *80960KB Hardware Designer's Reference Manual* describes the requirements that external logic must meet to perform these same functions.

Sending External IACs

Sending an external IAC message is similar to sending an internal IAC message, except that the address of the receiving agent is specified in a slightly different way. Figure 13-2 shows the required encoding of the address for the receiving agent.

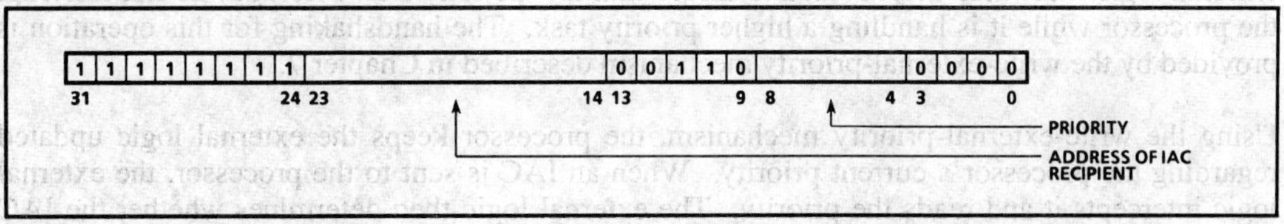

Figure 13-2: Encoding of Address for Processor Receiving an IAC

At initialization each agent on the bus is assigned a unique address in the range of $FF000C00_{16}$ to $FFFFCC00_{16}$. To send an IAC to an agent, the sending agent sends the message to the address assigned to the receiving agent. As shown in Figure 13-2, only bits 14 through 23 of this address are interpreted to determine the address of the receiving agent. Bits 4 through 8 of this address are used to encode the priority of the message.

For example, to send a priority 25_{10} IAC to the agent at address 0000000001_2, the message address would be $FF004D90_{16}$.

To send an external IAC from one 80960KB processor to another, software must perform the following steps:

1. Load the message into four consecutive words in memory, with the first word aligned on a word boundary.

2. Execute a **synmovq** instruction to move the message from its source address to the address of the receiving agent (encoded in the form shown in Figure 13-2).
3. Check the condition code in the arithmetic controls to determine if the message was received (010_2) or rejected (000_2).

The action of the **synmovq** move instruction insures that the sending processor does not execute any other instructions until the **synmovq** instruction is complete. It also sets the condition code bits to indicate whether or not the move was successful. A successful move is interpreted as the IAC being received by the processor.

Receiving and Handling an External IACs

A processor receives and handles an external IAC in somewhat the same manner as it receives and handles an interrupt. To configure a processor to receive external IACs, vector INT0 of the interrupt-control register (shown in Figure 8-3) is set to 0. The INT0 pin on the processor chip then becomes the $\overline{\text{IAC}}$ pin. (Refer to the section in Chapter 8 titled "Interrupts From Interrupt Pins" for further discussion of the interrupt pins and interrupt-control register.)

When the processor receives a signal on the $\overline{\text{IAC}}$ pin, it handles it initially as if it were receiving an interrupt. It reads the vector number associated with this pin (bits 0 through 7 of the interrupt-control register). If it is zero, the processor recognizes that it is receiving an external IAC. It then reads the four-word IAC message from the bus and performs the requested IAC.

The processor acts immediately on any IAC that it receives. For efficient system operation, external logic must thus be provided to insure that low priority IAC messages do not interrupt the processor while it is handling a higher priority task. The handshaking for this operation is provided by the write-external-priority mechanism described in Chapter 7.

Using the write-external-priority mechanism, the processor keeps the external logic updated regarding the processor's current priority. When an IAC is sent to the processor, the external logic intercepts it and reads the priority. The external logic then determines whether the IAC priority is above that of the processor or not. If the IAC has a higher priority, the external logic sends an acknowledge signal to the sending processor, then signals the receiving processor by asserting the IAC pin. If the IAC has an equal or lower priority, the external logic sends a non-acknowledge signal to the sending processor.

The sending processor uses the acknowledge or non-acknowledge signals to set the condition codes to complete the **synmovq** instruction.

While the processor is servicing an IAC, it performs some handshaking with the external logic so that the logic knows when the processor has finished work on an IAC. The external logic is then able to reject any IAC that it receives while the processor is servicing another IAC.

Refer to the *80960KB Hardware Designer's Reference Manual* for further information on the requirements for handling IAC messages.

SUMMARY OF IAC MESSAGES

Table 13-1 gives a list of the IAC messages that the processor can send either internally or externally. The following section provides detailed reference information on these messages.

Table 13-1: IAC Messages

Interrupt Handling	Processor Management
Interrupt	Purge Instruction Cache
Test Pending Interrupt	Set Breakpoint Register
	Store System Base
	Freeze
	Continue Initialization
	Reinitialize Processor

IAC MESSAGE REFERENCE

The following section provides detailed descriptions of the operations carried out for each of the IACs. This section is organized alphabetically by IAC title for easy reference.

Continue Initialization

Message Type: 92_{16}

Function: Carries out the initialization procedure that follows the processor self test. The processor executes the initialization procedure beginning with reading the initial memory image from ROM. The self test is not performed.

Refer to the section in Chapter 7 titled "Processor Initialization" for further details on the initialization process.

Freeze

Message Type: 91_{16}

Function: Stops the processor. The processor puts itself in the stopped state.

Interrupt

Message Type:	40_{16}	
Parameters:	Field 1	Interrupt vector
	Fields 2 - 5	Not Used

Function:

Generates an interrupt request. The interrupt vector is given in field 1 of the IAC message. The processor handles the interrupt request just as it does interrupts received from other sources. If the interrupt priority is higher than the processor's current priority, the processor services the interrupt request immediately. Otherwise, it posts the interrupt in the pending interrupts section of the interrupt table.

Refer to Chapter 8 for further information on the servicing of interrupt IACs.

Purge Instruction Cache

Message Type: 89_{16}

Function: Invalidates all entries in the processor's internal instruction cache.

Reinitialize Processor

Message Type:	93_{16}	
Parameters:	Fields 1 - 2	Not Used
	Field-3	Address of System Address Table
	Field-4	Address of Processor Control Block
	Field 5	Start Instruction IP

Function: Reestablishes the processor state. In reinitializing itself, the processor first locates the system address table and the processor control block in the IMI from the addresses given in fields 3 and 4.

The processor then begins executing the instruction list beginning with the IP given in field 5.

Set Breakpoint Register

Message Type:	$8F_{16}$	
Parameters:	Fields 1 - 2	Not Used
	Field 3	Breakpoint IP
	Field 4	Breakpoint IP
	Field 5	Not Used

Function: Enables or disables two breakpoints. When the processor receives this IAC, it conditionally loads the parameters from fields 3 and 4 into breakpoint registers 0 and 1, respectively. Field 3 provides a breakpoint IP for breakpoint register 0, and field 4 provides a breakpoint IP for breakpoint register 1. Bit 1 in each of these fields is a breakpoint disable flag.

If the disable flag in one of these fields is set, the breakpoint for the corresponding breakpoint register is disabled. Otherwise, the IP value in the field is loaded into the corresponding breakpoint register and the breakpoint is enabled.

Breakpoints are described in the section in Chapter 10 titled "Breakpoint-Trace Mode."

Store System Base

Message Type:	80_{16}	
Parameters:	Fields 1 - 2	Not Used
	Field 3	Destination Address
	Fields 4 - 5	Not Used

Function: Stores the current locations of the system address table and the PRCB in a specified location in memory. The address of the system address table is stored in the word starting at the byte specified in field 3, and the address of the PRCB is stored in the next word in memory (field 3 address plus 4).

Test Pending Interrupts

Message Type: 41_{16}

Function: Tests for pending interrupts. The processor checks the pending interrupt section of the interrupt table for a pending interrupt with a priority higher than the processor's current priority. If a higher priority interrupt is found, it is serviced immediately. Otherwise, no action is taken.

Appendix A
Instruction and Data Structure Quick Reference

APPENDIX A
INSTRUCTION AND DATA STRUCTURE QUICK REFERENCE

This appendix provides quick reference for the 80960KB instructions and data structures.

INSTRUCTION QUICK REFERENCE

This section provides two lists of 80960KB instructions: one sorted by assembly-language mnemonic and another sorted by machine-level opcode. In these lists, each entry includes the assembly-language mnemonic for an instruction; the operands (given in the required order); the machine-level opcode and instruction type (i.e., REG, MEM, COBR, CTRL); and the page number in Chapter 11 where the detailed description of the instruction is given.

Instruction List by Assembler Mnemonic

Mnemonic	Operands			Opcode	Inst. Type	Page
addc	*src1*,	*src2*,	*dst*	5B0	REG	11-6
addi	*src1*,	*src2*,	*dst*	591	REG	11-7
addo	*src1*,	*src2*,	*dst*	590	REG	11-7
addr	*src1*,	*src2*,	*dst*	78F	REG	11-8
addrl	*src1*,	*src2*,	*dst*	79F	REG	11-8
alterbit	*bitpos*,	*src*,	*dst*	58F	REG	11-10
and	*src1*,	*src2*,	*dst*	581	REG	11-11
andnot	*src1*,	*src2*,	*dst*	582	REG	11-11
atadd	*src/dst*,	*src*,	*dst*	612	REG	11-12
atanr	*src1*,	*src2*,	*dst*	680	REG	11-13
atanrl	*src1*,	*src2*,	*dst*	690	REG	11-13
atmod	*src*,	*mask*,	*src/dst*	610	REG	11-15
b	*targ*			08	CTRL	11-18
bal	*targ*			0B	CTRL	11-16
balx	*targ*,	*dst*		85	MEM	11-16
bbc	*bitpos*,	*src*,	*targ*	30	COBR	11-20
bbs	*bitpos*,	*src*,	*targ*	37	COBR	11-20
be	*targ*			12	CTRL	11-22
bg	*targ*			11	CTRL	11-22
bge	*targ*			13	CTRL	11-22
bl	*targ*			14	CTRL	11-22
ble	*targ*			16	CTRL	11-22
bne	*targ*			15	CTRL	11-22
bno	*targ*			10	CTRL	11-22
bo	*targ*			11	CTRL	11-22
bx	*targ*			84	MEM	11-18
call	*targ*			09	CTRL	11-25
calls	*targ*			660	REG	11-27
callx	*targ*			86	MEM	11-29
chkbit	*bitpos*,	*src*		5AE	REG	11-31
classr	*src*			68F	REG	11-32
classrl	*src*			69F	REG	11-32
clrbit	*bitpos*,	*src*,	*dst*	58C	REG	11-34
cmpdeci	*src1*,	*src2*,	*dst*	5A7	REG	11-36
cmpdeco	*src1*,	*src2*,	*dst*	5A6	REG	11-36
cmpi	*src1*,	*src2*		5A1	REG	11-35
cmpibe	*src1*,	*src2*,	*targ*	3A	COBR	11-42
cmpibg	*src1*,	*src2*,	*targ*	39	COBR	11-42
cmpibge	*src1*,	*src2*,	*targ*	3B	COBR	11-42
cmpibl	*src1*,	*src2*,	*targ*	3C	COBR	11-42
cmpible	*src1*,	*src2*,	*targ*	3E	COBR	11-42
cmpibne	*src1*,	*src2*,	*targ*	3D	COBR	11-42
cmpibno	*src1*,	*src2*,	*targ*	38	COBR	11-42
cmpibo	*src1*,	*src2*,	*targ*	3F	COBR	11-42

Mnemonic	Operands			Opcode	Inst. Type	Page
cmpinci	*src1*,	*src2*,	*dst*	5A5	REG	11-37
cmpinco	*src1*,	*src2*,	*dst*	5A4	REG	11-37
cmpo	*src1*,	*src2*		5A0	REG	11-35
cmpobe	*src1*,	*src2*,	*targ*	32	COBR	11-42
cmpobg	*src1*,	*src2*,	*targ*	31	COBR	11-42
cmpobge	*src1*,	*src2*,	*targ*	33	COBR	11-42
cmpobl	*src1*,	*src2*,	*targ*	34	COBR	11-42
cmpoble	*src1*,	*src2*,	*targ*	36	COBR	11-42
cmpobne	*src1*,	*src2*,	*targ*	35	COBR	11-42
cmpor	*src1*,	*src2*		684	REG	11-38
cmporl	*src1*,	*src2*		694	REG	11-38
cmpr	*src1*,	*src2*		685	REG	11-40
cmprl	*src1*,	*src2*		695	REG	11-40
concmpi	*src1*,	*src2*		5A3	REG	11-45
concmpo	*src1*,	*src2*		5A2	REG	11-45
cosr	*src*,	*dst*		68D	REG	11-46
cosrl	*src*,	*dst*		69D	REG	11-46
cpyrsre	*src1*,	*src2*,	*dst*	6E3	REG	11-48
cpysre	*src1*,	*src2*,	*dst*	6E2	REG	11-48
cvtilr	*src*,	*dst*		675	REG	11-49
cvtir	*src*,	*dst*		674	REG	11-49
cvtri	*src*,	*dst*		6C0	REG	11-50
cvtril	*src*,	*dst*		6C1	REG	11-50
cvtzri	*src*,	*dst*		6C2	REG	11-50
cvtzril	*src*,	*dst*		6C3	REG	11-50
daddc	*src1*,	*src2*,	*dst*	642	REG	11-52
divi	*src1*,	*src2*,	*dst*	74B	REG	11-53
divo	*src1*,	*src2*,	*dst*	70B	REG	11-53
divr	*src1*,	*src2*,	*dst*	78B	REG	11-54
divrl	*src1*,	*src2*,	*dst*	79B	REG	11-54
dmovt	*src*,	*dst*		644	REG	11-56
dsubc	*src1*,	*src2*,	*dst*	643	REG	11-57
ediv	*src1*,	*src2*,	*dst*	671	REG	11-58
emul	*src1*,	*src2*,	*dst*	670	REG	11-59
expr	*src*,	*dst*		689	REG	11-60
exprl	*src*,	*dst*		699	REG	11-60
extract	*bitpos*,	*len*,	*src/dst*	651	REG	11-62
faulte				1A	CTRL	11-63
faultg				19	CTRL	11-63
faultge				1B	CTRL	11-63
faultl				1C	CTRL	11-63
faultle				1E	CTRL	11-63
faultne				1D	CTRL	11-63
faultno				18	CTRL	11-63
faulto				1F	CTRL	11-63
flushreg				66D	REG	11-65
fmark				66C	REG	11-66

Mnemonic	Operands			Opcode	Inst. Type	Page
ld	*src,*	*dst*		90	MEM	11-67
lda	*src*	*dst*		8C	MEM	11-69
ldib	*src,*	*dst*		C0	MEM	11-67
ldis	*src,*	*dst*		C8	MEM	11-67
ldl	*src,*	*dst*		98	MEM	11-67
ldob	*src,*	*dst*		80	MEM	11-67
ldos	*src,*	*dst*		88	MEM	11-67
ldq	*src,*	*dst*		B0	MEM	11-67
ldt	*src,*	*dst*		A0	MEM	11-67
logbnr	*src,*	*dst*		68A	REG	11-70
logbnrl	*src,*	*dst*		69A	REG	11-70
logepr	*src1,*	*src2,*	*dst*	681	REG	11-72
logeprl	*src1,*	*src2,*	*dst*	691	REG	11-72
logr	*src1,*	*src2,*	*dst*	682	REG	11-75
logrl	*src1,*	*src2,*	*dst*	692	REG	11-75
mark				66B	REG	11-78
modac	*mask,*	*src,*	*dst*	645	REG	11-79
modi	*src1,*	*src2,*	*dst*	749	REG	11-80
modify	*mask,*	*src,*	*src/dst*	650	REG	11-81
modpc	*src*	*mask,*	*src/dst*	655	REG	11-82
modtc	*mask,*	*src,*	*dst*	654	REG	11-84
mov	*src,*	*dst*		5CC	REG	11-85
movl	*src,*	*dst*		5DC	REG	11-85
movq	*src,*	*dst*		5FC	REG	11-85
movr	*src,*	*dst*		6C9	REG	11-86
movre	*src,*	*dst*		6E9	REG	11-86
movrl	*src,*	*dst*		6D9	REG	11-86
movt	*src,*	*dst*		5EC	REG	11-85
muli	*src1,*	*src2,*	*dst*	741	REG	11-88
mulo	*src1,*	*src2,*	*dst*	701	REG	11-88
mulr	*src1,*	*src2,*	*dst*	78C	REG	11-89
mulrl	*src1,*	*src2,*	*dst*	79C	REG	11-89
nand	*src1,*	*src2,*	*dst*	58E	REG	11-91
nor	*src1,*	*src2,*	*dst*	588	REG	11-92
not	*src,*	*dst*		58A	REG	11-93
notand	*src,*	*dst*		584	REG	11-93
notbit	*bitpos,*	*src,*	*dst*	580	REG	11-94
notor	*src1,*	*src2,*	*dst*	58D	REG	11-95
or	*src1,*	*src2,*	*dst*	587	REG	11-96
ornot	*src1,*	*src2,*	*dst*	58B	REG	11-96
remi	*src1,*	*src2,*	*dst*	748	REG	11-97
remo	*src1,*	*src2,*	*dst*	708	REG	11-97
remr	*src1,*	*src2,*	*dst*	683	REG	11-98
remrl	*src1,*	*src2,*	*dst*	693	REG	11-98
ret				0A	CTRL	11-101
rotate	*len,*	*src,*	*dst*	59D	REG	11-103
roundr	*src,*	*dst*		68B	REG	11-104

Mnemonic	Operands			Opcode	Inst. Type	Page
roundrl	*src,*	*dst*		69B	REG	11-104
scaler	*src1,*	*src2,*	*dst*	677	REG	11-105
scalerl	*src1,*	*src2,*	*dst*	676	REG	11-105
scanbit	*src,*	*dst*		641	REG	11-107
scanbyte	*src1,*	*src2*		5AC	REG	11-108
setbit	*bitpos,*	*src,*	*dst*	583	REG	11-109
shli	*len,*	*src,*	*dst*	59E	REG	11-110
shlo	*len,*	*src,*	*dst*	59C	REG	11-110
shrdi	*len,*	*src,*	*dst*	59A	REG	11-110
shri	*len,*	*src,*	*dst*	59B	REG	11-110
shro	*len,*	*src,*	*dst*	598	REG	11-110
sinr	*src,*	*dst*		68C	REG	11-112
sinrl	*src,*	*dst*		69C	REG	11-112
spanbit	*src,*	*dst*		640	REG	11-114
sqrtr	*src,*	*dst*		688	REG	11-115
sqrtrl	*src,*	*dst*		698	REG	11-115
st	*src,*	*dst*		92	MEM	11-117
stib	*src,*	*dst*		C2	MEM	11-117
stis	*src,*	*dst*		CA	MEM	11-117
stl	*src,*	*dst*		9A	MEM	11-117
stob	*src,*	*dst*		82	MEM	11-117
stos	*src,*	*dst*		8A	MEM	11-117
stq	*src,*	*dst*		B2	MEM	11-117
stt	*src,*	*dst*		A2	MEM	11-117
subc	*src1,*	*src2,*	*dst*	5B2	REG	11-119
subi	*src1,*	*src2,*	*dst*	593	REG	11-120
subo	*src1,*	*src2,*	*dst*	592	REG	11-120
subr	*src1,*	*src2,*	*dst*	78D	REG	11-121
subrl	*src1,*	*src2,*	*dst*	79D	REG	11-121
syncf				66F	REG	11-123
synld	*src,*	*dst*		615	REG	11-124
synmov	*dst,*	*src*		600	REG	11-126
synmovl	*dst,*	*src*		601	REG	11-126
synmovq	*dst,*	*src*		602	REG	11-126
tanr	*src,*	*dst*		68E	REG	11-129
tanrl	*src,*	*dst*		69E	REG	11-129
teste	*dst*			22	COBR	11-131
testg	*dst*			21	COBR	11-131
testge	*dst*			23	COBR	11-131
testl	*dst*			24	COBR	11-131
testle	*dst*			26	COBR	11-131
testne	*dst*			25	COBR	11-131
testno	*dst*			20	COBR	11-131
testo	*dst*			27	COBR	11-131
xnor	*src1,*	*src2,*	*dst*	589	REG	11-133
xor	*src1,*	*src2,*	*dst*	586	REG	11-133

Instruction List by Opcode

Opcode	Inst. Type	Mnemonic	Operands			Page
08	CTRL	**b**	*targ*			11-18
09	CTRL	**call**	*targ*			11-25
0A	CTRL	**ret**				11-101
0B	CTRL	**bal**	*targ*			11-16
10	CTRL	**bno**	*targ*			11-22
11	CTRL	**bg**	*targ*			11-22
12	CTRL	**be**	*targ*			11-22
13	CTRL	**bge**	*targ*			11-22
14	CTRL	**bl**	*targ*			11-22
15	CTRL	**bne**	*targ*			11-22
16	CTRL	**ble**	*targ*			11-22
17	CTRL	**bo**	*targ*			11-22
18	CTRL	**faultno**				11-63
19	CTRL	**faultg**				11-63
1A	CTRL	**faulte**				11-63
1B	CTRL	**faultge**				11-63
1C	CTRL	**faultl**				11-63
1D	CTRL	**faultne**				11-63
1E	CTRL	**faultle**				11-63
1F	CTRL	**faulto**				11-63
20	COBR	**testno**	*dst*			11-131
21	COBR	**testg**	*dst*			11-131
22	COBR	**teste**	*dst*			11-131
23	COBR	**testge**	*dst*			11-131
24	COBR	**testl**	*dst*			11-131
25	COBR	**testne**	*dst*			11-131
26	COBR	**testle**	*dst*			11-131
27	COBR	**testo**	*dst*			11-131
30	COBR	**bbc**	*bitpos,*	*src,*	*targ*	11-20
31	COBR	**cmpobg**	*src1,*	*src2,*	*targ*	11-18
32	COBR	**cmpobe**	*src1,*	*src2,*	*targ*	11-42
33	COBR	**cmpobge**	*src1,*	*src2,*	*targ*	11-42
34	COBR	**cmpobl**	*src1,*	*src2,*	*targ*	11-42
35	COBR	**cmpobne**	*src1,*	*src2,*	*targ*	11-42
36	COBR	**cmpoble**	*src1,*	*src2,*	*targ*	11-42
37	COBR	**bbs**	*bitpos,*	*src,*	*targ*	11-20
38	COBR	**cmpibno**	*src1,*	*src2,*	*targ*	11-42
39	COBR	**cmpibg**	*src1,*	*src2,*	*targ*	11-42
3A	COBR	**cmpibe**	*src1,*	*src2,*	*targ*	11-42
3B	COBR	**cmpibge**	*src1,*	*src2,*	*targ*	11-42
3C	COBR	**cmpibl**	*src1,*	*src2,*	*targ*	11-42
3D	COBR	**cmpibne**	*src1,*	*src2,*	*targ*	11-42
3E	COBR	**cmpible**	*src1,*	*src2,*	*targ*	11-42
3F	COBR	**cmpibo**	*src1,*	*src2,*	*targ*	11-42
80	MEM	**ldob**	*src,*	*dst*		11-67

Opcode	Inst. Type	Mnemonic	Operands			Page
82	MEM	**stob**	*src,*	*dst*		11-117
84	MEM	**bx**	*targ*			11-18
85	MEM	**balx**	*targ,*	*dst*		11-16
86	MEM	**callx**	*targ*			11-29
88	MEM	**ldos**	*src,*	*dst*		11-67
8A	MEM	**stos**	*src,*	*dst*		11-117
8C	MEM	**lda**	*src*	*dst*		11-69
90	MEM	**ld**	*src,*	*dst*		11-67
92	MEM	**st**	*src,*	*dst*		11-117
98	MEM	**ldl**	*src,*	*dst*		11-67
9A	MEM	**stl**	*src,*	*dst*		11-117
A0	MEM	**ldt**	*src,*	*dst*		11-67
A2	MEM	**stt**	*src,*	*dst*		11-117
B0	MEM	**ldq**	*src,*	*dst*		11-67
B2	MEM	**stq**	*src,*	*dst*		11-117
C0	MEM	**ldib**	*src,*	*dst*		11-67
C2	MEM	**stib**	*src,*	*dst*		11-117
C8	MEM	**ldis**	*src,*	*dst*		11-67
CA	MEM	**stis**	*src,*	*dst*		11-117
580	REG	**notbit**	*bitpos,*	*src,*	*dst*	11-94
581	REG	**and**	*src1,*	*src2,*	*dst*	11-11
582	REG	**andnot**	*src1,*	*src2,*	*dst*	11-11
583	REG	**setbit**	*bitpos,*	*src,*	*dst*	11-109
584	REG	**notand**	*src,*	*dst*		11-93
586	REG	**xor**	*src1,*	*src2,*	*dst*	11-133
587	REG	**or**	*src1,*	*src2,*	*dst*	11-96
588	REG	**nor**	*src1,*	*src2,*	*dst*	11-92
589	REG	**xnor**	*src1,*	*src2,*	*dst*	11-133
58A	REG	**not**	*src,*	*dst*		11-93
58B	REG	**ornot**	*src1,*	*src2,*	*dst*	11-96
58C	REG	**clrbit**	*bitpos,*	*src,*	*dst*	11-34
58D	REG	**notor**	*src1,*	*src2,*	*dst*	11-95
58E	REG	**nand**	*src1,*	*src2,*	*dst*	11-91
58F	REG	**alterbit**	*bitpos,*	*src,*	*dst*	11-10
590	REG	**addo**	*src1,*	*src2,*	*dst*	11-7
591	REG	**addi**	*src1,*	*src2,*	*dst*	11-7
592	REG	**subo**	*src1,*	*src2,*	*dst*	11-120
593	REG	**subi**	*src1,*	*src2,*	*dst*	11-120
598	REG	**shro**	*len,*	*src,*	*dst*	11-110
59A	REG	**shrdi**	*len,*	*src,*	*dst*	11-110
59B	REG	**shri**	*len,*	*src,*	*dst*	11-110
59C	REG	**shlo**	*len,*	*src,*	*dst*	11-110
59D	REG	**rotate**	*len,*	*src,*	*dst*	11-103
59E	REG	**shli**	*len,*	*src,*	*dst*	11-110
5A0	REG	**cmpo**	*src1,*	*src2*		11-35
5A1	REG	**cmpi**	*src1,*	*src2*		11-35
5A2	REG	**concmpo**	*src1,*	*src2*		11-45

Opcode	Inst. Type	Mnemonic	Operands			Page
5A3	REG	**concmpi**	*src1*,	*src2*		11-45
5A4	REG	**cmpinco**	*src1*,	*src2*,	*dst*	11-37
5A5	REG	**cmpinci**	*src1*,	*src2*,	*dst*	11-37
5A6	REG	**cmpdeco**	*src1*,	*src2*,	*dst*	11-36
5A7	REG	**cmpdeci**	*src1*,	*src2*,	*dst*	11-36
5AC	REG	**scanbyte**	*src1*,	*src2*		11-108
5AE	REG	**chkbit**	*bitpos*,	*src*		11-31
5B0	REG	**addc**	*src1*,	*src2*,	*dst*	11-6
5B2	REG	**subc**	*src1*,	*src2*,	*dst*	11-119
5CC	REG	**mov**	*src*,	*dst*		11-85
5DC	REG	**movl**	*src*,	*dst*		11-85
5EC	REG	**movt**	*src*,	*dst*		11-85
5FC	REG	**movq**	*src*,	*dst*		11-85
600	REG	**synmov**	*dst*,	*src*		11-126
601	REG	**synmovl**	*dst*,	*src*		11-126
602	REG	**synmovq**	*dst*,	*src*		11-126
610	REG	**atmod**	*src*,	*mask*,	*src/dst*	11-15
612	REG	**atadd**	*src/dst*,	*src*,	*dst*	11-12
615	REG	**synld**	*src*,	*dst*		11-124
640	REG	**spanbit**	*src*,	*dst*		11-114
641	REG	**scanbit**	*src*,	*dst*		11-107
642	REG	**daddc**	*src1*,	*src2*,	*dst*	11-52
643	REG	**dsubc**	*src1*,	*src2*,	*dst*	11-57
644	REG	**dmovt**	*src*,	*dst*		11-56
645	REG	**modac**	*mask*,	*src*,	*dst*	11-79
650	REG	**modify**	*mask*,	*src*,	*src/dst*	11-81
651	REG	**extract**	*bitpos*,	*len*,	*src/dst*	11-62
654	REG	**modtc**	*mask*,	*src*,	*dst*	11-84
655	REG	**modpc**	*mask*,	*src/dst*		11-82
660	REG	**calls**	*targ*			11-27
66B	REG	**mark**				11-78
66C	REG	**fmark**				11-66
66D	REG	**flushreg**				11-65
66F	REG	**syncf**				11-123
670	REG	**emul**	*src1*,	*src2*,	*dst*	11-59
671	REG	**ediv**	*src1*,	*src2*,	*dst*	11-58
674	REG	**cvtir**	*src*,	*dst*		11-49
675	REG	**cvtilr**	*src*,	*dst*		11-49
676	REG	**scalerl**	*src1*,	*src2*,	*dst*	11-105
677	REG	**scaler**	*src1*,	*src2*,	*dst*	11-105
680	REG	**atanr**	*src1*,	*src2*,	*dst*	11-13
681	REG	**logepr**	*src1*,	*src2*,	*dst*	11-72
682	REG	**logr**	*src1*,	*src2*,	*dst*	11-75
683	REG	**remr**	*src1*,	*src2*,	*dst*	11-98
684	REG	**cmpor**	*src1*,	*src2*		11-38
685	REG	**cmpr**	*src1*,	*src2*		11-40
688	REG	**sqrtr**	*src*,	*dst*		11-115

Opcode	Inst. Type	Mnemonic	Operands			Page
689	REG	**expr**	*src*,	*dst*		11-60
68A	REG	**logbnr**	*src*,	*dst*		11-70
68B	REG	**roundr**	*src*,	*dst*		11-104
68C	REG	**sinr**	*src*,	*dst*		11-112
68D	REG	**cosr**	*src*,	*dst*		11-46
68E	REG	**tanr**	*src*,	*dst*		11-129
68F	REG	**classr**	*src*			11-32
690	REG	**atanrl**	*src1*,	*src2*,	*dst*	11-13
691	REG	**logeprl**	*src1*,	*src2*,	*dst*	11-72
692	REG	**logrl**	*src1*,	*src2*,	*dst*	11-75
693	REG	**remrl**	*src1*,	*src2*,	*dst*	11-98
694	REG	**cmporl**	*src1*,	*src2*		11-38
695	REG	**cmprl**	*src1*,	*src2*		11-40
698	REG	**sqrtrl**	*src*,	*dst*		11-115
699	REG	**exprl**	*src*,	*dst*		11-60
69A	REG	**logbnrl**	*src*,	*dst*		11-70
69B	REG	**roundrl**	*src*,	*dst*		11-104
69C	REG	**sinrl**	*src*,	*dst*		11-112
69D	REG	**cosrl**	*src*,	*dst*		11-46
69E	REG	**tanrl**	*src*,	*dst*		11-129
69F	REG	**classrl**	*src*			11-32
6C0	REG	**cvtri**	*src*,	*dst*		11-50
6C1	REG	**cvtril**	*src*,	*dst*		11-50
6C2	REG	**cvtzri**	*src*,	*dst*		11-50
6C3	REG	**cvtzril**	*src*,	*dst*		11-50
6C9	REG	**movr**	*src*,	*dst*		11-86
6D9	REG	**movrl**	*src*,	*dst*		11-86
6E2	REG	**cpysre**	*src1*,	*src2*,	*dst*	11-48
6E3	REG	**cpyrsre**	*src1*,	*src2*,	*dst*	11-48
6E9	REG	**movre**	*src*,	*dst*		11-86
701	REG	**mulo**	*src1*,	*src2*,	*dst*	11-88
708	REG	**remo**	*src1*,	*src2*,	*dst*	11-97
70B	REG	**divo**	*src1*,	*src2*,	*dst*	11-53
741	REG	**muli**	*src1*,	*src2*,	*dst*	11-88
748	REG	**remi**	*src1*,	*src2*,	*dst*	11-97
749	REG	**modi**	*src1*,	*src2*,	*dst*	11-80
74B	REG	**divi**	*src1*,	*src2*,	*dst*	11-53
78B	REG	**divr**	*src1*,	*src2*,	*dst*	11-54
78C	REG	**mulr**	*src1*,	*src2*,	*dst*	11-89
78D	REG	**subr**	*src1*,	*src2*,	*dst*	11-121
78F	REG	**addr**	*src1*,	*src2*,	*dst*	11-8
79B	REG	**divrl**	*src1*,	*src2*,	*dst*	11-54
79C	REG	**mulrl**	*src1*,	*src2*,	*dst*	11-89
79D	REG	**subrl**	*src1*,	*src2*,	*dst*	11-121
79F	REG	**addrl**	*src1*,	*src2*,	*dst*	11-8

SUMMARY OF SYSTEM DATA STRUCTURES

The following pages provide a collection of the system data structures presented in this manual. They are are grouped by function. The chapter reference below each data structure shows where in this manual this data structure is described.

Execution Environment

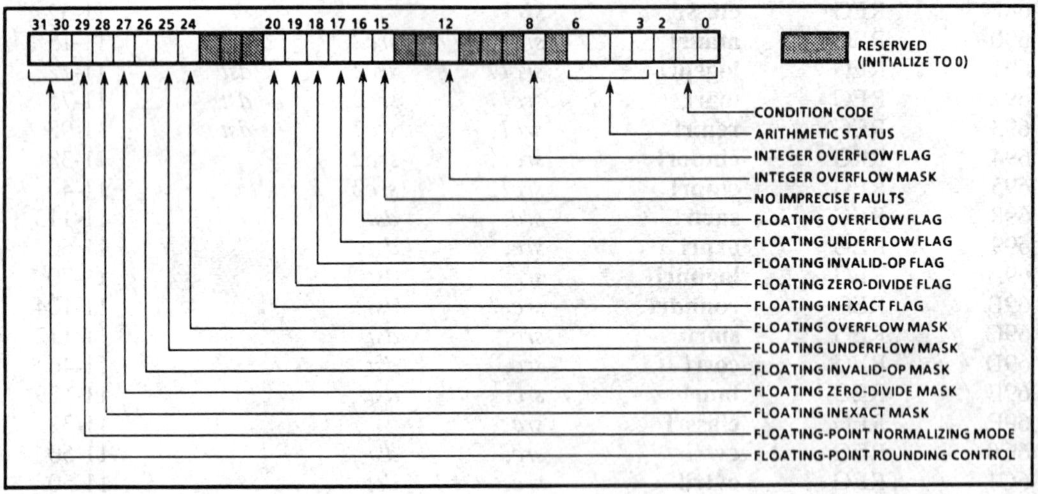

Figure A-1: Arithmetic Controls (Chapter 3)

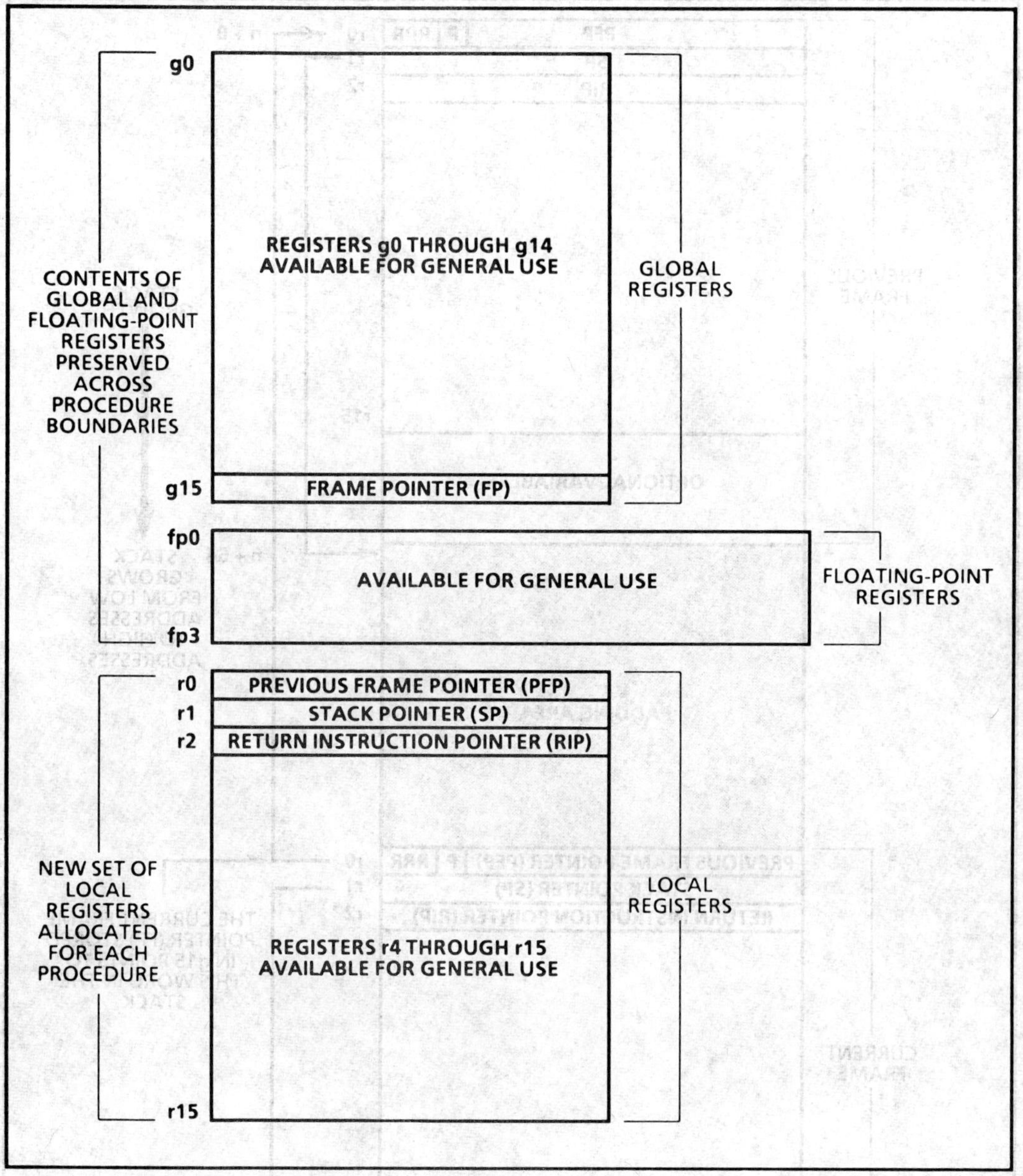

Figure A-2: Registers Available to a Single Procedure (Chapter 3)

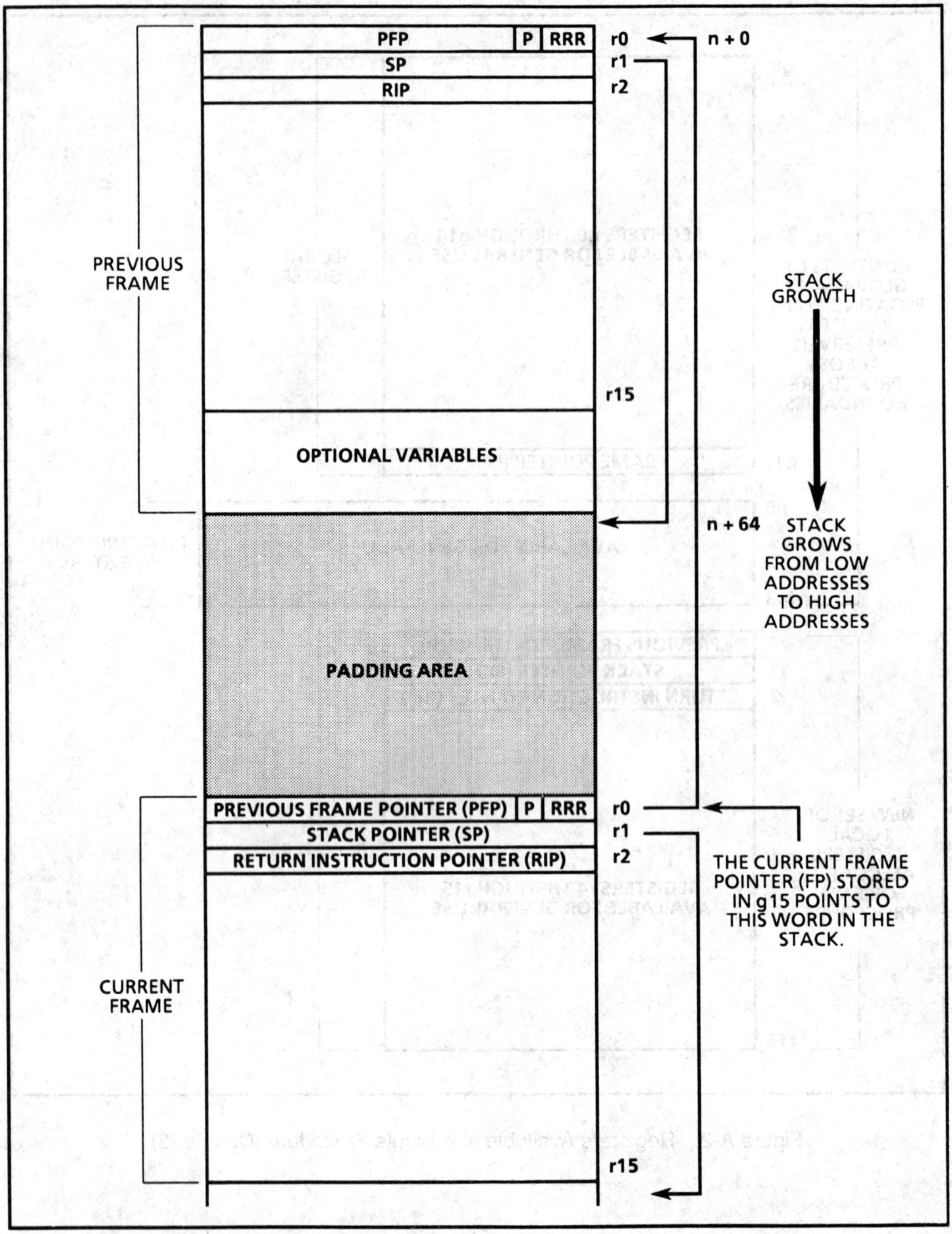

Figure A-3: Procedure Stack Structure (Chapter 4)

Processor Management

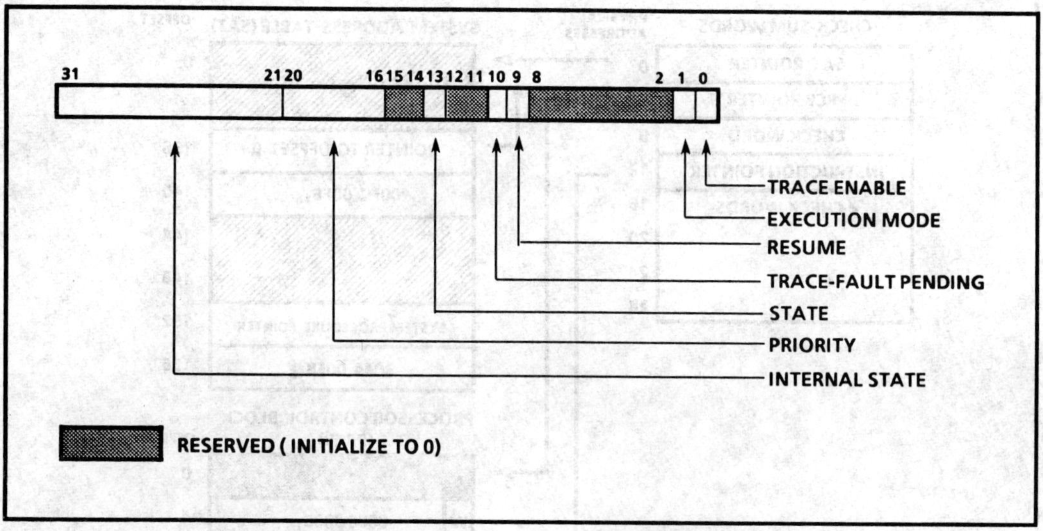

Figure A-4: Process Controls (Chapter 7)

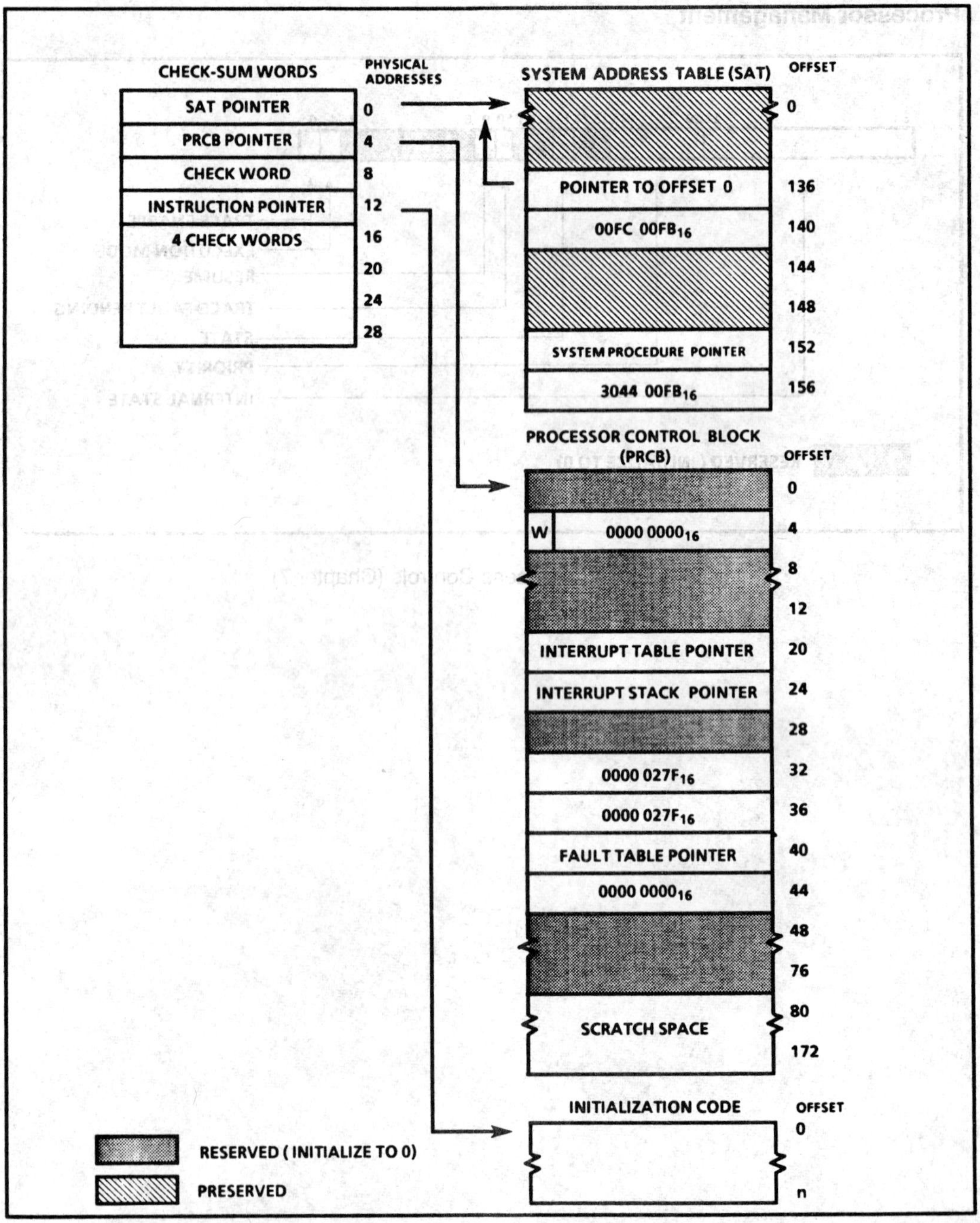

Figure A-5: Initial Memory Image (Chapter 7)

Interrupt Handling

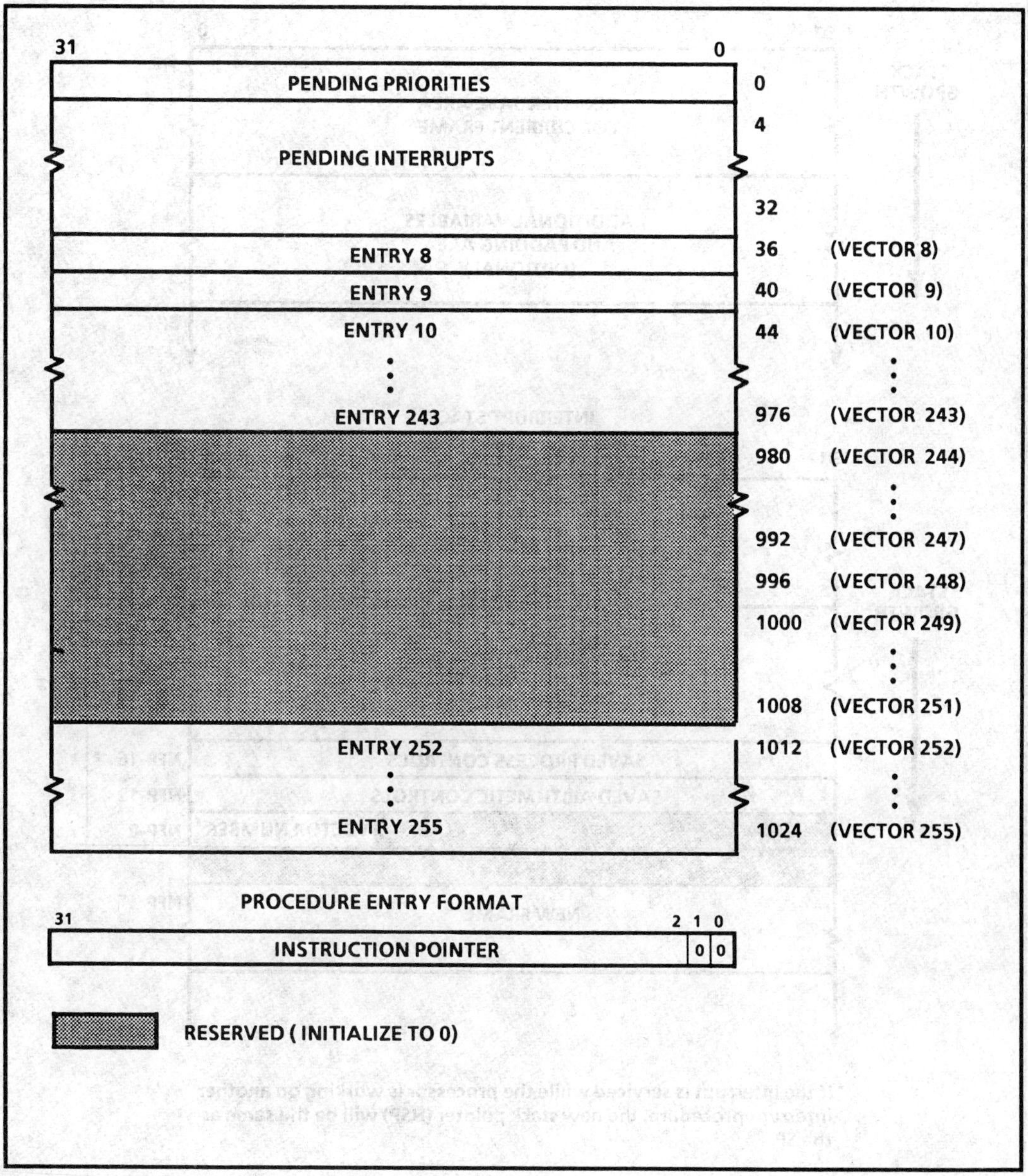

Figure A-6: Interrupt Table (Chapter 8)

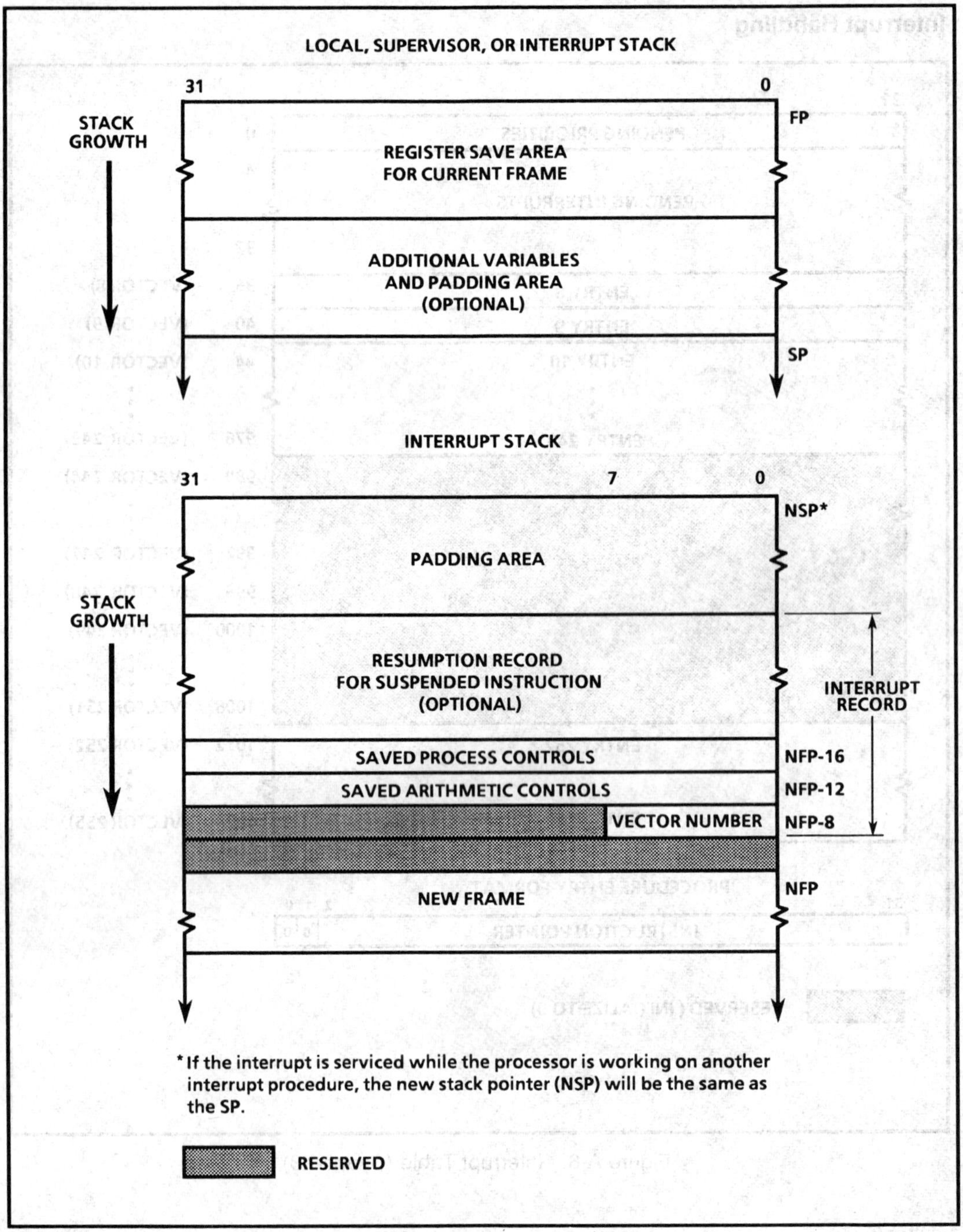

Figure A-7: Interrupt Record on Stack (Chapter 8)

IACs

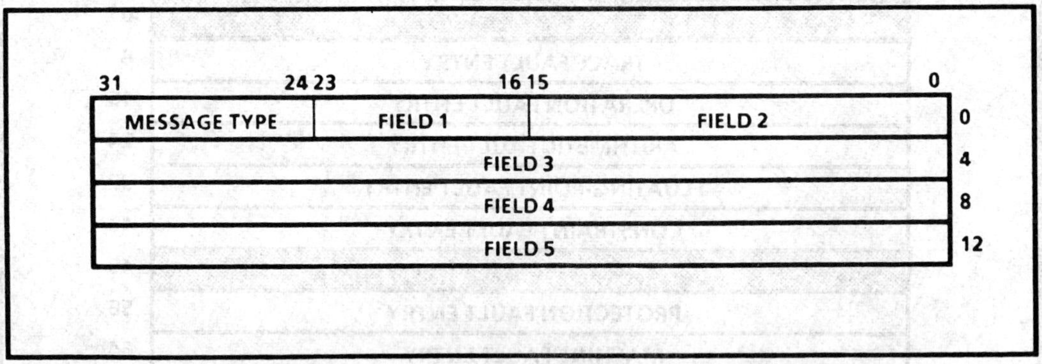

Figure A-8: IAC Message Format (Chapter 13)

Fault Handling

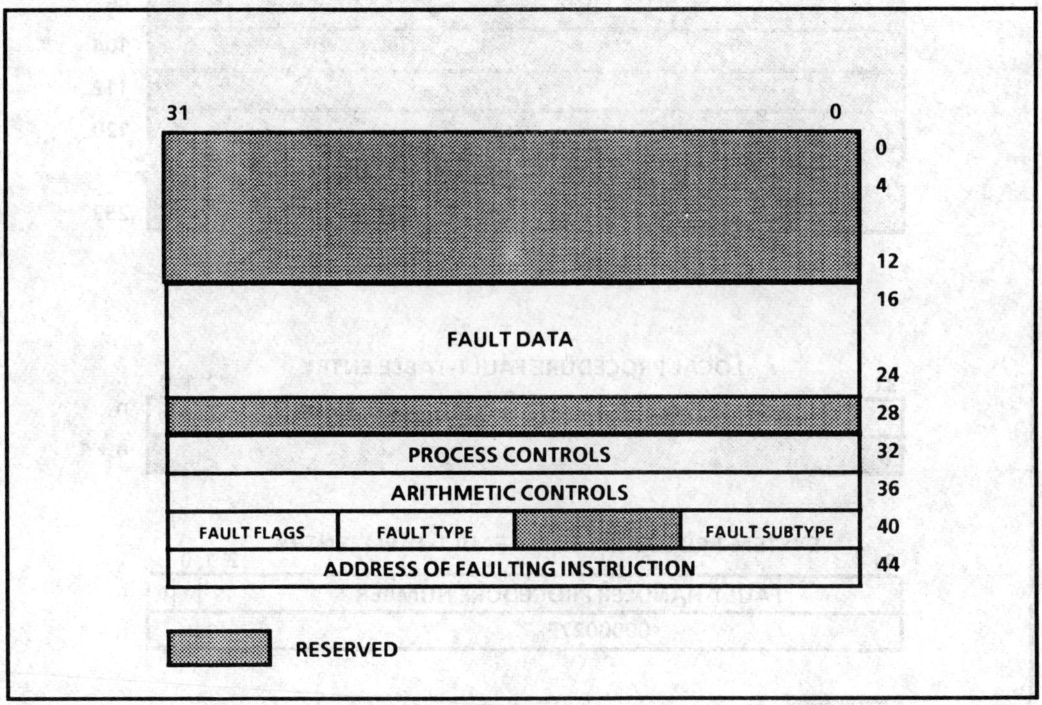

Figure A-9: Fault Record (Chapter 9)

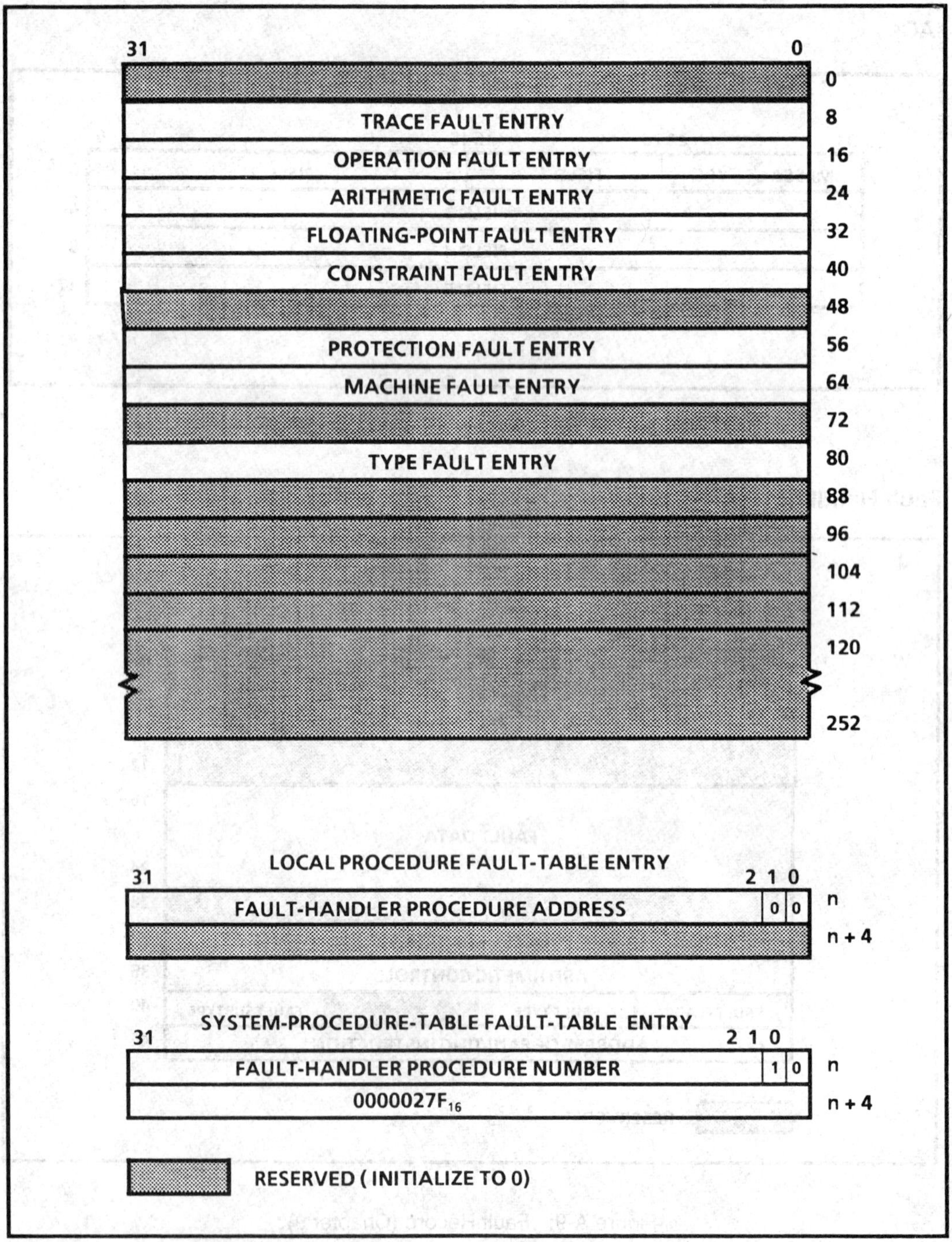

Figure A-10: Fault Table and Fault-Table Entries (Chapter 9)

Trace Control

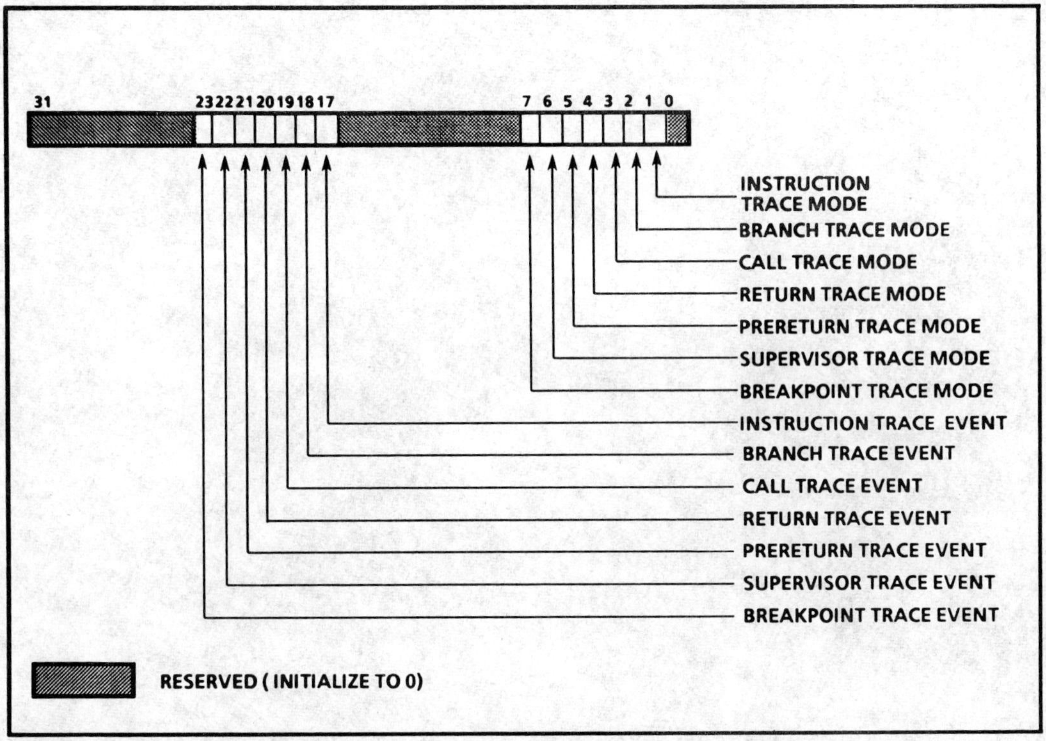

Figure A-11: Trace Controls (Chapter 10)

Appendix B
Machine-Level Instruction Formats

APPENDIX B
MACHINE-LEVEL INSTRUCTION FORMATS

This appendix describes the machine-level format for 80960KB instructions. Included is a description of the four instruction formats and how the addressing modes relate to these formats. Also, a table is given that shows the relationship between the machine-level instruction operands and the assembly-language-level instruction operands.

GENERAL INSTRUCTION FORMAT

At the machine-level, all the 80960KB instructions are one word long and begin on word boundaries. (One group of instructions allows a second word, which contains a 32-bit displacement.)

There are four basic instruction formats: REG, COBR, CTRL, and MEM. Figure B-1 shows these formats. Each instruction has only one format, which is defined by the opcode field of the instruction.

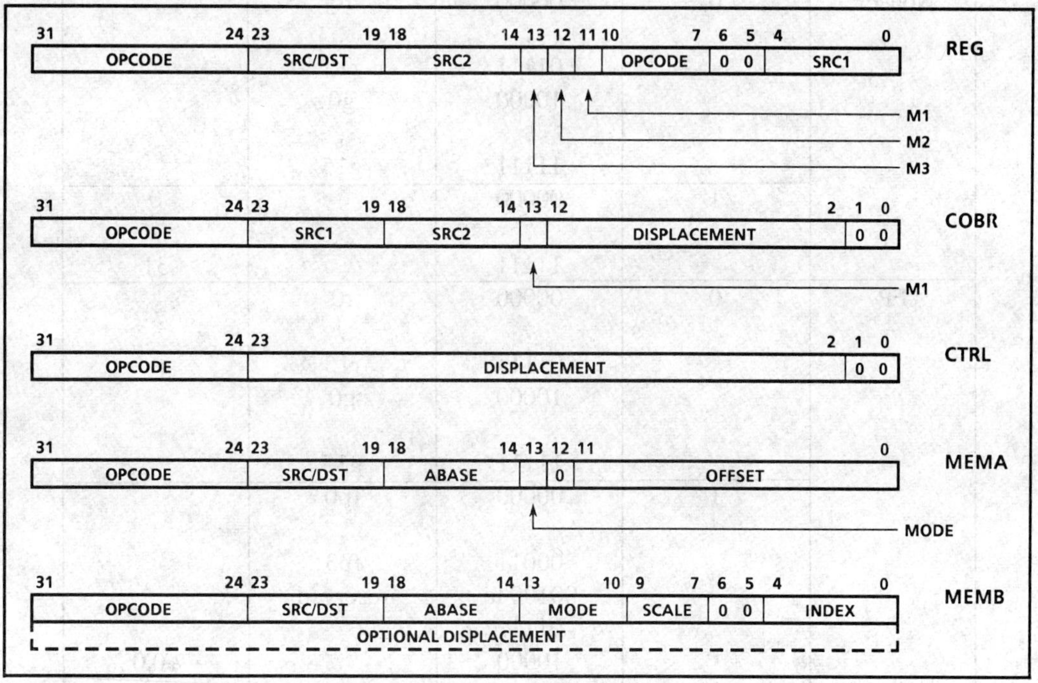

Figure B-1: Instruction Formats

The following sections describe the fields in the instruction word for each format.

REG FORMAT

The REG format is for operations that are performed on data contained in the global, local, and floating-point registers. The majority of the 80960KB instructions use this format.

The opcode for the REG instructions is 12 bits long (3 hexadecimal digits) and is split between bits 7 through 10 and bits 24 through 31. For example, the opcode for the **addi** instruction is 591_{16}. Here, 59_{16} is contained in bits 24 through 31 and 1_{16} is contained in bits 7 through 10.

The *src1* and *src2* fields specify source operands for the instruction. The operands can be either registers or literals. The mode bits (m1 for src1 and m2 for src2) and the instruction type (non-floating point or floating point) determine whether an operand is a register or a literal. Table B-1 shows the relationship between the instruction type, the mode bits, and the src1 and src2 operands.

Table B-1: Encoding of Src1 and Src2 Fields in REG Format

Inst. Type	M1 or M2	Src1 or Src2 Operand Value	Register Number	Literal Value
Non-FP	0	00000	r0	
		.	.	
		01111	r15	
		10000	g0	
		.	.	
		11111	g15	
	1	00000		0
		.	.	
		11111		31
FP	0	00000	r0	
		.	.	
		01111	r15	
		10000	g0	
		.	.	
		11111	g15	
	1	00000	fp0	
		.	.	
		00011	fp3	
		00100 to 01111	reserved	
		10000		+0.0
		10001 to 10101	reserved	
		10110		+1.0
		10111 to 11111	reserved	

For non-floating-point instructions, if a mode bit is set to 0, the respective src1 or src2 field specifies a global or local register. If the mode bit is set to 1, the field specifies an ordinal literal in the range of 0 to 31.

For floating-point instructions, if the mode bit is set to 0, the respective src1 or src2 field specifies a global or local register (just as it does for non-floating-point instructions). If the mode bit is set to 1, the field specifies either a floating-point register or one of two real-number literals (+0.0 or +1.0). All of the other encoding when the mode bit is set to 1 are reserved. When a reserved encoding is used as a source, the processor either signals an invalid opcode fault or produces an undefined value.

The src/dst field can specify either a source operand or a destination operand or both, depending on the instruction. Here again, the mode bit (m3) and the instruction type (non-floating point or floating point) determine how this field is used. Table B-2 shows this relationship.

Table B-2: Encoding of Src/Dst Field in REG Format

Inst. Type	m3	Src/Dst	Src Only	Dst Only
Non-FP	0	g0 .. g15 r0 .. r15	g0 .. g15 r0 .. r15	g0 .. g15 f0 .. r15
	1	NA	Literal	NA
FP	0	NA	NA	g0 .. g15 r0 .. r15
	1	NA	NA	fp0 .. fp4

Note: NA means not allowed

For non-floating-point instructions, if M3 is clear, the src/dst operand is a global or local register that is encoded as shown in Table B-1. If M3 is set, the src/dst operand can be used only as a src operand that is an ordinal literal.

For floating-point instructions, the src/dst field is only used to encode destination operands. Here, the encoding is the same as shown in Table B-1, except that the encodings for floating-point literals are not allowed. That is, if M3 is clear, the destination operand is a global or local register; if M3 is set, the destination operand is a floating-point register. When a reserved encoding or literal encoding is used as a destination, the processor either signals an invalid opcode fault or produces an undefined result.

COBR FORMAT

The COBR format is used primarily for control-and-branch instructions. (The test-if instructions also use this format.) The opcode field for this format is 8 bits (two hexadecimal digits).

The src1 and src2 fields specify source operands for the instruction. The src1 field can specify either a global or local register or a literal as determined by mode bit m1. (The encoding of the src1 field is the same as is shown in Table B-1 for the non-floating point instructions.) The src2 field can only specify a local or global register.

The displacement field contains a signed, twos complement number that specifies a word displacement. The processor uses this value to compute the address of a target instruction that the processor goes to as the result of a comparison. The displacement field can range from -2^{10} to (2^{10} -1). To determine the IP of the target instruction, the processor converts the displacement value to a byte displacement (i.e., multiplies the value by 4). It then adds the resulting byte displacement to the IP of the next instruction.

Note

To allow labels or absolute addresses to be used in the assembly-language version of the COBR format instructions, the Intel 80960KB Assembler converts a *targ* (target) operand value in an assembly-language instruction into the displacement value required for the COBR format, using the following calculation:

displacement = (*targ*/4) - (IP + 4)

For the test-if instructions, only the src1 field is used. Here, this field specifies a destination global or local register (m1 is ignored).

CTRL FORMAT

The CTRL format is used for instructions that branch to a new IP, including the branch, branch-if, **bal**, and **call** instructions. The **return** instruction also uses this format. The opcode field for this format is 8 bits (two hexadecimal digits).

The instructions that use this format have no operands. The target address for a branch is specified with the displacement field in the same manner as is done with the COBR format instructions. Here, the displacement field specifies a word displacement (also a signed, twos complement number) that can range from -2^{21} to 2^{21} -1.

The processor ignores the displacement field for the **return** instruction.

MEM FORMAT

The MEM format is used for instructions that require a memory address to be computed. These instructions include the load, store, and **lda** instructions. Also, the extended versions of the branch, branch-and-link, and call instructions (**bx**, **balx**, and **callx**) uses this format.

There are two MEM formats, MEMA and MEMB. The MEMB format offers the option of including a 32-bit displacement (contained in a second word) to the instruction. Bit 12 of the first word of the instruction determines whether the format is MEMA (clear) or MEMB (set).

For both formats the opcode field is 8 bits long. The src/dst field specifies a global or local register. For load instructions, the src/dst field specifies the destination register for a word loaded into the processor from memory or, for operands larger than one word, the first of successive destination registers. For store instructions, this field specifies the register or group of registers that contain the source operand to be stored in memory.

The mode bit (or bits for the MEMB format) determine the address mode used for the instruction. Table B-3 summarizes the addressing modes for the two versions of the MEM format. The fields used in these addressing modes are described in the following sections.

Table B-3: Addressing Modes for MEM Format Instructions

Format	Mode Bit(s)	Address Computation
MEMA	0	offset
	1	(abase) + offset
MEMB	0100	(abase)
	0101	(IP) + displacement + 8
	0110	reserved
	0111	(abase) + (index) * 2^{scale}
	1100	displacement
	1101	(abase) + displacement
	1110	(index) * 2^{scale} + displacement
	1111	(abase) + (index) * 2^{scale} + displacement

Notes:
1. In the address computations above, a field in parentheses (e.g., (abase)) indicates that the value in the specified register is used in the computation.
2. The use of a reserved encoding causes an invalid opcode fault to be signaled.

MEMA Format Addressing

The MEMA format provides two addressing modes:

- absolute offset
- register indirect with offset

The offset field specifies an unsigned byte offset from 0 to 4096. The abase field specifies a global or local register that contains an address in memory. The address is interpreted as either a virtual address or a physical address depending on whether the processor is operating in virtual-addressing or physical-addressing mode, respectively.

For the absolute offset addressing mode (the mode bit is clear), the processor interprets the offset field as an offset from byte 0 of the current process address space. The abase field is ignored. Using this addressing mode along with the **lda** instruction allows a constant of from 0 to 4096 to be loaded into a register.

For the register indirect with offset addressing mode (the md bit is set), the value in the offset field is added to the address in the abase register. Setting the offset value to zero creates a register indirect addressing mode, however, this operation can generally be carried out faster by using the MEMB version of this addressing mode.

MEMB Format Addressing

The MEMB format provides the following seven addressing modes:

- absolute displacement
- register indirect
- register indirect with displacement
- register indirect with index
- register indirect with index and displacement
- index with displacement
- IP with displacement

The abase and index fields specify local or global registers, the contents of which are used in the address computation. When the index field is used in an addressing mode, the processor automatically scales the value in the index register by the amount specified in the scale field. Table B-4 gives the encoding of the scale field. The optional displacement field is contained in the word following the instruction word. The displacement is a 32-bit, signed, twos complement value.

Table B-4: Encoding of Scale Field

Scale	Scale Factor (Multiplier)
000	1
001	2
010	4
011	8
100	16
101 to 111	reserved

Note:
The use of a reserved encoding causes an invalid opcode fault to be signaled.

For the IP with displacement mode, the value of the displacement field plus 8 is added to the address of the current instruction.

Appendix C
Instruction Timing

APPENDIX C
INSTRUCTION TIMING

This appendix describes the 80960KB processor's instruction pipeline and how it affects the timing of instructions. The number of clock cycles required for each instruction are also given here.

INTRODUCTION

The 80960 architecture defines several mechanisms for increasing processor performance through the use of pipelining and parallel execution of instructions. This appendix describes how these mechanisms have been incorporated into the design of the 80960KB processor and provides information to help programmers maximize the performance of the processor.

INTERNAL STRUCTURE OF THE 80960KB PROCESSOR

The 80960KB processor is composed of the following six major functional units (shown in Figure C-1):

- Bus Control Logic
- Instruction Fetch Unit and Instruction Cache
- Instruction Decoder
- Micro-Instruction Sequencer and ROM
- Instruction Execution Unit
- Floating Point Unit

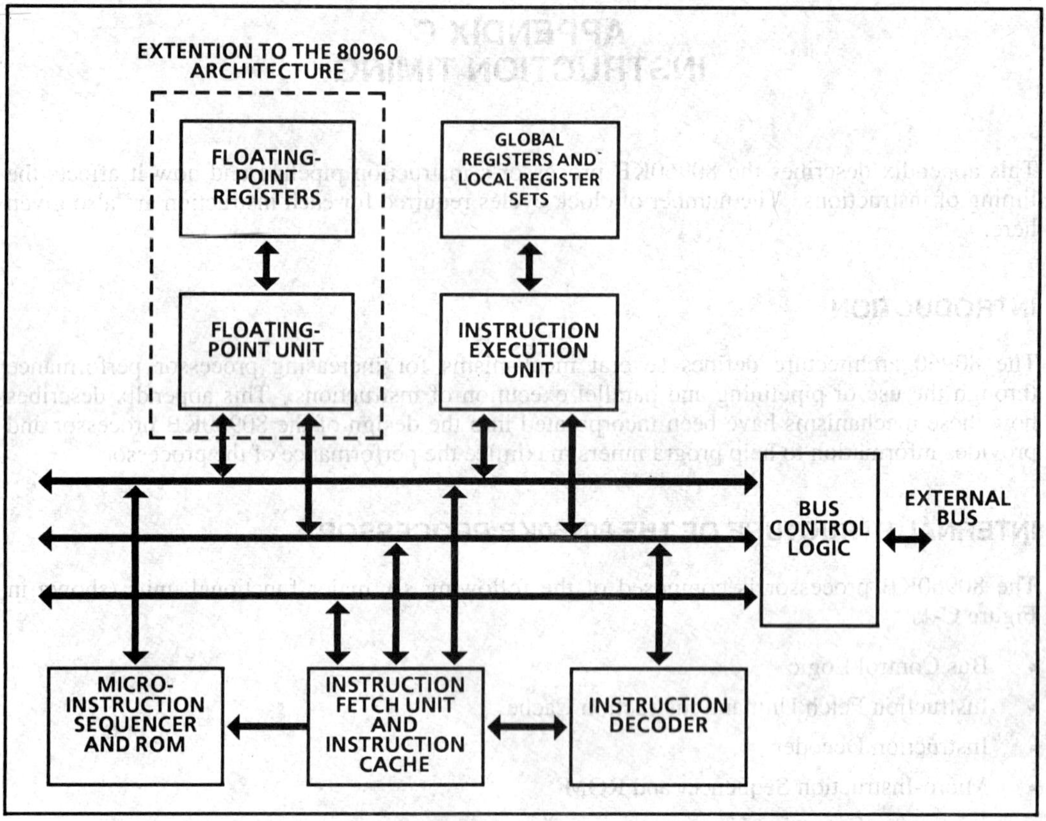

Figure C-1: Block Diagram of the 80960KB Processor

These units function independently from one another, but in close cooperation. The functions of each of these units is described in the following sections.

Bus Control Logic

The Bus Control Logic (BCL) provides the interface between the processor and the external world. This interface consists of a multiplexed, burst bus, which is capable of memory-access rates of over 53 Megabytes/second (with a 20 Mhz CPU clock). The BCL accepts requests from other units within the 80960KB, prioritizes them, and executes them. It attempts to maximize bus access efficiency through buffering and burst accesses.

The BCL provides a queuing mechanism that can buffer up to three outstanding requests at any given time. This mechanism, coupled with other 80960KB features (such as scoreboarding, which is discussed later), allow other units in the 80960KB to continue operation without waiting for bus requests to be completed. As a result, the execution of most memory reference instructions require little or no delay in the instruction execution pipeline.

The BCL generates burst cycles on the external bus, which allow from one to 16 bytes of data to be read or written in a single operation. The processor takes advantage of burst transfers in several ways. First, multiple-register load or store operations can be carried out in a single bus operation, using the **ldl** (load long), **ldt** (load triple), and **ldq** (load quad) instructions and the corresponding **stl** (store long) **stt** (store triple), and **stq** (store quad) instructions. Second, instructions can be fetched in 16-byte bursts, thereby reducing bus traffic for instruction fetches. Third, floating-point values of 32, 64 or 80 bits can be stored in a single bus operation.

Instruction Fetch Unit and Instruction Cache

The Instruction Fetch Unit (IFU) acts as an intelligent "buffer" for the Instruction Decoder (ID). Its purpose is to present the instruction stream to the ID in the fastest and most transparent way possible. The IFU uses several mechanisms to accomplish this goal, as described in the following paragraphs.

The IFU maintains a 512 byte, direct-mapped instruction cache. This cache allows very fast access to instructions. While the other units in the processor are executing instructions, the IFU looks ahead in flow of instructions stored in the instruction cache. If a cache miss is detected (that is, an instruction that will soon be needed is not in the instruction cache), the IFU issues a prefetch request to the BCL. Upon receiving the requested instruction, the IFU updates the instruction cache. In most cases, this fetch and load will take place before the ID requires the instruction. The major exception to this rule happens on branch conditions.

The IFU works closely with the ID in handling branch conditions. The ID informs the IFU of any branch operations that are about to take place. Such notifications take place on unconditional branches and on conditional branches in which the condition code is valid. When the IFU is notified of a branch, it checks for a cache hit on the desired instruction. If the instruction is not present, the IFU begins fetching instructions for the new control path.

To further minimize delays in the instruction pipeline, the ID sends a special signal to the IFU whenever instructions are required immediately. The IFU then passes the fetched instructions to the ID directly, rather than writing them to the cache and reading them back out again. This technique is called an instruction-cache bypassing.

The instruction pointer (IP) register in the processor and the IFU maintain several instruction pointers. These pointers point to instructions at various stages of the fetch-decode-execute pipeline. If a fault is signaled from any unit, the processor uses these pointers to determine the problem and preserve the state of the processor.

Instruction Decoder

The ID decodes the instructions it receives from the IFU and routes them to the appropriate execution units. In doing this, it attempts to keep the computing resources of the processor working at the highest possible levels.

Instructions are decoded into the following four groups, according to how the instructions are executed:

- Simple Instructions
- Floating Point and Branch Instructions
- Complex Instructions
- Load and Store Instructions

The following paragraphs list the instructions in each of these groups and describe how the ID handles them.

Simple Instructions

The instructions in the simple-instruction group require very little decoding. These instructions include logical; comparison; shift; integer add and subtract; and ordinal add and subtract instructions. The ID decodes these instructions and passes them to the instruction execution unit (IEU), where they are executed, usually in a single clock period.

Floating Point and Branch Instructions

All floating-point instructions are executed by the floating-point unit (FPU). Often, the execution of floating-point instructions requires interaction between the FPU, ID, and Micro-Instruction Sequencer (MIS). For example, the FPU may require access to the general-purpose registers (maintained by the IEU). Here, the ID assists in supplying data to the FPU. Also, many of the floating-point instructions are executed by means of microcode. The FPU gets the microcode from the MIS.

The ID executes branch instructions directly. If the branches are unconditional, no interaction with the processor's other execution units is required.

On conditional branch instructions, the ID uses a condition code scoreboard to streamline the branching process. Scoreboarding is a mechanism by which various resources within the processor can be marked as *in use* (or *pending a result*). When one of the execution units in the processor is in the process of altering the condition code, it marks the condition code scoreboard. When the ID prepares to execute a conditional branch instruction, it checks the condition code scoreboard. If the scoreboard is marked as in use, the ID waits for the result before proceeding. If the condition code scoreboard is clear, the ID signals the IFU immediately if a change in program flow is about to happen.

Conditional fault instructions (fault-if instructions) are also executed in the ID. These operations differ from conditional branches in that they result in a fault event being generated, followed by an implicit call to the appropriate fault-handler routine.

As a result of the pipelining described above, branches can often be carried out in zero clock cycles. For example, the branch instruction (**b**) shown below will execute in zero cycles, since the branch time is overlapped completely by the execution time of the floating-point instruction (**sinr**).

```
        sinr    g0, g1
        b       some_location
            .
            .
            .
    some_location:
        mov     g1,g2
```

The branch-if instruction (**be**) in the following example is also executed in zero cycles:

```
        cmp     0x10, r9
        divi    r10, r11, r10
        be      go_here
            .
            .
            .
    go_here:
        mov     g1,g2
```

Here, the comparison instruction (**cmp**) is placed early in the instruction stream, allowing the branch condition based on the value of r9 to take place while the integer divide instruction (**divi**) is being executed.

Complex Instructions

Complex instructions are those that are executed using one or more microcode instructions. Examples of such instructions are the **flushreg** (flush local registers), **mark**, and **fmark** (force mark) instructions. The ID decodes complex instructions and forwards them to the MIS unit. The MIS then sends the equivalent microcode to the IEU.

Load and Store Instructions

Load and store instructions are those that request data to be read from or written into memory. The ID sends these instructions directly to the BCL, which executes them.

The ID is responsible for converting the addressing information encoded in load, store, branch, and call instructions into an effective memory addresses. The circuitry that actually performs effective-address calculations resides in the IFU, but the ID oversees these operations. The generation of effective addresses is performed within a separate carry look-ahead adder, used with hardware shift logic. The ability to calculate effective addresses independently from instruction execution allows address calculation to be overlapped with computation. The time required to calculate an effective address ranges from zero to four cycles; but, for the most commonly used addressing modes, this time is less than two cycles.

Instructions that require effective addresses are executed by either the ID or the BCL, thus preserving the pipeline and eliminating delays or resource constraints on the IEU or FPU.

Micro-Instruction Sequencer and ROM

The MIS is a multipurpose unit designed to help in the execution of instructions that use microcode. All of the processor's microcode is stored in ROM, which is accessed through the MIS. When the ID receives a complex instruction (one that requires microcode to be executed), the MIS supplies the microcode to the IEU as described earlier in the discussion of complex instructions.

The MIS also supplies microcode for floating-point instructions; the power-up and self-test performed during processor initialization; interrupt handling; and fault handling.

Instruction Execution Unit

The IEU contains the Arithmetic Logic Unit (ALU) and the mechanism for register and condition-code scoreboarding. It also manages the 16 global registers and the 4 sets of 16 local registers.

The ALU performs the following functions for the IEU:

- Addition and subtraction of integers and ordinals
- Moves between registers
- Logical operations
- Bit operations
- Shifts and rotates
- Comparisons

It is capable of performing any of these operations in a single clock cycle.

The IEU can also work with integer literals in the range of -16 to +31, which are encoded in the REG instruction format. This method of encoding literals performs two functions. First, it provides a more compact instruction stream. Second, when a literal is used as an argument for an instruction, the IEU is able to execute the instruction in one less clock cycle.

The IEU handles the reading and writing of global and local registers. It also handles the allocation of local registers sets on procedure calls. The IEU allocates a new set of local registers on each procedure call. If all four register sets become allocated, the IEU automatically flushes the oldest frame to the stack on the next procedure call. The IEU also automatically retrieves any local register frame from the stack when required by a return operation. The majority of procedure calls or returns do not require the processor to flush local registers to memory. Call instructions that can be executed without flushing a register set require only 9 cycles to complete, with the corresponding return taking only 7 cycles.

The register scoreboard provides scoreboarding for the global and local registers. When, one or more registers are being used in an operation, they are marked as in use. The register scoreboarding mechanism allows the processor to continue executing subsequent instructions, as long as those instructions do not require the contents of the scoreboarded registers.

A typical event that would cause scoreboarding is a load operation. For a load from memory, the contents of the affected registers are not valid until the BCL fetches the data and the registers are loaded. For example, consider the sequence:

```
ld      g0, (g1)
addi    g2, g3, g4
addi    g5, g4 ,g6
subi    g0, g6, g6
```

Here, when the BCL initiates the **ld** operation, register g0 is scoreboarded. As long as subsequent instructions do not require the contents of g0, the ID continues to dispatch instructions. For example, the two **addi** instructions above are executed while the BCL is fetching the data for g0. If g0 is not loaded by the time the **subi** instruction is ready to be executed, the IEU delays execution of the instruction until the loading of g0 has been completed.

If an operation accesses a single register, only that register is scoreboarded. However, if multiple registers are accessed (such as, with the **ldl**, **lit**, or **ldq** instructions), registers are scoreboarded as shown in Table C-1, according to the base register of the the group being accessed.

Table C-1: Registers Scoreboarded According to Registers Referenced

Base Register Accessed	Block of Registers Scoreboarded
g0	0-3
g2	0-3
g4	0-7
g6	0-7
g8	8-11
g10	8-11
g12	12-15
g14	12-14

Instruction Execution Unit Performance Enhancements

The execution times of instructions in the IEU are dependent on the instruction flow. Two features in the IEU that can enhance the performance of instruction execution are:

- Register Bypassing
- Condition Code Scoreboarding

Register Bypassing. Register bypassing is a mechanism that allows an instruction that would ordinarily require source operands to be placed in registers to be executed without accessing one or both of the source registers. Register bypassing occurs in either of two circumstances. First, when the IEU executes an instruction with two source operands, register bypassing occurs if one or both of the operands are literals. Second, register bypassing will also occur when the second of two source operands is the result of the previous instruction. The net result of register bypassing is the saving of one clock cycle. Most instructions that the IEU executes can be executed in a single cycle when register bypassing occurs.

Condition Code Scoreboarding. The processor requires one clock cycle to set the condition code bits as the result of an instruction. If one of the instructions that follows depends on the condition code, condition-code scoreboarding can be used to save one cycle of execution time. The following example illustrates this technique:

Case 1 – 5 cycles

```
addc    r4, r5, r10
mov     g10, g12
addc    r6, r7, r11
```

Case 2 – 6 cycles

```
addc    r4, r5, r10
addc    r6, r7, r11
mov     g10, g12
```

Here, both Case 1 and Case 2 accomplish the same task. However, Case 2 requires a wait of one clock cycle between the first and second **addc** instruction, while the condition code is set. Case 1, on the other hand, takes advantage of condition code scoreboarding by executing the move (**mov**) instruction while the condition code is being set. The code in Case 1 thus executes one clock cycle faster than the code in Case 2.

Floating Point Unit

The FPU performs all the floating-point computations for the processor, as well as the integer multiply and divide operations. It also manages the four 80-bit floating-point registers, which it uses for extended-precision, floating-point calculations.

The FPU shares the resources of the processor. For example, it can use the global and local registers as operands for floating-point operations. It also gets microcode for the execution of complex floating-point instructions from the MIS.

To perform integer multiplication and several floating-point calculations, the FPU contains a 32-bit integer Booth-Multiplier. This multiplier performs integer multiplication operation in a variable amount of time, depending on the number of significant bits. It is used for integer multiplications and several floating-point calculations.

EXECUTION TIMES

The following section describes the execution times that can be expected for the various instructions in the 80960KB processor. As illustrated in the previous sections of this appendix, the execution time for each instruction can vary considerably, for two reasons. First, many instructions can vary in execution time, depending on their arguments and the state of the on-chip resources being used. Second, by taking advantage of pipelining and overlapping of operations, a program can be written in which some instructions, in effect, take no clock cycles to execute.

In the following discussion of instruction timing, the execution time of an instruction is defined as the time between the beginning of actual execution of a decoded instruction and the beginning of execution for the next decoded instruction. For example, the illustration in Figure C-2 shows the execution time of a two operand instruction to be two clocks, with respect to the next instruction to be executed.

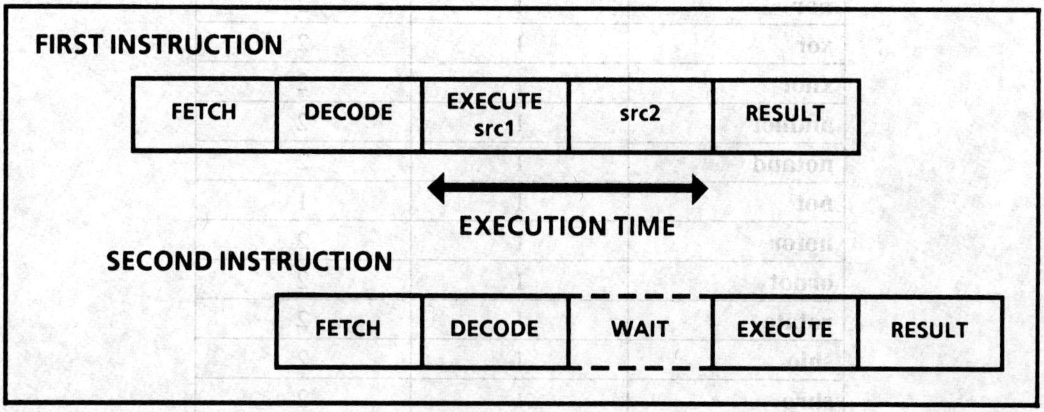

Figure C-2: Execution Time of an Instruction

Execution times for the 80960 Architecture Instructions

The following paragraphs show the instruction times for the instructions defined in the 80960 architecture.

Logical instructions

The timing of the logical instructions depends on the IEU bypass mechanism described earlier in this appendix, in particular for any instruction of the form:

alu_instruction *src1*, *src2*, *dst*

If *src1* or *src2* is a literal or if *src2* is the result of the previous operation, a bypass hit occurs. Otherwise, there is no bypass hit and the instruction requires an extra clock to load the second operand. Table C-2 shows the timing of the logical instructions depending on whether or not a bypass hit occurs.

Note

In all the following tables, execution time is given in number of clock cycles.

Table C-2: Logical Instruction Timing

Instruction	Normal Case Execution Time (Bypass Hit)	Worst Case Execution Time (Bypass Miss)
and	1	2
nand	1	2
or	1	2
nor	1	2
xor	1	2
xnor	1	2
andnot	1	2
notand	1	2
not	1	1
notor	1	2
ornot	1	2
rotate	1	2
shlo	1	2
shro	1	2
shli	2	3
shri	2	3
shrdi	2	3

Bit Instructions

The execution times for the bit instructions are also dependent on whether or not a register bypass has occurred or not, as is shown in Table C-3.

Table C-3: Bit Instruction Timing

Instruction	Normal Case Execution Time (Bypass Hit)	Worst Case Execution Time (Bypass Miss)
notbit	2	3
setbit	2	3
clrbit	2	3
alterbit	2	3
chkbit	2	3
extract	7	7
modify	8	8

The execution times of the **scanbit** and **spanbit** instructions (shown in Table C-4 depend on condition code scoreboarding. If the condition code is not set by the previous instruction execution, the instruction will complete in one less clock cycle. Execution time is also dependent on the number of bits operated upon.

Table C-4: Scan and Span Bit Instruction Timing

Instruction	Best Case Execution Time	Normal Case Execution Time	Worst Case Execution Time
scanbit	8	11	14
spanbit	8	11	14

Register Moves

The timing of instructions that move data between registers is directly related to the number of words moved. One clock cycle is required to move one (as shown in Table C-5).

Table C-5: Move Instruction Timing

Instruction	Execution Time
mov	1
movl	2
movt	3
movq	4

Integer and Ordinal Arithmetic

The execution times for the basic add, subtract, and comparison instructions (as shown in Table C-6) depend on register bypass. The normal-case results are achieved when a register bypass occurs.

Table C-6: Integer and Ordinal Arithmetic Instruction Timing

Instruction	Normal Case Execution Time (Bypass Hit)	Worst Case Execution Time (Bypass Miss)
addo	1	2
addi	1	2
subo	1	2
subi	1	2
cmpo	1	2
cmpi	1	2
cmpinco	2	3
cmpdeco	2	3
cmpinci	2	3
cmpdeci	2	3

The execution times for the add and subtract with carry and conditional compare instructions (shown in Table C-7) depend on condition code scoreboarding. If the instruction executed prior to any of these instructions sets the condition code (CC), the worst case instruction execution time occurs; if an instruction is inserted between the instruction that sets the condition code and one of the instructions listed in Table C-7, the instruction is executed in the normal case time.

Table C-7: Add/Subtract With Carry, Conditional Compare Instruction Timing

Instruction	Normal Case Execution Time (CC Available)	Worst Case Execution Time (CC Not Available)
addc	1	2
subc	1	2
subi	1	2
concmpi	1	2

Multiply and Divide Instructions

Table C-8 shows the typical instruction execution times for the multiply and divide instructions:

Table C-8: Multiply and Divide Instruction Timing

Instruction	Range of Significant Bits	Typical Case Execution Time
mulo	9 to 21	18
muli	9 to 21	18
divi	37	37
divo	37	37
remo	37	37
remi	37	37
modi	37	37
emul	37	24
ediv	37	40

Since the processor contains a Booth Multiplier with early out, the execution times on the multiply and divide instructions (shown in Table C-8) depend on the number of significant bits in the *src1* operand. For example, Table C-9 shows the execution times based on the number of significant bits in *src1*:

Table C-9: Multiply/Divide Execution Times Based on Significant Bits

Src1 Significant Bits	Execution Time
2	9
4	10
8	11
32	21

Note that the shift instructions or the add and subtract instructions may be faster than the multiply instructions in certain instances (for example, when multiplying by 3, 5, 15, etc.).

Branching

Branch instructions are executed directly by the ID and do not require IEU or FPU resources. Because of this, branch instructions can in most cases be programmed so that their execution is overlapped with other operations. Table C-10 lists the ranges of times for execution of branch instructions, from best (maximum overlap) to worst (no overlap). (The instructions in capital letters indicate groups of instructions that branch on condition codes, such the BRANCH IF instructions, **be**, **bg**, **bl**, etc.)

Table C-10: Branch Instruction Timing

Instruction	Best Case Execution Time (CC Available)	Worst Case Execution Time (CC Not Available)
b	0 to 2 (0 to 2)	0 to 2 (0 to 2)
BRANCH IF	0 to 2 (0 to 1)	0 to 3 (0 to 2)
bx	0 to 6 (0 to 6)	0 to 6 (0 to 6)
BRANCH AND LINK	2 to 8 (2 to 8)	2 to 8 (2 to 8)
COMPARE AND BRANCH	3 to 5 (3 to 4)	3 to 5 (3 to 4)
TEST IF	0 to 3 (0 to 2)	0 to 4 (0 to 3)
FAULT IF	0 to 2 (0 to 1)	0 to 3 (0 to 2)

The second column of numbers lists execution-time ranges for conditional branches in which the condition code was not set in the previous instruction, and the third column lists ranges for branches in which the condition code was set by the previous instruction. Also, the first range in each column is for the case in which the branch is taken, and the range in parentheses is for the case in which the branch is not taken.

When writing optimized code for the 80960KB processor, it is best to perform conditional tests at least one instruction before a conditional branch. This practice allows the execution times in column two to be achieved. It is also important to note that the "not taken" branch case executes in one less cycle, because there is no break in the pipeline. (Remember, instruction time is defined as the time from the start of execution of one instruction to the start of execution of the next instruction. If the pipeline is stalled, the fetch of the next instruction will be delayed one clock. This delay may or may not be hidden by the parallelism of the 80960KB processor).

Call/Return Instructions

As described earlier in this appendix, the 80960KB processor provides four sets of local registers. When a call instruction is executed, the processor allocates a new set of local registers to the called procedure or interrupt routine. If, when a **call** or **callx** instruction is executed, a set of local registers is available, the processor executes the instruction in 9 clock cycles.

If a set of local registers is not available, the processor flushes the oldest set of registers to the stack in memory to free up a register set. Flushing a set of local registers requires four quad-word stores to memory. Assuming zero-wait-state memory, this operation adds 24 clocks to the 9 clocks normally required to execute a call.

The **ret** (return) instruction normally requires 7 clock cycles. If the local registers being returned to have been flushed to the stack, an additional 24 clocks must be added to this execution time (with zero-wait-state memory) for the processor to reload the local registers from the stack. It is important to note that the processor only reloads the local registers when they are required, thus eliminating unnecessary memory cycles.

Load Instructions

A load instruction requires the following steps:

1. Instruction Fetch
2. Decode
3. Compute Effective Address/Scoreboard Register(s)
4. Place Address on Bus
5. Wait State(s)
6. Receive Data on Bus
7. Place Data in target register

Of these steps, only steps 3 through 7 are included in the definition of execution time for an instruction. The following figures show several examples of load instruction timing depending on where the load instruction is placed in the instruction stream.

The example in Figure C-3 illustrates a load instruction where the instruction that follows requires the fetched data. Here, the pipeline is stalled while the processor waits for the load to complete. Assuming a one-clock-cycle effective-address calculation, the load will require 4 or 5 clock cycles to be executed, depending on whether or not zero-wait-state memory is used.

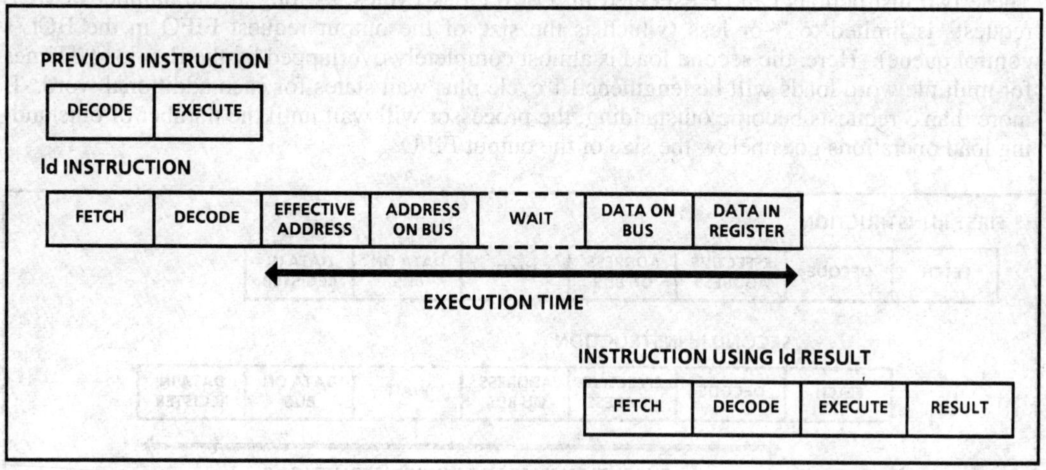

Figure C-3: Load Where the Next Instruction Requires the Fetched Data

Figure C-4 gives an example of a load instruction where the instruction that follows does not require the data being fetched from memory. Here, the unrelated instruction can be executed while the load is being completed. The 2 clock cycles required to execute the unrelated instruction are then overlapped with the 4 or 5 cycles required to execute the load (again depending on whether or not zero-wait-state memory is used). The load instruction thus requires a net of 1 or 2 clock cycles from the pipeline to be executed.

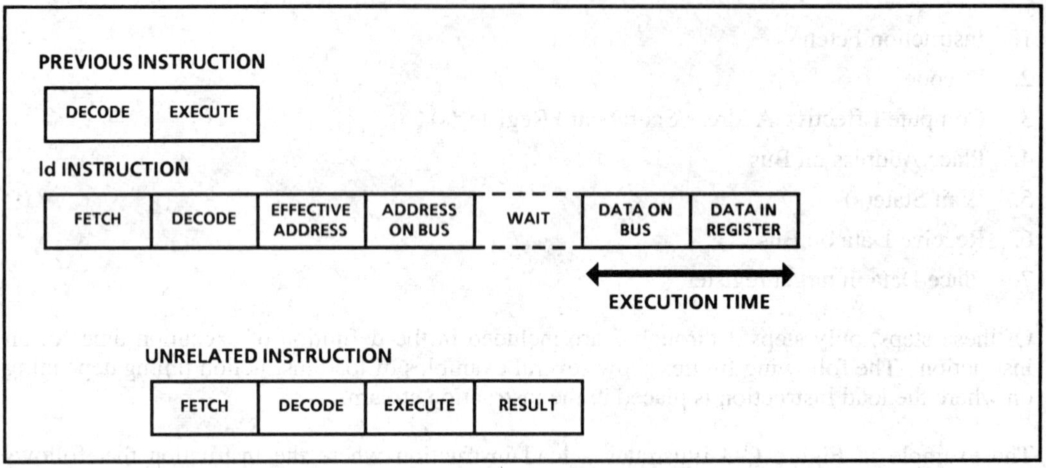

Figure C-4: Load Where the Next Instruction Does Not Require the Fetched Data

Finally, Figure C-5 shows an example of two load instructions being executed back-to-back. These two instructions can be executed in 5 or 6 clock cycles, as long as the number of BCL requests is limited to 3 or less (which is the size of the output request FIFO in the BCL's control queue). Here, the second load is almost completely overlapped by the first load. Times for multiple word loads will be lengthened 1 cycle plus wait states for each additional word. If more than 3 requests become outstanding, the processor will wait until the number of outstanding load operations goes below the size of the output FIFO.

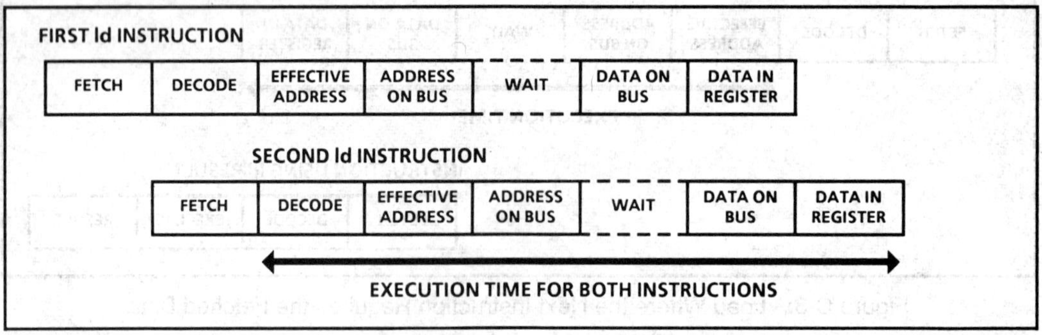

Figure C-5: Back-to-Back Load Instructions

Store Operations

Store instructions involve a posting of an address and data request to the BCL and are usually executed in 2 to 3 clock cycles. (They do not require register scoreboarding.) If the instruction following a store instruction is another store instruction, the second store instruction is usually executed in 2 clock cycles. If the following instruction uses the IEU, the execution time is 3 clock cycles. The only case in which this time will increase is when the three-request output FIFO in the BCL becomes full. Here, if another store instruction is issued, the processor waits for the BCL to complete its operations before other instructions can execute.

Execution times for the Extended Instructions

The following paragraphs show the execution times for those 80960KB instructions that are extensions to the 80960 architecture.

Decimal Instructions

Table C-11 shows the instruction times for the decimal instructions.

Table C-11: Decimal Instruction Timing

Instruction	Execution Time
dmovt	7
daddc	8
dsubc	8

Floating-Point Instructions

Table C-12 shows the instruction execution times for the simple floating-point instructions. Where applicable, a range and a typical observed average are given.

Table C-12: Simple Floating-Point Instruction Timing

Instruction	Execution Time
movr	5
movrl	5 to 7
movre	7 to 8
cpysre	8
cpyrsre	8
addr	9 to 17 (typical 10)
addrl	12 to 20 (typical 13)
subr	9 to 17 (typical 10)
subrl	12 to 20 (typical 13)
mulr	11 to 22 (typical 20)
mulrl	14 to 43 (typical 36)
divr	35
divrl	77
cmpr	10
cmprl	12
cmpor	10
cmporl	12
cvtri	25 to 33
cvtril	26 to 35
cvtilr	41 to 45
cvtilr	42 to 46
cvtzri	41 to 45
cvtzril	42 to 46
roundr	56 to 69
roundrl	56 to 70
scaler	28
scalerl	30
logbnr	32 to 41
logbnrl	32 to 43

The instructions given in Table C-13 consist of the complex floating point instructions. Only typical instruction execution rates are given here. In many cases, the clock count can vary by 30-40%. Execution time is dependent on the operands.

Table C-13: Complex Floating-Point Instruction Timing

Instruction	Execution Time
sqrtrl	104
expr	300
exprl	334
logepr	400
logeprl	420
logr	438
logrl	438
remr	(67 to 75878)
remrl	(67 to 75878)
atanr	267
atanrl	350
cosr	406
cosrl	441
tanr	293
tanrl	323

It is important to note that these floating-point instructions are interruptible. When an interrupt is received while one of these instructions is being executed, the processor can suspend execution, service the external request, then resume execution of the instruction.

Appendix D
Initialization Code

APPENDIX D
INITIALIZATION CODE

This appendix provides an example of the initialization code required to initialize the 80960KB processor.

OVERVIEW

The code given in this appendix demonstrates one of the methods that can be used to initialize the 80960KB processor. To use this code, the programmer must assemble (and compile, in the case of the C program modules) the individual files into object modules. These modules must then be loaded into ROM (generally EPROM). The resulting EPROM will contain an IMI (as shown in Figure 7-3; an interrupt table; a fault table; and a system procedure table; a set of dummy interrupt and fault handler routines; and a set of dummy system procedures. (The dummy interrupt and fault handler routines merely perform a return to the initialization code if an interrupt or fault occurs during initialization. Likewise, the dummy system procedures perform returns. These routines may be changed to suit the needs of a particular application.)

When the RESET pin on the processor is asserted, the processor performs its self test, then begins executing the initialization code. This code directs the processor to perform the following rudimentary steps of initialization:

1. Copy the PRCB from the IMI into RAM.
2. Copy the interrupt table into RAM.
3. Execute a reinitialize processor IAC, to enable the processor to load the new pointers to the PRCB and interrupt table.

The PRCB and interrupt table are copied into RAM because both of these data structures have fields that the processor must be able to write.

Once these first steps of initialization have been completed, the processor is able to execute additional initialization steps to configure the processor for a particular application. The following items are examples of further initialization actions that might be included in the initialization code:

- Copy new interrupt handler routines into RAM and change the pointers in the interrupt table to point to these new routines.
- Copy the fault table into RAM; copy new fault handler routines into RAM; change the pointers in the fault table to point to the new fault handler routines; and change the pointer in the PRCB to point to the relocated fault table.
- Create a new system procedure table in RAM; copy the system procedures into RAM; change the pointer in the PRCB to point to the new system procedure table.

Alternatively, the interrupt handler routines, fault handler routines, and system procedures can all be loaded into ROM. Here, execution of an application program can begin directly following the reinitialization of the processor.

EXAMPLE CODE

The example code consists of the following six files:

- example.lst
- f_table.lst
- i_table.lst
- f_handler.c
- i_handler.c
- cold.ld

The first three files are listings from the Intel 80960KB Assembler. These listings include assembly code (such as would be included in an ".s" file) and the resulting object code. The fourth and fifth files are C program modules. The sixth file is a load module.

The following steps describe how to use the code in these files:

1. Assemble the assembly code in files *example.s*, *f_table.s*, and *i_table.s*. (Here the ".s" files are made up of the assembly code only from the ".lst" files listed above.)
2. Compile the C code in files *f_handler.c* and *i_handler.c*.
3. Link the object modules (*example.o*, *f_table.o*, *i_table.o*, *f_handler.o*, and *i_handler.o*), using the 80960 Linker and the script in the *cold.ld* file. The script in *cold.ld* directs the linker to locate the linked code at address 0.
4. Burn the output file from the linker in an EPROM.

example.lst

```
0000          ####################################################################
0000          #
0000          #  Below is example system initialization code and tables.
0000          #  The code builds the prcb in memory, sets up the stack frame,
0000          #  the interrupt, fault, and system procedure tables, and
0000          #  then vectors to a user defined routine.
0000          #
0000          ####################################################################
0000
0000          # ------ declare the below symbols public
0000
0000           .globl  system_address_table
0000           .globl  prcb_ptr
0000           .globl  start_ip
0000           .globl  cs1
0000
0000           .globl  user_stack
0000           .globl  sup_stack
```

```
0000                        .globl  intr_stack
0000
0000                    # ------ define IAC address
0000
0000                        .set    local_IAC, 0xff000010
0000
0000                    # ------ core initialization block (located at address 0)
0000                    # ------    ( 8 words)
0000
0000                        .text
0000  00000140              .word   system_address_table    # SAT pointer
0004  00000020              .word   prcb_ptr                # PRCB pointer
0008  00000000              .word   0
000c  000001e8              .word   start_ip                # Pointer to first IP
0010  00000000              .word   cs1             # calculated at link time
0014  00000000              .word   0               # cs1 = -(segtab + PRCB + startup)
0018  00000000              .word   0
001c  ffffffff              .word   -1
001c
001c
001c                    # ------ initial PRCB
001c                    #
001c                    # ------ This is our startup PRCB.  After initialization, this will
001c                    # ------ Be copied to RAM
0020                    prcb_ptr:
0020  00000000              .word   0x0             #   0 - reserved
0024  00000000              .word   0x0             #   4 - initialize to 0
0028  00000000              .word   0x0             #   8 - reserved
002c  00000000              .word   0x0             #  12 - reserved
0030  00000000              .word   0x0             #  16 - reserved
0034  00000000              .word   intr_table      #  20 - interrupt table address
0038  00000f50              .word   intr_stack      #  24 - interrupt stack pointer
003c  00000000              .word   0x0             #  28 - reserved
0040  0000027f              .word   0x0000027f      #  32 -
0044  0000027f              .word   0x0000027f      #  36 -
0048  00000000              .word   fault_table     #  40 - fault table
004c  00000000              .word   0x0             #  44 - reserved
0050                        .space  12              #  48 - reserved
005c  00000000              .word   0x0             #  60 - reserved
0060                        .space  8               #  64 - reserved
0068  00000000              .word   0x0             #  72 - reserved
006c  00000000              .word   0x0             #  76 - reserved
0070                        .space  48              #  80 - scratch space (resumption)
00a0                        .space  44              # 128 - scratch space ( error)
00a0
00a0
00a0                    # The system procedure table will only be used if software puts the
00a0                    # processor into user mode and makes a supervisor procedure call
00a0
00cc                        .align 6
0100                    sys_proc_table:
0100  00000000              .word   0               # Reserved                      0
0104  00000000              .word   0               # Reserved                      4
0108  00000000              .word   0               # Reserved                      8
010c  00001150              .word   sup_stack       # Supervisor stack pointer     12
0110  00000000              .word   0               # Preserved
0114  00000000              .word   0               # Preserved
0118  00000000              .word   0               # Preserved
011c  00000000              .word   0               # Preserved
0120  00000000              .word   0               # Preserved
0124  00000000              .word   0               # Preserved
0128  00000000              .word   0               # Preserved
012c  00000000              .word   0               # Preserved
0130  000001e0              .word   proc_entry_0            # Procedure entry 0 (user)
0134  000001e6              .word   (proc_entry_1 + 0x2)    # Procedure entry 1 (sup.)
0134
0134
0134                    # ---------------- initial segment table
0134
0138                        .align  6
0140                    system_address_table:
0140                        .space 136                      # reserve 136 bytes
0140
01c8  00000140              .word system_address_table
01cc  00fc00fb              .word 0x00fc00fb                # initialization words
01d0                        .space 8
01d0
```

```
01d8  00000100                  .word sys_proc_table          # initialization words
01dc  304400fb                  .word 0x304400fb
01dc
01dc
01dc                         #
01dc                         # -- Below are two "dummy" system procedures.  In reality, these
01dc                         # -- would contain the real system code, rather than returns
01e0                            .align 4
01e0                            .text
01e0                          proc_entry_0:
01e0  0a000000                  ret                      #  These pointers are to dummy
01e4                          proc_entry_1:                       #  supervisor routines. They
01e4  0a000000                  ret                      #  are for example only
01e4
01e4                         # --- Processor starts execution at this spot after reset.
01e4                         # ---
01e8                         start_ip:
01e8
01e8                         # --
01e8                         # --   copy the interrupt table to RAM
01e8                         # --
01e8  8c800400                          lda     1024, g0          # load length of int. table
01ec  8ca00000                          lda     0, g4             # initialize offset to 0
01f0  8c883000 00000000                 lda     intr_table, g1    # load source
01f8  8c903000 00000290                 lda     intr_ram, g2      # load addrss of new table
0200  000040 0b                         bal     loop_here         # branch to move routine
0200
0200                         # --
0200                         # -- Processor will copy PRCB to ram space, located at prcb_ram
0200                         # --
0204  8c8000b0                          lda     176, g0           # load length of prcb
0208  8ca00000                          lda     0, g4             # initialize offset to 0
020c  8c883000 00000020                 lda     prcb_ptr, g1      # load source
0214  8c903000 00000690                 lda     prcb_ram, g2      # load destination
021c  000024 0b                         bal     loop_here         # branch to move routine
021c                         # --
021c                         # --  fix up the prcb to point to a new interrupt table
021c                         # --
0220  8ce03000 00000290                 lda     intr_ram, g12     # load address
0228  92e4a014                          st      g12,20(g2)        # store into PRCB
0228
0228
0228                         #
0228                         # --  At this point, the prcb, and interrupt table have
0228                         # --  been moved to RAM.  It is time
0228                         # --  to issue a REINITIALIZE IAC, which will start us anew with
0228                         # --  our RAM based prcb.
0228                         # --
0228                         # --  The IAC message, found in the 4 words locatad at the
0228                         # --  reinitialize_iac label, contain pointers to the current
0228                         # --  System address table, the new, RAM based PRCB, and to
0228                         # --  the instruction pointer labeled start_again_ip
0228                         #
0228
022c                         iac:
022c  8ca83000 ff000010                 lda local_IAC, g5
0234  8cb03000 00000280                 lda reinitialize_iac, g6
023c  6005a115                          synmovq  g5, g6
023c
023c                         # --
023c                         # --   Below is the software loop to move data
023c                         # --
0240                         loop_here:
0240  b0c45c14                          ldq     (g1)[g4*1], g8  # load 4 words into g8
0244  b2c49c14                          stq     g8, (g2)[g4*1]  # store to ram proc. block
0248  59a41094                          addi    g4,16, g4         # increment index
024c  39851ff4                          cmpibg  g0,g4, loop_here  # loop until done
0250  84079000                          bx      (g14)
0250
0250
0250                         #
0250                         # --  The processor will begin execution here after being
0250                         # --  reinitialized.  We will now set up the stacks and continue
0250
0254                         start_again_ip:
0254  8cf83000 00000750                 lda     user_stack,fp     # set up user stack space
025c  8c07f400 ffffffc0                 lda     -0x40(fp), pfp  # load pfp (just in case)
```

```
0264  8c0fe040                      lda     0x40(fp), sp     # set up current stack ptr
0264
0264
0268  5cf01e00                      mov     0, g14           # g14 used by C compiler
0268                                                         # for arguement lists past
0268                                                         # 13 arguements.
0268                                                         # Initialize to 0
0268
026c  8c803000 3b001000             lda     0x3b001000, g0   # set up arith. controls
0274  64840290                      modac   g0, g0, g0       # to mask unwanted
0274                                                         # exceptions
0274
0274                        #
0274                        # --   call main code from here
0274                        #
0274                        # --   Note: This setup assumes a main module "main()" written in
0274                        # --   C.  Also, no opens are done for stdin, stdout, or stderr.
0274                        # --   If I/O is required, the devices would need to be opened
0274                        # --   before the call to main.
0274
0278  86003000 00000000             callx    _main
0278
0278
0278
0280                        reinitialize_iac:
0280  93000000                      .word 0x93000000         # reinitialize iac message
0284  00000140                      .word system_address_table
0288  00000690                      .word prcb_ram           # use newly copied prcb
028c  00000254                      .word start_again_ip     # start here
028c
028c                        # -------------- other misc. stuff
028c

0290                           .data
0290                        # -- define RAM area to copy the prcb  & intr to after initial bootup
0290
0290                           .align 6
0290                        intr_ram:
0290                           .space 1024
0290
0690                        prcb_ram:
0690                           .space 176
0690
0740                           .align 6
0740
0750                        user_stack:         # reserved area for the user stack
0750                                    # this can be located anywhere in memory
0750                                    #    Size is set depending on application needs
0750                           .space 0x800
0750
0f50                        intr_stack:         # reserved area for the interrupt stack
0f50                                    # this can be located anywhere in memory
0f50                           .space 0x200
0f50                        #
0f50
1150                        sup_stack:
1150                           .space  0x400         #  Reserve stack space for
1150                                                 #     supervisor stack
1150
1150                        # the end
1150
```

f_table.lst

```
0000                     /* ******************************************************** */
0000                     /*       User Fault Table                                    */
0000                        .globl  fault_table
0000                        .align  8
0000                     fault_table:
0000  00000000              .word   _user_reserved   # Type 0 Reserved Fault Handler
0004  00000000              .word   0                # 4
0008  00000000              .word   _user_trace;     # 8
000c  00000000              .word   0                #
0010  00000000              .word   _user_operation;         #
0014  00000000              .word   0                #
0018  00000000              .word   _user_arithmetic;
001c  00000000              .word   0                #
0020  00000000              .word   _user_real_arithmetic;
0024  00000000              .word   0                #
0028  00000000              .word   _user_constraint;
002c  00000000              .word   0                #
0030  00000000              .word   _user_reserved   # Type 6 Reserved Fault Handler
0034  00000000              .word   0                #
0038  00000000              .word   _user_protection;
003c  00000000              .word   0                #
0040  00000000              .word   _user_machine;   #
0044  00000000              .word   0                #
0048  00000000              .word   _user_reserved;
004c  00000000              .word   0                #
0050  00000000              .word   _user_type;
0054  00000000              .word   0                #
0058  00000000              .word   _user_reserved   # Type 11 Reserved Fault Handler
005c  00000000              .word   0                #
0060  00000000              .word   _user_reserved   # Type 12 Reserved Fault Handler
0064  00000000              .word   0                #
0068  00000000              .word   _user_reserved   # Type 13 Reserved Fault Handler
006c  00000000              .word   0                #
0070  00000000              .word   _user_reserved   # Type 14 Reserved Fault Handler
0074  00000000              .word   0                #
0078  00000000              .word   _user_reserved   # Type 15 Reserved Fault Handler
007c  00000000              .word   0                #
0080  00000000              .word   _user_reserved   # Type 16 Reserved Fault Handler
0084  00000000              .word   0                #
0088  00000000              .word   _user_reserved   # Type 17 Reserved Fault Handler
008c  00000000              .word   0                #
0090  00000000              .word   _user_reserved   # Type 18 Reserved Fault Handler
0094  00000000              .word   0                #
0098  00000000              .word   _user_reserved   # Type 19 Reserved Fault Handler
009c  00000000              .word   0                #
00a0  00000000              .word   _user_reserved   # Type 20 Reserved Fault Handler
00a4  00000000              .word   0                #
00a8  00000000              .word   _user_reserved   # Type 21 Reserved Fault Handler
00ac  00000000              .word   0                #
00b0  00000000              .word   _user_reserved   # Type 22 Reserved Fault Handler
00b4  00000000              .word   0                #
00b8  00000000              .word   _user_reserved   # Type 23 Reserved Fault Handler
00bc  00000000              .word   0                #
00c0  00000000              .word   _user_reserved   # Type 24 Reserved Fault Handler
00c4  00000000              .word   0                #
00c8  00000000              .word   _user_reserved   # Type 25 Reserved Fault Handler
00cc  00000000              .word   0                #
00d0  00000000              .word   _user_reserved   # Type 26 Reserved Fault Handler
00d4  00000000              .word   0                #
00d8  00000000              .word   _user_reserved   # Type 27 Reserved Fault Handler
00dc  00000000              .word   0                #
00e0  00000000              .word   _user_reserved   # Type 28 Reserved Fault Handler
00e4  00000000              .word   0                #
00e8  00000000              .word   _user_reserved   # Type 29 Reserved Fault Handler
00ec  00000000              .word   0                #
00f0  00000000              .word   _user_reserved   # Type 30 Reserved Fault Handler
00f4  00000000              .word   0                #
00f8  00000000              .word   _user_reserved   # Type 31 Reserved Fault Handler
00fc  00000000              .word   0                #
```

i_table.lst

```
0000                 /*     Initial Interrupt Table         */
0000                      .globl  intr_table
0000                      .align  6
0000                 intr_table:
0000   00000000           .word   0       # Pending Priorities     0
0004                      .fill   8,4,0   # pending Interrupts    4 + (0->7)*4
0024   00000000           .word   _user_intrh;    # interrupt table entry  8
0028   00000000           .word   _user_intrh;    # interrupt table entry  9
002c   00000000           .word   _user_intrh;    # interrupt table entry  10
0030   00000000           .word   _user_intrh;    # interrupt table entry  11
0034   00000000           .word   _user_intrh;    # interrupt table entry  12
0038   00000000           .word   _user_intrh;    # interrupt table entry  13
003c   00000000           .word   _user_intrh;    # interrupt table entry  14
0040   00000000           .word   _user_intrh;    # interrupt table entry  15
0044   00000000           .word   _user_intrh;    # interrupt table entry  16
0048   00000000           .word   _user_intrh;    # interrupt table entry  17
004c   00000000           .word   _user_intrh;    # interrupt table entry  18
0050   00000000           .word   _user_intrh;    # interrupt table entry  19
0054   00000000           .word   _user_intrh;    # interrupt table entry  20
0058   00000000           .word   _user_intrh;    # interrupt table entry  21
005c   00000000           .word   _user_intrh;    # interrupt table entry  22
0060   00000000           .word   _user_intrh;    # interrupt table entry  23
0064   00000000           .word   _user_intrh;    # interrupt table entry  24
0068   00000000           .word   _user_intrh;    # interrupt table entry  25
006c   00000000           .word   _user_intrh;    # interrupt table entry  26
0070   00000000           .word   _user_intrh;    # interrupt table entry  27
0074   00000000           .word   _user_intrh;    # interrupt table entry  28
0078   00000000           .word   _user_intrh;    # interrupt table entry  29
007c   00000000           .word   _user_intrh;    # interrupt table entry  30
0080   00000000           .word   _user_intrh;    # interrupt table entry  31
0084   00000000           .word   _user_intrh;    # interrupt table entry  32
0088   00000000           .word   _user_intrh;    # interrupt table entry  33
008c   00000000           .word   _user_intrh;    # interrupt table entry  34
0090   00000000           .word   _user_intrh;    # interrupt table entry  35
0094   00000000           .word   _user_intrh;    # interrupt table entry  36
0098   00000000           .word   _user_intrh;    # interrupt table entry  37
009c   00000000           .word   _user_intrh;    # interrupt table entry  38
00a0   00000000           .word   _user_intrh;    # interrupt table entry  39
00a4   00000000           .word   _user_intrh;    # interrupt table entry  40
00a8   00000000           .word   _user_intrh;    # interrupt table entry  41
00ac   00000000           .word   _user_intrh;    # interrupt table entry  42
00b0   00000000           .word   _user_intrh;    # interrupt table entry  43
00b4   00000000           .word   _user_intrh;    # interrupt table entry  44
00b8   00000000           .word   _user_intrh;    # interrupt table entry  45
00bc   00000000           .word   _user_intrh;    # interrupt table entry  46
00c0   00000000           .word   _user_intrh;    # interrupt table entry  47
00c4   00000000           .word   _user_intrh;    # interrupt table entry  48
00c8   00000000           .word   _user_intrh;    # interrupt table entry  49
00cc   00000000           .word   _user_intrh;    # interrupt table entry  50
00d0   00000000           .word   _user_intrh;    # interrupt table entry  51
00d4   00000000           .word   _user_intrh;    # interrupt table entry  52
00d8   00000000           .word   _user_intrh;    # interrupt table entry  53
00dc   00000000           .word   _user_intrh;    # interrupt table entry  54
00e0   00000000           .word   _user_intrh;    # interrupt table entry  55
00e4   00000000           .word   _user_intrh;    # interrupt table entry  56
00e8   00000000           .word   _user_intrh;    # interrupt table entry  57
00ec   00000000           .word   _user_intrh;    # interrupt table entry  58
00f0   00000000           .word   _user_intrh;    # interrupt table entry  59
00f4   00000000           .word   _user_intrh;    # interrupt table entry  60
00f8   00000000           .word   _user_intrh;    # interrupt table entry  61
00fc   00000000           .word   _user_intrh;    # interrupt table entry  62
0100   00000000           .word   _user_intrh;    # interrupt table entry  63
0104   00000000           .word   _user_intrh;    # interrupt table entry  64
0108   00000000           .word   _user_intrh;    # interrupt table entry  65
010c   00000000           .word   _user_intrh;    # interrupt table entry  66
0110   00000000           .word   _user_intrh;    # interrupt table entry  67
0114   00000000           .word   _user_intrh;    # interrupt table entry  68
0118   00000000           .word   _user_intrh;    # interrupt table entry  69
011c   00000000           .word   _user_intrh;    # interrupt table entry  70
0120   00000000           .word   _user_intrh;    # interrupt table entry  71
0124   00000000           .word   _user_intrh;    # interrupt table entry  72
0128   00000000           .word   _user_intrh;    # interrupt table entry  73
012c   00000000           .word   _user_intrh;    # interrupt table entry  74
0130   00000000           .word   _user_intrh;    # interrupt table entry  75
```

```
0134  00000000        .word   _user_intrh;    # interrupt table entry  76
0138  00000000        .word   _user_intrh;    # interrupt table entry  77
013c  00000000        .word   _user_intrh;    # interrupt table entry  78
0140  00000000        .word   _user_intrh;    # interrupt table entry  79
0144  00000000        .word   _user_intrh;    # interrupt table entry  70
0148  00000000        .word   _user_intrh;    # interrupt table entry  71
014c  00000000        .word   _user_intrh;    # interrupt table entry  72
0150  00000000        .word   _user_intrh;    # interrupt table entry  73
0154  00000000        .word   _user_intrh;    # interrupt table entry  74
0158  00000000        .word   _user_intrh;    # interrupt table entry  75
015c  00000000        .word   _user_intrh;    # interrupt table entry  76
0160  00000000        .word   _user_intrh;    # interrupt table entry  77
0164  00000000        .word   _user_intrh;    # interrupt table entry  78
0168  00000000        .word   _user_intrh;    # interrupt table entry  79
016c  00000000        .word   _user_intrh;    # interrupt table entry  80
0170  00000000        .word   _user_intrh;    # interrupt table entry  81
0174  00000000        .word   _user_intrh;    # interrupt table entry  82
0178  00000000        .word   _user_intrh;    # interrupt table entry  83
017c  00000000        .word   _user_intrh;    # interrupt table entry  84
0180  00000000        .word   _user_intrh;    # interrupt table entry  85
0184  00000000        .word   _user_intrh;    # interrupt table entry  86
0188  00000000        .word   _user_intrh;    # interrupt table entry  87
018c  00000000        .word   _user_intrh;    # interrupt table entry  88
0190  00000000        .word   _user_intrh;    # interrupt table entry  89
0194  00000000        .word   _user_intrh;    # interrupt table entry  90
0198  00000000        .word   _user_intrh;    # interrupt table entry  91
019c  00000000        .word   _user_intrh;    # interrupt table entry  92
01a0  00000000        .word   _user_intrh;    # interrupt table entry  93
01a4  00000000        .word   _user_intrh;    # interrupt table entry  94
01a8  00000000        .word   _user_intrh;    # interrupt table entry  95
01ac  00000000        .word   _user_intrh;    # interrupt table entry  96
01b0  00000000        .word   _user_intrh;    # interrupt table entry  97
01b4  00000000        .word   _user_intrh;    # interrupt table entry  98
01b8  00000000        .word   _user_intrh;    # interrupt table entry  99
01bc  00000000        .word   _user_intrh;    # interrupt table entry 100
01c0  00000000        .word   _user_intrh;    # interrupt table entry 101
01c4  00000000        .word   _user_intrh;    # interrupt table entry 102
01c8  00000000        .word   _user_intrh;    # interrupt table entry 103
01cc  00000000        .word   _user_intrh;    # interrupt table entry 104
01d0  00000000        .word   _user_intrh;    # interrupt table entry 105
01d4  00000000        .word   _user_intrh;    # interrupt table entry 106
01d8  00000000        .word   _user_intrh;    # interrupt table entry 107
01dc  00000000        .word   _user_intrh;    # interrupt table entry 108
01e0  00000000        .word   _user_intrh;    # interrupt table entry 109
01e4  00000000        .word   _user_intrh;    # interrupt table entry 110
01e8  00000000        .word   _user_intrh;    # interrupt table entry 111
01ec  00000000        .word   _user_intrh;    # interrupt table entry 112
01f0  00000000        .word   _user_intrh;    # interrupt table entry 113
01f4  00000000        .word   _user_intrh;    # interrupt table entry 114
01f8  00000000        .word   _user_intrh;    # interrupt table entry 115
01fc  00000000        .word   _user_intrh;    # interrupt table entry 116
0200  00000000        .word   _user_intrh;    # interrupt table entry 117
0204  00000000        .word   _user_intrh;    # interrupt table entry 118
0208  00000000        .word   _user_intrh;    # interrupt table entry 119
020c  00000000        .word   _user_intrh;    # interrupt table entry 120
0210  00000000        .word   _user_intrh;    # interrupt table entry 121
0214  00000000        .word   _user_intrh;    # interrupt table entry 122
0218  00000000        .word   _user_intrh;    # interrupt table entry 123
021c  00000000        .word   _user_intrh;    # interrupt table entry 124
0220  00000000        .word   _user_intrh;    # interrupt table entry 125
0224  00000000        .word   _user_intrh;    # interrupt table entry 126
0228  00000000        .word   _user_intrh;    # interrupt table entry 127
022c  00000000        .word   _user_intrh;    # interrupt table entry 128
0230  00000000        .word   _user_intrh;    # interrupt table entry 129
0234  00000000        .word   _user_intrh;    # interrupt table entry 130
0238  00000000        .word   _user_intrh;    # interrupt table entry 131
023c  00000000        .word   _user_intrh;    # interrupt table entry 132
0240  00000000        .word   _user_intrh;    # interrupt table entry 133
0244  00000000        .word   _user_intrh;    # interrupt table entry 134
0248  00000000        .word   _user_intrh;    # interrupt table entry 135
024c  00000000        .word   _user_intrh;    # interrupt table entry 136
0250  00000000        .word   _user_intrh;    # interrupt table entry 137
0254  00000000        .word   _user_intrh;    # interrupt table entry 138
0258  00000000        .word   _user_intrh;    # interrupt table entry 139
025c  00000000        .word   _user_intrh;    # interrupt table entry 140
0260  00000000        .word   _user_intrh;    # interrupt table entry 141
0264  00000000        .word   _user_intrh;    # interrupt table entry 142
```

```
0268  00000000          .word   _user_intrh;    # interrupt table entry 143
026c  00000000          .word   _user_intrh;    # interrupt table entry 144
0270  00000000          .word   _user_intrh;    # interrupt table entry 145
0274  00000000          .word   _user_intrh;    # interrupt table entry 146
0278  00000000          .word   _user_intrh;    # interrupt table entry 147
027c  00000000          .word   _user_intrh;    # interrupt table entry 148
0280  00000000          .word   _user_intrh;    # interrupt table entry 149
0284  00000000          .word   _user_intrh;    # interrupt table entry 150
0288  00000000          .word   _user_intrh;    # interrupt table entry 151
028c  00000000          .word   _user_intrh;    # interrupt table entry 152
0290  00000000          .word   _user_intrh;    # interrupt table entry 153
0294  00000000          .word   _user_intrh;    # interrupt table entry 154
0298  00000000          .word   _user_intrh;    # interrupt table entry 155
029c  00000000          .word   _user_intrh;    # interrupt table entry 156
02a0  00000000          .word   _user_intrh;    # interrupt table entry 157
02a4  00000000          .word   _user_intrh;    # interrupt table entry 158
02a8  00000000          .word   _user_intrh;    # interrupt table entry 159
02ac  00000000          .word   _user_intrh;    # interrupt table entry 160
02b0  00000000          .word   _user_intrh;    # interrupt table entry 161
02b4  00000000          .word   _user_intrh;    # interrupt table entry 162
02b8  00000000          .word   _user_intrh;    # interrupt table entry 163
02bc  00000000          .word   _user_intrh;    # interrupt table entry 164
02c0  00000000          .word   _user_intrh;    # interrupt table entry 165
02c4  00000000          .word   _user_intrh;    # interrupt table entry 166
02c8  00000000          .word   _user_intrh;    # interrupt table entry 167
02cc  00000000          .word   _user_intrh;    # interrupt table entry 168
02d0  00000000          .word   _user_intrh;    # interrupt table entry 169
02d4  00000000          .word   _user_intrh;    # interrupt table entry 170
02d8  00000000          .word   _user_intrh;    # interrupt table entry 171
02dc  00000000          .word   _user_intrh;    # interrupt table entry 172
02e0  00000000          .word   _user_intrh;    # interrupt table entry 173
02e4  00000000          .word   _user_intrh;    # interrupt table entry 174
02e8  00000000          .word   _user_intrh;    # interrupt table entry 175
02ec  00000000          .word   _user_intrh;    # interrupt table entry 176
02f0  00000000          .word   _user_intrh;    # interrupt table entry 177
02f4  00000000          .word   _user_intrh;    # interrupt table entry 178
02f8  00000000          .word   _user_intrh;    # interrupt table entry 179
02fc  00000000          .word   _user_intrh;    # interrupt table entry 170
0300  00000000          .word   _user_intrh;    # interrupt table entry 171
0304  00000000          .word   _user_intrh;    # interrupt table entry 172
0308  00000000          .word   _user_intrh;    # interrupt table entry 173
030c  00000000          .word   _user_intrh;    # interrupt table entry 174
0310  00000000          .word   _user_intrh;    # interrupt table entry 175
0314  00000000          .word   _user_intrh;    # interrupt table entry 176
0318  00000000          .word   _user_intrh;    # interrupt table entry 177
031c  00000000          .word   _user_intrh;    # interrupt table entry 178
0320  00000000          .word   _user_intrh;    # interrupt table entry 179
0324  00000000          .word   _user_intrh;    # interrupt table entry 180
0328  00000000          .word   _user_intrh;    # interrupt table entry 181
032c  00000000          .word   _user_intrh;    # interrupt table entry 182
0330  00000000          .word   _user_intrh;    # interrupt table entry 183
0334  00000000          .word   _user_intrh;    # interrupt table entry 184
0338  00000000          .word   _user_intrh;    # interrupt table entry 185
033c  00000000          .word   _user_intrh;    # interrupt table entry 186
0340  00000000          .word   _user_intrh;    # interrupt table entry 187
0344  00000000          .word   _user_intrh;    # interrupt table entry 188
0348  00000000          .word   _user_intrh;    # interrupt table entry 189
034c  00000000          .word   _user_intrh;    # interrupt table entry 190
0350  00000000          .word   _user_intrh;    # interrupt table entry 191
0354  00000000          .word   _user_intrh;    # interrupt table entry 192
0358  00000000          .word   _user_intrh;    # interrupt table entry 193
035c  00000000          .word   _user_intrh;    # interrupt table entry 194
0360  00000000          .word   _user_intrh;    # interrupt table entry 195
0364  00000000          .word   _user_intrh;    # interrupt table entry 196
0368  00000000          .word   _user_intrh;    # interrupt table entry 197
036c  00000000          .word   _user_intrh;    # interrupt table entry 198
0370  00000000          .word   _user_intrh;    # interrupt table entry 199
0374  00000000          .word   _user_intrh;    # interrupt table entry 200
0378  00000000          .word   _user_intrh;    # interrupt table entry 201
037c  00000000          .word   _user_intrh;    # interrupt table entry 202
0380  00000000          .word   _user_intrh;    # interrupt table entry 203
0384  00000000          .word   _user_intrh;    # interrupt table entry 204
0388  00000000          .word   _user_intrh;    # interrupt table entry 205
038c  00000000          .word   _user_intrh;    # interrupt table entry 206
0390  00000000          .word   _user_intrh;    # interrupt table entry 207
0394  00000000          .word   _user_intrh;    # interrupt table entry 208
0398  00000000          .word   _user_intrh;    # interrupt table entry 209
```

```
039c  00000000          .word   _user_intrh;    # interrupt table entry 210
03a0  00000000          .word   _user_intrh;    # interrupt table entry 211
03a4  00000000          .word   _user_intrh;    # interrupt table entry 212
03a8  00000000          .word   _user_intrh;    # interrupt table entry 213
03ac  00000000          .word   _user_intrh;    # interrupt table entry 214
03b0  00000000          .word   _user_intrh;    # interrupt table entry 215
03b4  00000000          .word   _user_intrh;    # interrupt table entry 216
03b8  00000000          .word   _user_intrh;    # interrupt table entry 217
03bc  00000000          .word   _user_intrh;    # interrupt table entry 218
03c0  00000000          .word   _user_intrh;    # interrupt table entry 219
03c4  00000000          .word   _user_intrh;    # interrupt table entry 220
03c8  00000000          .word   _user_intrh;    # interrupt table entry 221
03cc  00000000          .word   _user_intrh;    # interrupt table entry 222
03d0  00000000          .word   _user_intrh;    # interrupt table entry 223
03d4  00000000          .word   _user_intrh;    # interrupt table entry 224
03d8  00000000          .word   _user_intrh;    # interrupt table entry 225
03dc  00000000          .word   _user_intrh;    # interrupt table entry 226
03e0  00000000          .word   _user_intrh;    # interrupt table entry 227
03e4  00000000          .word   _user_intrh;    # interrupt table entry 228
03e8  00000000          .word   _user_intrh;    # interrupt table entry 229
03ec  00000000          .word   _user_intrh;    # interrupt table entry 230
03f0  00000000          .word   _user_intrh;    # interrupt table entry 231
03f4  00000000          .word   _user_intrh;    # interrupt table entry 232
03f8  00000000          .word   _user_intrh;    # interrupt table entry 233
03fc  00000000          .word   _user_intrh;    # interrupt table entry 234
0400  00000000          .word   _user_intrh;    # interrupt table entry 235
0404  00000000          .word   _user_intrh;    # interrupt table entry 236
0408  00000000          .word   _user_intrh;    # interrupt table entry 237
040c  00000000          .word   _user_intrh;    # interrupt table entry 238
0410  00000000          .word   _user_intrh;    # interrupt table entry 239
0414  00000000          .word   _user_intrh;    # interrupt table entry 240
0418  00000000          .word   _user_intrh;    # interrupt table entry 241
041c  00000000          .word   _user_intrh;    # interrupt table entry 242
0420  00000000          .word   _user_intrh;    # interrupt table entry 243
0424  00000000          .word   _user_intrh;    # interrupt table entry 244
0428  00000000          .word   _user_intrh;    # interrupt table entry 245
042c  00000000          .word   _user_intrh;    # interrupt table entry 246
0430  00000000          .word   _user_intrh;    # interrupt table entry 247
0434  00000000          .word   _user_intrh;    # interrupt table entry 248
0438  00000000          .word   _user_intrh;    # interrupt table entry 249
043c  00000000          .word   _user_intrh;    # interrupt table entry 250
0440  00000000          .word   _user_intrh;    # interrupt table entry 251
0444  00000000          .word   _user_intrh;    # interrupt table entry 252
0448  00000000          .word   _user_intrh;    # interrupt table entry 253
044c  00000000          .word   _user_intrh;    # interrupt table entry 254
0450  00000000          .word   _user_intrh;    # interrupt table entry 255
```

f_handler.c

```
user_reserved()          {}
user_machine()           {}
user_trace()             {}
user_operation()         {}
user_arithmetic()        {}
user_real_arithmetic()   {}
user_constraint()        {}
user_protection()        {}
user_type()              {}
```

i_handler.c

```
user_intrh()
{
}
```

cold.ld

```
MEMORY
{
        rom: o=0x0,l=0x40000
        ram: o=0x40000,l=0x40000
}

SECTIONS
{
        .text :
        {
        } >rom

        .data :
        {
        } >ram

        .bss :
        {
        } >ram
}

cs1 = -(system_address_table + prcb_ptr + start_ip);
```

Appendix E
Considerations for Writing Portable Software

APPENDIX E
CONSIDERATIONS FOR WRITING PORTABLE SOFTWARE

This appendix describes those parts of the 80960KB processor design that are implementation dependent. This information is provided to facilitate the design of programs and kernel code that will be portable to other implementations of the 80960 architecture.

ARCHITECTURE RESTRICTIONS

The following aspects of the 80960KB's operation are deviations from the 80960KB architecture:

1. On all bus write operations except those of the **synmov**, **synmovl**, and **synmovq** instructions, the processor ignores the BADAC pin (i.e., errors signaled on "normal" writes are ignored).
2. The check for out-of-range input values for the **expr**, **exprl**, **logepr**, and **logeprl** instructions is omitted; out-of-range inputs yield an undefined result.
3. Bits 5 and 6 of a machine-level instruction word in the REG and MEMB formats and bits 0 and 1 of the CTRL format are provided to designate special function registers. The 80960KB processor has no special function registers.
4. The 80960KB processor does not guarantee that the value in register r2 of the current frame is predictable.
5. (The following is a note rather than a restriction.) When using the REG-format instructions, the m bit for every operand that is not defined by the instruction should be set (e.g., code the unused operand as an arbitrary literal). This practice may reduce overhead in some situations.

SALIGN PARAMETER

Stack frames in the 80960KB architecture are aligned on (SALIGN*16) byte boundaries. SALIGN is an implementation defined parameter. For the 80960KB processor, SALIGN is 4. Stack frames for this processor are thus aligned on 64 byte boundaries.

The low-order N bits of the FP are ignored and always interpreted to be zero. The N parameter is defined by the following expression: $SALIGN*16 = 2^N$. Thus for the 80960KB processor, N is 6.

BOUNDARY ALIGNMENT

The physical-address boundaries on which an operand begins has an impact on processor performance. For the 80960KB processor, the following is true:

- An operand that spans more word boundaries than necessary (e.g., addressing a 32-bit operand on a nonword boundary) suffers a moderate cost in speed because of extra bus and memory cycles.

- An operand that spans a 16-byte boundary suffers a large cost in speed.
- String operands that begin on nonword boundaries suffer a moderate cost in speed. String operands that begin on word boundaries but not on 16-byte boundaries suffer a small cost in speed.

FAULTS

The size of resumption records conditionally placed on the stack during faults and interrupts is 16 bytes.

PHYSICAL MEMORY

The upper 16M bytes of physical memory are reserved for special functions of local-bus components and IACs.

IACS

The mechanism for sending, receiving, and handling IAC messages is not defined in the 80960 architecture. It is a special implementation of the 80960KB processor.

The write-external-priority flag in the IMI controls is not defined in the 80960 architecture.

INTERRUPTS

The interrupt IAC message, the interrupt pins, and the interrupt register are not defined in the 80960 architecture. They are special implementations for the 80960KB processor.

INITIALIZATION

The 80960 architecture does not define an initialization mechanism. The initialization mechanism and procedures described in this manual are implementation dependent for the 80960KB processor.

BREAKPOINTS

The breakpoint registers in the 80960KB processor are not defined in the 80960 architecture.

IMPLEMENTATION DEPENDENT INSTRUCTIONS

The **synmov**, **synmovl**, **synmovq**, and **synld** instructions are not defined in the 80960 architecture and are implementation dependent in the 80960KB processor.

LOCK PIN

The $\overline{\text{LOCK}}$ pin is not defined in the 80960 architecture and is implementation dependent in the 80960KB processor.

Index

INDEX

G

I

S

W

X

intel

LITERATURE SALES FORM (EUROPE)

NAME: ____________________

COMPANY: ____________________

ADDRESS: ____________________

____

____

PHONE NO.: ____________________

ORDER NO.	TITLE	QTY.		PRICE		TOTAL
☐☐☐☐☐₋☐☐☐	______	____	×	____	=	____
☐☐☐☐☐₋☐☐☐	______	____	×	____	=	____
☐☐☐☐☐₋☐☐☐	______	____	×	____	=	____
☐☐☐☐☐₋☐☐☐	______	____	×	____	=	____
☐☐☐☐☐₋☐☐☐	______	____	×	____	=	____
☐☐☐☐☐₋☐☐☐	______	____	×	____	=	____
☐☐☐☐☐₋☐☐☐	______	____	×	____	=	____
☐☐☐☐☐₋☐☐☐	______	____	×	____	=	____
☐☐☐☐☐₋☐☐☐	______	____	×	____	=	____
☐☐☐☐☐₋☐☐☐	______	____	×	____	=	____
☐☐☐☐☐₋☐☐☐	______	____	×	____	=	____

Subtotal ____________

Your Local Sales Tax ____________

Postage ____________

Total ____________

PAYMENT

Cheques should be made payable to your local Intel Sales Office.

Other forms of payment may be available in your country. Please contact the Literature Coordinator at your local Intel Sales Office for details.

The Completed form should be marked for the attention of the LITERATURE CO-ORDINATOR and returned to your local Intel Sales Office.

intel®

DOMESTIC SALES OFFICES

ALABAMA

†Intel Corp.
5015 Bradford Dr., #2
Huntsville 35805
Tel: (205) 830-4010

ARIZONA

†Intel Corp.
11225 N. 28th Dr., #D214
Phoenix 85029
Tel: (602) 869-4980

Intel Corp.
1161 N. El Dorado Place
Suite 301
Tucson 85715
Tel: (602) 299-6815

CALIFORNIA

†Intel Corp.
21515 Vanowen Street
Suite 116
Canoga Park 91303
Tel: (818) 704-8500

†Intel Corp.
2250 E. Imperial Highway
Suite 218
El Segundo 90245
Tel: (213) 640-6040

Intel Corp.
1510 Arden Way, Suite 101
Sacramento 95815
Tel: (916) 920-8096

†Intel Corp.
4350 Executive Drive
Suite 105
San Diego 92121
Tel: (619) 452-5880

Intel Corp.*
400 N. Tustin Avenue
Suite 450
Santa Ana 92705
Tel: (714) 835-9642
TWX: 910-595-1114

†Intel Corp.*
San Tomas 4
2700 San Tomas Expressway
Santa Clara, CA 95051
Tel: (408) 986-8086
TWX: 910-338-0255

COLORADO

Intel Corp.
4445 Northpark Drive
Suite 100
Colorado Springs 80907
Tel: (303) 594-6622

†Intel Corp.*
650 S. Cherry St., Suite 915
Denver 80222
Tel: (303) 321-8086
TWX: 910-931-2289

CONNECTICUT

†Intel Corp.
26 Mill Plain Road
Danbury 06811
Tel: (203) 748-3130
TWX: 710-456-1199

FLORIDA

†Intel Corp.
242 N. Westmonte Dr.
Suite 105
Altamonte Springs 32714
Tel: (305) 869-5588
FAX: 305-682-6047

Intel Corp.
6363 N.W. 6th Way, Suite 100
Ft. Lauderdale 33309
Tel: (305) 771-0600
TWX: 510-956-9407
FAX: 305-772-8193

Intel Corp.
11300 4th Street North
Suite 170
St. Petersburg 33702
Tel: (813) 577-2413
FAX: 813-578-1607

GEORGIA

†Intel Corp.
3280 Pointe Parkway
Suite 200
Norcross 30092
Tel: (404) 449-0541

ILLINOIS

Intel Corp.
300 N. Martingale Road, Suite 400
Schaumburg 60173
Tel: (312) 310-8031

INDIANA

†Intel Corp.
8777 Purdue Road
Suite 125
Indianapolis 46268
Tel: (317) 875-0623

IOWA

Intel Corp.
St. Andrews Building
1930 St. Andrews Drive N.E.
Cedar Rapids 52402
Tel: (319) 393-5510

KANSAS

†Intel Corp.
8400 W. 110th Street
Suite 170
Overland Park 66210
Tel: (913) 345-2727

MARYLAND

Intel Corp.*
7321 Parkway Drive South
Suite C
Hanover 21076
Tel: (301) 796-7500
TWX: 710-862-1944

Intel Corp.
5th Floor
7833 Walker Drive
Greenbelt 20770
Tel: (301) 441-1020

MASSACHUSETTS

†Intel Corp.*
Westford Corp. Center
3 Carlisle Road
Westford 01886
Tel: (617) 692-3222
TWX: 710-343-6333

MICHIGAN

†Intel Corp.
7071 Orchard Lake Road
Suite 100
West Bloomfield 48033
Tel: (313) 851-8096

MINNESOTA

Intel Corp.
3500 W. 80th St., Suite 360
Bloomington 55431
Tel: (612) 835-6722
TWX: 910-576-2867

MISSOURI

Intel Corp.
4203 Earth City Expressway
Suite 131
Earth City 63045
Tel: (314) 291-1990

NEW JERSEY

Intel Corp.*
Parkway 109 Office Center
328 Newman Springs Road
Red Bank 07701
Tel: (201) 747-2233

Intel Corp.
280 Corporate Center
75 Livingston Avenue
First Floor
Roseland 07068
Tel: (201) 740-0111

NEW MEXICO

Intel Corp.
8500 Menual Boulevard N.E.
Suite B 295
Albuquerque 87112
Tel: (505) 292-8086

NEW YORK

Intel Corp.
127 Main Street
Binghamton 13905
Tel: (607) 773-0337

Intel Corp.*
850 Cross Keys Office Park
Fairport 14450
Tel: (716) 425-2750
TWX: 510-253-7391

Intel Corp.*
300 Motor Parkway
Hauppauge 11787
Tel: (516) 231-3300
TWX: 510-227-6236

Intel Corp.
Suite 2B Hollowbrook Park
15 Myers Corners Road
Wappinger Falls 12590
Tel: (914) 297-6161
TWX: 510-248-0060

NORTH CAROLINA

Intel Corp.
5700 Executive Center Drive
Suite 213
Charlotte 28212
Tel: (704) 568-8966

†Intel Corp.
2700 Wycliff Road
Suite 102
Raleigh 27607
Tel: (919) 781-8022

OHIO

Intel Corp.*
3401 Park Center Drive
Suite 220
Dayton 45414
Tel: (513) 890-5350
TWX: 810-450-2528

Intel Corp.*
25700 Science Park Dr., Suite 100
Beachwood 44122
Tel: (216) 464-2736
TWX: 810-427-9298

OKLAHOMA

Intel Corp.
6801 N. Broadway
Suite 115
Oklahoma City 73116
Tel: (405) 848-8086

OREGON

†Intel Corp.
15254 N.W. Greenbrier Parkway, Bldg. B
Beaverton 97006
Tel: (503) 645-8051
TWX: 910-467-8741

PENNSYLVANIA

Intel Corp.
1513 Cedar Cliff Drive
Camp Hill 17011
Tel: (717) 737-5035

Intel Corp.*
455 Pennsylvania Avenue
Fort Washington 19034
Tel: (215) 641-1000
TWX: 510-661-2077

Intel Corp.*
400 Penn Center Blvd., Suite 610
Pittsburgh 15235
Tel: (412) 823-4970

PUERTO RICO

Intel Microprocessor Corp.
South Industrial Park
P.O. Box 910
Las Piedras 00671
Tel: (809) 733-8616

TEXAS

†Intel Corp.
313 E. Anderson Lane
Suite 314
Austin 78752
Tel: (512) 454-3628

†Intel Corp.*
12300 Ford Road
Suite 380
Dallas 75234
Tel: (214) 241-8087
TWX: 910-860-5617

Intel Corp.*
7322 S.W. Freeway
Suite 1490
Houston 77074
Tel: (713) 988-8086
TWX: 910-881-2490

UTAH

Intel Corp.
5201 Green Street
Suite 290
Murray 84123
Tel: (801) 263-8051

VIRGINIA

†Intel Corp.
1504 Santa Rosa Road
Suite 108
Richmond 23288
Tel: (804) 282-5668

WASHINGTON

Intel Corp.
155-108 Avenue N.E.
Suite 386
Bellevue 98004
Tel: (206) 453-8086
TWX: 910-443-3002

Intel Corp.
408 N. Mullan Road
Suite 102
Spokane 99206
Tel: (509) 928-8086

WISCONSIN

†Intel Corp.
330 S. Executive Dr.
Suite 102
Brookfield 53005
Tel: (414) 784-8087
FAX: (414) 796-2115

CANADA

BRITISH COLUMBIA

Intel Semiconductor of Canada, Ltd.
4585 Canada Way, Suite 202
Burnaby V5G 4L6
Tel: (604) 298-0387
FAX: (604) 298-8234

ONTARIO

†Intel Semiconductor of Canada, Ltd.
2650 Queensview Drive
Suite 250
Ottawa K2B 8H6
Tel: (613) 829-9714
TLX: 053-4115

†Intel Semiconductor of Canada, Ltd.
190 Attwell Drive
Suite 500
Rexdale M9W 6H8
Tel: (416) 675-2105
TLX: 06983574
FAX: (416) 675-2438

QUEBEC

†Intel Semiconductor of Canada, Ltd.
620 St. Jean Boulevard
Pointe Claire H9R 3K3
Tel: (514) 694-9130
TWX: 514-694-9134

†Sales and Service Office
*Field Application Location

intel®

DOMESTIC DISTRIBUTORS

ALABAMA

Arrow Electronics, Inc.
1015 Henderson Road
Huntsville 35816
Tel: (205) 837-6955

†Hamilton/Avnet Electronics
4940 Research Drive
Huntsville 35805
Tel: (205) 837-7210
TWX: 810-726-2162

Pioneer/Technologies Group Inc.
4825 University Square
Huntsville 35816
Tel: (205) 837-9300
TWX: 810-726-2197

ARIZONA

†Hamilton/Avnet Electronics
505 S. Madison Drive
Tempe 85281
Tel: (602) 968-1461
TWX: 910-950-0077

Kieruff Electronics, Inc.
4134 E. Wood Street
Phoenix 85040
Tel: (602) 437-0750
FAX: 602-252-9109

Wyle Distribution Group
17855 N. Black Canyon Highway
Phoenix 85023
Tel: (602) 866-2888
FAX: 602-866-6937

CALIFORNIA

Arrow Electronics, Inc.
19748 Dearborn Street
Chatsworth 91311
Tel: (818) 701-7500
FAX: 818-772-8930

Arrow Electronics, Inc.
9511 Ridgehaven Court
San Diego 92123
Tel: (619) 565-4800
FAX: 619-279-0862

†Arrow Electronics, Inc.
521 Weddell Drive
Sunnyvale 94089
Tel: (408) 745-6600
FAX: 408-743-4770

Arrow Electronics, Inc.
2961 Dow Avenue
Tustin 92680
Tel: (714) 838-5422
FAX: 714-838-4151

†Avnet Electronics
350 McCormick Avenue
Costa Mesa 92626
Tel: (714) 754-6051
FAX: 714-754-6007

Hamilton/Avnet Electronics
1175 Bordeaux Drive
Sunnyvale 94089
Tel: (408) 743-3300
FAX: 408-745-6679

†Hamilton/Avnet Electronics
4545 Viewridge Avenue
San Diego 92123
Tel: (619) 571-7500
FAX: 619-277-6136

†Hamilton/Avnet Electronics
9650 Desoto Ave.
Chatsworth 91311
Tel: (818) 700-1222, 6500
FAX: 818-700-6553

†Hamilton/Avnet Electronics
4103 Northgate Boulevard
Sacramento 95834
Tel: (916) 920-3150
FAX: 916-925-3478

†Hamilton/Avnet Electronics
3002 G Street
Ontario 91311
Tel: (714) 989-9411
FAX: 714-980-7129

†Hamilton/Avnet Electronics
10950 W. Washington Blvd.
Culver City 90230
Tel: (213) 558-2458
FAX: 213-558-2248

†Hamilton Electro Sales
3170 Pullman Street
Costa Mesa 92626
Tel: (714) 641-4150
FAX: 714-641-4122

CALIFORNIA (Cont'd.)

Kierulff Electronics, Inc.
10824 Hope Street
Cypress 90430
Tel: (714) 220-6300
FAX: 714-821-8420

†Kierulff Electronics, Inc.
1180 Murphy Avenue
San Jose 95131
Tel: (408) 971-2600
FAX: 408-947-3432

†Kierulff Electronics, Inc.
14242 Chamber Rd.
Tustin 92680
Tel: (714) 731-5711
FAX: 714-669-4235

†Kierulff Electronics, Inc.
9800 Variel St.
Chattsworth 91311
Tel: (213) 725-0325
FAX: 818-407-0803

Wyle Distribution Group
26677 W. Agoura Rd.
Calabasas 91302
Tel: (818) 880-9000
FAX: 818-880-5510

†Wyle Distribution Group
17872 Cowan Avenue
Irvine 92714
Tel: (714) 863-9953
FAX: 714-863-0473

Wyle Distribution Group
11151 Sun Center Drive
Rancho Cordova 95670
Tel: (916) 638-5282
FAX: 916-638-1491

†Wyle Distribution Group
9525 Chesapeake Drive
San Diego 92123
Tel: (619) 565-9171
TWX: 910-371-9592
FAX: 619-565-9171 ext. 274

†Wyle Distribution Group
3000 Bowers Avenue
Santa Clara 95051
Tel: (408) 727-2500
FAX: 408-727-5896

Wyle Military
18910 Teller Avenue
Irvine 92715
Tel: (714) 851-9958
TWX: 310-371-9127
FAX: 714-851-8366

Wyle Systems
7382 Lampson Avenue
Garden Grove 92641
Tel: (714) 891-1717
FAX: 714-895-9038

COLORADO

Arrow Electronics, Inc.
1390 S. Potomac Street
Suite 136
Aurora 80012
Tel: (303) 696-1111

†Hamilton/Avnet Electronics
8765 E. Orchard Road
Suite 708
Englewood 80111
Tel: (303) 740-1017
TWX: 910-935-0787

†Wyle Distribution Group
451 E. 124th Avenue
Thornton 80241
Tel: (303) 457-9953
TWX: 910-936-0770

CONNECTICUT

†Arrow Electronics, Inc.
12 Beaumont Road
Wallingford 06492
Tel: (203) 265-7741
TWX: 710-476-0162

Hamilton/Avnet Electronics
Commerce Industrial Park
Commerce Drive
Danbury 06810
Tel: (203) 797-2800
FAX: 203-797-2866

†Pioneer Northeast Electronics
112 Main Street
Norwalk 06851
Tel: (203) 853-1515
TWX: 710-468-3373

FLORIDA

†Arrow Electronics, Inc.
350 Fairway Drive
Deerfield Beach 33441
Tel: (305) 429-8200
TWX: 510-955-9456

Arrow Electronics, Inc.
1001 N.W. 62nd St., Ste. 108
Ft. Lauderdale 33309
Tel: (305) 475-4297
TWX: 510-955-9456

†Arrow Electronics, Inc.
1530 Bottlebrush N.E.
Palm Bay 32905
Tel: (305) 725-1480

†Hamilton/Avnet Electronics
6801 N.W. 15th Way
Ft. Lauderdale 33309
Tel: (305) 971-2900
TLX: 510-956-3097

Hamilton/Avnet Electronics
3245 Tech Drive North
St. Petersburg 33702
Tel: (813) 576-3930
TWX: 810-863-0374

Hamilton/Avnet Electronics
6947 University Boulevard
Winterpark 32792
Tel: (305) 628-3888
FAX: 305-628-3888 ext. 40

†Pioneer Electronics
337 N. Lake Blvd., Ste. 1000
Alta Monte Springs 32701
Tel: (305) 834-9090
TWX: 810-853-0284

Pioneer Electronics
674 S. Military Trail
Deerfield Beach 33442
Tel: (305) 428-8877
TWX: 510-955-9653

GEORGIA

†Arrow Electronics, Inc.
3155 Northwoods Parkway
Suite A
Norcross 30071
Tel: (404) 449-8252
FAX: 404-242-6827

Hamilton/Avnet Electronics
5825 D. Peachtree Corners East
Norcross 30092
Tel: (404) 447-7500
TWX: 810-766-0432

Pioneer Electronics
3100 F. Northwoods Place
Norcross 30071
Tel: (404) 448-1711
FAX: 404-446-8270

ILLINOIS

†Arrow Electronics, Inc.
2000 E. Alonquin Street
Schaumberg 60173
Tel: (312) 397-3440
FAX: 312-397-3550

†Hamilton/Avnet Electronics
1130 Thorndale Avenue
Bensenville 60106
Tel: (312) 860-7780
TWX: 910-227-0060

Kierulff Electronics, Inc.
1140 W. Thorndale
Itasca 60143
Tel: (312) 250-0500
FAX: 312-250-0916

MTI Systems Sales
1100 West Thorndale
Itasca 60143
Tel: (312) 773-2300

†Pioneer Electronics
1551 Carmen Drive
Elk Grove Village 60007
Tel: (312) 437-9680
TWX: 910-222-1834

INDIANA

†Arrow Electronics, Inc.
2495 Directors Row, Suite H
Indianapolis 46241
Tel: (317) 243-9353
TWX: 810-341-3119

INDIANA (Cont'd.)

Hamilton/Avnet Electronics
485 Gradle Drive
Carmel 46032
Tel: (317) 844-9333
FAX: 317-844-5921

†Pioneer Electronics
6408 Castleplace Drive
Indianapolis 46250
Tel: (317) 849-7300
TWX: 810-260-1794

KANSAS

†Hamilton/Avnet Electronics
9219 Quivera Road
Overland Park 66215
Tel: (913) 888-8900
FAX: 913-541-7951

Pioneer Electronics
10551 Lackman Rd.
Lenexa 66215
Tel: (913) 492-0500
FAX: 913-492-7832

KENTUCKY

Hamilton/Avnet Electronics
805-A Newtown Circle
Lexington 40511
Tel: (606) 259-1475
FAX: 606-252-3238

MARYLAND

Arrow Electronics, Inc.
8300 Guilford Road, Ste. H
Rivers Center
Columbia 21046
Tel: (301) 995-6002
TWX: 710-236-9005
FAX: 301-381-3854

†Hamilton/Avnet Electronics
6822 Oak Hall Lane
Columbia 21045
Tel: (301) 995-3500
FAX: 301-995-3593

†Mesa Technology Corp.
9720 Patuxent Woods Dr.
Columbia 21046
Tel: (301) 720-5020
TWX: 710-828-9702

†Pioneer Electronics
9100 Gaither Road
Gaithersburg 20877
Tel: (301) 921-0660
TWX: 710-828-0545

MASSACHUSETTS

†Arrow Electronics, Inc.
1 Arrow Drive
Woburn 01801
Tel: (617) 933-8130
TWX: 710-393-6770

†Hamilton/Avnet Electronics
10D Centennial Drive
Peabody 01960
Tel: (617) 532-3701
TWX: 710-393-0382

Kierulff Electronics, Inc.
13 Fortune Dr.
Billerica 01821
Tel: (617) 667-8331
TWX: 710-390-1449
FAX: 617-663-1754

Pioneer Northeast Electronics
44 Hartwell Avenue
Lexington 02173
Tel: (617) 861-9200
FAX: 617-863-1547

MICHIGAN

Arrow Electronics, Inc.
755 Phoenix Drive
Ann Arbor 48108
Tel: (313) 971-8220
FAX: 313-971-2633

†Hamilton/Avnet Electronics
32487 Schoolcraft Road
Livonia 48150
Tel: (313) 522-4700
TWX: 810-242-8775
FAX: 313-522-2624

Hamilton/Avnet Electronics
2215 29th Street S.E.
Space A5
Grand Rapids 49508
Tel: (616) 243-8805
TWX: 810-273-6921
FAX: 616-243-0028

MICHIGAN (Cont'd.)

Pioneer Electronics
4505 Broadmoor Ave. S.E.
Grand Rapids 49508
Tel: (616) 698-1800
FAX: 616-698-1831

†Pioneer Electronics
13485 Stamford
Livonia 48150
Tel: (313) 525-1800
TWX: 810-242-3271

MINNESOTA

†Arrow Electronics, Inc.
5230 W. 73rd Street
Edina 55435
Tel: (612) 830-1800
FAX: 612-830-1856

Hamilton/Avnet Electronics
12400 White Water Drive
Minnetonka 55343
Tel: (612) 932-0600
FAX: 612-932-0613

†Pioneer Electronics
10203 Bren Road East
Minnetonka 55343
Tel: (612) 935-5444
FAX: 612-935-1921

MISSOURI

†Arrow Electronics, Inc.
2380 Schuetz
St. Louis 63146
Tel: (314) 567-6888
FAX: 314-567-1164

†Hamilton/Avnet Electronics
13743 Shoreline Court East
Earth City 63045
Tel: (314) 344-1200
FAX: 314-291-8889

Kierulff Electronics, Inc.
11804 Borman Dr.
St. Louis 63146
Tel: (314) 997-4956
FAX: 314-567-0860

NEW HAMPSHIRE

†Arrow Electronics, Inc.
3 Perimeter Road
Manchester 03103
Tel: (603) 668-6968
FAX: 603-668-3484

Hamilton/Avnet Electronics
444 E. Industrial Drive
Manchester 03103
Tel: (603) 624-9400
FAX: 603-624-2402

NEW JERSEY

†Arrow Electronics, Inc.
6000 Lincoln Drive East
Marlton 08053
Tel: (609) 596-8000
FAX: 609-596-5632

†Arrow Electronics, Inc.
6 Century Drive
Parsipanny 07054
Tel: (201) 538-0900
FAX: 201-538-4962

†Hamilton/Avnet Electronics
1 Keystone Ave., Bldg. 36
Cherry Hill 08003
Tel: (609) 424-0110
TWX: 710-940-0262
FAX: 609-751-8624

†Hamilton/Avnet Electronics
10 Industrial
Fairfield 07006
Tel: (201) 575-3390
FAX: 201-575-5839

†Pioneer Northeast Electronics
45 Route 46
Pinebrook 07058
Tel: (201) 575-3510
FAX: 201-575-3454

†MTI Systems Sales
37 Kulick Rd.
Fairfield 07006
Tel: (201) 227-5552
FAX: 201-575-6336

†Microcomputer System Technical Distributor Centers

DOMESTIC DISTRIBUTORS

NEW MEXICO

Alliance Electronics Inc.
11030 Cochiti S.E.
Albuquerque 87123
Tel: (505) 292-3360
FAX: 505-292-6537

Hamilton/Avnet Electronics
2524 Baylor Drive S.E.
Albuquerque 87106
Tel: (505) 765-1500
FAX: 505-243-1395

NEW YORK

Arrow Electronics, Inc.
25 Hub Drive
Melville 11747
Tel: (516) 694-6800
TWX: 510-224-6126
FAX: 516-391-1401

†Arrow Electronics, Inc.
3375 Brighton-Henrietta Townline Rd.
Rochester 14623
Tel: (716) 427-0300
FAX: 716-427-0735

Arrow Electronics, Inc.
20 Oser Avenue
Hauppauge 11788
Tel: (516) 231-1000
FAX: 516-231-1072

Hamilton/Avnet Electronics
2060 Townline Rd.
Rochester 14623
Tel: (716) 475-9130
FAX: 716-475-9119

†Hamilton/Avnet Electronics
103 Twin Oaks Drive
Syracuse 13206
Tel: (315) 437-2641
FAX: 315-432-0740

†Hamilton/Avnet Electronics
933 Motor Parkway
Hauppauge 11788
Tel: (516) 231-9800
FAX: 516-434-7426

†MTI Systems Sales
38 Harbor Park Drive
P.O. Box 271
Port Washington 11050
Tel: (516) 621-6200
FAX: 516-625-3039

†Pioneer Northeast Electronics
68 Corporate Dr.
Binghamton 13904
Tel: (607) 722-9300
FAX: 607-722-9562

†Pioneer Northeast Electronics
60 Crossway Park West
Woodbury, Long Island 11797
Tel: (516) 921-8700
TWX: 510-221-2184
FAX: 516-921-2143

†Pioneer Northeast Electronics
840 Fairport Park
Fairport 14450
Tel: (716) 381-7070
FAX: 716-381-5955

NORTH CAROLINA

†Arrow Electronics, Inc.
5240 Greens Dairy Road
Raleigh 27604
Tel: (919) 876-3132
FAX: 919-876-3132, ext. 200

†Hamilton/Avnet Electronics
3510 Spring Forest Drive
Raleigh 27609
Tel: (919) 878-0819
TWX: 510-928-1836

NORTH CAROLINA (Cont'd.)

Pioneer Electronics
9801 A-Southern Pine Blvd.
Charlotte 28217
Tel: (704) 527-8188
TWX: 810-621-0366

OHIO

Arrow Electronics, Inc.
7620 McEwen Road
Centerville 45459
Tel: (513) 435-5563
FAX: 513-435-2049

†Arrow Electronics, Inc.
6238 Cochran Road
Solon 44139
Tel: (216) 248-3990
FAX: 216-248-1106

Hamilton/Avnet Electronics
777 Brooksedge Blvd.
Westerville 43081
Tel: (614) 882-7004
FAX: 614-882-8650

†Hamilton/Avnet Electronics
954 Senate Drive
Dayton 45459
Tel: (513) 439-6700
FAX: 513-439-6711

†Hamilton/Avnet Electronics
30325 Bainbridge Rd., Bldg. A
Solon 44139
Tel: (216) 349-5100
FAX: 216-349-1894

†Pioneer Electronics
4433 Interpoint Blvd.
Dayton 45424
Tel: (513) 236-9900
FAX: 513-236-8133

†Pioneer Electronics
4800 E. 131st Street
Cleveland 44105
Tel: (216) 587-3600
TWX: 810-422-2211
FAX: 216-587-3906

OKLAHOMA

Arrow Electronics, Inc.
3158 S. 108 East Ave., Ste. 210
Tulsa 74146
Tel: (918) 665-7700
FAX: 918-665-7700

OREGON

†Almac Electronics Corp.
1885 N.W. 169th Place
Beaverton 97006
Tel: (503) 629-8090
FAX: 503-645-0611

†Hamilton/Avnet Electronics
6024 S.W. Jean Road
Bldg. C, Suite 10
Lake Oswego 97034
Tel: (503) 635-7848
FAX: 503-636-1327

Wyle Distribution Group
5250 N.E. Elam Young Parkway
Suite 600
Hillsboro 97124
Tel: (503) 640-6000
FAX: 503-640-5846

PENNSYLVANIA

Arrow Electronics, Inc.
650 Seco Road
Monroeville 15146
Tel: (412) 856-7000
FAX: 412-856-5777

Hamilton/Avnet Electronics
2800 Liberty Ave., Bldg. E
Pittsburgh 15222
Tel: (412) 281-4150
FAX: 412-281-8662

PENNSYLVANIA (Cont'd.)

Pioneer Electronics
259 Kappa Drive
Pittsburgh 15238
Tel: (412) 782-2300
TWX: 710-795-3122
FAX: 412-963-8255

†Pioneer Electronics
261 Gibraltar Road
Horsham 19044
Tel: (215) 674-4000
TWX: 510-665-6778
FAX: 215-674-3107

TEXAS

†Arrow Electronics, Inc.
3220 Commander Drive
Carrollton 75006
Tel: (214) 380-6464
FAX: 214-248-7208

†Arrow Electronics, Inc.
10899 Kinghurst Dr.
Suite 100
Houston 77099
Tel: (713) 530-4700
FAX: 713-568-8518

†Arrow Electronics, Inc.
2227 W. Braker Lane
Austin 78758
Tel: (512) 835-4180
FAX: 512-832-9875

†Hamilton/Avnet Electronics
1807A W. Braker Lane
Austin 78758
Tel: (512) 837-8911
FAX: 512-339-6232

†Hamilton/Avnet Electronics
2111 W. Walnut Hill Lane
Irving 75038
Tel: (214) 550-6111
FAX: 214-550-6172

†Hamilton/Avnet Electronics
4850 Wright Road, Ste. 190
Stafford 77477
Tel: (713) 240-7733
FAX: 713-240-0582

Kierulff Electronics, Inc.
2010 Merritt Dr.
Garland 75040
Tel: (214) 840-0110
FAX: 214-278-0928

†Pioneer Electronics
1826-D Kramer Lane
Austin 78758
Tel: (512) 835-4000
FAX: 512-835-9829

†Pioneer Electronics
13710 Omega Road
Dallas 75244
Tel: (214) 386-7300
FAX: 214-490-6419

†Pioneer Electronics
5853 Point West Drive
Houston 77036
Tel: (713) 988-5555
FAX: 713-988-1732

UTAH

†Hamilton/Avnet Electronics
1585 West 2100 South
Salt Lake City 84119
Tel: (801) 972-2800
FAX: 801-974-9675

Kierulff Electronics, Inc.
1946 W. Parkway Blvd.
Salt Lake City 84119
Tel: (801) 973-6913
FAX: 801-972-0200

Wyle Distribution Group
1325 West 2200 South
Suite E
Salt Lake City 84119
Tel: (801) 974-9953
FAX: 801-972-2524

WASHINGTON

†Almac Electronics Corp.
14360 S.E. Eastgate Way
Bellevue 98007
Tel: (206) 643-9992
FAX: 206-643-9709

Arrow Electronics, Inc.
14320 N.E. 21st Street
Bellevue 98007
Tel: (206) 643-4800
FAX: 206-746-3740

Hamilton/Avnet Electronics
14212 N.E. 21st Street
Bellevue 98005
Tel: (206) 453-5874
FAX: 206-643-0086

Wyle Distribution Group
1750 132nd Ave., N.E.
Bellevue 98005
Tel: (206) 453-8300
FAX: 206-453-4071

WISCONSIN

†Arrow Electronics, Inc.
200 N. Patrick Blvd., Ste. 100
Brookfield 53005
Tel: (414) 792-0150
FAX: 414-792-0156

Hamilton/Avnet Electronics
2975 Moorland Road
New Berlin 53151
Tel: (414) 784-4510
FAX: 414-784-9509

Kierulff Electronics, Inc.
2238-E W. Bluemound Rd.
Waukesha 53186
Tel: (414) 784-8160
FAX: 414-784-0409

CANADA

ALBERTA

Hamilton/Avnet Electronics
2816 21st Street N.E.
Calgary T2E 6Z2
Tel: (403) 250-9380
FAX: 403-250-1591

Zentronics
6815 8th Street, N.E., Ste. 100
Calgary T2E 7H7
Tel: (403) 295-8838
FAX: 403-295-8714

BRITISH COLUMBIA

Hamilton/Avnet Electronics
2550 Boundary Rd., Ste. 115
Burnaby V5M 3Z3
Tel: (604) 437-6667
FAX: 604-437-4712

Zentronics
108-11400 Bridgeport Road
Richmond V6X 1T2
Tel: (604) 273-5575
FAX: 604-273-2413

MANITOBA

Zentronics
60-1313 Border Street
Winnipeg R3H 0X4
Tel: (204) 694-1957
FAX: 204-633-9255

ONTARIO

Arrow Electronics Inc.
1093 Meyerside Dr.
Unit 2
Mississauga LST 1M4
Tel: (416) 672-7769
FAX: 416-672-0489

Arrow Electronics Inc.
Nepean K2E 7W5
Tel: (613) 226-6903
FAX: 613-723-2018

†Hamilton/Avnet Electronics
6845 Rexwood Road
Units 3-5
Mississauga L4V 1R2
Tel: (416) 677-7432
FAX: 416-677-0940

Hamilton/Avnet Electronics
3688 Nashua Dr.
Units 9 and 10
Mississauga L4V 1M5
Tel: (416) 677-0484
FAX: 416-677-0627

†Hamilton/Avnet Electronics
190 Colonnade Road South
Nepean K2E 7J5
Tel: (613) 226-1700
FAX: 613-226-1184

†Zentronics
8Tilbury Court
Brampton L6T 3T4
Tel: (416) 451-9600
FAX: 416-451-8320

†Zentronics
155 Colonnade Road
Unit 17
Nepean K2E 7K1
Tel: (613) 226-8840
FAX: 613-226-6350

SASKATCHEWAN

Zentronics
173-1222 Alberta Avenue
Saskatoon S7K 1R4
Tel: (306) 955-2202, 2207
FAX: (306) 244-3731

QUEBEC

†Arrow Electronics Inc.
4050 Jean Talon Quest
Montreal H4P 1W1
Tel: (514) 735-5511
FAX: 514-341-4821

Arrow Electronics Inc.
909 Charest Blvd.
Quebec 61N 269
Tel: (418) 687-4231
FAX: 418-687-5348

Hamilton/Avnet Electronics
2795 Rue Halpern
St. Laurent H4S 1P8
Tel: (514) 335-1000
FAX: 514-335-2481

Zentronics
817 McCafrey St.
St. Laurent H4T 1N4
Tel: (514) 737-9700
FAX: 514-737-5212

†Microcomputer System Technical Distributor Centers

intel®

EUROPEAN SALES OFFICES

DENMARK

Intel
Glentevej 61, 3rd Floor
2400 Copenhagen NV
Tel: (01) 19 80 33
TLX: 19567

FINLAND

Intel
Ruosilantie 2
00390 Helsinki 39
Tel: (0) 54 46 44
TLX: 123332

FRANCE

Intel
1, rue Edison-BP 303
78054 St Quentin-en-Yvelines Cedex
Tel: (1) 30 57 70 00
TLX: 699016

Intel
Immeuble BBC
4, Quai des Etroits
69005 Lyon
Tel: 78 42 40 89
TLX: 305153

WEST GERMANY

Intel*
Seidlstrasse 27
8000 Muenchen 2
Tel: (089) 5 38 90
TLX: 523177

Intel
Hohenzollern Strasse 5
3000 Hannover 1
Tel: (051) 1 34 40 81
TLX: 923625

Intel
Abraham Lincoln Strasse 16-18
6200 Wiesbaden
Tel: (061) 217 60 50
TLX: 4186183

Intel
Bruckstrasse 61
7012 Fellbach
Stuttgart
Tel: (071) 158 00 82
TLX: 7254826

ISRAEL

Intel*
Attidim Industrial Park
P.O. Box 43202
Tel Aviv 61430
Tel: (03) 49 80 80
TLX: 371215

ITALY

Intel*
Milanofiori Palazzo E
20090 Assago
Milano
Tel: (02) 824 40 71
TLX: 341286

NETHERLANDS

Intel*
Alexander Poort Building
Marten Meesweg 93
3068 AV Rotterdam
Tel: (010) 421 23 77
TLX: 22283

NORWAY

Intel
Hvamveien 4-P.O. Box 92
2013 Skjetten
Tel: (6) 842 420
TLX: 78018

SPAIN

Intel
Calle Zurbaran no. 28-1 Isq
28010 Madrid
Tel: (1) 410 40 04
TLX: 46880

SWEDEN

Intel*
Dalvagen 24
17136 Solna
Tel: (08) 734 01 00
TLX: 12261

SWITZERLAND

Intel*
Talackerstrasse 17
8065 Zurich
Tel: (01) 829 29 77
TLX: 57989

UNITED KINGDOM

Intel*
Pipers Way
Swindon, Wiltshire SN3 1RJ
Tel: (0793) 69 60 00
TLX: 444447

EUROPEAN DISTRIBUTORS/REPRESENTATIVES

AUSTRIA

Bacher Electronics GmbH
Rotenmuehlgasse 26
1120 Wien
Tel: (0222) 835 64 60
TLX: 131532

BELGIUM

Inelco Belgium S.A.
Av. des Croix de Guerre 94
1120 Bruxelles
Tel: (02) 216 01 60
TLX: 64475

DENMARK

ITT-Multikomponent A/S
Naverland 29
2600 Glostrup
Tel: (02) 45 66 45
TLX: 33355

FINLAND

OY Fintronic AB
Melkonkatu 24A
00210 Helsinki 21
Tel: (0) 692 60 22
TLX: 124224

FRANCE

Generim
Z.A. de Courtaboeuf
Av. de la Baltique-BP 88
91943 Les Ulis Cedex
Tel: (1) 69 07 78 78
TLX: 691700

Jermyn S.A.
73-79, rue des Solets
Silic 585
94663 Rungis Cedex
Tel: (1) 45 60 04 00
TLX: 260967

Metrologie
Tour d'Asnieres
4, av. Laurent-Cely
92606 Asnieres Cedex
Tel: (1) 47 90 62 40
TLX: 611448

Tekelec-Airtronic
Cite des Bruyeres
Rue Carle-Vernet - BP 2
92310 Sevres
Tel: (1) 45 34 75 35
TLX: 204552

WEST GERMANY

Electronic 2000 Vertriebs-AG
Stahlgruberring 12
8000 Muenchen 82
Tel: (089) 42 00 10
TLX: 522561

ITT Multikomponent GmbH
Bahnhofstrasse 44
7141 Moeglingen
Tel: (071) 41 48 79
TLX: 7264399

Jermyn GmbH
Im Dachsstueck 9
6250 Limburg
Tel: (064) 31 50 80
TLX: 415257-0

Metrologie GmbH
Meglingerstrasse 49
8000 Muenchen 71
Tel: (089) 78 04 20
TLX: 5213189

Proelectron Vertriebs GmbH
Max Planck Strasse 1-3
6072 Dreieich
Tel: (061) 03 30 43 43
TLX: 417972

IRELAND

Micro Marketing
Glenageary Office Park
Glenageary
Co Dublin
Tel: (1) 85 62 88
TLX: 31584

ISRAEL

Eastronics Ltd.
11 Rozanis Street
P.O. Box 39300
Tel Aviv 61392
Tel: (03) 47 51 51
TLX: 33638

ITALY

Intesi Corporation Italia S.A.
Milanofiori Palazzo E/5
20090 Assago
Milano
Tel: (02) 82 47 01
TLX: 311351

ITALY (Cont'd.)

Lasi Elettronica S.p.a.
Viale Fulvio Testi 126
20092 Cinisello Balsamo
Milano
Tel: (02) 244 00 12
TLX: 352040

NETHERLANDS

Koning en Hartman
Energieweg 1
2627 AP Delft
Tel: (015) 60 99 06
TLX: 38250

NORWAY

Nordisk Elektronik A/S
P.O. Box 122
Smedsvingen 4
1364 Hvalstad
Tel: (2) 84 62 10
TLX: 77546

PORTUGAL

Ditram
Av. M. Bombarda, 133-1 D
1000 Lisboa
Tel: (1) 54 53 13
TLX: 14182

SPAIN

ATD Electronica S.A.
Plaza Ciudad de Viena no. 6
28040 Madrid
Tel: (1) 234 40 00
TLX: 42477

ITT-SESA
Calle Miguel Angel no. 21-3
28010 Madrid
Tel: (1) 419 09 57
TLX: 27461

SWEDEN

Nordisk Elektronik A.B.
Huvudstagatan 1
P.O. Box 1409
17127 Solna
Tel: (8) 734 97 70
TLX: 10547

SWITZERLAND

Industrade A.G.
Hertistrasse 31
8304 Wallisellen
Tel: (01) 8 30 50 40
TLX: 56788

UNITED KINGDOM

Accent Electronic Components Ltd.
Jubilee House, Jubilee Way
Letchworth, Herts SG6 1QH
Tel: (0462) 68 66 66
TLX: 626923

Bytech Comway Ltd.
Unit 2 The Western Centre
Western Road
Bracknell
Berks RG12 1RW
Tel: (0344) 48 22 11
TLX: 848215

Jermyn
Vestry Estate
Otford Road
Sevenoaks
Kent TN14 5EU
Tel: (0732) 45 01 44
TLX: 95142

Rapid Silicon
Rapid House
Denmark St.
High Wycombe
Bucks HP11 2ER
Tel: (0494) 44 22 66
TLX: 837931

Rapid Systems
Rapid House
Denmark St.
High Wycombe
Bucks HP11 2ER
Tel: (0494) 45 02 44
TLX: 837931

YUGOSLAVIA

H.R. Microelectronics Corp.
2005 de la Cruz Blvd., Ste. 223
Santa Clara, CA 95050
U.S.A.
Tel: (408) 988-0286
TLX: 387452

*Field Application Location

intel®

INTERNATIONAL SALES OFFICES

AUSTRALIA

Intel Australia Pty. Ltd.*
Spectrum Building
200 Pacific Hwy., Level 6
Crows Nest, NSW, 2065
Tel: (2) 957-2744
TLX: 20097
FAX: (2) 923-2632

BRAZIL

Intel Semicondutores do Brasil LTDA
Av. Paulista, 1159-CJS 404/405
01311 - Sao Paulo - S.P.
Tel: 55-11-287-5899
TLX: 1153146
FAX: 55-11-212-7631

CHINA

Intel PRC Corporation
15/F, Office 1, Citic Bldg.
Jian Guo Men Wai Street
Beijing, PRC
Tel: (1) 500-4850
TLX: 22947 INTEL CN
FAX: (1) 500-2953

HONG KONG

Intel Semiconductor Ltd.*
1701-3 Connaught Centre
1 Connaught Road
Tel: (5) 844-4555
TWX: 63869 ISLHK HX
FAX: (5) 294-589

JAPAN

Intel Japan K.K.
5-6 Tokodai Toyosato-machi
Tsukuba-gun, Ibaraki-ken 300-26
Tel: 029747-8511
TLX: 3656-160
FAX: 029747-8450

Intel Japan K.K.*
Daiichi Mitsugi Bldg.
1-8889 Fuchu-cho
Fuchu-shi, Tokyo 183
Tel: 0423-60-7871
FAX: 0423-60-0315

Intel Japan K.K.*
Flower-Hill Shin-machi Bldg.
1-23-9 Shinmachi
Setagaya-ku, Tokyo 154
Tel: 03-426-2231
FAX: 03-427-7620

Intel Japan K.K.*
Bldg. Kumagaya
2-69 Hon-cho
Kumagaya-shi, Saitama 360
Tel: 0485-24-6871
FAX: 0485-24-7518

Intel Japan K.K.*
Mitsui-Seimei Musashi-kosugi Bldg.
915 Shinmaruko, Nakahara-ku
Kawasaki-shi, Kanagawa 211
Tel: 044-733-7011
FAX: 044-733-7010

JAPAN (Cont'd)

Intel Japan K.K.
Nihon Seimei Atsugi Bldg.
1-2-1 Asahi-machi
Atsugi-shi, Kanagawa 243
Tel: 0462-29-3731
FAX: 0462-29-3781

Intel Japan K.K.*
Ryokuchi-Eki Bldg.
2-4-1 Terauchi
Toyonaka-shi, Osaka 560
Tel: (06) 863-1091
FAX: 06-863-1084

Intel Japan K.K.
Shinmaru Bldg.
1-5-1 Marunouchi
Chiyoda-ku, Tokyo 100
Tel: 03-201-3621
FAX: 03-201-6850

Intel Japan K.K.
Tokai Bldg.
1-16-30 Meieki Minami
Nakamura-ku, Nagoya-shi
Aichi 450
Tel: 052-561-5181
FAX: 052-561-5317

KOREA

Intel Technology Asia Ltd.
Room 906, Singsong Bldg.
25-4, Yoido-Dong, Youngdeungpo-ku
Seoul 150
Tel: (2) 784-8186
TLX: 29312 INTELKO
FAX: (2) 784-8096

SINGAPORE

Intel Singapore Technology, Ltd.
101 Thomson Road #21-06
Goldhill Square
Singapore 1130
Tel: 250-7811
TLX: 39921 INTEL
FAX: 250-9256

TAIWAN

Intel Technology (Far East) Ltd.
Taiwan Branch
10/F., No. 205, Tun Hua N. Road
Taipei, R.O.C.
Tel: 886-2-716-9660
TLX: 13159 INTELTWN
FAX: 886-2-717-2455

INTERNATIONAL DISTRIBUTORS/REPRESENTATIVES

ARGENTINA

DAFSYS S.R.L.
Chacabuco, 90-4 PISO
1069-Buenos Aires
Tel: 54-1-334-1871
54-1-34-7726
TLX: 25472

Reycom Electronica S.R.L.
Arcos 3631
1429-Buenos Aires
Tel: 54 (1) 701-4462/66
FAX: 54 (1) 11-1722
TLX: 22122

AUSTRALIA

Total Electronics
P.M.B. 250
9 Harker Street
Burwood, Victoria 3125
Tel: 61-3-288-4044
TLX: AA 31261

Total Electronics
P.O. Box 139
Artamon, N.S.W. 2064
Tel: 61-02-438-1855
TLX: 26297

BRAZIL

Elebra Microelectronica
R. Geraldo Flausino Gomes, 78
9 Andar
04575 - Sao Paulo - S.P.
Tel: 55-11-534-9522
TLX: 1154591 or 1154593BR
FAX: 55-11-534-9637

CHILE

DIN Instruments
Suecia 2323
Casilla 6055, Correo 22
Santiago
Tel: 56-2-225-8139
TLX: 440422 RUDY CZ

CHINA

Novel Precision Machinery Co., Ltd.
Flat D, 20 Kingsford Ind. Bldg.
Phase 1, 26 Kwai Hei Street
N.T., Kowloon
Hong Kong
Tel: 852-0-223-222
TWX: 39114 JINMI HX
FAX: 852-0-261-602

CHINA (Cont'd)

Schmidt & Co. Ltd.
18/F Great Eagle Centre
23 Harbour Road
Wanchai, Hong Kong
Tel: 852-5-833-0222
TWX: 74766 SCHMC HX
FAX: 852-5-891-8754

INDIA

Micronic Devices
Arun Complex
No. 65 D.V.G. Road
Basavanagudi
Bangalore 560 004
Tel: 91-812-600-631
TLX: 0845-8332 MD BG IN

Micronic Devices
403, Gagan Deep
12, Rajendra Place
New Delhi 110 008
Tel: 91-58-97-71
TLX: 03163235 MDND IN

Micronic Devices
No. 516 5th Floor
Swastik Chambers
Sion, Chambray Road
Bombay 400 071
Tel: 91-52-39-63
TLX: 9531 171447 MDEV IN

JAPAN

Asahi Electronics Co. Ltd.
KMM Bldg. 2-14-1 Asano
Kokurakita-ku
Kitakyushu-shi 802
Tel: 093-511-6471
FAX: 093-551-7861

C. Itoh Techno-Science Co., Ltd.
C. Itoh Bldg., 2-5-1 Kita-Aoyama
Minato-ku, Tokyo 107
Tel: 03-497-4840
FAX: 03-497-4969

JAPAN (Cont'd)

Dia Semicon Systems, Inc.
Wacore 64, 1-37-8 Sangenjaya
Setagaya-ku, Tokyo 154
Tel: 03-487-0386
FAX: 03-487-8088

Okaya Koki
2-4-18 Sakae
Naka-ku, Nagoya-shi 460
Tel: 052-204-2911
FAX: 052-204-2901

Ryoyo Electro Corp.
Konwa Bldg.
1-12-22 Tsukiji
Chuo-ku, Tokyo 104
Tel: 03-546-5011
FAX: 03-546-5044

KOREA

J-Tek Corporation
6th Floor, Government Pension Bldg.
24-3 Yoido-Dong
Youngdeungpo-ku
Seoul 150
Tel: 82-2-782-8039
TLX: 25299 KODIGIT
FAX: 82-2-784-8391

Samsung Semiconductor &
Telecommunications Co., Ltd.
150, 2-KA, Tafpyung-ro, Chung-ku
Seoul 100
Tel: 82-2-751-3987
TLX: 27970 KORSST
FAX: 82-2-753-0967

MEXICO

Dicopel S.A.
Tochtli 368 Fracc. Ind. San Antonio
Azcapotzalco
C.P. 02760-Mexico, D.F.
Tel: 52-5-561-3211
TLX: 1773790 DICOME

NEW ZEALAND

Northrup Instruments & Systems Ltd.
459 Kyber Pass Road
P.O. Box 9464, Newmarket
Auckland 1
Tel: 64-9-501-219, 501-801
TLX: 21570 THERMAL

Northrup Instruments & Systems Ltd.
P.O. Box 2406
Wellington 856658
Tel: 64-4-856-658
TLX: NZ3380
FAX: 64-4-857276

SINGAPORE

Francotone Electronics Pte Ltd.
17 Harvey Road #04-01
Singapore 1336
Tel: 283-0888, 289-1618
TWX: 56541 FRELS
FAX: 2895327

SOUTH AFRICA

Electronic Building Elements, Pty. Ltd.
P.O. Box 4609
Pine Square, 18th Street
Hazelwood, Pretoria 0001
Tel: 27-12-469921
TLX: 3-227786 SA

TAIWAN

Mitac Corporation
No. 585, Ming Shen East Rd.
Taipei, R.O.C.
Tel: 886-2-501-8231
FAX: 886-2-501-4265

VENEZUELA

P. Benavides S.A.
Avilanes a Rio
Residencia Kamarata
Locales 4 AL 7
La Candelaria, Caracas
Tel: 58-2-571-0396
TLX: 28450
FAX: 58-2-572-3321

*Field Application Location

intel

DOMESTIC SERVICE OFFICES

ALABAMA

Intel Corp.
5015 Bradford Drive, #2
Huntsville 35805
Tel: (205) 830-4010

ARIZONA

Intel Corp.
11225 N. 28th Dr., #D214
Phoenix 85029
Tel: (602) 869-4980

Intel Corp.
500 E. Fry Blvd., Suite M-15
Sierra Vista 85635
Tel: (602) 459-5010

ARKANSAS

Intel Corp.
P.O. Box 206
Ulm 72170
Tel: (501) 241-3264

CALIFORNIA

Intel Corp.
21515 Vanowen St.
Suite 116
Canoga Park 91303
Tel: (818) 704-8500

Intel Corp.
2250 E. Imperial Highway
Suite 218
El Segundo 90245
Tel: 1-800-468-3548

Intel Corp.
1900 Prairie City Rd.
Folsom 95630-9597
Tel: (916) 351-6143

Intel Corp.
2000 E. 4th Street
Suite 110
Santa Ana 92705
Tel: (714) 835-5789
TWX: 910-595-2475

Intel Corp.
2700 San Tomas Expressway
Santa Clara 95051
Tel: (408) 970-1740

Intel Corp.
4350 Executive Drive
Suite 105
San Diego 92121
Tel: (619) 452-5880

COLORADO

Intel Corp.
650 South Cherry
Suite 915
Denver 80222
Tel: (303) 321-8086
TWX: 910-931-2289

CONNECTICUT

Intel Corp.
26 Mill Plain Road
Danbury 06811
Tel: (203) 748-3130
TWX: 710-456-1199

FLORIDA

Intel Corp.
1500 N.W. 62, Suite 104
Ft. Lauderdale 33309
Tel: (305) 771-0600
TWX: 510-956-9407

Intel Corp.
242 N. Westmonte Drive
Suite 105
Altamonte Springs 32714
Tel: (305) 869-5588

GEORGIA

Intel Corp.
3280 Pointe Parkway
Suite 200
Norcross 30092
Tel: (404) 441-1171

ILLINOIS

Intel Corp.
300 N. Martingale Rd.
Suite 300
Schaumburg 60194
Tel: (312) 310-5733

INDIANA

Intel Corp.
8777 Purdue Rd., #125
Indianapolis 46268
Tel: (317) 875-0623

KANSAS

Intel Corp.
8400 W. 110th Street
Suite 170
Overland Park 66210
Tel: (913) 345-2727

KENTUCKY

Intel Corp.
3525 Tatescreek Road, #51
Lexington 40502
Tel: (606) 272-6745

MARYLAND

Intel Corp.
5th Floor
7833 Walker Drive
Greenbelt 20770
Tel: (301) 441-1020

MASSACHUSETTS

Intel Corp.
Westford Corp. Center
3 Carlisle Road
Westford 01886
Tel: (617) 692-1060

MICHIGAN

Intel Corp.
7071 Orchard Lake Road
Suite 100
West Bloomfield 48033
Tel: (313) 851-8905

MISSOURI

Intel Corp.
4203 Earth City Expressway
Suite 143
Earth City 63045
Tel: (314) 291-2015

NEW JERSEY

Intel Corp.
385 Sylvan Avenue
Englewood Cliffs 07632
Tel: (201) 567-0821
TWX: 710-991-8593

Intel Corp.
Raritan Plaza III
Raritan Center
Edison 08817
Tel: (201) 225-3000

NORTH CAROLINA

Intel Corp.
2306 W. Meadowview Road
Suite 206
Greensboro 27407
Tel: (919) 294-1541

Intel Corp.
2700 Wycliff Rd., Suite 102
Raleigh 27607
Tel: (919) 781-8022

OHIO

Intel Corp.
Chagrin-Brainard Bldg.
Suite 305
28001 Chagrin Boulevard
Cleveland 44122
Tel: (216) 464-6915
TWX: 810-427-9298

Intel Corp.
6500 Poe
Dayton 45414
Tel: (513) 890-5350

OREGON

Intel Corp.
15254 N.W. Greenbrier Parkway, Bldg. B
Beaverton 01886
Tel: (503) 645-8051
TWX: 910-467-8741

Intel Corp.
5200 N.E. Elam Young Parkway
Hillsboro 97123
Tel: (503) 681-8080

PENNSYLVANIA

Intel Corp.
201 Penn Center Boulevard
Suite 301 W
Pittsburgh 15235
Tel: (313) 354-1540

TEXAS

Intel Corp.
313 E. Anderson Lane
Suite 314
Austin 78752
Tel: (512) 454-3628
TWX: 910-874-1347

Intel Corp.
12300 Ford Road
Suite 380
Dallas 75234
Tel: (214) 241-2820
TWX: 910-860-5617

Intel Corp.
8815 Dyer St., Suite 225
El Paso 79904
Tel: (915) 751-0186

VIRGINIA

Intel Corp.
1603 Santa Rosa Rd., #109
Richmond 23288
Tel: (804) 282-5668

WASHINGTON

Intel Corp.
110 110th Avenue N.E.
Suite 510
Bellevue 98004
Tel: 1-800-468-3548
TWX: 910-443-3002

WISCONSIN

Intel Corp.
330 S. Executive Dr.
Suite 102
Brookfield 53005
Tel: (414) 784-8087

CANADA

Intel Corp.
190 Attwell Drive, Suite 500
Rexdale, Ontario
Canada M9W 6H8
Tel: (416) 675-2105

Intel Corp.
620 St. Jean Blvd.
Pointe Claire, Quebec
Canada H9R 3K3
Tel: (514) 694-9130

Intel Corp.
2650 Queensview Drive, #250
Ottawa, Ontario,
Canada K2B 8H6
Tel: (613) 829-9714

CUSTOMER TRAINING CENTERS

CALIFORNIA

2700 San Tomas Expressway
Santa Clara 95051
Tel: (408) 970-1700

ILLINOIS

300 N. Martingale, #300
Schaumburg 60173
Tel: (312) 310-5700

MASSACHUSETTS

3 Carlisle Road
Westford 01886
Tel: (617) 692-1000

MARYLAND

7833 Walker Dr., 4th Floor
Greenbelt 20770
Tel: (301) 220-3380

SYSTEMS ENGINEERING OFFICES

CALIFORNIA

2700 San Tomas Expressway
Santa Clara 95051
Tel: (408) 986-8086

ILLINOIS

300 N. Martingale, #300
Schaumburg 60173
Tel: (312) 310-8031

MASSACHUSETTS

3 Carlisle Road
Westford 01886
Tel: (617) 692-3222

NEW YORK

300 Motor Parkway
Hauppauge 11788
Tel: (516) 231-3300